Japanese: The Spoken Language

PART 3

Eleanor Harz Jorden
with Mari Noda

Yale University Press
New Haven and London

Special thanks are due the Secretarial Services Division
of Williams College—Donna Chanail, Peggy Bryant,
Shirley Bushika, and Lori Tolle—for their assistance in
preparing sample drafts of this material. The
professionalism of their work, their cooperation, and
their enthusiasm were deeply appreciated.

Designed by Sally Harris
and set in Baskerville type by
Brevis Press, Bethany, Connecticut.
Printed in the United States of America by
Murray Printing Co., Westford, Mass.

Library of Congress Cataloging-in-Publication Data
(Revised for volume 3)
Jorden, Eleanor Harz.
  Japanese, the spoken language.

  (Yale language series)
  1. Japanese language—Textbooks for foreign
speakers—English. 2. Japanese language—Spoken
Japanese. I. Noda, Mari. II. Title. III. Series.
PL539.3.J58 1987   495.6'83421   86–15890
  ISBN 0–300–03831–3 (v. 1 : alk. paper)
  ISBN 0–300–03834–8 (pbk. : v. 1 : alk. paper)
  ISBN 0–300–04186–1 (v. 2 : alk. paper)
  ISBN 0–300–04188–8 (pbk. : v. 2 : alk. paper)
  ISBN 0–300–04189–6 (v. 3 : alk. paper)
  ISBN 0–300–04191–8 (pbk. : v. 3 : alk. paper)

The paper in this book meets the guidelines for
permanence and durability of the Committee on
Production Guidelines for Book Longevity
of the Council on Library Resources.

10 9 8 7 6 5 4 3 2 1

To
THE TEAM—
its concept and its realization

NOTE

This volume is a continuation of
JAPANESE: THE SPOKEN LANGUAGE, Parts 1 and 2.
A description of romanization, special symbols, procedures, etc.,
appears in the introduction to Part 1.

Contents

Lesson 25

Core Conversations

1(N)   Tuukiñ wa, tikátetu da sòo desu
ğa; otáku karà wa, arûite mo
korárèru desyoo?

(J)   Êe. Arûite kuru koto mo arímàsu
yo

2(J)a. Kotira ni syuúsyoku-sitài to iû
no wa, dôo site desu ka

(N)a. Mâa, nihoñğo ğa sukôsi hanásèru
no de, eeğo to nihoñğo o ikâsita
siğóto ğa sitài to omóimàsite . .

b. Yômu koto mo dekímàsu ka

b. Tasyóo wa yomemàsu ğa, mâda
'sore hodo . .

c. Mâa, utí dè wa, yomîkaki ğa
hitúyoo na kotò wa, amári nài
desu kedo ne! Koñpyùtaa wa?

c. Tyôtto narâtta koto ğa arímàsu no
de, tukáeru kotò wa tukáeru to
omoimàsu.

. . .

d. Râiğetu kara hazímeraremàsu
ka

d. Hâi, îtu kara de mo.

3(J)a. Kôndo no utí no sèminaa de,
Amérika-kèezai ni tuite
hanásèru katâ o sağásite (i)rù ñ
desu ğa; onéğai-dekìnai desyoo
ka.

(N)a. Kamáimasèñ kedo, îtu desu ka

1

b. Sań-syùukañ-hodo sakí nà ñ
   desu ğa; |anô desu ne!| nihóñğo
   de site hosìi to iú kotò na ñ
   desu.

        b. Nihoñğo de? Iya, watasi wa, yatto
        sukôsi hanásèru yoo ni nâtta kedo,
        seńmoñ-teki na kotò wa, mâda
        tyôtto . .

c. Nâñ to ka onéğai-dekimasèñ ka↙

        c. Tûuyaku o tukêru koto wa
        dekímasèñ ka↙

d. Sôo desu nêe. Tekítoo na hitò ğa
   sağáserù ka dôo ka wakárimasèñ
   ğa, sağasite mimasyo(o)?

ENGLISH EQUIVALENTS

1(N)   I hear you commute to work by
       subway, but from your house, you
       can also walk here—right?

        (J)   Yes. There are (also) times when I
        do walk here.

2(J)a. Why would you like to come to
       work here?

        (N)a. Well, since I can speak Japanese a
        little, [I've been] thinking I'd like to
        do work that uses (*lit.* has brought
        into use) English and Japanese.

b. Can you read, too?

        b. I can read more or less (at least),
        but not that much yet.

c. Well, at our place, there aren't
   very many occasions when reading
   and writing are required, but . . .
   (I asked anyway). What about the
   computer?

        c. I have studied it a little, so I *can* use
        one, I believe, (but not well).

        . . .

d. Can you begin, starting next
   month?

        d. Yes, starting any time.

3(J)a. (It's that) I'm looking for a person
   who can talk about the American
   economy at our seminar this next
   time; could(n't) I ask you?

b. It's about three weeks from now,
   but, you know, the fact is they
   want to have it done in Japanese.

        (N)a. That's no problem, but when is it?

        b. In Japanese? Oh, no! I've just barely
        reached the point where I can speak
        a little, but specialized things are
        still a bit [of a problem].

c. Can't I ask you somehow?

d. I wonder. It's not clear whether or not I'll be able to track down a suitable person, but why don't I try looking for one.

c. Is it impossible to provide an interpreter?

BREAKDOWNS
(AND SUPPLEMENTARY VOCABULARY)

1. **tuukiñ**	commuting to work
ko(rá)rêru[1]**/-ru; korâreta ~ kôreta/** (SP1)	can come
arûite mo ko(rá)rêru	can come also/even having walked
kûru koto ǧa âru (SP3)	there are occasions when [I] come; [I] sometimes come
2. **syuusyoku-suru**	find or seek employment
+ **tutómèru /-ru; tutômeta/**	become employed
+ **hataraku /-u; hataraita/**	work
syuúsyoku-sitài to iû no	the thing described as wanting to find employment
hanásèru /-ru; hanâseta/	can speak
nihóñǧo ǧa hanasèru	can speak Japanese
ikâsu /-u; ikâsita/	bring to life; make the most of, bring into use
eeǧo to nihoñǧo o ikâsita siǧoto	work that has brought English and Japanese into use
yômu koto mo dekîru (SP2)	can also read (*lit.* the act of reading is also possible)
tasyoo	more or less, somewhat
yomêru /-ru; yômeta/	can read
yômîkaki	reading and writing
yômîkaki ǧa hitúyoo na kotò wa nâi (SP3)	there aren't any occasions when reading and writing are necessary
narâu /-u; narâtta/	learn, study, take lessons
narâtta koto ǧa âru (SP3)	have ever studied
tukaeru /-ru; tukaeta/	can use
tukáeru kotò wa 'tukaeru (SP4)	can use, at least
hazimeru /-ru; hazimeta/	begin [something]
+ **hazimaru /-u; hazimatta/**	[something] begins

---

1. This accent represents the alternates **korárèru** and **korêru**.

hazime(ra)reru /-ru; hazime(ra)reta/	can begin [something]
3. **kôñdo**	this time; this next time
sêminaa	seminar
Amérika-kèezai ni tuite (SP5)	concerning the American economy
sáñ-syùukañ-hodo saki	about three weeks ahead (from now)
hosîi /-katta/ (SP6)	want; is wanted
sité hosìi	want to have it done
sité hosìi to iú kotò da	it's a fact described as wanting to have it done
yatto	finally, with difficulty; barely, only just
señmoñ/goseñmoñ	specialization
señmoñ-teki /na/	specialized
nâñ to ka	somehow
tûuyaku	interpreter; interpretation
+ **hoñyaku**	translation
tukêru koto ḡa dekîru	can attach (*lit.* the act of attaching is possible)
tekitoo /na/	suitable
saḡaseru /-ru; saḡaseta/	can look for; can track down
hito ḡa saḡaseru	can track down a person

MISCELLANEOUS NOTES

1. In CC1, a single exchange between Smith and his sponsor, Mr. Suzuki, the commuting patterns Mr. Suzuki uses are described. The style is careful, with distal-style predicates.

(N) **Tuukiñ**: Note also **tuukiñ-suru** 'commute to work'; **tuuḡaku-suru** 'commute to school.' Note again the use of **dà** before **sôo**, an example of the rare use of this form preceding the nominal it modifies. Ordinarily the **no** or **na** alternate occurs in this position. **Arûite mo** 'even/also having walked,' that is, as of the time of occurrence of **ko(rá)rèru**: 'you can get here even/also having walked.'

2. CC2 is an excerpt from a job interview. Smith, the graduate student, is seeking employment at the bank where his sponsor, Mr. Suzuki, works. We can presume that Mr. Suzuki arranged the interview. Japanese society works with heavy emphasis on connections (**kône**, a shortening of **konêkusyoñ**), without which little can be accomplished. A connection that contributes to an introduction may sometimes be rather indirect—a friend of a friend of a friend—but without some form of personal connection, one remains very much outside. (Contrast the American system of sending copies of one's résumé to countless unknown prospective employers in the hope of employment based on background, experience, and recommendations.)

The kinds of questions included in Japanese interviews and application forms are culture-specific and may surprise the foreigner. For example, job seekers from some societies resent questions relating to marital status or father's occupation. Probing of this kind indicates the importance the Japanese place on being able to define the setting that encompasses the interviewee, but the same questions may strike an American as an invasion of privacy that has no relation to employment. Frequently job interviews are conducted in the presence of several interviewers, some of whom may remain silent during the entire interview.

Note how Smith modestly plays down his abilities without suggesting that he can't do the job. He answers the questions directed to him with promptness and firmness, fully aware of the importance of the impression he makes through his manner, appearance, gestures, and, of course, language.

Both Smith and the **butyoo** use careful-style with distal-style final predicates, as we would expect in view of the social distance between them. But what about Smith's three minor sentences? (N)a and b both trail off politely, indicating an assumption that the hearer knows exactly what is implied without explicit expression of it; (N)d assumes the addition of the same final predicate as that of the preceding question. Smith's use of a distal-style final gerund in (N)a and a distal-style imperfective before **no de** in (N)c are indicators of extremely careful style. However, he does not use polite-style. In his utterances, there does not happen to be any opportunity for polite equivalents that would not be too polite in the situation.

(J)a. **Kotira ni** expresses goal: 'come into this place for employment.'
Tutómèru is an operational, intransitive vowel verbal. In its **-te (i)ru** form, it regularly refers to current employment. Note **X ni tutômete (i)ru** 'be employed in behalf of X,' in which X indicates the organization *for* which one works.
Hataraku, an operational, intransitive consonant-verbal, refers to working or laboring. Note **yôku hataraku** 'work hard'; **határakisuḡìru** 'overwork'; **X de hataraku** 'work at X (= place)'; **atámà no határaku hitò** 'a bright, clever person' (that is, one whose head works!).

(N)a. **Ikásu** is an operational, transitive consonant verbal whose basic meaning involves sparing or bringing to life. The use of the perfective **ikâsita** before **siḡoto** implies that the work, at the time it is done, will have brought Japanese and English together to their best advantage. The imperfective **ikâsu** is also possible in this utterance, indicating repeated occurrences. Note also **hima o ikâsite tukau** 'use leisure wisely,' **okane o ikâsite tukau** 'put money to good use.'
Siḡoto ḡa sitai: Remember the alternation of **ḡa** and **o** before **-tai** forms. The nominal gains independent focus with the **ḡa** alternate.

(N)b. **Mâda 'sore hodo . .** assumes **yomémasèn** as a final predicate.

(J)c. **Uti** here refers to the office as in-group.
Yômîkaki is a compound nominal derived from two verbal stems. It occurs with particle **ḡa** as the affect of the affective predicate **hitúyoo dà**: 'reading and writing are necessary.' That sequence, because it modifies the nominal **kotô**, assumes the pre-nominal form **hituyoo na**.

(N)c. **Naráu** is an operational, transitive **w**-consonant verbal. Whereas **beñkyoo-suru** regularly refers to more academic kinds of study, **naráu** implies the acquisition of skills: practicing, taking lessons, and so on. Some subjects (language study, for example) may occur with either verbal, reflecting the complex aspects of the subject—"fact" and "act."

(J)d. **Hazimeru**, an operational vowel verbal, is the transitive partner of intransitive, affective **hazimaru**, a consonant verbal. Note: **X o hazimeru** 'begin X'; **X ḡa hazimaru** 'X (= the beginning *thing*) begins'; **hazime** 'the beginning'; **hazime ni** 'in the beginning.' Compare the accents of **hazimete**, the gerund of **hazimeru**, and of the special nominal **hazîmete** '[for] the first time.'

3. In CC3, Ms. Morimoto discusses an upcoming seminar with Sue Brown, attempting to convince her to participate in a meeting that will be conducted in Japanese. Sue Brown's reluctance to agree to speak is softened by her suggestion of another solution, the use of an interpreter. That she is entitled to refuse tells us that Ms. Morimoto is a colleague at a level only a bit higher than Sue Brown's. If the request had originated with a division chief,

we can imagine her beginning some hurried, intensive study of specialized economics-related Japanese!

The style is careful, with distal-style final predicates. In the questions that are requests ([J]a and c), note that Ms. Morimoto uses humble-polite forms. In (N)b, Sue Brown's refusal (implied in **mâda tyôtto . .**) is polite, as it trails off without actually saying no.

(J)a. Compare **sêminaa**, a small study group or public seminar, borrowed from English, and **zêmi**, a college seminar, an abbreviated form of a German borrowing. **Utí no sèminaa** refers to a seminar at 'our place,' 'our institution.' Note the form of the request: a description of what is required followed by **ḡa** (or **kedo**) and then the actual request in polite-style.

(J)b. /Extent expression of time + **saki**/ refers to the period of time ahead.

The insert |**anô desu ne!**| puts focus on what is about to be said. What follows is introduced with some reluctance since the speaker recognizes it as a possible cause for refusal. **Anô** is obviously related to the more deliberate **anoo . .**

The sequence /**X to iú kotò da**/, in which **X** is a sentence ending in the perfective or imperfective, often reports information (**X**) that has been heard, is being said, etc.—another pattern for relaying information.

(N)b. **Señmoñ**: Note **X o 'señmoñ ni suru** 'make X a specialty,' 'specialize in X'; **señmoñḡo** 'specialized vocabulary.' **Señmoñ-teki**: /Nominal X + **-teki**/ is a **na**-nominal meaning 'pertaining to X,' 'derived from X,' or 'related to X.' Examples: **keezai-teki** 'economic' or 'economical'; **seezi-teki** 'political.' Nominals in **teki** may also form compounds with following nominals, thus resulting in /**X na Y**/ and /**XY**/ alternates (e.g., **seezi-teki na moñdai** and **seeziteki-moñdai** 'political problems').

Tyôtto . ., you will remember, suggests 'a bit' + something negative, in conflict, impossible, contrary. Here Sue Brown is trying to excuse herself from speaking at the seminar now that she has learned she would be expected to speak in Japanese. She is careful to attribute her reluctance to her incompetence, not to a lack of interest in or willingness to accede to her colleague's request.

(J)c. Ms. Morimoto tries once more, with a humble-polite request, further softened by **nâñ to ka** 'somehow,' 'one way or another.' There is the possibility that Sue Brown is being modest and needs only a bit of encouragement. The **to** of **nâñ to ka** is a derived use of the quotative, with **ka** making the **nâñ** into an indefinite.

(N)c. Since Sue Brown is serious about her refusal to attempt to participate in the panel to be conducted in Japanese, the most appropriate procedure is for her to suggest an alternate solution to the problem—the use of an interpreter.

Tûuyaku can refer to interpretation or interpreter(s). As an alternate for 'interpreter(s),' **tûuyaku no hito** also occurs. Note: **tuuyaku-suru** 'interpret,' 'serve as an interpreter'; **X no tûuyaku de Y to hanâsu** 'speak with Y, with X interpreting (*lit.* by means of X's interpretation).'

Hoñyaku: note also **hoñyaku-suru** 'translate'; **X kara 'Y ni hoñyaku-suru** 'translate from X to Y.'

Structural Patterns

1. THE POTENTIAL

In English, our pattern for indicating ability to do things is very easy to form: we use the auxiliary verb 'can' followed immediately by the base form of the activity verb. Japanese, on the other hand, has special verbals—hereafter called POTENTIALS—which are derived from basic verbals according to regular, predictable patterning. These new potential verbals, corresponding more or less to English 'can do' sequences, are formed as follows:

Vowel-verbals. /verbal root (= **-ru** form minus **-ru**) + **-rare** (*or* **-re**) + **-ru**/
Examples:

   tabé-(ra)rè-ru 'can eat'

   ake-(ra)re-ru 'can open (something)'

   okí-(ra)rè-ru 'can get up'

Consonant verbals. /verbal root (= **-u** form minus **-u**) + **-e** + **-ru**/
Examples:

   nom-ê-ru 'can drink'

   hanás-è-ru 'can talk'

   kaér-è-ru 'can return (home)'

   mat-ê-ru 'can wait'

(All **w**-consonant verbals again lose their /**w**/, in this case before the /**-e**/ of the potential. Examples are **ka-e-ru** (from **kaw-e-ru*) 'can buy' and **a-ê-ru** (from **aw-ê-ru*) 'can meet.' In the distal-style forms of these potentials, it is often difficult for English speakers to distinguish the vowel sequence of the potential from that of the corresponding basic verbal. The following types of pairs frequently cause confusion:

   kaímàsu 'buy' and **kaémàsu** 'can buy'

   aímàsu 'meet' and **aémàsu** 'can meet'

   omóimàsu 'think' and **omóemàsu** 'can think'

   suímàsu 'smoke' and **suémàsu** 'can smoke')

Special polite verbals. Formation is the same as for consonant verbals, but occurrences, except for **irássyarèru**, are extremely rare.

Irregular verbals. For **kûru**, the **ko-** root is used: **ko-rárè-ru** *or* **ko-rê-ru** 'can come.' For **suru**, the verbal **dekîru** is used in place of a derived potential.

If the basic verbal is unaccented, its potential is also unaccented; otherwise, the derived potential is accented, and the accent occurs on the next-to-last mora of the citation form, following the accent pattern of **tabêru**.

All potentials, then, consist of a verbal root, a "root-extender"—which is either **-(ra)re-** or **-e-**, and, in their citation form, the **-ru** ending. Potentials are all vowel verbals, patterning like **tabêru** and **akeru**. Compare:

Basic Verbal	Potential Equivalent
mîseta (from **misêru**)	**misê(rà)reta** (from **misé(ra)rèru**)
nônde (from **nômu**)	**nômete** (from **nomêru**)
kaérimàsu (from **kâeru**)	**kaéremàsu** (from **kaérèru**)
matânai (from **mâtu**)	**matênai** (from **matêru**)
ki-sôo (from **kûru**)	**ko(rá)re-sòo** (from **ko(rá)rêru**)

Some important points about the potential:

   a. The shorter form of the potential of vowel verbals, which uses the single-mora root-extender **-re-**, is becoming increasingly popular, particularly among younger Japenese. Its patterning is parallel to the single-mora extender that occurs with consonant verbals.

b. Many potentials coincide in form with entirely unrelated basic verbals or with potentials of unrelated verbals. Examples:

> **kaeru** 'change [something]' *or* 'can buy' (from **kau**)
>
> **kakêru** 'hang [something]' *or* 'can write'
>
> **tatêru** 'stand [something] up' *or* 'can stand'

Kir-ê-ru 'can cut' (from **kîr-u**) and **ki-re-ru** 'can put on or wear' (short form of **ki-rare-ru**, from **ki-ru**) are distinguished by accent, but in many derived forms the two potentials coincide: **kirémàsu**, for example, is the distal-style potential of both verbals. Distinguishing between members of these pairs in the spoken language depends on context.

c. For the most part it is operational verbals that have potential derivatives. Affective verbals like **aku, kieru, simâru**, and **wakâru**, for example, have no corresponding potentials. Once again a warning about direct translation from English is in order. Note these examples:

> 'Can you understand?' 'Do you understand?' 'Is this comprehensible?' > **Wakárimàsu ka⌐**
>
> 'Can that window open?' 'Does that window open?' 'Will that window open?' > **Anó màdo, akímàsu ka⌐**

The meaning of these basic affective verbals includes the idea that occurrence is possible.

d. Potential verbals, even if derived from operational verbals, are themselves affective verbals, for they describe conditions, not self-determined operations. We cannot suggest that we be able to do something, nor can we tell someone to have a particular ability. Rarely do we find a potential in the **-tai** form. Instead, to express desire to be able to do something, the /—— **yòo ni nâru**/ pattern is used: **Zyoózù ni hanásèru yoo ni narítài ñ desu kedo . .** 'I'd like to reach the point where [*lit.* become in a manner that] I can speak well, but . . .' (I don't know if I can).

e. As affective verbals, potentials have traditionally NOT occurred in combination with /nominal + **o**/ phrases. Compare:

> **kâre ĝa yômu** '*he* reads it' (operational verbal with an operator)
>
> **siñbuñ o yòmu** 'I read *newspapers*' (operational verbal with an operand); *but*
>
> **kâre ĝa yomêru** '*he* can read it' (affective verbal with a primary affect)
>
> **siñbuñ ĝa yomèru** 'I can read *newspapers*' (*lit.* '*newspapers* are readable') (affective verbal with a secondary affect)

Recently the use of /nominal + **o** + potential/ has begun to gain acceptance among some speakers of Japanese, but this pattern is not yet considered standard. This new alternation between /**siñbuñ ĝa yomèru**/ and /**siñbuñ o yomèru**/ is reminiscent of a similar alternation with **-tai** forms: /**siñbuñ ĝa kaitai**/ and /**siñbuñ o kaitai**/. Assuming that the meaning differences are parallel, we can analyze the alternate with **ĝa** as **siñbuñ ĝa / yomèru** 'what I am able to read is newspapers,' with focus on **siñbuñ,** and the alternate with **o** as **siñbuñ o yom/èru** 'what I am able to do is read newspapers' with focus on the operation expressed by **siñbuñ o yom**. In sequences with particle **o**, the potential has moved over to the operational class in terms of its basic root.

f. As indicated above, affective potentials may occur as double **-ğa** verbals: **Itóo-sañ ğa eeğo ğa hanasèru kara . .** 'Since Mr/s. Ito can speak English . . .'

Also possible with some potentials is the use of the particle **ni** of reference following the nominal that indicates the person for whom the ability exists, i.e., the primary affect: **akátyañ ni nomèru** 'it is possible for babies to drink it,' 'babies can drink it.'

g. Note the difference in meaning between

Mi(rá)rémasèñ. 'I can't look at [it].' *and*

Miémasèñ. 'I can't see it.'

Kikémasèñ. 'I can't ask *or* listen to it.' *and*

Kikóemasèñ. 'I can't hear it.'

2. /—— kotô ğa dekîru/

We have already met the nominal **kotô** 'act,' 'fact' as part of a number of special combinations: /—— **kotô ni suru**/; /—— **kotô ni nâru**/; /—— **kotô ni kimaru**/; /—— **kotô ni kimeru**/. We will now examine one such special combination which alternates with the potential.

An already familiar pattern is /nominal + **ğa** + **dekîru**/, as in **nihóñğo ğa dekìru, koñna siğoto ğa dekìru, uñteñ ğa dekìru**. We are also familiar with the use of the nominal **kotô** preceded by a sentence modifier. If we now combine these two patterns, we arrive at combinations like **waápuro o tukau kotô ğa dekîru**, *lit.* 'the act of using a word processor is possible,' 'I can use a word processor'; **nihôñğo o sukôsi yômu koto ğa dekîru**, *lit.* 'the act of reading Japanese a little is possible,' 'I can read Japanese a little.'

In these examples, the /imperfective verbal + **kotò ğa dekîru**/ can be replaced by the corresponding potential forms **tukaeru** and **yomêru,** which probably occur more commonly. Because the **kotô ğa dekîru** pattern is much easier for foreigners to form, we tend to overuse it, sometimes to the exclusion of the potential. This practice does not affect the basic meaning of one's message, but in many contexts it will seem rather stiff and formal.

For most speakers the potential is an affective verbal ('the word processor [**waapuro ğa**] can undergo using'), while the pattern with **dekîru** refers to the ability to perform an operational activity ('using the word processor [**waapuro o tukau**] is possible'). Thus

waapuro ğa tukaeru (standard pattern)

waapuro o tukaeru   (newer pattern; not yet universally accepted)

waápuro o tukau kotò ğa dekîru (**ğa** impossible here in place of **o**)

All three alternatives occur as the equivalent of '[I] can use a word processor.'

In situations in which an ability is being qualified or compared, the **kotô ğa dekîru** pattern (with appropriate particle changes as necessary) is regularly used.

Tyuúğokuğo (ğa) dekimàsu ka⤹ 'Do you know Chinese?'

Hanâsu koto wa dekímàsu kedo . . 'I can speak it (at least), but . . .'

Tyuúğokuğo (wa) dekìru desyoo? 'You know Chinese—right?'

Hanâsu koto mo yômu koto mo sukôsi dekîru kedo, kâku koto wa zeñzeñ dekimasèñ. 'I can speak it and read it a little, but I can't write it at all.'

The verbal preceding **kotô** in this pattern is regularly an operational verbal, never a potential. The notion of ability is conveyed by the appropriate form of **dekîru**. Compare

Anó màdo (ğa) akímàsu ka⤹ 'Does that window open?' *and*

Anó màdo (o) akémàsu ka⤸ 'Are you going to open that window.?' *with*

Anó màdo (ğa [*or* o]) aké(ra)remàsu ka⤸ *or*

Anó màdo (o) akéru kotò ğa dekímàsu ka⤸ 'Can you open that window?'

As with the potential, the nominal representing the person having the ability may occur as a primary affect (followed by **ğa**) or as a referent (followed by **ni**):

Kodomo ğa końna monò o tabêru koto ğa dekîru kara . . 'Children can eat things like this, so . . .' *or*

Kodomo ni końna monò o tabêru koto ğa dekîru kara . . 'It is possible for children to eat things like this, so . . .'

3. /—— kotô ğa âru/

A sequence like **wasyóku o tabemàsu**, depending on context, can refer to a single future occurrence or to repeated occurrences, which may or may not have already begun: 'I'm going to eat Japanese food (once or repeatedly)' *or* 'I eat Japanese food (repeatedly).' The perfective equivalent, **wasyóku o tabemàsita**, can also refer to a single occurrence or repeated occurrences, in this case completed one(s): 'I ate ~ have eaten Japanese food.'

Compare now the use of /sentence modifier + **kotô ğa âru**/, another pattern that includes **kotô**. This pattern refers to the existence (**âru**) of the occurrence of particular acts (**kotô**): the combination relates to whether or not the specified activity ever occurs (with an imperfective sentence modifier) or ever has occurred (with a perfective sentence modifier). Study the following examples carefully, noting the particle changes following **kotô**, which indicate shifts in focus.

(1) **Wasyóku o tabèru koto ğa arímàsu ka⤸** 'Do you ever eat Japanese food?' (*lit.* 'Does the act of eating Japanese food exist?')

Êe, tabêru koto ğa arímàsu. 'Yes, there are occasions when I eat it.'

Iie, tabêru koto wa arímasèñ. 'No, there aren't any occasions when I eat it.'

(2) **Wasyóku o tàbeta koto ğa arímàsu ka⤸** 'Have you ever eaten Japanese food?' (*lit.* 'Does the act of having eaten Japanese food exist?')

Êe, tàbeta koto ğa arímàsu. 'Yes, I have eaten it.'

Iie, tâbeta koto wa arímasèñ. 'No, I've never eaten it.'

(3) **Wasyóku o tabènai koto mo arímàsu ka⤸** 'Do you ever not eat Japanese food?' (i.e., are there also occurrences of not eating Japanese food, assuming you usually do?)

Êe, tabênai koto mo arímàsu. 'Yes, there are also occasions when I don't eat it.'

Iie, tabênai koto wa arímasèñ. 'No, there are no occasions when I don't eat it.'

(4) **Wasyóku o tabènakatta koto mo arímàsu ka⤸** 'Did you ever not eat Japanese food?' (i.e., are there also any occasions when you didn't eat Japanese food?)

Êe, tabênakatta koto mo arímàsu. 'Yes, I have on occasion(s) not eaten it.'

Iie, tabênakatta koto wa arímasèñ. 'No, there are no occasions when I didn't eat it.'

In this pattern, **âru** and its derived forms are regularly imperfective unless there is reference to occurrences as of a time already completed. Thus: **Nihôñ e hazîmete iťta tokì ni wa, wasyóku o tàbeta koto ğa arímàsita ka** 'When you first went to Japan, had you ever eaten Japanese food?'

*4. /PREDICATE X + **kotô wa** + PREDICATE X/*

Yet another special combination with **kotô** consists of **kotô wa** preceded by an imperfective predicate and followed by a repetition of that predicate in the same or a derived form. The combination implies that the predicate at least (**wa**) is valid in terms of its repeated form, but any more general related extensions must not be assumed. If the nonapplicable extension is not specifically stated, it may be inferred from the context. Examples:

Sakana o tabêru koto wa tabêru kedo, amári sukì zya nâi desu. 'I DO EAT fish, but I don't like it very much.'

Takâi koto wa takâi desu ğa . . 'It IS EXPENSIVE, but . . .' (it's worth the price).

Kono wasyoku wa, kîree na koto wa kîree desyoo? 'This Japanese food IS (at least) BEAUTIFUL, isn't it?'

Yasúmì no koto wa yasúmì datta kedo . . 'It WAS a VACATION, but . . .' (I didn't have a very good time).

Yaménai kotò wa yamémasèñ ğa, koré karà wa, amári miènai to omoimasu. 'S/he's NOT going to QUIT, but from now on, I don't think s/he'll appear very often.'

*5. /**X ni tûite**/*

The sequence /nominal X + **ni** + **tûite**/ = 'concerning X,' 'about X,' 'regarding X.' In origin, **tûite** is undoubtedly the gerund of **tûku** 'become attached,' and the /**X ni**/ phrase that precedes it supports this interpretation: 'being attached to (i.e., concerned with) X.'

Most of the patterns in which the /**X ni tûite**/ combinations occur are typical gerund patterns, but sometimes they are nominal patterns. The occurrence of /**X ni tûite + dà** (including its **no** and **na** alternates)/, however, suggests that the whole combination occurs within a larger context, as if it were a "super-nominal." Note the following types of usage.

(1) Followed directly by the copula **dà** (NOT a typical gerund pattern).

Konó hòñ wa tuyú ni tùite desu. 'This book is about the rainy season.'

Tuyú ni tùite no hôñ desu. 'It's a book (which is) about the rainy season.'

(2) Hooking up directly with a predicate as an expression of manner (a pattern shared by nominals and verbal gerunds).

Tuyú ni tùite hanásimàsita. 'I talked about the rainy season.'

Îtu kara sonó siğoto o hazimerù ka to iú kotò ni tuite soódañ-simas-yòo. 'Let's discuss (concerning the matter described as) when we're going to start that work.'

(3) Followed by phrase-particles **wa** and **mo** (patterns also shared by nominals and verbal gerunds).

Nihóñ no tuyu ni tùite wa tyôtto hanáseru to omóimàsu kedo . . 'About the rainy season in Japan (at least) I think I can talk a little, but . . .'

> **Raíneñ no kàiḡi ni tuite mo kañḡàete okimasyoo.** 'Let's do some advance thinking about next year's conference, too.'
>
> **Nâni/nâñ ni tuite mo hanásànakatta.** 'I didn't talk about anything.'

6. **hosîi**

The affecive adjectival **hosîi** functions as a double-**ḡa**, affective predicate:

> **Dâre ḡā hosîi?** 'Who wants it?'
>
> **Nâni ḡa hosîi?** 'What do you want?'
>
> **Nakamura-kuñ ḡa koré ḡa hosìi kara . .** 'Nakamura wants this, so . . .'

These combinations are direct and assertive. They should not be considered exact equivalents of the more polite **onéḡai-simàsu, moraitai, itadakitai,** and so on when used in reference to what the speaker or members of his/her in-group want. Unlike the more polite forms, **hosîi** also frequently refers to the desires of the out-group.

The sequence /verbal gerund + **hosîi**/ expresses a desire to have the action of the verbal performed by others:

> **Kono hako o hakóñde hosìi.** 'I want this box carried.'
>
> **Konó nìmotu o todôkete hosîi.** 'I want this luggage delivered.'

When the desire is for something NOT to be done, /-**(a)nai de** + **hosîi**/ occurs:

> **Soó iwanài de hosîi.** 'I want [you] not to say that.'

If a nominal expresses the person by whom the action is or is not to be performed, it is followed by particle **ni**:

> **Arúbàito ni konó koñpyùutaa no 'tukaikata o narâtte hosîi.** 'I want the part-timer to learn how to use this computer.'

Note that the combination /gerund + **hosîi** + **to iú kotò da**/ regularly refers to the wishes of third parties (cf. CC3[J]b).

⚠WARNING: Do not confuse -**tai** forms with /gerund + **hosîi**/ patterns. Compare **tukúritài** 'I want to make it' and **tukûtte hosîi** 'I want to have it made' (by someone else).

In all /gerund + **hosîi**/ patterns, the substitution of **moraitai** or **itadakitai**↓ for **hosîi** results in a less demanding expression that indicates desire on the part of the speaker in terms of being a beneficiary of an action.

Drills

In all the following drills, practice both the full form (with -**rare**-) and the abbreviated form (with -**re**-) of vowel verbal potentials.

A 1. **Mâiniti ko(rá)rémàsu ka**↗
    'Is it possible to come every day?'

    Êe, tâbuñ ko(rá)rèru daroo to omóimàsu.
    'Yes, I think it probably is possible (to come).'

  2. **Asoko ni sumémàsu ka**↗
    'Is it possible to live there?'

    Êe, tâbuñ sumêru daroo to omóimàsu.
    'Yes, I think it probably is possible (to live).'

3. **kore naósemàsu**; 4. **ni-sâñ-niti yasúmemàsu**; 5. **eéḡo mo naraemàsu**; 6. **îma sûḡu kañḡae(ra)remàsu**; 7. **môtto sôba made tikázukemàsu**

B 1. **Asítà mo kimásèñ ka**   **Ainiku ko(rá)rênai ñ desu.**
'Won't you come tomorrow, too?'   'Unfortunately, (it's that) I can't (come).'

2. **Asítà mo reñsyuu-simasèñ ka**   **Ainiku reñsyuu-dekìnai ñ desu.**
'Won't you practice tomorrow too?'   'Unfortunately, (it's that) I can't practice.'

3. **dekákemasèñ**; 4. **deñwa iremasèñ**; 5. **azúkarimasèñ**; 6. **todókemasèñ**; 7. **torímasèñ**; 8. **iímasèñ**; 9. **tukúrimasèñ**; 10. **maḡárimasèñ**

● Repeat the preceding drill, replacing the potential in each response with the appropriate corresponding /—— **kotô ḡa dekîru**/ pattern. (Examples: 1. **Ainiku kûru koto wa dekînai ñ desu.** 2. **Ainiku reñsyuu-suru kotò wa dekìnai ñ desu.**)

C 1. **Kotíra è wa irássyarànakatta yoo desu nêe.**   **Êe, ko(rá)rênakute nêe.**
'It seems that you didn't come here (at least), did you!'   'That's right. Being unable to come . . .' (I didn't).

2. **Atíra è wa oyóri ni narànakatta yoo desu nêe.**   **Êe, yorénàkute nêe.**
'It seems that you didn't stop by over there (at least), did you!'   'That's right. Being unable to stop by . . .' (I didn't).

3. **ano heñ/osáḡasi ni narànakatta**; 4. **gozeñ-tyuu ni/oházime ni narànakatta**; 5. **zêñbu/oáruki ni narànakatta**; 6. **añmari takusañ/onókosi ni narànakatta**; 7. **sûḡu ni/oákirame ni narànakatta**

● Repeat the preceding drill, replacing the potential in each response with the appropriate corresponding /—— **kotô ḡa dekîru**/ pattern. (Examples: 1. **Êe, kûru koto ḡa dekînakute nêe.** 2. **Êe, yorú kotò ḡa dekînakute nêe.**)

D 1. **Kinoo 'kita?**   **Kitâkatta kedo, ko(rá)rênakatta no.**
'Did you come yesterday?'   'I wanted to (come), but (it's that) I couldn't (come).'

2. **Kyôneñ 'turete itta?**   **Turéte ikitàkatta kedo, turéte ikenàkatta no.**
'Did you take her/him last year?'   'I wanted to (take), but (it's that) I couldn't (take).'

3. **kêsa imóotosañ ni àtta**; 4. **ototoi zêmi ni dêta**; 5. **señsyuu 'yoyaku-sita**; 6. **môo kíppu tòtta**; 7. **getúyòobi ni apâato 'saḡasita**

● The responses above are gentle-style. To form the corresponding blunt-style responses, change sentence-final **no** to **ñ da**.

E 1. **Yômu koto mo dekímàsu ka**   **Tasyóo wa yomemàsu ḡa, mâda 'sore hodo . .**
'Can you read (*lit.* is the act of reading possible), too?'   'I can read more or less, but not that well yet.'

2. **Kâku koto mo dekímàsu ka**〰
'Can you write (*lit.* is the act of writing possible), too?'

Tasyóo wa kakemàsu g̃a, mâda 'sore hodo . .
'I can write more or less, but not that well yet.'

3. **tukûru**; 4. **syabêru**; 5. **tabêru**; 6. **hanâsu**; 7. **tûuyaku-suru**

F 1. **Yômu koto wa dekímàsu ka**〰
'Can you read it (*lit.* is the act of reading possible)?'

Sâa, yomêru ka dôo ka tyôtto sin̄pai dèsu g̃a, yôn̄de mimásyòo ka.
Hmm, I'm uneasy about whether I can (read) or not, but shall I try (reading)?'

2. **Osíeru kotò wa dekímàsu ka**〰
'Can you give me instructions (*lit.* is the act of instructing possible)?'

Sâa, osíe(ra)rerù ka dôo ka tyôtto sin̄pai dèsu g̃a, osíete mimasyòo ka.
'Hmm, I'm uneasy about whether I can (give instructions) or not, but shall I try (instructing)?'

3. **nômu**; 4. **naraberu**; 5. **ireru**; 6. **môtu**; 7. **tatêru**

G 1. **Yômu koto wa dekímàsu ka**〰
'Can you read (*lit.* is the act of reading possible)?'

Êe, okag̃esama de, tasyóo wa yomèru yoo ni narímàsita.
'Yes, thanks (for asking), I've reached the point where I can read to some extent (at least).'

2. **Tukáu kotò wa dekímàsu ka**〰
'Can you use it (*lit.* is the act of using possible)?'

Êe, okag̃esama de, tasyóo wa tukaeru yòo ni narímàsita.
'Yes, thanks (for asking), I've reached the point where can use it to some extent (at least).'

3. **tukûru**; 4. **kâku**; 5. **okuru**; 6. **kiku**; 7. **dekakeru**

H 1. **A, yomémasèn̄.**
'Oh, I can't read this.'

Nâni g̃a yomênai n̄ desu ka〰
'What is it that you can't read?'

2. **A, tukúremasèn̄.**
'Oh, I can't make this.'

Nâni g̃a tukúrènai n̄ desu ka〰
'What is it that you can't make?'

3. **kakémasèn̄**; 4. **tabé(ra)remasèn̄**; 5. **mi(rá)rémasèn̄**; 6. **kikémasèn̄**

I 1. **Kon̄na kikài tukáimasu ka**〰
'Do you use machines like these?'

Êe, mâa, tukáu kotò mo arímàsu yo〰
'Yes, well, there are (also) times when I use them.'

2. **Òobaa kimâsu ka**〰
'Do you wear a coat?'

Êe, mâa, kirú kotò mo arímàsu yo〰
'Yes, well, there are (also) times when I wear one.'

3. **huran̄sug̃o syabérimasu**; 4. **tikátetu ni norimàsu**; 5. **tosyôkan̄ ni yorímàsu**; 6. **tênisu simàsu**; 7. **hutón̄ ni nemàsu**; 8. **kamínarì narímàsu**

● a. Repeat the preceding drill, replacing the affirmative responses with negatives in the

/—— **kotô wa arímasèñ**/ pattern. Examples: 1. **Ie, tukáu kotò wa arímasèñ.** 'No, I never use them.' (*lit.* 'There aren't any occasions when I use them.') 2. **Ie, kirú kotò wa arímasèñ.** 'No, I never wear one.' (*lit.* 'There aren't any occasions when I wear one.')

   b. Repeat the preceding drill, replacing the responses with new responses according to the following pattern: 1. **Êe, hotôñdo mâiniti tukáimàsu kedo, tukáwanai kotò mo arímàsu nêe.** 'Yes, I use them almost every day, but there are also times when I don't use them.' 2. **Êe, hotôñdo mâiniti kimâsu kedo, kinái kotò mo arímàsu nêe.** 'Yes, I wear one almost every day, but there are also times when I don't wear one.'

J 1. **Koñna kikài wa tukáwanài desyoo.**
   'You probably don't use machines like these.'

    Iya, tukáu kotò ğa âru ñ desu yo⤳
   'No, (it's that) there are times when I do use them, you know.'

2. **Byóoki nì wa narânai desyoo.**
   'You probably don't get sick.'

    Iya, nâru koto ğa âru ñ desu yo⤳
   'No, (it's that) there are times when I do get [sick], you know.'

3. **señsèe ni/omé ni kakarànai**; 4. **ûmi e/ikanai**; 5. **kono osara/kowárènai**; 6. **kâre no koto/siñpai-sinai**; 7. **soñna monò/yakû ni tatânai**; 8. **zyâñpaa/nuğânai**

K 1. **Îtu mo koñpyùutaa o tukáù ñ desu ka⤳**
   '(Is it that) you always use a computer?'

    Êe, tukáwanai kotò wa nâi desu ne!
   'Yes, there aren't any occasions when I don't (use).'

2. **Îtu mo tûuyaku o tanômu ñ desu ka⤳**
   '(Is it that) you always hire an interpreter?'

    Êe, tanómànai koto wa nâi desu ne!
   'Yes, there aren't any occasions when I don't (hire).'

3. **gôhañ o nokôsu**; 4. **boósi o kabùtte (i)ru**; 5. **syosai ni iru**; 6. **taíhùu ğa kûru**; 7. **koko ni yoru**

L 1. **Asóko karà wa, arûite mo ko(rá)rêru desyoo?**
   'From there, you can also walk here, can't you?'

    Êe, arûite kûru koto mo arímasu yo⤳
   'Yes, I sometimes do (*lit.* there are also times when I come having walked), you know.'

2. **Asóko màde wa, zitêñsya de mo ikérù desyoo?**
   'That far, you can also go by bicycle, can't you?'

    Êe, zitêñsya de ikú kotò mo arímàsu yo⤳
   'Yes, I sometimes do (*lit.* there are also times when I go by bicycle), you know.'

3. **koñna hòñ/tosyôkañ kara karite/yomêru**; 4. **anó heñ no heyà/hudóosañya ni tanòñde/sağaseru**

M 1. **Watasi, nihoñğo ğa hâyâku yomênai ñ desu ğa ..**
   '(It's that) I can't read Japanese fast, but . . .' (is that all right?)

    Âa, hâyâku yomêru hituyoo wa arímasèñ kara, daízyòobu desu yo⤳
   'Oh, there is no need to be able to read fast, so it's all right.'

2. **Watasi, keésàñki g̃a ûmâku tukáenài
ñ desu g̃a . .**
'(It's that) I can't use a calculator with
any skill, but . . .' (is that all right?)

**Âa, ûmâku tukaeru hituyoo wa arímasèñ
kara, daízyòobu desu yo⌄**
'Oh, there is no need to be able to use one
skillfully, so it's all right.'

3. **kotóbà/ûmâku hanásènai;** 4. **kimono/tyañto ʹki(ra)renai;** 5. **atárasìi namae/sûg̃u
obóe(ra)rènai;** 6. **sig̃oto/sûg̃u ʹhazime(ra)renai;** 7. **yâtiñ/zêñbu haráènai**

N 1. **Koñpyùutaa tukáemàsu?**
'Can you use a computer?'

Mâa, tukáeru kotò wa tukáemàsu kedo . .
'Well, I *can use* one, but . . .' (not very well).

2. **Wasyoku tabémàsu?**
'Do you eat Japanese food?'

Mâa, tabêru koto wa tabémàsu kedo . .
'Well, I *do eat* it, but . . .' (not very much).

3. **tûuyaku muzúkasìi desu;** 4. **sûg̃u hazíme(ra)remàsu;** 5. **tokee naórimàsu;** 6. **kitá
no hòo sag̃ásemàsu;** 7. **kotóbà ni narémàsu;** 8. **zêñbu haírimàsu;** 9. **go-róku-niñ
nokoremàsu;** 10. **kore súppài desu;** 11. **asoko nig̃îyaka desu**

O 1. **Yôku ʹsag̃asita?**
'Did you search well?'

Êe, sag̃ásu kotò wa sag̃ásità ñ desu yo⌄
'Yes, (it's that) I *did search* (at least).'

2. **Kimatta zikañ ni ʹtyañto
ʹhazimatta?**
'Did it start promptly at the
scheduled time?'

**Êe, hazímaru kotò wa hazímattà ñ desu
yo⌄**
'Yes, (it's that) it *did start,* (at least).'

3. **señmoñ no hitò ni kiíte mìta;** 4. **syokúdoo no dèñki ʹkesita;** 5. **nâñ-tubo âru ka
ʹhudoosàñya ni ʹkiita;** 6. **sîñg̃uru o hutâ-heya tanôñda;** 7. **kuúkoo màde ʹdemu-
kaeta;** 8. **ano hoñyaku taíheñ dàtta;** 9. **kinoo no kooeñ nihóñg̃o dàtta**

P 1. **Mâda koñpyùutaa no tukaikata
narâtte (i)nâi desyoo?**
'You haven't studied how to use a
computer yet, have you?'

**Iya, zitû wa ʹiti-do narâtta koto g̃a âru ñ
desu.**
'No, actually, (it's that) I've had instruction
once.'

2. **Mâda señsèe no otaku ni ukág̃atte
(i)nài desyoo?**
'You haven't visited the professor's
home yet, have you?'

**Iya, zitû wa ití-do ukag̃atta kotò g̃a âru ñ
desu.**
'No, actually, (it's that) I have visited it
once.'

3. **Nihoñ no kaisya ni ʹsyuusyoku-site (i)nai;** 4. **huráñsug̃o karà no hoñyaku wa ʹsite
(i)nai;** 5. **rêe no supóotukàa, notte (i)nai[2];** 6. **Hoḱkàidoo no hoo ʹryokoo-site (i)nai;**
7. **Oóta-señsèe no zyûg̃yoo, dête (i)nai[2]**

Q 1. **Koñpyùutaa no ʹtukaikata wa,
gozôñzi desu neʕ**
'You know how to use a computer,
right?'

**Ie, zitû wa tukátta kotò g̃a nâi no de,
añmari . .**
'No, actually I've never used one, so [I
don't know] very much [about them].'

2. **Mêziro made no ʹikikata wa,
gozôñzi desu neʕ**

**Ie, zitû wa iṫta kotò g̃a nâi no de,
añmari . .**

---

2. Note the occurrence of the goal, without following particle **ni**, as a general topic of discussion.

'You know how to go to Mejiro, right?'

'No, actually I've never gone [there], so [I don't know] very much [about it].'

3. **hikôoki no kippu/toríkàta**; 4. **demae/tanómikàta**; 5. **yukata/kikata**; 6. **konó màdo/ akekata**; 7. **omiyaǧe/watasikata**

R 1. **Kimúra-señsèe ǧa hôñ o kâite (i)ru-rasii desu yo**

'Say, Professor Kimura apparently is writing a book.'

Sôo desu ka. Nâñ/nâni ni tuite kâite (i)rássyàru ñ desyoo nêe.

'Is that right. I wonder what it is s/he's writing about.'

2. **Butyoo ǧa arúbàito no ko to hanâsite (i)ru-rasii desu yo**

'Say, the division chief apparently is talking with that part-timer.'

Sôo desu ka. Nâñ/nâni ni tuite hanâsite (i)rássyàru ñ desyoo nêe.

'Is that right. I wonder what it is s/he's talking about.'

3. **Hasimoto-sañ/keñkyuuzyò ni 'deñwa-site (i)ru**; 4. **Nôǧuti-sañ/komâtte (i)ru**; 5. **Suǧîura-sañ/kañǧàete (i)ru**; 6. **Kodáma-señsèe/yôñde (i)ru**; 7. **Nakáda-señsèe/ Osámu-kuñ no oyà ni 'soodañ-site (i)ru**

S 1. **Omósiròi kooeñ o kikímàsita yo**

'Say, I heard an interesting lecture.'

Nâñ/nâni ni tuite no kóoeñ dèsu ka

'(It's) a lecture about what?'

2. **Omósiròi zadâñkai o mimâsita yo**

'Say, I saw an interesting round-table discussion.'

Nâñ/nâni ni tuite no zadâñkai desu ka

'(It's) a round-table discussion about what?'

3. **hanási o kikímàsita**; 4. **hôñ o yomímàsita**; 5. **zyûǧyoo ni demâsita**; 6. **bañǧumi o mimàsita**; 7. **nyûusu o kikímàsita**

T 1. **Anâta wa, tâsika huráñsuǧo ǧa señmoñ dèsita neʕ**

'You, as I recall, had French as your specialty, didn't you?'

Êe. Dâ kara, huráñsuǧo ni tùite siʕte (i)ru kotò o ikásèru siǧoto ǧa sitâi to omôtte (i)masu.

'Yes. Therefore I've been thinking that I'd like to do work where I will be able to make use of what I know about French.'

2. **Anâta wa, tâsika doítuǧo ǧa señmoñ dèsita neʕ**

'You, as I recall, had German as your specialty, didn't you?'

Êe. Dâ kara, doítuǧo ni tùite siʕte (i)ru kotò o ikásèru siǧoto ǧa sitâi to omôtte (i)masu.

'Yes. Therefore I've been thinking that I'd like to do work where I will be able to make use of what I know about German.'

3. **seezi**; 4. **gaikokuǧo**; 5. **kêezai**

U 1. **Itú-ǧoro màde ni sumásemasyòo ka—kono siǧoto.**

'By (approximately) when shall I finish—this work?'

Narubeku koñsyuu-tyuu ni sumàsete hosîi desu neʕ

'I want it finished within this week, as nearly as possible.'

2. **Itú-ǧoro màde ni soózi-site okimasyòo ka—syosai.**

Narubeku koñsyuu-tyuu ni soozi-sit(e) òite hosîi desu neʕ

'By (approximately) when shall I take care of cleaning—the study?'

'I want it cleaned within this week, as nearly as possible.'

3. **saḡásimasyòo/kôñpa no heyâ**; 4. **kañḡàete okímasyòo/kooeñ no naiyoo**; 5. **haráimasyòo/ yâtiñ**; 6. **tôri ni ikímasyòo/kippu**

V 1. **Kimi ḡa suru?**

'Are *you* going to do it?'

Iya, warûi kedo, sité hosìi no.

'No, I'm sorry to say this, but I want you to do it.'

2. **Kimi ḡa hazimeru?**

'Are *you* going to start it?'

Iya, warûi kedo, hazímete hosìi no.

'No, I'm sorry to say this, but I want you to start it.'

3. **nokôru**; 4. **saḡasu**; 5. **kañḡaèru**; 6. **harâu**; 7. **mawasu**; 8. **môtu**

W1. **Mîte hosìi?**

'Do you want [someone] to look at it?'

Ñ, yáppàri dâre ka ni mîte moraitai naʃ

'Yeah, after all, I would like to have someone look at it, you know?'

2. **Osíete hosìi?**

'Do you want [someone] to give you instruction?'

Ñ, yáppàri dâre ka ni osíete moraitài naʃ

'Yeah, after all, I would like to have someone give me instruction, you know?'

3. **okôsite**; 4. **tetúdàtte**; 5. **obôete (i)te**; 6. **naôsite**; 7. **tukatte**

Application Exercises

A1. Take turns asking and answering questions involving ability, for example, to write Japanese; to read Russian; to speak French; to translate from English into Japanese; to make sushi; to buy fresh fish in this area; to use a word processor; to come here by 8:30 tomorrow morning; to begin work earlier on Friday than today; to go from place X to place Y by subway; to buy English–Japanese dictionaries in bookstores in this town; to study Japanese history at this university; to talk about Japanese economics; etc. Practice both the potential and the /—— **kotô ḡa dekîru**/ pattern. Make your replies conversationally natural (using echo questions and appropriate qualifiers and hesitation noises), expansive ('I can write, but not very well'; 'I can speak *and* read'; 'I *have* made it, but I'm not very good at it'; 'I couldn't do it before, but now I've reached the point where I can'; etc.), and accurate in reflecting what you would actually say in the situation. Don't grind out answers as if a computer were performing mechanical drills of the kind we have carefully avoided in this text (for example, 'Is the book on the table interesting?' . . . 'Yes, the book on the table is interesting.' No native speaker would ordinarily use language in that way!!!). TALK NATURALLY! COMMUNICATE!

2. Take turns asking and answering questions relating to past or recurring experiences, involving, for example, going to Europe; coming here by bus; speaking French in France; reading a Chinese newspaper; using a computer; working in Japan; playing golf in Japan; riding on the **siñkàñseñ**; making **teñpura**; watching a Japanese soap opera; not commuting by car; not drinking coffee in the morning; not using a word processor in writing letters; etc. Practice both the perfective and the imperfective with the /**kotô ḡa âru**/ pattern. Again, make your replies conversationally natural, expansive, and representative of what you would say in the situation.

3. Take turns asking general, unqualified questions and providing answers that include qualifications. For example:

Kore, ano hako ni hâiru desyoo ka. 'Do you suppose this will go into that box?'
Hâiru koto wa haírimàsu kedo, kowáreyasùi monô da kara, môtto oókìi hako no hôo ǧa îi to omóimàsu yo✓ 'It will go in, but since it's (a) breakable (thing), a bigger box would be better, I think.

4a. Take turns describing activities that you want to have performed, using the /gerund + **hosîi**/ pattern, and replying appropriately. For example, state that you want to have this letter translated into Japanese; this box delivered to the teacher's home; a new secretary looked for; books about Japanese history collected; **sìṅkàṅseṅ** tickets bought; the second floor straightened up; the broken window in the next room fixed; etc. In providing answers, again be natural, expansive, and communicate what you really would say. You may suggest appropriate places or people for handling the task in question, or you may offer your own services.

b. Next cover similar topics, assuming that you are reporting someone else's wishes. Use the /gerund + **hosîi to iú kotò da**/ pattern.

5. Practice conducting job interviews. Distribute cards to each interviewee that provide the background information s/he is to use during the interview—name, age, marital status, educational background, experience, foreign-language ability, the kind of position sought, etc. At the conclusion of each interview, ask and answer questions about the contents of the interview.

6. Practice polite refusals. Take turns setting up situations in which one member of the group is asked to do something. Have that person refuse politely by identifying a problem with his/her taking it on (other than personal convenience!) and suggesting another individual or course of action that is more appropriate. Some possible situations: a request to correct the English in this letter about next month's conference; a request to speak in Japanese about American and British English to the students in Professor Nakamura's linguistics seminar; a request to be(come) the interpreter at tomorrow's sociology conference; a request to write this on a word processor; a request to make a pie (e.g., for a party that is being planned). Remember that in all these situations, the relationship between the participants should be such that refusal in a Japanese context is not unthinkable.

B. Core Conversations: Substitution
In practicing the Core Conversations with appropriate substitutions, follow each new version with questions relating to the new contents.

SECTION B

Core Conversations

1(J)a. **Burâuṅ-saṅ. Îma nâni site (i)ru?**   (N)a. **Eeǧo no sikéṅ-mòṅdai tukûtte (i)ru tokoro.**

b. **Âto de îi kara, kore mo 'waapuro de kâite moraenai?**   b. **Êe, îi wa yo✓**

2(N)a. Morimoto-sañ. Yuuḡata tyôtto
ozîkañ o itádakemasèñ ka↙
Anâta ni zêhi syoókai-site hosìi
to iu hitô ḡa irû ñ desu yo.

       (J)a. Sôo desu ka↙ Kamáimasèñ yo↙ Dâ
kedo, kotíra no hòo made kitê
itádakemàsu ka↙

b. Motîroñ soó simàsu yo. Dôo mo
kyoósyuku dèsu.

. . .

Osóku nàtte sumímasèñ. Tyoodo
deyôo to sita tokorô ni deńwa ḡa
hàitte simatte . .

       b. Iya. Koʿtì mo tyoódo ìma owátta
tokorò desu kara . .

3(J)a. Mîraa-sañ. Kokó nì mo ni-sáñ-
kai kità koto no âru
ryuúḡàkùsee ḡa itâ desyoo—
nihoñḡo ḡa perapera no hito.
Obôete (i)ru?

      (N)a. Ñ. |Eeto| Nâñ te iʿtà kke. Namáe
wa omoidasènai kedo, Rińkaañ-
dàiḡaku no hitô desyoo?

b. Sôo sôo. Teḡámi kakòo to omôtta
ñ da kedo, zyûusyo ḡa
wakáranakute . . Mîraa-sañ
siranai?

      b. Watási wa siranài kedo, Toodai no
buńḡakùbu ni kitê (i)ta ñ da kara,
asóko de osiete moraerù ñ zya nai
ka sira.

c. Âa, îma ʼbetu no yoozi de
ʼToodai ni deńwa kakeyòo to
omôtte (i)ta tokórò na no.

      c. Tyoódo yòkatta desu ne!

ENGLISH EQUIVALENTS

1(J)a. What are you doing (now), Sue
(*lit.* Ms. Brown)?

      (N)a. I'm (just now) making up English
test questions.

b. Later on will be fine, but (*lit.* so)
can('t) I have you write *this* on the
word processor, too?

      b. O.K.

2(N)a. Ms. Morimoto, could(n't) I have a
little of your time in the evening?
(It's that) there's someone (*lit.* a
person) who very much wants to
be introduced to you.

    (J)a. Really? That will be fine. But can I
have you come here?

  b. Of course I'll do that. I'm very
grateful to you.

We're sorry to be late. Just as we
were about to leave, a phone call
came in, and . . . (you know what
that means).

   . . .

    b. No problem. I (too) just now
finished [what I was doing], so
(there's no need to apologize).

3(J)a. Ms. Miller, there was an exchange
student who has come here (too)
two or three times—you know—
one who is really good in
Japanese. Do you remember?

    (N)a. Yeah. Uh, what was her/his
name. . . . The name I can't recall,
but s/he's from Lincoln University—
right?

  b. That's right! I thought I would
write a letter [to her/him], but not
knowing the address. . . . You
don't know it, Ms. Miller?

    b. I don't know it, but s/he was (*lit.* had
come) in the literature department
at Tokyo University, so I wonder if
it isn't the case that you can get
information there.

  c. Oh, (it's that) I was just now
thinking of calling Tokyo
University on another matter.

    c. Then that's just great!

BREAKDOWNS
(AND SUPPLEMENTARY VOCABULARY)

1. **sikêñ**
   sikéñ-mòñdai
   tokórò (SP1)

   tukûtte (i)ru tokórò da
   kâite moraeru (SP2)

exam, test
test problem, test question
stage in a sequence; the very moment (of
an activity)
is just now making
can have [it] written

kâite moraenai?	can('t) [I] have [it] written?
2. **yuuǧata**	evening
ozîkañ o itádakemasèñ↓ ka⤳	can('t) I have [some of] your time? /polite/
zêhi syoókai-site hosìi	wants to be introduced by all means
dâ kedo (SP3)	however
kitê itádakemàsu↓ ka⤳	will I be able to have you come? /polite/
kyoósyuku dà	is grateful, appreciative; is obliged; is apologetic
deyôo to suru (SP4)	be about to leave; try to leave
deyôo to sita tokórò ni	at the very moment when [I] had been about to leave
deńwa ǧa hàiru	telephone calls come in
owaru /-u; owatta/	finish, terminate
owátta tokorò da	is the very moment when [I] finished; just finished
3. **ryuúǧàkùsee**	student studying abroad
perapera	fluent
nihóñǧo ǧa perapera no hitò	person whose Japanese is fluent
Nâñ te (i)ttà kke. (SP5)	What was his/her name (I can't recall)!
omóidàsu /-u; omóidàsita/	recall
Rińkaañ-dàgiǧaku	Lincoln University/College
zyûusyo	address
+ **gakubu**	academic department; college (within a university)
buńǧàkùbu	literature department
+ **kyoóyoogàkùbu**	liberal arts department or college
deńwa ǧa hàiru	telephone calls come in
osiete moraeru	can have [someone] teach; can get information
X zya nai ka sira. (SP5)	I wonder if it isn't X.
betu	separate; different
omôtte (i)ta tokórò da	is the very moment when [I] was just thinking

Academic Disciplines

zińrùiǧaku	anthropology
seébutùǧaku	biology
sêebutu	living things
kâǧaku	chemistry
kooǧaku	engineering

tîri	geography
rekisi	history
hooḡaku	law, jurisprudence
hooritu	a law, the law
geńḡòḡaku	linguistics
suuḡaku	mathematics
îḡaku	medicine
tetûḡaku	philosophy
butúrìḡaku	physics (as an academic subject)
sińrìḡaku	psychology
syuúkyòoḡaku	religion (as an academic subject)
syûukyoo	religion
kâḡaku	science

MISCELLANEOUS NOTES

1. In CC1, Kato asks his fellow graduate student, Sue Brown, who is busy at a university word processor, to write something for him. The style is casual, with direct-style final predicates. Sue Brown's use of sentence-final **wa yo** ([N]b) is feminine.

Note the patterning of this request: before making his request, Kato checks that circumstances are appropriate to it.

(J)b. Kato's request addressed to Sue Brown follows a **kara** sequence that would ordinarily be described as causal: /perfective or imperfective predicate X + **kara . . /** = 'X, so . . . ,' 'because X, ...' But the fundamental difference between English cause and Japanese **kara** sequences of this kind becomes clear in this kind of example. We cannot say that it is '*because* later on will be fine' that Kato makes his request. What we can say is that his request is to be carried out stemming from—based on—that fact. In other words, 'Would you do this for me, keeping in mind the fact that later on will be fine?' Note that in English, *'Would you write this for me, because later on will be fine?' would make no sense.

2. In CC2, Sue Brown asks Ms. Morimoto, her female colleague at work, to meet an acquaintance of hers who wants to be introduced. The meeting is set up for the evening. The late arrival of Sue and her friend calls for an apology. Sue also offers an excuse, as often occurs in such situations, although it is not absolutely required. Note how Ms. Morimoto politely turns the apology aside by reassuring Sue and her friend that she had just finished her work, implying that she had not been kept waiting.

As usual, Sue Brown and Ms. Morimoto use careful-style in speaking with each other, with distal-style final predicates; Ms. Morimoto also uses distal-style before **kara** in (J)b. In stating her personal request for the benefit of a friend of hers, Sue Brown uses a polite request pattern.

Observe the pattern of this request: (1) statement of the request; (2) explanation for it; (3) basic agreement from the person receiving the request; (4) introduction of a minor qualification by that person; (5) resolution and expression of thanks by the person making the request. The final exchange of the CC is an example of an apology plus explanation pattern followed by a response that politely dismisses the apology as unnecessary.

(N)a. The polite **ozikań** refers to the addressee's time. Note that Sue Brown and Ms.

Morimoto are close enough in rank to permit the use of **anâta** as a generally polite but nondeferential form of address.

(J)a. **Kotíra no hòo** contrasts the location of the speaker with that of others involved, in this case, Sue Brown and her friend.

(N)b. **Kyoosyuku** is another example of a Japanese expression which, through the concept of obligation, incorporates apology and gratitude. It is a very polite, formal—and often businesslike—expression. It may express thanks to the addressee and/or apologize for causing trouble or inconvenience. Compare **sumímasèñ** and **osôre-irimasu**, both of which also share this range of meaning.

Sue Brown's excuse for being late ends with a gerund pattern, **hâitte simatte . .** The preceding apology has already covered the implied conclusion.

(J)b. **Kottì mo** implies that 'here, too,' as well as on your side, things are running late. Ms. Morimoto's use of **iya** and **kottì** shows a slight movement toward a more casual style.

The verbal **owaru** occurs commonly in reference to inanimates (**kâiḡi ḡa 'owatta, eeḡa ḡa hâyâku owaru**, etc.), but also possible are occurrences like **siḡoto o owaru, sâñ-zi made ni 'owaritai, hâyâku owárimasyòo**, etc., indicating that the verbal is indeed operational. Its meaning is close to that of the **sûmu/sumáseru** pair, but **owaru** usually implies ending at a concluding point. Note the derivative nominal **owari** 'the end.'

3. In CC3, Ms. Tanaka, the consultant, is trying to locate someone's address. Deborah Miller suggests that she ask the literature department at Tokyo University to give it to her. Note carefully the speech style of these two women. Ms. Tanaka uses casual style with direct-style verbal predicates but sentence-final **desyoo**, an indication that in this casual-style context the style is also gentle; Ms. Miller's style is essentially the same, with both sentence-final **desyoo** and **ka sira** (see SP5, following) marking gentle-style. The distal-style final adjectival predicate **yokatta desu ne!** suggests closure of the conversational unit with a distal form that sets up linguistic separation from later conversation and matches the rather gentle style of the conversation. The direct-style equivalent of this utterance would be quite blunt in this context.

Note how this CC, an example of a request for information, is constructed: (1) background information meant to orient the addressee is followed by (2) a check by the addressee on her understanding of that information; (3) an explanation for the request and the actual request follow; (4) the negative response by the addressee is supplemented by her suggestion for another way to get the desired information; (5) support for the alternate solution comes from the requester; (6) closure on a pleasant note.

(J)a. **Kokó nì mo** 'also/even to this place,' i.e., in addition to various other assumed places. **Kitâ koto no âru** ends the sentence modifier describing the nominal **ryuúḡàkùsee**; the **no** here can be replaced by **ḡa**. **Perapera**, another example of onomatopoeia, is used in reference to speech that is glib, fluent, voluble. In **nihóñḡo ḡa perapera no hitò, no** is the special pre-nominal alternate of **dà**, and **nihoñḡo ḡa** is the affect of the affective predicate **perapera dà/no**: 'a Japanese-is-fluent person.'

(N)a. **Namae wa** '[his/her] name, at least,' i.e., in contrast with other things I may be able to recall. Note the use of **namae** without **o-** in reference to a third person, not present, to whom no special deference is owed by either of the participants in the conversation. **Omóidàsu** and **obóèru**, both of which may occur in situations covered by 'remember' in English, are carefully distinguished in Japanese. **Omóidàsu** refers to calling to mind—bringing back to one's thoughts—something that was previously known. **Obóèru** pertains to an initial committing to memory—learning, memorizing.

(N)b. **Watasi wa** 'I, at least,' in contrast with the Toodai office I'm about to mention. Note the use of **kitê** in reference to motion to a place where the speaker is not presently located: in this case, Ms. Miller talks about the student as 'coming [from points outside Japan] to the literature department at Tokyo University.' **Asoko** refers to a place already familiar to the speaker and addressee.

(J)c. **Betú no yoozi dè** 'because of a different/separate matter.' Compare **zîko de okú-rete kùru** 'come late because of an accident.'

Academic Disciplines: Note the difference between medicine that one takes (**kusuri**) and medicine as a field of study (**iĝaku**).

Kâĝaku 'chemistry' and **kâgaku** 'science' are distinguished in the spoken language only by context. However, both occur commonly in compounds that immediately differentiate them. In the written language different symbols represent the **ka** of these two words.

Structural Patterns

1. /—— **tokórò da/**

We have previously encountered **tokórò** as a general spatial nominal meaning 'place'; we now examine its extended use referring to place in a situational sense—stage in a sequence—from which it moves to a temporal meaning referring to the very moment when something occurs. **Tokórò** is just another Japanese item that can refer to both location in space and location in time. Compare **mâe** 'place in front' and 'time before'; **aida** 'space between' and 'interval of time'; **-zyuu** 'throughout (of space and time).'

We have already been introduced to a number of different words referring to time: **zikañ** indicates a period of time (**zikáñ ĝa kakáru** 'it takes time') or a time on the clock (**zikáñ dà**) 'it's time [to go, to do something, etc.]'; **tokî** refers to time as the time or occasion when something occurs or applies (**byoóki ni nàtta toki** '[occasions] when one has become sick'; **kodómo no tokì** 'childhood'). In contrast, **tokórò** as a time word refers to the very moment of an occurrence. Its most frequent use is as part of a nominal predicate (i.e., followed by a form of the copula **dà**) with a preceding modifier, specifically a sentence modifier. The form of the final predicate of this modifier is crucial in interpreting the meaning of the sequence. Study the following examples carefully:

Teĝámi o kàku tokórò desu. 'I'm just about to write a letter.' (*lit.* 'It's the very moment when I'm going to write a letter.')

Teĝámi o kàite (i)ru tokórò desu. 'I'm just now writing a letter.' (*lit.* 'It's the very moment when I'm writing a letter.')

Teĝámi o kàita tokórò desu. 'I just wrote a letter.' (*lit.* 'It's the very moment when I wrote a letter.')

Teĝámi o kàite (i)ta tokórò desu. 'I have just been writing a letter.' (*lit.* 'It's the very moment when I was writing a letter.')

Teĝámi o kàku tokórò desita. 'I was just going to write a letter.' (*lit.* 'It was the very I-will-write-a-letter moment.')

Teĝámi o kàite (i)ru tokórò desita. 'I was just writing a letter.' (*lit.* 'It was the very I-am-writing-a-letter moment.')

Teḡámi o kàita tokórò desita. 'I had just written a letter.' (*lit.* 'It was the very I-wrote-a-letter moment.')

Teḡámi o kàite (i)ta tokórò desita. 'I had just been writing a letter.' (*lit.* 'It was the very I-was-writing-a-letter moment.')

Tokórò with its preceding modifier may also occur followed by phrase-particles, for example, **ni** and **e**, and a motion verbal, indicating the precise moment of occurrence of the motion:

Teḡámi o kàite (i)ru tokórò e/ni, tomódati ḡa hàitte kimasita. 'Just as I was writing a letter, a friend came in.'

A **tokórò** pattern may also occur as an operand, followed by phrase-particle **o**:

Nakamura-sañ ḡa koñpyùutaa o tukátte (i)ru tokorò o mimâsita. 'I saw Mr/s. Nakamura at the very moment when s/he was using the computer.'

The association of **tokórò** with 'the very moment' is so strong that it affects the meaning of motion verbals in the **-te (i)ru** form. Ordinarily, such combinations indicate a state resulting from a previous occurrence (on one or more occasions), but when joined with **tokórò**, they refer to the time of motion. Compare: **Yuúbìñkyoku ni iťte (i)màsu.** 'S/he has gone to the post office.' and **Yuúbìñkyoku ni iťte (i)ru tokorò desu.** 'S/he is just now going to the post office.'

In the ritualized utterance **Oísoḡasii tokorò (o) ariḡatoo gozaimasita.** 'Thank you for giving me your time when you are busy,' the **tokórò** pattern with following **o** assumes an operational activity which, though not expressed, is understood in the context.

These **tokórò** patterns remind us again of the importance of context. Many of the above examples, depending on context, might also refer to the place where the specified activities take place. **Teḡámi o kàku tokórò desu** may also mean 'It's the place where I write (or am going to write) letters.' Perhaps a more accurate way of describing a question of this kind is to point out that a Japanese item like **tokórò** covers location as a broad concept with both time and space implications, and only context makes it possible to distinguish further.

2. REQUEST PATTERNS IN **moraeru ~ itadakeru** ↓

We now add yet another request pattern, in this case viewing the desired thing or action as something to be received by the requester rather than given to him/her. The new pattern uses the potential of **morau** or **itadaku** ↓, i.e., **moraeru** or **itadakeru** ↓. Just as requests that someone give something occur in the negative, really as a suggestion or invitation to the addressee to give (e.g., . . . **kudásaimasèñ ka**⤳), requests that the speaker receive something follow the same pattern. Note that this is one of the rare cases where a question with a predicate in the perfective or imperfective usually refers to the speaker. Compare the following pairs:

Sonó zìsyo (o) kudásaimasèñ ka⤳ 'Would(n't) you be kind enough to give me that dictionary?'

Sonó zìsyo (o) itádakemasèñ ↓ **ka**⤳ 'May(n't) I have that dictionary?' (*lit.* 'Can['t] I receive that dictionary?')

Asítà mo kitê kudásaimasèñ ka⤳ 'Would(n't) you be kind enough to come here tomorrow, too?'

Asítà mo kitê itádakemasèñ↓ **ka**↙ 'Could(n't) I have you come here tomorrow, too?'

Waápuro de kàite kurémasèñ ka↙ 'Will (*lit.* won't) you write this on the word processor for me?'

Waápuro de kàite moráemasèñ ka↙ 'Can('t) I have you write this on the word processor for me?'

Ano hako 'hakoñde kurenai? 'Will (*lit.* won't) you carry that box for me?'

Ano hako 'hakoñde moraenai? 'Can('t) I have you carry that box for me?'

Note how the substitution of an affirmative form of a giving or receiving verbal alters the meaning:

Sonó zìsyo (o) kudásaimàsu ka↙ 'Are you going to be so kind as to give me that dictionary?'

Sonó zìsyo (o) itádakemàsu↓ **ka**↙ 'Am I going to be able to have that dictionary?'

Ano hako 'hakoñde kureru? 'Are you going to carry that box for me?'

Ano hako 'hakoñde moraeru? 'Will I be able to have you carry that box for me?'

Strictly speaking, such questions simply seek information, and in many contexts, that is all they do. But often their real function is to convey the speaker's wishes through a pattern that is interpreted as a request. Their negative equivalents, which in a sense *invite* the addressee to perform the desired action, are softer expressions of request.

WARNING: Be sure to distinguish **morawanai** and (potential) **moraenai**; **itadakanai**↓ and (potential) **itadakenai**↓. There are NO such forms as *MORAINAI and *ITADAKINAI.

3. SENTENCE CONNECTORS

If we rely simply on putting together isolated sentences, we can never produce normal conversation in any language. This is why Core Conversations are used as the basic unit for memorization. A sentence within a conversation is linked to what precedes through such features as special introductory expressions, words like **sore** and **soko** that refer to earlier items in the conversation, intonation, and so on.

Among the special Japanese sentence-initial connecting expressions is a group whose members have one common feature: they appear to have lost an introductory **sore** or **sôo** that refers to what has just been stated. Thus, **dâ kedo** occurring at the beginning of a sentence means something like 'it is that (which was just said), but . . . ,' i.e., 'however.' Its direct-style copula form **dà** can be replaced by **dêsu** or **de gózaimàsu** in very careful and polite style.

Note also **dâ kara** 'since it is that (which was just stated),' 'therefore'; **dê mo** 'even/also if it is that (which was just stated),' 'even so,' 'however'; **dê wa**, or contracted **zyâ(a)** 'granted its being that (at least),' 'in that case,' 'then.' Even the copula gerund **dê** alone may occur initially in a sentence as a conjoining element, similar in meaning to **soré dè** 'being that (just stated),' 'that being the case.'

Sentence connectors occur commonly at the beginning of responses to something said by a conversation partner. They may occur with **sore** or **sôo** included (**sôo da kara, sôo da kedo, soré dè mo, soré dè wa ~ soré zyà(a), soré dè**) with no appreciable difference in meaning beyond being more explicit.

4. /——(y)oo to suru/

We have already encountered the pattern /verbal gerund X + **mîru**/ 'do X and see (how it turns out),' 'try doing X.' It implies the actual occurrence of the action of the gerund with a following check on the result.

We now introduce a new pattern with a similar English equivalent but a different implication. This pattern covers decisions to act in a particular way—decisions regarding what one is about to do or what one will try to do. It is often followed by a statement that a past attempt was unsuccessful either because of an interruption or because of inability. In the imperfective, the pattern covers future endeavors.

The pattern consists of /direct-style verbal consultative (vowel-verbal root + **-yoo**; consonant-verbal root + **-oo**; cf. 20A-SP6) + particle **to** + **suru**/ 'be about to X,' 'try to X.' Note how the pattern is constructed: 'do, act; decide' (= **suru**) + namely (= **to**) + "I guess I'll X" (= ——[**-yoo**]).' The underlying equivalence of quotative **to** and **to**, the particle of accompaniment/manner, becomes more evident in a pattern like this.

A usually unaccented consultative may acquire an accent in this pattern, resulting in alternate accents. Thus: **tukaoo to suru** or **tukáòo to suru**. Study the following examples carefully:

Anó màdo, akéyòo to simâsita ğa, yaṕpàri akánài ñ desu ne! 'I tried to open that window, but the fact is it doesn't open, does it!'

Seńsèe kara no 'teğami o yomôo to simâsita kedo, zeñzeñ yomemasèñ desita. 'I tried to read the letter from the teacher, but I couldn't read it at all.'

Nihóñğo de kakòo to sitê mo, kakênai to omoimasu. 'Even if I try to write it in Japanese, I don't think I can (write).'

Utí e kaeròo to sita tokî ni, gakusee ğa soódañ ni kimàsita. 'When I was about to go home, a student came to talk things over.'

Tyoodo neyóo to sita tokorò ni, deńwa ğa hàitte kimasita. 'Just at the point when/where I was about to go to bed, a call came in.'

5. —— kke; —— ka sira

Ever since lesson 1, we have been introducing sentence-final items that in some way qualify the meaning of a sentence, making it different from a simple sentence like **Dekîru.** For example, compare:

Dekîru yo✓	**Dekîru ne!**
Dekîru ne↗	**Dekîru nêe.**
Dekîru daroo.	**Dekîru daroo?**
Dekîru hazu da.	**Dekîru soo da.**
Dekísòo da.	**Dekîru yoo da.**
Dekîru-rasìi.	**Dekîru tte.**
Dekîru to omôu.	**Dekîru ka mo sirenai.**

In this lesson, we introduce two more sentence-final items, **kke** and **ka sira**.

Kke is an interrogative sentence-particle used when the speaker is attempting to recall the answer to a question, to revive information previously known, with the implication that s/he should know it. Since recall is involved, **kke** is frequently accompanied by the perfective of recall. It may also follow the imperfective direct-style copula **dà**.

When a **kke** question is addressed to oneself, it regularly ends in period intonation; when it involves the addressee as well, /⤳/ intonation may also occur. Examples:

Anó zìsyo, nâñ te itta kke. 'What *was* the name of that dictionary?'

Itoo-sañ no bôttyañ, Tâkasi tte iímàsita kke⤳ 'Was the name of Mr/s. Ito's son Takashi (as I recall)?'

Anó zèmi no kyoositu, dôko da kke. 'Where *is* the classroom for that seminar?'

Nâñ-zi ni kûru ñ da kke⤳ 'What time *is* it that s/he's coming?'

Omósiròi ñ da kke⤳ '*Is* it (the case that it's) interesting?'

Ka sira occurs as a gentle-style sentence-final expression similar in meaning to the blunt-style **ka nâa**. It marks deliberation addressed to oneself, requiring no particular answer from anyone within hearing, and may be preceded by a perfective, an imperfective, or a consultative predicate, direct- or distal-style. As usual, the **dà** form of the copula is regularly dropped before **ka**.

Ka sira and **ka mo sirenai** look a lot alike. Obviously both are ultimately derived from a negative of **siru** and have to do with not knowing or not having found out for certain. Accentuation before both is the same. Examples:

Sâa. Dekîru ka sira. 'Hmm. I wonder if it's possible.'

Kâre wa, gêñki ni narímàsita ka sira. 'I wonder if he got better.'

Ikôo ka sira. 'I wonder if I/we should go.'

Dôtti no hoo ǧa tâkâkatta ka sira. 'I wonder which one was more expensive.'

Kore wa nâñ te iu îmi ka sira. 'I wonder what this means.'

Sôo ka sira. 'I wonder if it's like that.'

Drills

A 1. **Môo sikéñ-mòñdai o tukúrimàsita?**
'Did you make up the examination questions already?'

Ie, îma tukûtte (i)ru tokórò desu.
'No, I'm just now making them up.'

2. **Môo kowâreta têrebi o naôsimàsita?**
'Did you repair the broken television already?'

Ie, îma naôsite (i)ru tokórò desu.
'No, I'm just now repairing it.'

3. **teǧámi no naiyoo o kañǧaemàsita;** 4. **demáe o tyuumoñ-simàsita;** 5. **kakíkàta o osíete moraimàsita;** 6. **isu o tonári ni hakobimàsita**

A′1. **Môo sikéñ-mòñdai o tukúrimàsita?**
'Did you make up the examination questions already?'

Ie, koré kara tukùru tokórò desu.
'No, I'm just now going to make them up.'

2. **Môo kowâreta têrebi o naôsimàsita?**
'Did you repair the broken television already?'

Ie, koré kara naôsu tokórò desu.
'No, I'm just now going to repair it.'

3–6. Repeat the stimulus questions of drill A 3–6.

B 1. **Asíta no sikèñ, môo tukúrimàsita?**
'Tomorrow's examination—did you make it up yet?'

Êe, tukûtta tokórò desu ğa, nâni ka . .
'Yes, I just made it up, but [is there] something [you are concerned about]?'

2. **Teğami, môo yuúbìñkyoku e motte ikimàsita?**
'The letter—did you take it to the post office yet?'

Êe, motte ìtta tokórò desu ğa, nâni ka . .
'Yes, I just took it, but [is there] something [you are concerned about]?'

3. **kikâi/katázukemàsita;** 4. **kâiği/hazímarimàsita;** 5. **okyákusàma/okáeri ni narimàsita;** 6. **ni-kái no dèñki/kesímàsita;** 7. **syuúsyoku-suru tokoro/kimárimàsita**

C 1. **Sikéñ-mòñdai, môo tukûtte simáttà desyoo ka.**
'The examination questions—would you have finished making them up yet?'

Ie, tukúròo to omôtte (i)ru tokórò desu ğa, mâda . .
'No, I'm just now thinking of making them up, but [I haven't made them up] yet.'

2. **Îma katta kêeki, môo tâbete simáttà desyoo ka.**
'The cake [I] just bought—would you have finished eating it already?'

Ie, tabéyòo to omôtte (i)ru tokórò desu ğa, mâda . .
'No, I'm just now thinking of eating it, but [I haven't eaten it] yet.'

3. **iranai tte itta hako/kowâsite;** 4. **syuúsyoku ni tùite/reñraku-site;** 5. **rêe no mâñsyoñ no koto/hanâsite;** 6. **ryokóo no kotò/yakusoku-site;** 7. **kêsa no siñbuñ/sutete**

D 1. **Îtu syokúzi-sità ñ desu ka**
'When is it that you ate?'

Âa, sâkki 'tyoodo Suzúki-sañ mo syokuzi-siyòo to sité (i)ru tokorò datta kara, issyo ni . .
'Oh, a little while ago, it was just when Mr/s. Suzuki was also about to eat, so [we ate] together.'

2. **Îtu depâato e ittà ñ desu ka**
'When is it that you went to the department store?'

Âa, sâkki 'tyoodo Suzúki-sañ mo ikoo to site (i)ru tokorò datta kara, issyo ni . .
'Oh, a little while ago, it was just when Mr/s. Suzuki was also about to go, so [we went] together.'

3. **yasûñda;** 4. **dekaketa;** 5. **sonó hanà motte kita;** 6. **sikéñ-mòñdai 'watasita;** 7. **ryooğae-sita;** 8. **ağatta**

E 1. **Tyôtto, osáke moraemasèñ ka**
'Excuse me! Can('t) I have some sake?'

Osáke dèsu ka **Hâi. Kasíkomarimàsita.**
'Sake? Yes, certainly.'

2. **Tyôtto, tâbi itadakenai?**
'Excuse me! Could(n't) I have some tabi?'

Tâbi desu ka **Hâi. Kasíkomarimàsita.**
'Tabi? Yes, certainly.'

3. **hoká nò moraenai?** 4. **surîppa itádakemasèñ ka** 5. **ohâsi itádakenài desyoo ka.** 6. **h(u)ôoku moráenài desyoo ka.**

F 1. |Anoo| Îtu ka yomîkaki o osíete
moraemasèñ ka⤹

'Uh . . . could(n't) I have you teach
me reading and writing some time?'

Yomîkaki desu ka⤹ Itú dè mo yorókòñde
osíete aḡemàsu yo⤹

'Reading and writing? I'll be happy to
teach you any time.'

2. |Anoo| Îtu ka tûuyaku o saḡásite
itadakemasèñ ka⤹

'Uh . . . could(n't) I have you look for
an interpreter for me some time?'

Tûuyaku desu ka⤹ Itú dè mo yorókòñde
saḡásite aḡemàsu yo⤹

'An interpreter? I'll be happy to look for
one for you any time.'

3. hoñ́yaku o site moraenài desyoo ka. 4. buḱka o siràbete itádakenài desyoo ka.
5. heyâ o mîsete itadakenai? 6. yânusi o 'syookai-site moraenai? 7. kimóno o kasite
itadakenài desyoo ka.

G 1. Apâato wa, Yamâḡuti-sañ ni
saḡásite moraerù desyoo ne!

'An apartment—we can have Mr/s.
Yamaguchi look for for us, can't we.'

Êe, saḡásite kudasàru to omóimàsu yo⤹

'Yes, I think s/he will look for one for us.'

2. Yomîkaki wa, otôosañ ni osíete
moraerù desyoo ne!

'Reading and writing—we can have
Father teach us, can't we.'

Êe, osíete kurerù to omóimàsu yo⤹

'Yes, I think he will teach us.'

3. tûuyaku/señ́sèe ni tanôñde; 4. moñdai/Sâtoo-kuñ ni kâite; 5. wahuku/onêesañ ni
kasite; 6. nîmotu/ozisañ ni hakoñde; 7. nêko/tonári no òkusañ ni sewâ-site

H 1. Asita nâñ-zi ni okósimasyòo ka.
Sitî-zi de îi desu ka⤹

'What time shall I wake you up
tomorrow? Will seven o'clock be all
right?'

Êe. Zya, sitî-zi ni okôsite itádakemàsu
ka⤹ Moósiwake arimasèñ.

'Yes. Then will I be able to have you wake
me up at seven? I'm sorry [to bother you].'

2. Asita nâñ-zi made tetúdaimasyòo
ka. Syôogo made de îi desu ka⤹

'Until what time shall I help
tomorrow? Will (until) noon be all
right?'

Êe. Zya, syôoḡo made tetúdàtte
itádakemàsu ka⤹ Moósiwake arimasèñ.

'Yes. Then will I be able to have you help
me until noon? I'm sorry [to bother you].'

3. kore dôko ni simáimasyòo ka/hôñdana ni; 4. zisá-syùkkiñ îtu kara hazímemasyòo
ka/raísyuu karà; 5. koko ni îtu made imásyòo ka/yuúḡata màde; 6. donó heñ o
saḡasimasyòo ka/konó heñ dakè; 7. osûsi nañ́-niñmae tyuumoñ-simasyòo ka/yo-
niñmae

I 1. Mâda dête (i)nâi no?

'You mean you haven't left yet?'

Ñ. Tyoódo deyòo to sitá tokorò ni deń́wa
ḡa hàittyatte . .

'Right. Just as I was about to leave, a call
came in, and [I wasn't able to].'

Mâda reñraku-site (i)nài no?

'You mean you haven't gotten in

Ñ. Tyoódo reñraku-siyòo to sitá tokorò
ni deń́wa ḡa hàittyatte . .

touch yet?'

'Right. Just as I was about to make contact, a call came in, and [I wasn't able to].'

3. **sumâsete**; 4. **kiĝâete**; 5. **siite**; 6. **dâsite**

J 1. **Sikéñ-mòñdai tukúrimàsita?**
'Did you make up the exam questions?'

Tukúròo to sitâ ñ desu kedo ne! Yáppàri tukúremasèñ desita.
'(It's that) I tried to make them up, you know. But in the end, I couldn't (make them up).'

2. **Teĝami kakímàsita?**
'Did you write the letter?'

Kakôo to sitâ ñ desu kedo ne! Yáppàri kakémasèñ desita.
'(It's that) I tried to write it, you know. But in the end, I couldn't (write it).'

3. **hoñyaku tanómimàsita**; 4. **kuruma karímàsita**; 5. **yâtiñ tâkâku simâsita**; 6. **heyâ kaémàsita**

K 1. **Hâitte mimásèñ ka⤳**
'Won't you try going in?'

Dê mo, haíròo to sitê mo haírènai to omóimàsu yo⤳
'But even if I try to go in, I don't think I can (go in).'

2. **Tukûtte mimásèñ ka⤳**
'Won't you try making it?'

Dê mo, tukúròo to sitê mo tukúrènai to omóimàsu yo⤳
'But even if I try to make it, I don't think I can (make it).'

3. **naôsite**; 4. **omóidàsite**; 5. **narañde**; 6. **tikázùite**; 7. **siite**

L 1. **Kâre, îtu kûru tte?**
'When did he say he would come?'

Îtu tte itta kke. Îtu kûru no ka nâa.
'When *did* he say! I wonder when it is that he's coming.'

2. **Kâre, nâni kowâsita tte?**
'What did he say he broke?'

Nâni tte (~ nâñ te) itta kke. Nâni kowâsita no ka nâa.
'What *did* he say! I wonder what it is that he broke.'

3. **dôko ni sûñde (i)ru**; 4. **nâñ-niti yasûmu**; 5. **nâni ĝa kirai da**; 6. **nâni saĝasite (i)ru**; 7. **dôko ni syuusyoku-sitai**

● Repeat the preceding drill, replacing **ka nâa** in the responses with **ka sira**.

M 1. **Nâñ te ośsyaimàsita?**
'What did you say?'

E? Nâni ka iímàsita kke?
'What? Did I say something?'

2. **Dôtira e irássyaimàsita?**
'Where did you go?'

E? Dôko ka e ikímàsita kke?
'What? Did I go somewhere?'

3. **Nâni o tyuúmoñ-nasaimàsita?** 4. **Nâni o owásure ni narimàsita?**

N 1. **Goseñmoñ wa? Siṅrìĝaku desita kke?**

Êe, siṅrìĝaku o yatte (i)masu.
'Yes, I'm doing psychology.'

'Your specialization? Was it
psychology (as I recall)?'

2. **Goseñmoñ wa? Tîri desita kke?**   **Êe, tîri o yatte (i)masu.**
'Your specialization? Was it   'Yes, I'm doing geography.'
geography (as I recall)?'

3. **hoogaku**; 4. **zińrùigaku**; 5. **tetûgaku**; 6. **syakâigaku**

O 1. **Bûñgaku o señmoñ ni site (i)ru**   **Bûñgaku desu ka. Tâsika hitô-ri imâsita**
gakusee, sirímasèñ ka⤳ Arúbàito o   **kedo, îma tyôtto namáe ga**
sagásite (i)rù ñ desu ga . .   **omoidasemasèñ nêe. Nâñ te itta kke.**
'Do(n't) you know a student   'Literature? There was one, I'm quite sure,
specializing in literature? It's that I'm   but I can't remember the name now...
looking for a part-time assistant,   What *was* his/her name?'
but ...' (I don't know anyone).

2. **Hooritu o señmoñ ni site (i)ru**   **Hoóritu dèsu ka. Tâsika hitô-ri imâsita**
gakusee, sirímasèñ ka⤳ Arúbàito o   **kedo, îma tyôtto namáe ga**
sagásite (i)rù ñ desu ga . .   **omoidasemasèñ nêe. Nâñ te itta kke.**
'Do(n't) you know a student   'Law? There was one, I'm quite sure, but I
specializing in law? It's that I'm   can't remember the name now... What
looking for a part-time assistant,   *was* his/her name?'
but ...' (I don't know anyone).

3. **rekisi**; 4. **kâgaku**; 5. **geńgògaku**; 6. **seébutùgaku**; 7. **koogaku**

Application Exercises

A1. Collect or draw pictures that show people engaged in, or about to begin, or just completing various activities. Practice asking and answering appropriate questions, using **tokórò** in the responses.

2. After assigning to each member of the group a particular identification—close friend, professor, classmate, section chief, doctor, etc.—take turns making reasonable requests of them, using an appropriate **moraeru** ~ **itadakeru** pattern. Examples: correct this Japanese; translate this into Japanese; write Dr. Nakamura's address on the back of this envelope; read this letter written in Japanese; find out the name of the American exchange student who's specializing in anthropology at Tokyo University; meet with you some time next week; get in touch with you about employment; lend you a kimono; explain this test question; give you a map to the Keio Hospital. Wherever possible, modify the exchanges so that they fit actual situations that can be answered on the basis of reality. Be sure to include appropriate introductions to your requests.

3. Practice asking questions about whether the person addressed performed particular activities, with that person replying that s/he tried to but couldn't. Examples: make up next week's test questions; check on the Toranomon Hospital address; telephone the linguistics department at Waseda; attend Professor Sato's seminar; finish the work started this morning; straighten up the study; quit smoking; buy a timetable; check Dr. Ito's luggage; use the new computer; read this book that Professor Nakamura wrote; open the window in the

room next door; fix the calculator. Wherever possible, include an explanation for the fact that the attempt proved impossible.

4. Practice request situations, using CC2 and CC3 as general models for the organization of your conversations (look at the Miscellaneous Notes to these CCs). Make certain that the style used by each speaker reflects the assumed relationships of the participants. Suggested topics: ask a friend to correct the Japanese of a letter you have written to a Japanese friend; ask a classmate to serve as interpreter at next week's conference on American literature; ask a colleague for the telephone number of Section Chief Yamaguchi at Oriental Trade; ask a colleague for the name of the doctor you both met at the Yamamoto wedding reception last month.

SECTION C

Eavesdropping

(Answer the following on the basis of the accompanying tape. A = the first [or only] speaker and B the second speaker, in each conversation.)

1a. What does A want to find out about B?
  b. What does A learn?
  2. At what stage is B in going to the place assumed but not mentioned in this exchange?
  3. For what does A express gratitude?
4a. In what connection does A bring up the subject of letters?
  b. What was B's problem, and what was the result?
5a. What positive statement does A make about B's home?
  b. How does B receive A's comment?
6a. What compliment does A offer B?
  b. How does B modestly turn the compliment aside?
7a. Who is A?
  b. What is the probable setting of this conversation?
  c. What was B about to do when A arrived?
8a. Who is B?
  b. Why is A calling B?
  c. Who is Hayashi?
  d. What request does B make? Why?
9a. How is the weather?
  b. How does it seem to B?
  c. What effect does it have on A's tennis?
  d. How long has A been playing?
10a. What does B describe as too much to expect?
  b. In what connection is one and one-half hours mentioned?
11a. What is the topic of conversation?
  b. What is B doing today?
  c. What is B using for this, and why does B find it convenient?
12a. What does A ask B to do?
  b. What does B advise A to do?
  c. Why does B apologize?
13a. What is B concerned about?
  b. What kind of place is B interested in? Why?
  c. In what connection does B mention this year?

14a. Who does A think the interpreter is?
  b. What is B's opinion? Why?
  c. How does A react?
15a. What mistaken assumption does A check on?
  b. What is the actual situation?
  c. What is A's concern?
  d. How does B reassure A?
16a. What does A assume about B's daughter? Why?
  b. What would B like?
  c. Why does B doubt it will happen? Give two reasons.
17a. Why does A want a word processor?
  b. What word processor would A like to borrow?
  c. What is the objection?
18a. What has just come to an end today?
  b. What is B most concerned about?
  c. What went fairly well for B, with what one exception?
  d. What will B now be able to do?
19a. When can B begin work?
  b. What is the problem?
  c. When did this come about? Give details.
  d. How is the problem being handled?
20a. Who is being discussed by A and B?
  b. What is that person's true area of specialization?
  c. What else does that person know a great deal about?
  d. What project is that person engaged in?
  e. What request does B make of A?
  f. What is A's response?
21a. What is the topic of discussion?
  b. In that connection, what is B now able to do?
  c. What is A's reaction?
  d. How does B qualify the competence just described?
  e. What is A's reaction to that qualification?
  f. How does A feel about the topic of discussion?
22a. Who are A and B?
  b. Why is B calling?
  c. What time does A suggest?
  d. What is B's reaction?
  e. What is the final decision?
23a. Describe B's upcoming trip.
  b. Why is the first stopover being made?
  c. What is described as a pleasure?
  d. In what connection is employment mentioned?
24a. What function is A fulfilling?
  b. With what institution is Professor Ito connected?
  c. Name Professor Ito's two areas of specialization.
  d. On what topic has Professor Ito just written a book?
  e. What connection does that have with today's activities?
  f. Describe the immediately upcoming schedule. Give details.
25a. Why is the material under discussion considered difficult to translate? Give two reasons.
  b. Who will do the translation? Into what language?
  c. What does the translator request?

d. How is the request received?

26a. Compare B's competence in German and in English. Give details.

b. Compare B's background in German and in English.

c. What kind of work would B like to do?

Utilization

From now on, in this type of exercise, both a stimulus (a) and a response (b) are included. Wherever possible, the conversation should be continued beyond what is outlined here, as appropriate. Remember that the goal is NOT direct translation of the English that is given, but the transfer of the situational meaning into natural Japanese.

1a. Ask a friend if he can read French (language) newspapers.

b. Your friend replies that he did study French, but he's completely forgotten it, so he can't read it at all any more.

2a. Tell a colleague that you've heard he usually commutes to work by bus, but find out if he ever comes by subway.

b. Your colleague replies that he can't come from his house by subway, so he has to come by bus, even if it is slow.

3a. Ask a colleague about her competence in Chinese.

b. Your colleague replies that she can speak a little but can't read or write.

4a. Ask a job applicant if she can use a word processor.

b. The applicant replies that she has had some instruction, but she isn't that good yet.

5a. Ask a friend if she has ever made sushi.

b. Your friend replies that she has made it—but it wasn't very good.

6a. Ask a colleague if he knows anyone who can speak in Japanese about American politics at next week's seminar.

b. Your colleague replies that Carter knows a lot about American politics, and his Japanese is quite good, but he doesn't know whether or not he is free next week. The colleague offers to ask him and see.

7a. Tell an acquaintance that since you want to do work that puts Japanese and English to use, you've been thinking you'd like to become an interpreter.

b. Your acquaintance points out that people who can do that kind of work are needed, so she thinks it should be possible to find employment right away.

8a. Ask an acquaintance if she ever works on Saturdays.

b. Your acquaintance replies, with some surprise at the question, that there's never a time when she does NOT work on Saturdays. She adds that there are even times when she works on Sundays, too.

9a. During a job interview, explain that you can speak Japanese more or less, but ask if there are also occasions when reading and writing would be required.

b. The interviewer replies that reading is often necessary, but you don't have to be able to write.

10a. Point out to a friend, assuming agreement, that Americans who are employed in American companies usually don't become able to speak Japanese well even if they're in Japan.

b. Your friend agrees, commenting that it's too bad, since they've taken the trouble to come all the way to Japan.

11a. Ask a friend when the next (time) seminar on American literature will begin.

b. Your friend replies that it will begin about three months from now and that classes are held twice a week.

12a. Tell a colleague you are looking for someone who can translate an English-language book about U.S. law into Japanese. Ask if she knows anyone suitable.

b. Your colleague replies that she knows a Japanese professor whose specialty is U.S. law, but his English probably isn't good enough to be able to do that kind of translation.

13a. Tell an acquaintance you have finally reached the point where you can read Chinese newspapers.

b. Your acquaintance asks when you began your study of Chinese.

14a. Tell a colleague that the **katyoo** wants to have this computer repaired as soon as possible, but you don't know who will do that (for us) right away.

b. Your colleague replies that he has heard that Nakamura knows about things like that, so he'll try asking him. He adds that he doesn't know for sure whether he'll be able to locate anyone or not, but . . .

15a. Ask an acquaintance if she has ever studied Chinese.

b. Your acquaintance replies that she's studying right now—since she plans to go to China next year.

16a. Ask a colleague if he has finished that translation (the item in question is familiar to both conversation participants).

b. Your colleague expresses amazement at the suggestion. He replies that he is just about to begin it.

17a. Ask your professor—very politely!—for permission to borrow the book about American religion that he wrote.

b. Your professor agrees to the request, explaining that he isn't using the book right now.

18a. Ask a friend if she read the letter she received from a Chinese friend.

b. Your friend replies that she tried to read it but couldn't, because it was written in difficult Chinese.

19a. At a department store, ask if you can have this television set delivered to your home within this week.

b. The sales clerk replies that this week may be a bit of a problem (i.e., a strain, too much to expect), but by next Tuesday it will positively be delivered.

20a. Tell an acquaintance you've met on the street that you were just thinking of stopping in at a **kissaten**. Invite her to join you.

b. Your acquaintance refuses politely on the grounds that she has a 2:30 appointment.

21a. Ask a friend if he has telephoned Mr. Miyaji yet.

b. Your friend replies that just as he was about to call, a letter from Mr. Miyaji arrived, so he doesn't have to call.

22a. Ask a Japanese colleague which he uses—Japanese or English—when speaking to Ms. Carter.

b. Your colleague replies that since he is going to the trouble of studying English, he is trying to use it as much as possible.

23a. Tell a colleague you are going to the Ginza to buy an English–Japanese dictionary. Invite her to go with you.

b. Your colleague accepts with enthusiasm, pointing out that she was just thinking of going to the Ginza on other business.

24a. Ask a colleague if he knows the name of that German exchange student at Keio who is fluent in both English and Chinese.

b. Your colleague replies that he has been introduced to him, but he can't recall his name.

25a. Ask the secretary to write this on the word processor—tomorrow will be fine.

b. The secretary replies that she can do it right away, because she's not especially busy today.

26a. Ask a friend what Mr. Nakamura specializes in.

b. After wondering aloud, trying to recall the answer, your friend replies that he thinks Mr. Nakamura is studying: (1) law; (2) linguistics; (3) medicine; (4) physics; (5) engineering; (6) biology; (7) philosophy; (8) mathematics.

27a. Ask a fellow student if her exams are over.

b. Your fellow student replies that they are over, but they were terribly difficult. In particular, literature is a worry.

28a. Ask a fellow student if he can write Chinese.

b. Your fellow student replies that simple things like letters and messages he can write, but specialized things are still a bit [too difficult].

29a. Complain to a friend that you tried to open that window but couldn't.

b. Your friend informs you that that window doesn't open.

30a. Inquire of a friend where it is that Kato studied economics.

b. Your friend wonders aloud, trying to recall. She suggests Waseda as a possible answer.

31a. Wonder aloud whether Kei is going to the student party.

b. Your close friend comments that she thinks Kei will come. She adds that the truth of the matter is that she would like her not to come, but . . .

Check-up

1. Describe how the potential of the verbal is formed in Japanese. What is the potential of **kau**? of **kûru**? What serves as the potential of **suru**? What is meant by the "short form of the vowel-verbal potential?" (A-SP1)

2. Out of context, verbals like **kaeru**, **kakêru**, and **tatêru** may be analyzed in two different ways with two very different meanings. Explain. (A-SP1)

3. Are the verbals from which potentials are derived, for the most part, affective or operational? Are potential derivatives themselves affective or operational? Give an example of a potential occurring as a double-**ḡa** verbal. (A-SP1)

4. What pattern is regularly used to indicate the desire to become able to do something? (Example: 'I'd like to be[come] able to read.') (A-SP1)

5. Describe an alternate to the potential verbal for expressing ability in Japanese. In what types of contexts is it most commonly used? (A-SP2)

6. Describe the phrase-particles that occur following **siñbuñ** in the Japanese equivalents of '[he] reads newspapers' and '[he] can read newspapers.' For the latter, cover both patterns for expressing ability in Japanese. What particles follow a nominal expressing the person having ability? (A-SP2)

7. What is the difference in meaning between **Tukau.** and **Tukáu kotò ḡa âru.**; between **Tukái-màsita ka**✔ and **Tukátta kotò ḡa arímàsu ka**✔; **Tukáu kotò ḡa nâi.** and **Tukáwanai kotò mo âru**; **Tukátta kotò ḡa âru.** and **Tukátta kotò ḡa âtta.** (A-SP3)

8. How does one distinguish in Japanese between a simple statement of fact and a statement that stresses that only what is mentioned is to be assumed, implying that there are reservations about broadening the meaning? Give equivalents for: 'I did read it, but . . .' (I didn't really understand it); 'It is cheap, but . . .' (it isn't very pretty); 'It is pretty, but . . .' (it's terribly expensive.) (A-SP4)

9. What is the basic meaning of the pattern /**X ni tûite**/? Give an example of its use (a) before **dà**, **no**, and **na**; (b) before particles **wa** and **mo**; (c) hooked up to a predicate. What is unusual about its occurrences before the copula? (A-SP5)

10. **Hosîi** is described as a double-**ḡa**, affective adjectival. Explain. (A-SP6)

11. What is the meaning of the pattern /verbal gerund + **hosîi**/? How does it compare with the **-tai** form of the verbal alone? With the pattern /verbal gerund + **moraitai**/? What pattern expresses a desire for something *not* to be done? What phrase-particle follows the agent by whom a desired action is performed? (A-SP6)

12. To what may **tokórò** refer in addition to a specific place? In this connection, describe its use followed by particle **o**; particle **e**. What is the difference in meaning between **tabêru tokórò desita** and **tâbeta tokórò desu?** (B-SP1)

13. Motion verbals in the **-te (i)ru** form usually refer to a state that results from previous action (example: **kâette (i)ru** '[s/he] has returned,' '[s/he] is back'. What change in meaning occurs when this pattern is hooked up to a following **tokórò**? (B-SP1)

14. Describe a Japanese request pattern that focuses on the requester as receiver rather than the person asked as giver. (B-SP2)

15. What is the difference in implication between **sité moraemasèñ ka** and **sité moraemàsu ka**? (B-SP2)

16. Why is the study of a foreign language through isolated, independent sentences alone a problem? (B-SP3)

17. In sentence connectives like **dâ kedo**, **dâ ḡa**, **dê mo**, and **dè**, what nominal is assumed preceding the copula? (B-SP3)

18. How does Japanese distinguish between 'try' in the sense of 'try doing,' 'do and see how it turns out,' as opposed to 'try to do,' 'act as if to do,' 'try (unsuccessfully) to do'? (B-SP4)

19. What interrogative sentence-particle indicates questioning while attempting to recall? What predicate forms precede this particle? (B-SP5)

20. What gentle-style sentence-final element indicates wondering or pondering addressed to oneself? What predicate forms precede it? What is the blunt-style equivalent? (B-SP5)

Lesson 26

SECTION A

Core Conversations

1(J)a. **Isôḡu yoo ni iťt(e) òita no ni, Yamada-kuñ wa osôi wa nêe.**
  b. **Soré ni sitè mo, osôi wa yo.**

(N)a. **Îma mití ḡa kòñde (i)ru kara . .**
  b. **Âto gô-huñ mâtte kônakattara, saki ni hazimemasyo(o)?**

2(J)a. **Kono botañ o osu to, kotâe ḡa demasu.**

  b. **Watási o yoñde kudasài.**

(N) **Kotâe ḡa dênakattara, dôo simasyoo.**

3(N)a. **Tyôtto gosóodañ-sitai kotò ḡa âru ñ desu ḡa . .**
  b. **|Anoo| Uti no señpai no Mîzuno-sañ nêe.**
  c. **Kono-ḡoro tyôtto yoósu ḡa hèñ na ñ desu.**
  d. **Nań to nàku, tumétaku nàtta yoo na ki ḡá surù ñ desu yo.**
  e. **Êe. Sekkaku tomódati to site tukiaèru yoo ni nâtte kitâ to omôttara[1] |dêsu nêe|. Kyuú ni mata kyòri ḡa dêkita-mitai de . .**

(J)a. **Nâñ desyoo.**

  b. **Êe.**

  c. **Hêñ to iu to?**

  d. **Tumétaku nàtta?**

  e. **Âa, môsi ka suru to, koóhai to sitè wa hanásikàta ḡa sitási-sùḡita ñ zya arimaseñ ka⤸**

---

1. The accompanying video has an alternate pattern: **omôtta ñ desu nêe.**

f. Watási ḡà desu ka⤸

g. Âa. Naruhodo nêe.

f. Êe. Dôñna ni sitâsìku nâtte mo, koohai wa koóhai-ràsìku |dêsu nêe|. Hanásikàta nañka mo, tyôtto ki ó tukèru yoo ni sité mìtara dôo desyoo.

ENGLISH EQUIVALENTS

1(J)a. Even though I told him to hurry, Yamada is late, isn't he!
  b. Even so, he's late!

(N)a. The roads are crowded now, so . . .
  b. If he doesn't come after we've waited for the next five minutes, shall we begin?

2(J)a. When you push this button, the answer comes out.

  b. Call me.

(N)a. Supposing the answer doesn't come out, what should I do?

3(N)a. There's a matter I'd like to discuss with you, but . . . (is it all right?)
  b. Uh, my senior colleague, Mr. Mizuno, you know.
  c. It's that his manner is a bit strange these days.

(J)a. What is it?

  b. Yes.

  c. When you say strange, (what do you mean)?

  d. It's that somehow I have the feeling that he's become cold.
  e. Yes. [Just] when I thought I had at last become able to associate [with him] as a friend, you know. Suddenly it's (lit. being) as if distance [between us] has developed again.

  d. He's become cold?

  f. I ['ve done this]?

  e. Oh, isn't it perhaps the case that your way of talking has been too familiar for a junior colleague?
  f. Yes. No matter how familiar you become, juniors [should act] like juniors, you know. Why don't you try to be a bit careful even about things like your way of talking, and see (how that works out).

  g. Oh. Of course (I might have known).

BREAKDOWNS
(AND SUPPLEMENTARY VOCABULARY)

1. í't(e) òita no ni (SP1)   in spite of having said in advance

soré ni sitè mo (SP4)	even so, nevertheless (*lit.* even having made it into that)
âto gô-huñ mâtte	having waited the next five minutes
kônakattara (SP2)	if/when/supposing/assuming [someone] hasn't come
2. botañ	button
osu /-u; osita/	push
+hiku /-u; hiita/	pull
osu to (SP3)	with pushing, when [someone] pushes
kotâe	answer
+kotáèru /-ru; kotâeta/	answer [verbal]
dênakattara	if/when/supposing/assuming [someone] hasn't come out
3. señpai	senior colleague
uti no señpai	senior colleague within the in-group
uti no señpai no Mîzuno-sañ	Mr/s. Mizuno who is my senior
yoosu	the state of things; manner; appearance
X to iu to?	when you say (*lit.* with the saying of) X; what do you mean by X?
nań to nàku	somehow, in some (vague) way (*lit.* there not being [a clear] 'what')
ki ğa suru	have a feeling
tomodati to site (SP4)	in the capacity of a friend, as a friend
tukíàu /-u; tukíàtta/	associate, interact, socialize
tomódati to site tukiaèru	be able to associate as a friend
tukíaèru yoo ni nâtte kuru	gradually reach the point where [one] can associate
omôttara	if/when/supposing/assuming [someone] has thought
kyuu /na/	sudden, without warning; urgent
kyôri	distance
kyôri ğa dekîru	distance develops
môsi	supposing
môsi ka suru to	perhaps; it may be the case that . . . (*lit.* with making a 'supposing')
koohai	junior colleague
+doohai *or*	
+dooryoo	colleague of equal status
koohai to site	in the capacity of a junior, as a junior
sitásìi /-katta/	is familiar, intimate, close

sitásisuğìru	be too familiar
X nâñka *or*	
+X nâdo (SP5)	X, etc.; X, and so forth; X, for example
ki ó tukèru yoo ni sité mìru	try to be careful and see (how it turns out)
sité mìtara	if/when/supposing/assuming [someone] has tried doing
sité mìtara dôo desyoo	how would it be if [you] tried doing? why don't you try doing?

Supplementary Activity Verbals

hanâsu /-u; hanâsita/	let go, release, detach, separate
hanárèru /-ru; hanâreta/	become detached, separated
hirou /-u; hirotta/	pick up
mağeru /-ru; mağeta/	bend [something]
mağaru /-u; mağatta/	[something] bends, makes a turn
mazêru /-ru; mâzeta/	mix [something]
mazîru /-u; mazîtta/	[something] gets mixed; [something] mixes
otôsu /-u; otôsita/	drop [something]
otîru /-ru; ôtita/	[something] drops, falls
sibâru /-u; sibâtta/	bind, tie up
taôsu /-u; taôsita/	fell, knock down
taórèru /-ru; taôreta/	fall down, collapse
tatâku /-u; tatâita	beat, knock, tap
tôosu /-u; tôosita/	pass [something] through
tôoru /-u; tôotta/	go through; pass through [something]
ûtu /-u; ûtta/	hit, strike

MISCELLANEOUS NOTES

1. In CC1, Deborah Miller and her supervisor, Ms. Sakamoto, are waiting for Mr. Yamada, who is late. Ms. Miller suggests an explanation, but her supervisor does not accept it as an adequate excuse. The final suggestion is to go ahead without him if he doesn't come in the next five minutes. The supervisor, in her frank complaining to her employee, uses direct feminine-style (with sentence-final **wa nêe** and **wa yo**). Miller's use of direct-style before **kara** and the distal-style of a sentence-final consultative is typical of moderately careful speech for a woman.

(J)a. Note the female supervisor's use of **-kuñ** in reference to Yamada, which indicates both that he is male and that she need not defer to him. That she told him to hurry is further evidence of relative rank.

(N)b. **Âto gô-huñ** refers to the five-minute period coming up, which will mark the end of waiting for Mr. Yamada.

2. In CC2, Sue Brown is receiving instruction in the use of a computer from her colleague at work. The style is careful, with distal-style final predicates and one direct-style—but polite—imperative (**kudásài**).

(J)a. **Osu** and **hiku** are transitive, operational verbals, both of which have derived meanings beyond physical motor activity. **Osu** refers to pushing, shoving, jostling—and pushing oneself in the sense of exerting oneself beyond normal limits. **Hiku** covers pulling, dragging, drawing from behind, conducting—and drawing in or away from. Note the following combinations, which suggest the broadly extended usage of this verbal: **hûne o hiku** 'tow a boat'; **kodomo o tê de hiku** 'lead a child by the hand'; **deñwa o hiku** 'install a telephone'; **kawa no mizu o hiku** 'draw off river water'; **piano o hiku** 'play the piano'; **kaze o hiku** 'catch a cold'; **kyaku o hiku** 'attract customers'; **zîsyo o hiku** 'look up in a dictionary'; **sâñzyuu kara zyûugo o hiku** 'subtract 15 from 30'; **gohyákù-eñ hiku** 'take off ¥500.'
Kotâe is a nominal derivative of the operational vowel-verbal **kotáèru**. Note: **teǵámi ni kotáèru** 'answer a letter'; **hitô ni kotáèru** 'answer a person'; **iîè to kotáèru** 'answer "no."'

3. In CC3 Mr. Carter, who has become confused by the sudden coolness of a senior colleague with whom he thought he had established a relaxed, friendly relationship, seeks advice from Professor Ono. Note that he does not ask Mr. Mizuno, the person directly involved, what the problem is. He chooses the route preferred by the Japanese: avoiding confrontation and going through a third party. Professor Ono suspects that Mr. Carter has made the kind of mistake some foreigners frequently make—believing that the requirements of hierarchy, including deference in speech style, can be ignored among colleagues of differing rank once they get to know each other and associate on a regular basis.

Note the difference in the speech-styles of Mr. Carter and Professor Ono. Mr. Carter uses careful-style with distal-style final predicates, but in several of his utterances he departs from the use of major sentences: In (N)a, he introduces his topic of conversation with a minor sentence ending in **ǵa** that sets the stage for what follows. In N(b), with polite hesitation, he further prepares Professor Ono for what is to come by naming (as a fragment) the senior colleague he will discuss. In N(e), his speech is interrupted by Professor Ono's suggestion for an explanation, resulting in a minor sentence. His final exclamatory **Naruhodo nêe** is a fragment. Mr. Carter's frequent use of extended predicates, given the nature of this conversation, is to be expected.

Professor Ono's style of speech is more casual, reflecting his superior position. He begins with an utterance in distal-style, but in (J)c and (J)d, he shifts to a minor sentence and a major sentence in direct-style, both of which occur at a point where he is anxious to show concern and sincere interest in Mr. Carter's problems. When he turns to offering his interpretation of the problem and his advice for its solution, he reverts to a more careful style, with distal-style final predicates ([J]e and f). His advice is offered gently as a suggestion: 'how would it be if ——?'

Distinguishing among **señpai**, **dooryoo** (or **doohai**), and **koohai** is crucial in Japanese society. This relationship affects interaction at every turn within many spheres—the workplace, school, clubs, and so on. What is often surprising to the foreigner is the persisting awareness of these relationships among the Japanese. It is not unusual for a middle-aged Japanese to introduce a former schoolmate, who was only one year his senior at school, in terms of these categories.

(N)c. The nominal **yoosu** occurs in reference both to the manner or appearance of people and to the condition of things (**kono mati no yoosu, hurísòo na yoosu**).

(N)d. **Ki ǵa suru** 'have a feeling,' yet another special combination that includes **ki** 'spirit,' 'mind,' 'feeling,' must not be confused with **ki ni suru** 'mind,' 'worry about,' 'concern oneself about.'

(J)e,f. Note how Professor Ono offers his interpretation of the situation and his advice:

(1) 'Isn't it the case that ——?' (2) 'Let X be X-like,' and (3) 'How would it be if ——?' A very clear meaning is delivered in structural patterns that are indirect.

(N)f. **Watasi ḡa** functions here as the primary affect of an affective predicate which is understood from the context: 'Do you mean that *I* am the one being described?'

Supplementary activity verbals: The verbals in this list cover common motor activities and, in many cases, have extended derivative meanings. The list includes several transitive/intransitive pairs. Consider the following:

Hanâsu (transitive) covers the notion of letting go what is being held, releasing, but note also: **mê/tê o hanâsu** 'take one's eyes/hands off.'

Hanárèru (intransitive) refers to separation from a physical location, leaving, quitting, and becoming cut off from. Note **êki o hanárèru** 'get clear of the station'; **tê o hanárèru** 'get to be out of one's hands'; **hanâreta matî** 'an isolated town'; **Tookyoo kara 'deñsya de itízikañ-ḡùrai hanârete (i)ru** 'be about one hour from Tokyo by train.'

Hirou (transitive) refers basically to picking up tangible objects, but extends to picking up in the sense of finding: **miti de 'okane o hirou** 'find money on the street.' Note the Japanese version of "finders, keepers": **Hirótta monò wa, zibuñ no mono**.

Maḡeru is the transitive partner of **maḡaru**, which appeared earlier in reference to making a turn at a corner. In its basic sense, **maḡeru** refers to the bending and twisting of tangible objects—pipes, wires, and the like—but by extension it covers distorting and perverting: **kotóbà no îmi o maḡeru** 'twist the meaning of words.' Paralleling these usages, **maḡaru** also refers to becoming bent or twisted—or distorted or perverted: **miti ḡa maḡatte (i)ru** 'the road is curved'; **nêkutai ḡa maḡatte (i)ru** '[his] necktie is twisted'; **kosí no maḡatta tosiyòri** 'an old person with a bent back'; **maḡátta kotò o suru** 'do something not above-board.'

Mazêru (transitive) refers to the mixing or blending of items—tangible or intangible. Thus: **mizú o mazèru** 'dilute (*lit.* mix water)'; **gurêe ni guriîñ o mazèru** 'blend green into the gray'; **nihóñḡo o màzeta eeḡo** 'English that has mixed in Japanese.'

Mazîru[2] (an intransitive consonant verbal) or, less commonly, **mazâru**, paralleling its transitive partner, refers to tangible or intangible items' becoming mixed or blended: **ûmâku mazîru irô** 'colors that blend well'; **yukî no mazîtta âme** 'rain mixed with snow'; **eéḡo to nihoñḡo ḡa mazìtte (i)ru hanásì** 'a talk in which English and Japanese are mixed.' The derived nominal **mazírì** has the basic meaning 'mixture' and extends to include impurity and adulteration. The cultural implications of this are important to note: the Japanese love of conformity includes a strong preference for the pure and unmixed in all aspects of life.

Otôsu (transitive) in its basic meaning refers to the dropping or letting go of tangible objects, but extends to a more generalized dropping off, removing, omitting, letting go, lowering, and detracting (from). Thus: **sará o otòsu** 'drop a plate'; **kôe o otôsu** 'lower one's voice'; **namáe o otòsu** 'drop (i.e., omit) a name'; **ki ó otòsu** 'lose heart.'

Otîru[3] (intransitive) parallels its transitive partner in the scope of its meanings. This includes the falling of leaves and apples from trees and of humans from horses, but note also: **hî ḡa nisí ni otìru** 'the sun sets in the west'; **aráttè mo otínài** 'it [a stain, for example] doesn't come out even if you wash it'; **sikêñ ni otîru** 'fail in an exam.'

2. Note how Hepburn romanization (i.e., **mazeru, majiru**) obscures the connection between the roots of these verbals. Besides its *not* being an obvious indicator of accurate pronunciation—a claim that is often made—Hepburn romanization inaccurately represents the roots as different.

3. Again Hepburn romanization (**otosu, ochiru**) obscures the similarity between the roots of the two verbals. (Cf. n. 2.)

Sibâru (transitive) covers physical binding and tying and extends to tying up in work, rules, and so forth.

Taôsu (transitive) covers knocking or throwing down a tangible item—felling a tree (**kî o taôsu**), razing a house (**iê o taôsu**), throwing down a person (**hitô o taôsu**)—and can also mean bringing down a person in power or overthrowing a government: **kaísya no syatyoo o taòsu** 'unseat the president of a company.'

Taórèru (intransitive) parallels its transitive partner and covers the falling down, collapsing, dropping down, and toppling of tangible items. It extends to the bankruptcy of companies and the fall of governments: **zisiñ de iê ga taórèru** 'houses collapse in earthquakes'; **kazé de taòreta kî** 'a tree that toppled over in the wind'; **taóresòo na kaisya** 'a company that looks as if it will fail.'

Tatâku (transitive) covers such activities as knocking on a door (**dôa o tatâku**), pounding on someone's shoulders to promote relaxation (**kâta o tatâku**),[4] clapping hands to summon someone (**tê o tatâku**), drumming on the table (**teéburu o tatàku**), pecking away at a typewriter (**taípuràitaa o tatâku**), and slapping someone's face (**hitó no kao o tatàku**); in extended usage, it can refer to taking a slap at, censuring, criticizing: **gakútyoo o tatâku** '(verbally) attack the university president.'

Tôosu (transitive) denotes the activity involved in permitting or causing a tangible entity to pass through or along an area—**âme o tôosu** 'let in the rain'; **mizú o toosànai** 'be waterproof'; **kaígìsitu ni okyákusàma o tôosu** 'show a guest to the conference room.' Note also: **mê o tôosu** 'glance at' (*lit.* 'pass one's eyes along'). The combination **X (o) tôosite** 'through the medium of X,' 'having passed through X' occurs as a manner expression, linked up to a following predicate: **tûuyaku o tôosite hanâsu** 'speak through an interpreter'; **rokú-syùukañ tôosite 'asoko de hataraita** '[I] worked there for an uninterrupted period of six weeks.'

Tôoru (intransitive) refers to going or passing or getting through or along an area—**koóeñ o tòoru** 'go through the park'; **mití o tòoru** 'pass through a street'; **gakkoo no usiro o tòoru** 'pass in back of the school'; **Mêziro o tôotte iku** 'go by way of (i.e., having passed through) Mejiro'—and is also used in such combinations as **sikêñ o tôoru** 'pass an exam'; **îmi ga tôoru** 'the meaning is understood'; **Suzúki to iu namae de tòoru** 'pass as (go by the name of) Suzuki.'

Ûtu (transitive) covering striking and hitting tangible objects in general, also occurs in such combinations as: **taípuràitaa o ûtu** 'use a typewriter'; **pisútoru o ùtu** 'shoot a pistol'; **tokee ga kû-zi o ûtta** 'the clock struck 9:00.' In its extended usage, it may refer to striking in the sense of impressing.

Structural Patterns

1. iít(e) òita no ni

In lesson 20A-SP1, /imperfective verbal X + **no ni** / 'for doing X' was introduced. Example: **Końna keesàñki o naôsu no ni wa, tokúbetu no doogù ga irú to omoimàsu.** 'For repairing this kind of calculator, I believe you need special tools.' In this usage, the pattern is usually followed by particle **wa**.

With a change of context, the /**no** + **ni**/ combination can assume a very different mean-

---

4. The extended meaning of this combination is 'designate for separation out from the company.'

ing, indicating strong contrast: 'in spite of.' The predicate preceding **no** may be verbal, adjectival, or nominal, perfective or imperfective. It is usually direct-style, but in very careful style, a distal-style verbal may occur.

Note again the importance of always considering the particle **ni** in connection with both what precedes and what follows it. Its core meaning is location—literal or figurative—but depending on context, **ni** may designate either the goal or the source (**tomodati ni ağeta** 'I gave it *to* a friend,' but **tomodati ni moratta** 'I received it *from* a friend'; **gaiziñ ni osieta** 'I taught a foreigner,' but **gaíziñ ni naràtta** 'I received instruction *from* a foreigner'); the purpose for which or the situation contrary to which something occurs (**tukûri ni kita** 'I came to make it,' but **tukûru no ni tabênai** 'in spite of making it, I don't eat it'). This /predicate + **no ni**/ pattern expresses a much stronger contrast than that of /predicate + **kedo** or **ğa**/ when they are contrastive.

Note now what happens when a nominal predicate precedes these three alternates:

> **Eéğo dà kedo . .** *or*
>
> **Eéğo dà ğa . .** 'It's English, but' *versus*
>
> **Eéğo nà no ni . .** 'In spite of the fact that it's English'

Both **kedo** and **ğa** are particles. Before some particles, **dà** is deleted (cf. **Âa, sôo ka.**), but otherwise, it is unchanged. The **no** of **no ni**, however, is the nominal **no**, before which **dà** > **nà**. Examples:

> **Ki ó tukèru yoo ni iû no ni, kâre wa kikánài ñ desu.** 'In spite of the fact that I tell him/her to be careful, (the fact is that) s/he doesn't listen.'
>
> **Seḱkaku kèeki o tukûtta no ni, daré mo tabènakatta.** 'Here I took all the trouble to make a cake, but nobody ate it!'
>
> **Sûğôku samûi no ni, ôobaa o kinâi de dekáketa-rasìi desu.** 'In spite of the fact that it's terribly cold, s/he apparently went out without wearing a coat.'
>
> **Zeñzeñ wakarànai no ni, yôku wakâtta tte.** 'Even though s/he doesn't understand at all, s/he said s/he understood very well.'
>
> **Ano gakusee, nihóñzìñ na no ni, nihóñziñ-ràsìku miémasèñ nêe.** 'Even though that student is Japanese, s/he doesn't seem like a Japanese, does s/he!'
>
> **Byoóki dàtta no ni, zêmi ni dênakutya ikénàkatta.** 'Even though I was sick, I had to attend the seminar.'

Sequences ending in **no ni** frequently occur as minor sentences, implying that, in reality, the opposite is the true situation. Example: **Ki ó tukèru yoo ni iḱtà no ni . .** 'When (*lit.* in spite of the fact that) I told him/her to be careful . . .' (why isn't s/he)!

2. THE CONDITIONAL

We now introduce a new inflected form, the CONDITIONAL. It consists of (1) verbal root + **-tara**/, with the same sound changes occurring in the root as occur before all endings beginning with **t**; (2) adjectival root + **-kattara**/; and (3) for the copula, **dàttara**. The simplest way actually to form the conditional is /perfective predicate + **-ra**/; this analysis is also useful because it reminds us of the perfective content of the conditional.

The conditional is an accented form: its accent is on the same mora as in the related perfective, if that form is accented, and otherwise, on the /**ta**/ of /**-tara**/.

Kind of verbal	Imperfective	Perfective	Conditional	Basic meaning
Vowel	iru	ita	itâra	'be located (animate)'
	kariru	karita	karítàra	'borrow'
	neru	neta	netâra	'go to bed/sleep'
	tabêru	tâbeta	tâbetara	'eat'
Consonant	kâku	kâita	kâitara	'write'
	isôǧu	isôida	isôidara	'be in a hurry'
	hanâsu	hanâsita	hanâsitara	'talk' or 'let go'
	mâtu	mâtta	mâttara	'wait'
	kau	katta	kaítàra	'buy'
	iu	itta	iítàra	'say'
	iku	itta	iítàra	'go'
	iru	itta	iítàra	'need'
	yômu	yôñda	yôñdara	'read'
	yobu	yoñda	yoñdàra	'call'
Special polite[5]	irássyàru ↑	irássyàtta/ irâsita ↑	irássyàttara/ irâsitara ↑	'go,' 'come,' 'be located (animate)'
	kudásàru ↑	kudásàtta/ kudásùtta ↑	kusásàttara/ kudásùttara ↑	'give (to the in-group)'
	nasâru ↑	nasâtta/ nasûtta ↑	nasâttara/ nasûttara ↑	'do'
	ossyàru ↑	ossyàtta ↑	ossyàttara ↑	'say'
Irregular	kûru	kîtâ	kîtâra	'come'
	suru	sita	sitâra	'do'
Adjectivals	akai	akâkatta	akâkattara	'is red'
	takâi	tâkâkatta	tâkâkattara	'is expensive'
	dênai	dênakatta	dênakattara	'doesn't go out'
	sinai	sinâkatta	sinâkattara	'doesn't do'
	sitai	sitâkatta	sitâkattara	'wants to do'

There is also a distal-style conditional of verbals and the copula, occurring in very careful style, which is formed in much the same way: /distal-style perfective + **-ra**/. Examples: **dekímàsitara**, **gozáimàsitara**,[5] **ohíma dèsitara**.

Corresponding conditional forms for **-te (i)ru** patterns, the negative of adjectival and nominal predicates, the potential, the extended predicate, etc., and combinations of these also exist. Examples: **kâette (i)nâkattara**; **omosîrôku nâkattara**; **nihóñzìñ zya nâkattara**;

5. For the verbal **gozâru**, as usual, only a distal-style form is in current usage.

yômetara; **yomênakattara**; **isôg̃u n̄ dattara**; **hanáséru n̄ dattara**; **akérarenàkatta n̄ dattara**. But how are these conditional forms used, and what do they mean??

The Japanese conditional (which we will refer to as X temporarily) sets up an activity or condition which is supposed or assumed to have been realized (but not necessarily completed) by the time the next activity or condition (which we will call the outcome, or Y) occurs: 'given X, then Y'; 'if/when X is assumed, then Y'; 'if/when we presuppose the occurrence of X, then Y.' The conditional refers to an event or condition that is, if not certain, at least likely. The conditional situation may be a one-time event or a recurring one.

Consider now these examples:

(a) **Môtto tûyôku osítàra, dôa g̃a akímàsu yo⤴**

(b) **Môtto tûyôku osítàra, dôa g̃a akímàsita.**

(c) **Môtto tûyôku osítàra, dôa g̃a aítà n̄ desyoo g̃a . .**

In (a), the form of the outcome—**akímàsu**—indicates what is going to happen or what does happen, should the action of the conditional have already occurred at that point. 'If/when [you] (will have) push(ed) harder, the door will open (or opens).'

In (b), the form of the outcome—**akímàsita**—represents what has already actually happened, assuming the action of the conditional had already occurred by that time. 'When [I] pushed harder, the door opened.' When an occurrence has already taken place, as in this example, the outcome is usually beyond the direct control of the operator of the conditional. The operator of the conditional and of the following predicate in the outcome sequence are different, unless some special limiting factor is included in the outcome. For example, the inclusion of **sug̃u**, indicating immediacy, is one such factor. Compare

Den̄sya g̃a Toókyòo-eki ni tûitara, orímàsita. 'When the train arrived at Tokyo Station, they got off.'

Toókyòo-eki ni tûitara, sûg̃u orímàsita. 'As soon as they arrived at Tokyo Station, they got off.' *with*

Toókyòo-eki ni tûita tokî ni, sin̄bun̄ o kaimàsita. '(At the time) when they arrived at Tokyo Station, they bought a newspaper.'

In (c), the /extended predicate + g̃a/ in the outcome sequence—**aítà n̄ desyoo g̃a**—tells us that 'it's probably a case described as the occurrence of **aita**, if we assume that **osita** had occurred by that time, but . . . ,' implying that it may not have actually happened. Thus, *depending on how much I know about the situation,* the English equivalent of (c) may be a contrary-to-fact statement, 'If I (or someone) had pushed harder, the door would probably have opened, but . . .' (I [or someone] didn't push); or a noncommittal statement, 'If/when [someone] pushed the door harder, it's probably the case that it opened, but . . .' (I don't know whether [someone] pushed or not).

A pattern that regularly expresses contrary-to-fact conditions is /conditional X + predicate Y + **no ni**/. This says, 'in spite of the fact that Y would occur (or would have occurred), assuming the prior occurrence of X,' and always implies a contrary state of affairs. When predicate Y is a form of **îi**, the pattern expresses a contrary-to-fact wish: 'it would be (or would have been) good/nice/great, if X were (or had been) the case'; 'I wish X were (or had been) the case.' Examples:

Aá iu hitò to tukíàetara yôkatta no ni . . 'I wish (*lit.* it would have been great if) [you] could have associated with that kind of person.'

Môtto suzûsìkattara îi no ni . . 'I wish (*lit.* it would be good if) it were cooler.'

Môtto hâyâku hazímattè (i)tara, aṅna kotò ni wa narânakatta no ni nêe. 'If it had started earlier, it wouldn't have turned out that way, would it!'

What immediately strikes a native speaker of English is the fact that the English differentiation between 'if' and 'when' does not transfer to Japanese with any agreement or regularity. The **-tara** form in Japanese tells us that a particular occurrence or condition is to be assumed, and, given that, there is an outcome—which may or may not occur or have occurred. Depending on context, this Japanese conditional may have as its English equivalent 'if X' or 'when X.' The "when" that refers to a specific time rather than a condition is expressed by **tokî**, not the conditional. Compare

Kodómo dàttara, tetúdàtte kudasai. 'If/when it's a child (that's involved), please help him/her.' *with*

Kodómo no tokì ni, anó señsèe ni Kyôoto de aímàsita. 'When I was a child, I met that teacher in Kyoto.'

English requires a clear-cut differentiation between 'if' and 'when'; the Japanese conditional incorporates both notions. Knowledge of the situation is often required for the English speaker to sort out 'if' and 'when' distinctions when moving from Japanese to English. If, however, the optional **mosi** 'supposing' occurs at the beginning of a conditional sequence, one can assume that the sequence represents an 'if' situation.

It is important to distinguish between **-tara** sequences and corresponding sequences ending in **-te mo**. Compare

Kâre ḡa yamétàra, watási mo yameru tumori dèsu. 'If he quits, I plan to quit, too.' *with*

Kâre ḡa yamétè mo, watási mo yameru tumori dèsu. 'Even/also if he quits, I plan to quit, too.'

Note how these patterns interlock:

Kâre ḡa yamétàra, anâta mo yamérù ñ desu ka 'Is it that you are going to quit, too, if he quits?'

Iie, kâre ḡa yamétè mo, watási wa yamemasèñ. 'No, even if he quits, I (at least) am not going to (quit).'

Kâre ḡa yamétè mo, anâta mo yamérù ñ desu ka 'Is it that you are going to quit, too, even if he quits?'

Iie, kâre ḡa yamétàra, watási wa yamemasèñ. 'No, if he quits, I (at least) am not going to (quit).'

With a **-tara** pattern, only the particular action or condition of the root is under consideration as a condition leading to the outcome; with **-te mo**, it is *additionally* considered as one of several presumed possible conditions. (cf. 21B-SP1).

A conditional sequence followed by a **dôo**-question is a commonly occurring pattern of suggestion: 'how would it be if. . . ? 'why don't [you] . . . ?' In suggesting that the addressee perform some action, however, care must be taken that it is appropriate to make such a suggestion given relative rank, situation, and other circumstances. An important feature to consider is whether or not the activity is for the *benefit* of the addressee. Examples:

Waápuro tukattàra dôo? 'How about using a word processor?'

Okâsi no kawari ni, ohána o aĝetàra dôo desu ka. 'How would it be if you gave flowers instead of candy?'

Sore, watási ĝa tukùttara dôo desyoo. 'Why don't I make that.'

Frequently the **dôo**-question is omitted, resulting in a more casual-style, minor-sentence pattern of suggestion ending in question intonation. This is often used as an indirect form of request that avoids a direct request pattern. For example, a situation involving an English-language request to 'draw on this paper' might be rendered in Japanese as **Konó kamì ni kâitara?** Of course a request pattern in Japanese and a suggestion pattern in English *are* also possible in this situation, but what is significant is the frequency with which the suggestion pattern is chosen in Japanese. The following examples might all occur as indirect requests.

Asita moó sukòsi hâyâku kîtara? 'How about coming a little earlier tomorrow?'

Kokó de yattàra? 'Why don't you do it here?'

Yuúĝata màde irássyaрànakattara? 'How about not coming until evening?'

The conditional is also used in patterns that seek out suggestions, in which case the sequence ending in the conditional contains a question-word, and the outcome is a form of **îi**: 'assuming the prior occurrence of what, will it be good?' Thus:

Dôo sitara îi? 'What should I do?' (*lit.* 'if I have acted how, will it be good?')

Dôko e ittàra îi? 'Where should I go?' (*lit.* 'if I have gone where, will it be good?')

Nâñ to ittàra îi? 'What should I say?' (*lit.* 'if I have said what, will it be good?')

Mêziro e ikû no ni wa, dôno deñsya ni nottàra îi desyoo ka. 'To go to Mejiro, which train should I take?' (*lit.* 'if I have taken which train to go to Mejiro, would it be good?')

When the interrogative in these questions is replaced by a non-interrogative, the result is advice: 'assuming the prior occurrence of —, it will be good/fine/great.' Thus: **Koó sitàra îi.** 'You should do (*lit.* it will be good if you have done) it this way'; **Giñkoo e ittàra îi.** 'You should go (*lit.* it will be good if you have gone) to a bank'; **Dôo mo to ittàra îi.** 'You should say (*lit.* it will be good if you have said) "Dôo mo."'

Although this pattern, by indicating a condition for the situation to be described as **îi**, offers advice, it is a less strong statement than a /—— **sitá hòo ĝa îi**/ sequence, which states that 'the alternative of having done —— (as opposed to not having done it or to having done something else) will be good'; 'you'd better do ——.' The use of **hôo** 'alternative (of two)' narrows the field of options and makes the advice specific. The **-tara** pattern, on the other hand, simply states that 'if X, fine," but there may be many other actions or conditions not under consideration that would also be fine.

Compare now these three patterns, all of which occur as equivalents of English 'They say [one] should come by 9:00':

Kû-zi made ni kîtara îi tte. (it will be nice if it happens that way)

Kû-zi made ni kîtá hoo ĝa îi tte. (one had better do it)

Kû-zi made ni kûru hazú dà tte. (the general expectation is that this is what will happen)

In many contexts, the conditional sequence has a close relationship with what has preceded and provides a background for what follows (cf. CC3[N]e). Consider these examples:

Koñpyùutaa wa mâda tukáenài ñ desu ka⌐ '(Is it that) you can't use the computer
yet?'

**Êe. Sukôsi tukáeru yòo ni nâtta to omôttara, mata tukáenaku nàtte, komâtte
(i)masu.** 'That's right. [Just] when I thought I had reached the point where I
could use it a little, I again became unable to (use), and I'm upset.'

Kore kara sûupaa e kurúma de ikù kedo, issyo ni ikanai? 'I'm going to the supermarket by car now. Won't you go along?'

Âa, kurúma de ikù ñ dattara, yorókòñde . . 'Oh, if it's the case that you're going
by car, [I'll] gladly [go along].'

*3. PREDICATE + PHRASE-PARTICLE **to** OF ACCOMPANIMENT/: osu to*

The phrase-particle **to** of accompaniment has previously been introduced in several
contexts.

(a) Joining nominals: **suuḡaku to kâḡaku** 'science with math,' 'math and science';
tomodati to issyo 'together with a friend'

(b) Linking a nominal with a predicate: **keñtikuka to hanàsu** 'talk with an architect';
kore to tiḡau 'be different from this'

(c) In the combination /**X ni yoru to**/ 'according to X' (*lit.* 'with relying on X')

We now consider the kind of usage exemplified by (c)—**to** connecting predicates: /imper-
fective predicate X + **to** + predicate Y/ = 'with the occurrence of X, Y occurs,' 'when/if
X occurs, Y occurs,' 'upon the occurrence of X, Y occurs.' If X is distal-style, Y is also
regularly distal-style; if X is direct-style, Y may be either direct or distal. This pattern has
several special features.

1. The predicate before **to** is always imperfective, regardless of the form of the following
predicate. Thus:

Kono miti o maśsùḡu iku to, miḡí no hòo ni otéra ḡa miemàsu/miemàsita. 'Upon
going straight along this street, on the right a temple will come/came into view.'[6]

2. X and Y are always two distinct activities or states. In the sentence **Kâre to hanâsu
tokî ni wa, îtu mo nihóñḡo de hanasimàsu.** '(At times) when I speak with him, I always
speak in Japanese,' **hanâsu tokî** cannot be replaced by **hanâsu to** because both predicates
refer to the same activity, performed by the same operator.

3. The underlying notion of accompaniment that is present in this pattern implies a close
association between the events of the X and Y predicates, which follow on each other without
interruption. Sometimes the association is a regular, recurring one. Examples:

Hâha wa, sore o kiku to, taôreta ñ desu yo. 'You know, upon hearing that, my
mother collapsed.'

---

6. Note that in English this kind of sentence is considered incorrect because the agent of the first clause is not
the same as that of the main clause. In Japanese, however, such sentences are the norm.

Hâha g̃a heyâ ni hâiru to, sûg̃u sonó hañasì o yamétà ñ desu. 'What happened is that as soon as my mother entered the room, they stopped talking about that.'[7]

Himá dà to, iê ni ite, têrebi o mîru soo desu. 'Whenever s/he's free, s/he stays at home and watches television, I hear.'

Natû ni nâru to, Toókyoo o dète, môtto suzúsìi tokórò ni ikítaku nàru ñ desu. 'With the coming of summer, I get to want to leave Tokyo and go to a cooler place.'

4. The /imperfective predicate X + **to** + predicate Y/ pattern regularly puts focus on predicate Y as if it were a kind of climax: 'with the occurrence of X, *what then?*' Accordingly, we most often find this pattern in statements and questions of fact. It does not hook up with request patterns. Even when X occurs as the final predicate in a minor sentence, with Y left unexpressed, Y is understood from context and is the focus. Contrast this with the conditional, which permits focus either on the conditional sequence or on its outcome (which may be a request), depending on context. **Okyákusañ g̃a mìetara yoñde kudasài** can explain either (1) under what conditions the calling is to take place, or (2) what is to be done if a guest appears. The only difference in the two utterances is intonation: in (1), the accented portion of the outcome has reduced high pitch (i.e., significantly less high than the accented portion of the conditional sequence that precedes).

/Predicate + **to**/ followed by **îi** often expresses a hope or a wish.

Hâyâku owaru to îi desu g̃a nêe. 'I hope it ends early!' *or* 'It's nice when it ends early, but . . .' (*lit.* 'with ending early it is/will be nice, but . . .' [otherwise, not])

Iru to îi no ni . . 'I wish s/he were in.' (*lit.* 'in spite of the fact that it's nice with his/her being in . . .' [s/he isn't])

Compare these examples with:

Hâyâku owáttàra yôkatta no ni . . 'I wish it had ended early.'

The combination **soo suru to** '(with) that being the case,' '(with) considering it like that' (*lit.* 'with making [it] like that'), an example of this pattern, functions as a sentence connector (cf. drill L, following). Note also **môsi ka suru to**, a set phrase that occurs frequently in introducing a possibility: 'perhaps,' 'possibly' (*lit.* 'with making a "supposing"').

Compare now the three patterns introduced thus far that overlap with the area of English covered by 'when':

Êki ni tûita tokî ni, baiteñ de beñtòo o kaímàsita. 'When I arrived at the station, I bought a box lunch at the concession stand.' (**Tokî** refers specifically to the *time* when I bought the box lunch.)

Êki ni tûitara, sitî-zi hatu wa môo dête (i)masita. 'When I arrived at the station, the 7 o'clock had already left.' (The conditional tells what activity is to be assumed as realized prior to the departure of the 7 o'clock, an action not controlled by me.)

Êki ni tûkû to, sûg̃u orímàsita. 'When I arrived at the station, I got off right away.' (The **to** sequence leads up to what activity *accompanied* my arrival at the station.)

---

7. Note the difference in meaning (i.e., shift in operator) that is signaled by the use of **hâha** *wa* in the preceding sentence (*my mother* heard and *she* collapsed) and **hâha** *g̃a* in this sentence (*my mother* entered and *they* stopped). Compare 11A-SP2, which discusses this same distinction in reference to /predicate + **kara**/.

4. **/X to site/, /X ni site/**

As a manner construction, /nominal X + **to site**/ 'in the capacity of X,' 'as X,' 'for X' (*lit.* 'having made [it] or considered [it] as if X') hooks up directly with a following predicate:

> **arúbàito to site hataraku** 'work as a part-timer'
>
> **gaíkòokañ to site 'mukoo e iku** 'go abroad as a diplomat'

The **site** of this pattern is, of course, the gerund of **suru**, and as is typical of gerunds, it may be followed by phrase-particles **wa** and **mo**, with the usual change of focus:

> **konó heñ no utì to sitê wa yasûi** 'for a house in this area (at least) it's cheap'
>
> **hitó to sitè wa îi kedo** 'as a person (at least) s/he's nice, but'
>
> **gaíziñ to sitè wa zyoózù da** for a foreigner (at least) s/he's skillful'
>
> **Toókyoo no natù to sitê mo atûi** 'even/also for a Tokyo summer it's hot'
>
> **tuyú to sitè mo âme ğa oôi** 'even/also for the rainy season there's a lot of rain'

Compare now the combination /nominal X + *ni* **site**/. In this case, /**X ni**/ indicates an actual making into X, making or considering to be X, deciding on X, and the item directly affected (the operand) is often expressed. The two patterns are *not* interchangeable. Thus:

> **sono moñdai o 'owari ni site yameru** 'quit, having made that problem be the end'
>
> **kore o sikéñ-mòñdai ni sitê wa muzúkasisuğìru** 'be too difficult to make this into an exam question (at least)'
>
> **owári no sikèñ ni sitê mo mûri da** 'it's too much to expect even/also if we make it (to be) the final exam'

An example of this pattern, the sequence **soré ni sitè mo** 'even so,' is another commonly occurring sentence connector, used to introduce a counter-remark to what has preceded while allowing for its validity: 'even having decided on that (as valid).'

A sequence consisting of or ending with a predicate, perfective or imperfective, may also occur before /**ni site**/ and /**to site**/. Examples:

> **Kâre, arûite kuru ni sitê mo, osôi desu yo.** 'Even granted that he's walking here, he's late, I tell you.'
>
> **Sikêñ ğa muzúkasìkatta ni sitê mo, môtto dekîru hazú dèsita nêe.** Even granted that the test was difficult, s/he should have done better, shouldn't s/he!'
>
> **Huyû datta ni sitê mo, sâmûkatta yo** 'Even granted that it was winter, it was cold!'
>
> **Môo kimátta to sitè mo, mâda kañğaènakutya narânai moñdai ğa âru desyoo?** 'Even if we consider it as already decided, there are still problems we must think about—right?'
>
> **Sore wa, iyâ da to sitê mo, sité kureru to omoimàsu.** 'Even if they consider that as being unpleasant, I believe they will do it for us.'

5. **/X nàñka/**

Nàñka, or its more formal equivalent **nàdo**, following a single nominal or two or more nominals in a series, indicates that the nominal(s) mentioned do not comprise a complete list: other items are implied but not identified. The reader will be reminded of the particle **ya**, which connects at least two nominals in a series, and has a similar meaning. **Nàñka** and

nàdo often occur following such a sequence as a reinforcement of the 'and so forth,' 'and the like' meaning. Following an accented word, **nàñka** and **nàdo** lose their accent. Examples:

>**watási nàñka** 'I, among others'

>**kotósi nàdo** 'this year, for example'

>**kâĝaku, butúrìĝaku, seébutùĝaku nado** 'chemistry, physics, biology, etc.'

>**sûupaa ya depâato nañka** 'supermarkets and department stores and so forth'

The /nominal(s) + **nàñka** (or **nâdo**)/ sequence occurs in the same kinds of patterns as nominal(s) alone. Thus:

>**Koko wa, râzio ya têrebi nañka (o) uťte (i)ru misè desu.** 'This (place) is a shop that sells things like radios and televisions.'

>**Hisyô nañka wa, koo iu kaisya ĝa iyâ da soo desu.** 'I hear that secretaries, among others, don't like companies like this.'

>**Asoko wa, hôteru ryokáñ nàdo ĝa oôi matî desu.** 'That (place) is a town with lots of hotels and inns and the like.'

Drills

A 1. **Hayási-kuñ ĝa yòku wakâru tte?**
'They said that Hayasi understands well?'

    Êe, sońna ni yòku wakárànai no ni nêe.
'Yes, in spite of the fact that he doesn't understand that well.'

  2. **Nôguti-kuñ ĝa yòku yasûmu tte?**
'They said that Noguchi is absent often?'

    Êe, sońna ni yòku yasúmànai no ni nêe.
'Yes, in spite of the fact that he doesn't take off that often.'

  3. **konó kikài/sûĝu kowáréru;** 4. **anó rèsutorañ/mazûi;** 5. **asóko no hàru/kiree da;**
  6. **hiatari/warûi**

B 1. **Koko no bukka wa takâi tte, Nisida-sañ ĝa iťte (i)màsita yo**
'Say, Mr/s. Nishida was saying that prices here are high.'

    Iya, mûsiro yasûi no ni . . Nisida-sañ ĝa takâi to omôtte (i)ru dakê desu yo.
'When (*lit.* in spite of the fact that) on the contrary they are low (*lit.* cheap). It's just that Mr/s. Nishida has been thinking they are high.'

  2. **Kokó no àki wa atûi tte, Nakámura-kuñ ĝa itte (i)màsita yo**
'Say, Nakamura was saying that the fall here is hot.'

    Iya, mûsiro samûi no ni . . Nakámura-kuñ ĝa atùi to omôtte (i)ru dakê desu yo.
'When (*lit.* in spite of the fact that) on the contrary it's cold. It's just that Nakamura has been thinking it's hot.'

  3. **anó sikeñ-mòñdai wa 'muzukasii/Watanabe-kuñ;** 4. **anó utì wa hirôi/Kitamura-kuñ;** 5. **konó koñpyùutaa wa tukáinikùi/arúbàito no ko;** 6. **ano miti wa 'suite (i)ru/ Itóo-kàtyoo;** 7. **ni-kái no hòo ĝa hirôi/Hasimoto sañ**

C 1. **Oota-sañ wa, anó dañti ni haitta-rasìi desu nêe.**

    Êe, anó dañti nì wa haírànai hoo ĝa îi to iû no ni kikánài ñ desu yo.

'Mr/s. Ota apparently went into that apartment complex, didn't s/he!'

'Yes, in spite of my saying it would be better not to go into *that* apartment complex (at least); (it's that) s/he doesn't listen, you know.'

2. **Tâkasi-kuñ wa, anó kaisya ni syuusyoku-suru-rasìi desu nêe.**
'Takashi apparently is going to work for that company, isn't he!'

Êe, anó kaisya nì wa syuúsyoku-sinai hòo ḡa ìi to iû no ni kikánài ñ desu yo.
'Yes, in spite of my saying it would be better not to go to work for *that* company (at least); (it's that) he doesn't listen, you know.'

3. **Nakada-sañ/doituḡo o anó señsèe ni narâtte (i)ru**; 4. **Oono-sañ/Nârita de demú-kaèru**; 5. **Mîyazi-sañ/sebiro o anó misè de katta**; 6. **Kêe-tyañ/hooritu no gakkoo e iku**; 7. **Tanaka-sañ/anó màñsyoñ o dêru**

D 1. **Watasi, arúbàito no siḡoto o yamérù ka mo sirémasèñ.**
'Me—I may quit part-time work.'

Sôo desu ka. Sikâsi, anâta ḡa yamétàra, mińna yamerù ñ zya arímasèñ ka✓
'Oh? But if *you* quit, isn't it the case that everybody will quit?'

2. **Watasi, asítà wa yasùmu ka mo sirémasèñ.**
'Me—I may take the day off tomorrow.'

Sôo desu ka. Sikâsi, anâta ḡa yasûñdara, mińna yasùmu ñ zya arímasèñ ka✓
'Oh? But if *you* take the day off, isn't it the case that everybody will take the day off?'

3. **tûuyaku no siḡoto o hazimeru**; 4. **koko ni yuúḡata màde nokôru**; 5. **anó iḡakùbu o akíramèru**; 6. **waapuro o tukau**; 7. **kimono o kiru**

E 1. **Syuúsyoku-sitàra, kono beñkyoo yamérù ñ desu ka✓**
'Is it that you're going to quit these studies, once you become employed?'

Iya, syuúsyoku-sitè mo, kono beñkyoo wa yamémasèñ yo.
'No, even if/when I become employed, I won't give up these studies (at least).'

2. **Sikêñ ḡa sûñdara, kâeru ñ desu ka✓**
'Is it that you're going home, once the exams are over?'

Iya, sikêñ ḡa sûñde mo, kaérimasèñ yo.
'No, even if/when the exams are over, I'm not going home.'

3. **siḡóto ḡa dèkitara, katyoo ni misèru**; 4. **konó botañ o ositàra, kotâe ḡa dêru**; 5. **konó hoñyaku ḡa owattâra, yasûmu**; 6. **anó zimùsyo ni hâittara, seńmoñ ḡa ika-sèru**; 7. **anó señsèe ni kotóbà o narâttara, perápera ni nàru**

F 1. **Sonó botañ o ositè mo, kippu ḡa denâi ñ desu ḡa . .**
('It's that) a ticket won't come out even if/when I press that button, but . . .' (am I doing something wrong?)

Tyôtto mâtte kudasai✓ . . . A, moó iti-do ositàra, tyańto demâsita yo✓
'Wait a moment, please. . . . Oh, when I pressed [it] again, it came out the way it should.'

2. **Sonó hòñdana o saḡásitè mo, hôñ ḡa mitúkaranài ñ desu ḡa . .**

Tyôtto mâtte kudasai✓ . . . A, moó iti-do saḡasitàra, tyańto mitúkarimàsita yo✓

'(It's that) I can't find the book even if/when I search those bookshelves, but . . .' (is it really there?)

'Wait a moment, please. . . . Oh, when I looked [for it] again, it turned up as expected.'

3. **sonó zìsyo sirâbete/kâite nâi**; 4. **tûyôku hiite/dôa g̃a 'akanai**; 5. **ôoki na kôe de yoñde/daré mo kotaènai**; 6. **hanâsu yoo ni itte/hanásànai**; 7. **tûyôku osite/taórènai**

G 1. **Doó sitè mo apâato o sag̃ásu zikañ g̃a nàkute . .**

'No matter what, I have no time to look for an apartment, and . . .' (I'm concerned).

Zyâa, hoká no hitò ni sag̃ásite morattàra dôo desu ka

'Then how would it be if you had someone else look?'

2. **Doó sitè mo waápuro o ùtu zikáñ g̃a nàkute . .**

'No matter what, I have no time to put it on (*lit.* hit) the word processor, and . . .' (I'm concerned).

Zyâa, hoká no hitò ni ûtte moráttàra dôo desu ka

'Then how would it be if you had someone else put it on?'

3. **kono hoñyaku o suru**; 4. **kaimono ni iku**; 5. **señmoñ no hitò ni 'soodañ-suru**; 6. **okyákusañ ni tukiàu**; 7. **kâig̃i ni dêru**

H 1. **Nâñ-zi kara hazímemasyòo ka.**

'(From) what time shall we begin?'

Sôo desu nêe. Nâñ-zi kara hazímetàra îi desyoo nêe.

'Hmm. (From) what time do you suppose it *would* be good to begin?'

2. **Îtu made ni owárimasyòo ka.**

'By when shall we end?'

Sôo desu nêe. Îtu made ni owáttàra îi desyoo nêe.

'Hmm. By when do you suppose it *would* be good to end?'

3. **nâñ to nâni o mazémasyòo**; 4. **nâñ-zi made tukíaimasyòo**; 5. **nâñ de sibárimasyòo**; 6. **donó-g̃urai mag̃emasyòo**; 7. **nâñ ni ki ó tukemasyòo**; 8. **dôñna kao o simásyòo**; 9. **nâni o ikásimasyòo**

I 1. **Okâasañ wa, mâda okírarènai ñ desu ka**

'Is it that your mother is still unable to get up [out of bed]?'

Hâa. Tyôtto okírareru yoo ni nâtta to omôttara, matá okirarènaku narímàsite . .

'Yes. Just when I thought she had reached the point where she was able to get up a little, again she became unable to (get up), and . . .' (there has been no change since).

2. **Otôosañ wa, mâda yasúmènai ñ desu ka**

'Is it that your father is still unable to take any time off?'

Hâa. Tyôtto yasúmèru yoo ni nâtta to omôttara, matá yasumènaku narímàsite . .

'Yes. Just when I thought he had reached the point where he was able to take a little time off, again he became unable to (take time off), and . . .' (there has been no change since).

3. **âkatyañ/syabérènai**; 4. **onîisañ/reñsyuu-dekìnai**; 5. **señpai to/tukíaènai**; 6. **ôkusañ/dekakerarenai**; 7. **onêesañ/tabérarènai**

I '1. **Amari tumétaku nài yoo desu nêe.**   **Êe. Môtto tumétàkattara îi ñ desu kedo**
'It doesn't seem to be very cold, does   **nêe.**
it!'   'That's right. (It's that) it's nice if it's
    colder, but . . .' (it isn't).

2. **Amari kîree zya nâi yoo desu nêe.**   **Êe. Môtto kîree dattara îi ñ desu kedo**
'It doesn't seem to be very pretty,   **nêe.**
does it!'   'That's right. (It's that) it's nice if it's
    prettier, but . . .' (it isn't).

3. **sitâsiku nâi**; 4. **bêñri zya nâi**; 5. **mezúràsìku nâi**; 6. **hîrôku nâi**; 7. **kôku nâi**; 8. **buátuku nài**; 9. **zyoózù zya nâi**

I ''1. **Nakánaka owarimasèñ desita nêe.**   **Êe. Môtto hâyâku owâttè (i)tara, añna**
'It didn't end for quite a while, did it!'   **kotò ni wa narânakatta no ni nêe.**
    'That's right. If it had been over earlier,
    things wouldn't have turned out like that,
    but . . .' (what you said is true).

2. **Nakánaka ki ḡa tukimasèñ desita**   **Êe. Môtto hâyâku ki ḡá tùite (i)tara,**
nêe.   **añna kotò ni wa narânakatta no ni nêe.**
'They didn't notice for quite a while,   'That's right. If they had noticed earlier,
did they!'   things wouldn't have turned out like that,
    but . . .' (what you said is true).

3. **hazímarimasèñ**; 4. **wakárimasèñ**; 5. **omóidasimasèñ**

I '''1. **Ûmi e ikû no wa neˤ Yáppàri**   **Sôo desita ka. Íttàra yôkatta no ni . .**
yamétà ñ desu yo.   'You did? When (i.e., in spite of the fact
'About going to the beach, you know,   that) it would have been great if you had
I gave up [the idea].'   gone . . .'

2. **Tûuyaku o tukêru no wa neˤ**   **Sôo desita ka. Tukêtara yôkatta no ni . .**
Yáppàri yamétà ñ desu yo.   'You did? When (i.e., in spite of the fact
'About using (*lit.* attaching) an   that) it would have been great if you had
interpreter, you know, I gave up [the   used (*lit.* attached) one . . .'
idea].[7]

3. **atárasìi arúbàito o saḡasu**; 4. **Mîzuno-señpai ni 'soodañ-suru**; 5. **wâiñ to mizu o mazêru**; 6. **sûḡu 'siḡoto o hazimeru**

J 1. **Kono botañ o osíte mìte kudasai.**   **Osu to, dôo naru ñ desu ka⤳**
'Please try pushing this button.'   'What (is it that) will happen when I push
    it?'

2. **Kore to sore o mâzete mite kudasai.**   **Mazêru to, dôo naru ñ desu ka⤳**

'Please try mixing this and that.'	'What (is it that) will happen when I mix them?'

3. mukôo e 'mawasite; 4. kore, soko ni irete; 5. kotira o tukatte; 6. tê o hanâsite

K 1. Îi apâato ğa moó sùğu mitúkaru to omoimàsu yo⤹
I think a good apartment will turn up soon now.'

Âa, hâyâku mitukaru to îi desu nêe.
'Oh, it will be great if one turns up quickly, won't it!'

2. Siğoto ğa moó sùğu owáru to omoimàsu yo⤹
'I think the work will end soon now.'

Âa, hâyâku owaru to îi desu nêe.
'Oh, it will be great if it ends quickly, won't it!'

3. deñwa ğa moó sùğu hâiru; 4. syuusyoku ğa moó sùğu kimaru; 5. arúbàito no hitô ğa moó sùğu nârete kureru; 6. moó sùğu hârete kuru

L 1. Konó kutù wa, Yamáda-sañ nò zya nâi desyoo ka.
'Aren't these shoes Mr/s. Yamada's?'

Soo suru to, koíti no kutù wa dâre no desyoo ka.
'If that's the case, whose do you suppose these shoes over here are?'

2. Kono teğami wa, Kitámura-sañ karà zya nâi desyoo ka.
'Isn't this letter from Mr/s. Kitamura?'

Soo suru to, kotti no teğami wa dâre kara desyoo ka.
'If that's the case, who do you suppose this letter over here is from?'

3. hito/Sîkoku no hito; 4. hoñyaku/Watánabe-sañ ğa yattà no; 5. koppu/Osámu-kuñ ğa taòsita no; 6. tûaa/yoo-ka kara; 7. kaisya/sañ-ğai

M 1. Konó miti o itte kudasài—miñsyuku ğa mièru hazú dèsu kara.
'Go along this street—because there should be (lit. appear) a miñsyuku.'

Donó-ğurai iku to mièru ñ desu ka⤹—miñsyuku.
'How far do I go before I see it—the miñsyuku?'

2. Sonó kikài o tukátte kudasài—niôi ğa kiéru hazu dèsu kara.
'Please use that machine—because the odor should disappear.'

Donó-ğurai tukau to kierù ñ desu ka⤹—niôi.
'How long do I use it before it disappears—the odor?'

3. botañ o mawasite/dôa ğa aku; 4. yuíkkùri yasûñde/byoóki ğa naòru; 5. moó sibàr-aku mâtte/bañğòhañ ğa dekîru; 6. orée o harâtte/gôruhu 'osiete kureru

N 1. Waapuro, kowâretyatta ñ zya nâi desyoo ka.
'Don't you suppose that it's that the word processor ended up breaking down?'

Âa, môsi ka suru to, kowâretyatta no ka mo sirémasèñ nêe.
'Hmm, maybe it is the case that it ended up breaking down, I suppose.'

2. Señsèe, sêki o hazúsite (i)ràsita ñ zya nâi desyoo ka.

Âa, môsi ka suru to, hazúsite (i)ràsita no ka mo sirémasèñ nêe.

'Don't you suppose that it's that the professor was not at her/his seat?'

'Hmm, maybe it *is* the case that s/he was not at his/her seat, I suppose.'

3. **niwa no ki, taôrete simatta**; 4. **yâtiñ no koto, ki ni site (i)ru**; 5. **Kêe-tyañ, kutábì-retyatta**; 6. **kaminari, náttè (i)ta**; 7. **koko de noríkàetyatta**

O 1. **Anâta no baai, Toódai o dètara, kyôosi ni nâru ñ desu ka**✔

'In your case, once you graduate from (*lit.* leave) Tokyo University, (is it that) you are going to become an instructor?'

Êe, kyôosi to site siĝóto o suru kotò ni naru ki ĝá simàsu.

'Yes, I have a feeling that (it will come about that) I'll work as an instructor.'

2. **Anâta no baai, Kyoódai o dètara, gîsi ni nâru ñ desu ka**✔

'In your case, once you graduate from (*lit.* leave) Kyoto University, (is it that) you are going to become an engineer?'

Êe, gîsi to site siĝóto o suru kotò ni naru ki ĝá simàsu.

'Yes, I have a feeling that (it will come about that) I'll work as an engineer.'

3. **Hokudai/gaíkòokañ**; 4. **Kyuudai/keñtikuka**; 5. **Tukûba/beñĝòsi**

P 1. **Ano gaiziñ, nihoñĝo wa syabéremàsu ka**✔

'Can that foreigner speak Japanese?'

Êe, mâa, gaíziñ to sitè wa, kânari syabérèru to omoimasu.

'Yes, well, I think s/he can speak quite well, for a foreigner.'

2. **Anó kooĝakùbu no gakusee, bûñĝaku no kotô mo sítte (i)màsu ka**✔

'Does that engineering department student know about literature, too?'

Êe, mâa, koóĝakùbu no gakusee to sitê wa, kânari sítte (i)rù to omoimasu.

'Yes, well, I think s/he knows quite a bit for an engineering department student.'

3. **anó wañ-d(e)ii-kèe, yâtiñ wa takâi desu**; 4. **kotosi no Nihóñ no natù, suzúsìi desu**; 5. **ano Watánabe-señsèe no kooeñ, omósìròkatta desu**; 6. **kêsa no Hanéda-kùukoo, suíte (i)màsita**; 7. **anó yama no nàka, koótuu no bèñ wa îi desu**

Q 1. **Amérika è no ryuúĝakusee to sitè wa, kotóbà ĝa tyôtto dekînai desyoo ka.**

'As an exchange student [going] to America, do you suppose s/he is a little weak in language?'

Iya, dôko e no gakúsee to sitè mo, koré dè wa, tyôtto dekínasuĝimàsu yo.

'No, as a student [going] anywhere, if this is how s/he is (*lit.* being this), his/her proficiency is a bit too low.'

2. **Konó kaisya to sitè wa, tyôtto yasúmì ĝa ôôi desyoo ka.**

'For this company, do you suppose the holidays are a few [too] many?'

Iya, dôno kaísya to sitè mo, koré dè wa, tyôtto oósuĝimàsu yo.

'No, for *any* company, if this is how it is (*lit.* being this), there are a few too many holidays.'

3. konó arubàito/oree ğa sukúnài; 4. asóko no syàiñ/siğoto ğa dekînai; 5. asóko no okàsi/tyôtto amâi; 6. syatyóo no iè/semâi

R 1. Dêñsya ğa okúretà ñ da kara, osóku nàtte mo sikáta ga nài desyoo?

'Since (it's that) the train was behind schedule, even if I'm late, it can't be helped, can it?'

Dê mo, dêñsya ğa okúretà ni sitê mo, osósuğimàsu yo.

'But even if we grant that the train *was* behind schedule, you are too late.'

2. Kotóbà ğa wakáranakatta ñ da kara, matíğàete mo sikáta ga nài desyoo?

'Since (it's that) I didn't understand the language, even if I make mistakes, it can't be helped, can it?'

Dê mo, kotóbà ğa wakáranakatta ni sitê mo, matíğaesuğimàsu yo.

'But even if we grant that you *didn't* understand the language, you make too many mistakes.'

3. sêki o hazúsitè (i)ta/siránàkute; 4. kyôri o siránàkatta/zikáñ ğa kakàtte; 5. arúbàito o site (i)ru/yasûñde; 6. señmoñ no tùuyaku ğa inâkatta/îmi ga tuúzinàkute; 7. sikêñ ğa dekînakatta/gêñki ga nâkute

S 1. Dañti wa, iyâ na ñ desu ka‿

'(Is it that) you don't like apartment complexes?'

Sôo desu nêe. Dañti nàñka wa, nań to nàku iyâ da nâa to omôtte . .

'Well, places like apartment complexes for some reason don't appeal to me (do they!), [I keep] thinking . . .'

2. Señpai wa, tukíainikùi ñ desu ka‿

'(Is it that) your senior colleagues are hard to associate with?'

Sôo desu nêe. Señpai nàñka wa, nań to nàku tukíainikùi nâa to omôtte . .

'Well, people like my senior colleagues are for some reason hard to associate with (aren't they!), [I keep] thinking . . .'

3. seébutuğaku/damê na; 4. yomîkaki/sukî zya nâi; 5. Nihóñ-teki na monò/wakárinikùi; 6. gaíziñ-muki no iè/sumítaku nâi; 7. nôoka no siğoto/ki ni iranai

T 1. Konó-ğoro no sikêñ wa, muzúkasìi desu nêe.

'Examinations these days are difficult, aren't they!'

Êe, nań to nàku mâe yori muzúkasiku nàtta yoo na ki ğá simàsu nêe.

'Yes, for some reason, I do have the feeling that they have become more difficult than before.'

2. Konó-ğoro no ryuuğàkusee wa, kotóbà ğa yôku dekímàsu nêe.

'Exchange students these days are proficient in the language, aren't they!'

Êe, nań to nàku mâe yori dekîru yoo ni nàtta yoo na ki ğá simàsu nêe.

'Yes, for some reason, I do have the feeling that they have become more proficient than before.'

3. mâñsyoñ/sumíyasùi desu; 4. Matûzusi/azí ğa warùi desu; 5. arúbàito/yôku yasúmimàsu; 6. siñbuñ/tumáranai desu; 7. Yosida-kuñ/yôku syabérimàsu; 8. kôñpa/ oózee kimàsu

U 1. **Gakúsee nà ñ da kara, môtto**
   beñkyoo-site moraitài desu nêe.
   'It's that they are students, so I want
   them to study more.'

   Sôo desu yo. Gakusee wa gakúsee-ràsìku
   'beñkyoo-sinai to nêe.
   'You're right! Unless students study like
   students—[there's trouble,] isn't that true!'

2. **Señpai nà ñ da kara, môtto ki ó**
   tùkète moráitài desu nêe.
   'It's that they are seniors, so I want
   them to pay more attention.'

   Sôo desu yo. Señpai wa señpai-ràsìku ki
   ó tukènai to nêe.
   'You're right! Unless seniors pay attention
   like seniors—[there's trouble,] isn't that
   true!'

3. **koohai/kyôri o oite;** 4. **syatyoo/tyañto site;** 5. **dooryoo/sitâsìku tukíàtte;** 6. **señsèe/**
   kuwâsìku osiete

V 1. **Utímasyôo ka.**
   'Shall I hit it?'

   Êe, ûtte kudasai.
   'Yes, please do (hit).'

2. **Taósimasyòo ka.**
   'Shall I knock it over?'

   Êe, taôsite kudasai.
   'Yes, please do (knock over).'

3. **sibárimasyòo;** 4. **otósimasyòo;** 5. **hikímasyòo;** 6. **osímasyòo;** 7. **hiróimasyòo;**
   8. **hanásimasyòo;** 9. **kowásimasyòo;** 10. **mazémasyòo;** 11. **maĝémasyòo**

Application Exercises

A1. Using a detailed city map or the model town used in earlier lessons, ask and answer
questions that relate to a specific **-tara** conditional For example, (a) 'If I go along this street,
will I pass any hotels?' (b) 'I want to go from X to the station. How would it be fastest to
go? (*lit.* 'if I go how, would it be fastest?'); (c) 'If I walk from X to Y, about how long will it
take?' (d) 'I want to go to X, but I don't know the way (= street). Where would it be good
to ask?' (e) 'If I make a mistake and go too far along the streets of this city, can I make a
U-turn?'

2. Again on the basis of a map or model, practice asking directions for going to a particular place, using a **-tara** pattern, and answering appropriately.

3. In response to problem situations presented by one member of the group, offer
suggestions for solutions, using the **/-tara, dôo/** pattern. Examples of situations: 'I forgot
to bring my lunch'; 'I want to telephone Mr. Kato but I don't know his number'; 'I want to
send flowers to Mrs. Ono, but I don't know which hospital she's in'; 'I want to write a letter
to the exchange student I met last night, but I don't know her address'; 'I want to have this
camera repaired, but I don't know which place would be good'; 'I'm to go (i.e., it has been
decided that I will go) by car tomorrow to the company where Mr. Sato works, but I don't
have a clue as to the distance [Don't try to translate literally!!!], so I don't know how long
it will take.'

4. Practice describing events that take place (or did or will take place) as an accompaniment to a particular occurrence or condition, as, for example, when 4:00 (evening, De-
cember, summer) comes; when this class ends; when you graduate from school; when you
pushed that button; when you're free; when there's too much work for you; when a professor doesn't come to class; when you don't understand what your teacher has said; when

you get a headache; when you arrived in Nagoya; when the show ended. Incorporate each statement into a short conversation.

5. Using a variety of appropriate objects, request that particular activities be performed in reference to them, using the activity verbals introduced in this lesson. After the activity has been performed, have another member of the group describe what happened. Examples include: 's/he just picked up a magazine'; 's/he tried to bend that fork but couldn't'; 's/he tried to mix those things, but they wouldn't mix'; 's/he let go of the knife, and it fell into that box.'

B. Core Conversations: Substitution

Return now to the Core Conversations and practice them with appropriate substitutions. Include questioning on content. For CC3, include questions that involve background and interpretive information; for example: Why is Mr. Carter talking to Professor Ono instead of to Mr. Mizuno? What does Professor Ono suggest may be the problem? What does Mr. Carter think of this (the suggestion)? Give reasons for your opinion. How will Mr. Carter probably change from now on?

SECTION B

Core Conversations

1(N)a. **Gûamu wa, ikâḡa desita?**

   b. **Otêñki wa?**

   c. **Dê mo, onázi yòo na têñki bâkari tuzúityàa, omósìròku nâi desyoo.**

   d. **Kisêtu ni yotte, âtûku nattari sâmûku nattari surú hòo ḡa tanósìi to omóimasèñ ka⸜**

   e. **Soré wa sono tòori desu neʕ**

2(N)a. **Boku, konaida hiḱkosi-sita bàkari desyoo? Sokó no ue no kài ḡa urûsàkute nêe.**

(J)a. **Iyâa, siḡóto si ni ittà no ni, asóñde bàkari desita.**

   b. **Saíkoo dèsita yo⸝ Níppòñ mo, zuʃto añna tèñki da to îi no ni nêe.**

   c. **Soré wa sòo desu kedo, aá iu tèñki dattara, îi to omóimàsu kedo nêe.**

   d. **Sikâsi |dêsu neʕ| Tatôeba, Níppòñ ni iru to, mâiniti tèñki no kotó bàkari ki ní site (i)nàkutya(a) narânai desyoo.**

(J)a. **Ñ . . Môñku iú bèki desu yo—soó iu tokì wa.**

b. Iʹttà ñ desu yo. Deńwa kàketari,
tyokusetu ií ni ittàri . . Dê mo,
kâette hîdôku naru bâkari na ñ
desu.

                         b. Âa |ano nêe.| Soó iu tokì wa neʕ
                           Kańriniñ ni iù ñ desu yo.

c. Kañriniñ ni?

                         c. Êe. Aida ni hitó ni hàitte morátta
                         hòo ḡa sumûuzu ni ikû ñ desu
                         yo⤳

d. Hêe⤳ Naruhodo nêe.

ENGLISH EQUIVALENTS

1(N)a. How was Guam?

                         (J)a. Oh, even though I went to (do)
                         work, I did nothing but have a good
                         time.

b. [How was] the weather?

                         b. It was tops. Don't we wish Japan
                         would have that kind of weather all
                         the time, too!

c. But with nothing but the same
kind of weather continuing, it's
probably tiresome (*lit.* not
interesting).

                         c. That's so, but I think it's great if it's
                         weather like that, but—you know
                         what I mean.

d. Don't you think it's more
enjoyable for it to be hot
sometimes and cold sometimes,
depending on the season?

                         d. But, you know, for example, when
                         you're in Japan, all you seem to do
                         is have to worry about the weather
                         every day.

e. That's the way it is, isn't it?

2(N)a. I just moved recently—right? The
floor above me (*lit.* that place) is
noisy, and . . . (it's terrible).

                        (J)a. You ought to complain—at times
                         like that.

b. I did say [something].
Telephoning, and speaking
directly . . . But on the contrary,
all it does is get worse.

                        b. Oh, say, at times like that, you speak
                         to the apartment manager!

c. To the apartment manager?

                        c. Yes. [Things] will go more smoothly
                         if you have somebody be a go-
                         between.

d. Really? I should have known,
shouldn't I!

BREAKDOWNS
(AND SUPPLEMENTARY VOCABULARY)

1. **Gûamu** — Guam

   asobu /-u; asoñda/ — play, play around, amuse oneself; be off from work

   asóñde bàkari da (SP1) — it's nothing but playing

   saikoo — the highest, the maximum

   zutto — without interruption

   X ǧa tuzuku /-u; tuzuita/ — X continues

   + **X o tuzukeru /-ru; tuzuketa/** — continue X

   têñki bâkari tuzuku — nothing but good weather continues

   kisêtu — season

   âtûku nattari sâmûku nattari suru (SP2) — alternate between getting hot and getting cold

   tanósìi /-katta/ — is enjoyable, pleasant; is joyous

   + **urésìi /-katta/** — is happy, glad

   + **subárasìi /-katta/** — is splendid, wonderful, magnificent

   + **natúkasìi /-katta/** — is nostalgic

   + **sabísìi /-katta/** — is sad, desolate, lonely, solitary

   + **kowâi /-katta/** — is fearsome, frightening, terrible

   tatôeba — for example

   têñki no kotó bàkari ki ni suru — concern oneself about nothing but things pertaining to weather

   sonó tòori — that way, [just] like that

2. **hiќkòsu /-u; hiќkòsita/** *or*

   hikkosi-suru — move (to a new residence)

   hiќkosi-sita bàkari da — [I] just moved

   kâi — floor

   urúsài /-katta/ — is noisy, harassing, a nuisance

   + **yakámasìi /-katta/** — is noisy, loud; is fault-finding, strict

   + **sîzuka /na/** — quiet, calm, placid

   môñku — complaint

   + **iiwake** — excuse, explanation

   + **koozitu** — excuse, explanation, pretext

   iú bèki da (SP3) — [one] ought to/must/should say

   tyokusetu — direct

   tyokusetu iu — say directly

   deńwa kàketari, tyokusetu ií ni ittàri — telephoning, going in order to say directly [and the like]

   kâette — on the contrary, instead

hîdôku naru bâkari da	it just gets severe
kañriniñ	apartment manager, superintendent
aída ni hàiru	become a go-between
aida ni hitó ni hàitte morau	have someone become a go-between
aida ni hitó ni hàitte morátta hòo	the alternative of having had someone become a go-between
sumûuzu /na/	smooth
sumûuzu ni iku	go smoothly

Supplementary Vocabulary: Exercise

sañpo	a walk
sañpo-suru	take a walk
oyóğì	swimming
oyôğu /-u; oyôida/	swim
hâikiñğu	hiking
zyogiñğu	jogging

MISCELLANEOUS NOTES

1. In CC1, Smith, the graduate student, and his sponsor, Mr. Suzuki, discuss Suzuki's recent trip to Guam. The style is basically careful, with final predicates and predicates before **kedo** in distal-style. The conversation includes a question without a question-particle ([N]a), a fragment ([N]b), and several other minor sentences ([J]c,d). In other words, the two participants are speaking in a manner that reflects some relaxation but at the same time maintains an appropriate amount of distance between them.

This is a conversation of disagreement. The two participants politely express a difference of opinion on the subject of weather. Notice how this is handled in an indirect, nonthreatening, and nonconfrontational way. In (J)b, Suzuki makes his first comment about the weather in Japan—one with which Smith disagrees. Instead of responding with a clear contradiction, Smith makes a negative statement that indirectly supports Japan's climate and ends it with the tentative **desyòo**, suggesting that Suzuki probably would agree with what he just said. Suzuki's response ([J]c) makes very clear that he persists in his wish that Japan's weather were like that of Guam, but he softens his disagreement with Smith in three ways: (1) he allows for the validity of Smith's background comments; (2) he adds that his statement is an opinion (—— **to omóimàsu**); and (3) he ends his statement with two nonconfrontational elements: **kedo** (allowing for Smith to respond again) and **nêe** (suggesting assumed understanding of his position). Smith, pursuing his own contrary opinion, responds with a question that, by its form, also suggests that agreement by Suzuki can be assumed: 'Don't you think ——?' (implying that surely everyone would). Suzuki, as he takes his next turn, raises another objection to Smith's argument, but again carefully ends with the tentative **desyòo**. As the polite, nonconclusive end to the discussion, Smith, the lower-ranking member of the pair, agrees that 'that, at least' (i.e., the point just made by Suzuki) is something he accepts.

Note another significant feature of this conversation: Suzuki is complaining about something in his own culture that Smith, the foreigner, is defending. When this situation is reversed, even more care must be exerted to avoid confrontation and the threat of inflicting loss of face.

(N)a. The use of **ikâg̃a** rather than **dôo** fits in with the generally careful tone of the conversation. As the introduction to a topic of conversation—and one from Smith to his sponsor—it is particularly appropriate. The form of the question (lacking a question-particle), however, keeps it from being excessively stiff given the setting (drinking tea together in Suzuki's home).

(J)a. **Iyâa**, occurring here at the beginning of an answer to an information question, suggests something negative or apologetic about what is about to be said.

(J)b. **Zutto**, previously introduced in comparisons as an indication of marked difference (**konó hòo g̃a zuítto ìi** 'this one is much better, better by far'), also occurs as an indication of continuity, lack of interruption. It links with a predicate as a pattern of manner (**zuítto beñkyoo-sitè (i)ta** '[I] was studying the whole time, without interruption').

(N)c. **Tuzuku** '[X] continues' is the intransitive partner of transitive **tuzukeru** 'continue [X].' While both verbals are operational, examples in which **tuzuku** occurs with a person as operator are limited to those in which s/he continues to function in a particular capacity or follows in sequence, *not* continues a named or understood activity (= **tuzukeru**). The notion of continuation for these verbals includes occurrence without interruption or without intervention by others, animate or inanimate. Examples: **gakkoo o tuzukeru** 'continue school'; **hanásì o tuzukeru** 'continue a talk,' 'continue talking'; **têñki g̃a tuzuita** 'good weather continued'; **tuzúite hosìi** '[I] want [it/him/her] to continue'; **kânozyo mo 'tuzuite yameta** 'she, too, continuing [the trend], quit'; **tuzúita sèki**[8] 'adjoining (continuous) seats'; **tuzuita kooeñ**[8] 'lectures [given] one after the other.'

(N)c, (J)c. Compare Smith's use of /gerund + **wa**/ followed by a negative, describing a general, ongoing condition—'having continuation isn't interesting'—with Suzuki's suggestion in the conditional that '*if* it should be that kind of weather, it would be good.'

(N)d. **Kisêtu**: The Japanese place great emphasis on the seasons and what is appropriate to them. This is reflected in their diet (what foods are eaten in what season), the scrolls they hang in their **tokonoma**, and the art objects they display. Note: **kisêtu no mono** 'seasonal thing(s); **kisetu-teki** 'seasonal.'

Tanósìi, obviously related to **tanósìmì** 'a pleasure' and **tanósìmu** 'take pleasure in,' refers to things that are pleasurable: **tanósìi hi/tokî/iê** 'a happy day/time/home'; **Tanôsìkatta.** 'It was fun!' **tanôsìku asobu** 'play with enjoyment.'

Urésìi, on the other hand, indicates pleasure from the point of view of the person experiencing it: **Âa, urésìi.** 'Oh, I'm [so] happy!' **Señsèe g̃a irâsite urêsìkatta.** 'I was happy that the teacher came'; **urésisòo na kao** 'a happy-looking face (or expression).'

Subárasìi may refer to animate or inanimate items characterized as being splendid, wonderful, great, first-rate, superb, as, for example, **hôñ, kôog̃i, iê, kyoozyu**, and so forth.

Natúkasìi is used in reference to items, animate or inanimate, that are dear to one's heart, yearned for, or missed. Note the significant structural difference between personalized English 'I miss Tokyo' and Japanese **Toókyoo g̃a natukasìi**; between English 'How nostalgic I feel [to see this again]!' and Japanese **Âa, natúkasìi** [which refers to the item just met up with].

Sabísìi describes items and general situations that are lonely, desolate, solitary, cheerless:

8. For the use of the perfective here, see 21A-SP1.

sabísìi tokórò 'a lonely place,' sabísìi kao 'a cheerless face (or expression),' sabísìi kêsiki 'desolate scenery'; kânozyo ḡa inâkute sabísìi 'it's lonely with her not being here.'
Kowâi describes animate and inanimate things that are frightening, horrifying, weird, or eerie. Examples: kowâi hanásì/eeḡa/kaminari/seńsèe 'frightening story/movie/thunder/ teacher.' Note again that a more overtly personalized English pattern (describing a person as being afraid of or fearing X—'I'm afraid of X') is represented in Japanese by an affective pattern (X ḡa kowâi 'X is frightening'). If the person who is afraid is also expressed, a double-ḡa pattern results: Tâkasi-tyañ ḡa kamínarì ḡa kowâi kara.. 'since Takashi is afraid of thunder...'

(J)d. Suzuki's comment about constant concern for the weather points up the fact that among the Japanese there is a strong cultural awareness of weather and a fear of natural disasters like typhoons and earthquakes.

(N)e. Toori, a nominal derived from the stem of the verbal tôoru 'pass through,' has as its concrete meaning 'road,' 'thoroughfare,' 'avenue,' in the form toórì. By extension—and with a different accent (tôori)—it means 'way,' 'in accordance with.' Compare such sequences as yakúsoku no yòo and yakúsoku no tòori: yakúsoku no yòo refers to something that is 'like a promise,' 'as if a promise'; yakúsoku no tòori signifies 'accordance with a promise made.' As a pattern of manner, tôori is followed by phrase-particle ni. Examples of tôori: ossyàtta tôori da 'it's just as you said'; îtu mo no tôori 'just as always'; kâre no iú tòori ni suru 'do in accordance with what he says.' Tôori occurs as the second part of nominal compounds in the form -doori (zikáñ-dòori 'on time').

2. In CC2, Smith discusses with Mr. Suzuki the problems he is having with upstairs neighbors in his new apartment and his unsuccessful attempts at a solution. Mr. Suzuki offers advice on how to solve the problem. The style is basically careful, as is usual in conversations between these two people, with major sentences ending in distal-style. But a number of minor sentences, including fragments, and an inverted sentence, point to a style that is moving in the direction of casualness.

In this CC, as in lesson 26A, the importance of the use of go-betweens in Japanese society is stressed. For the injured party to confront an antagonist directly leads to loss of face, as s/he is directly charged with causing a problem. For the Japanese, this is inappropriate behavior. From their point of view, a go-between, who is not personally or emotionally involved in the problem, becomes a neutral buffer, able to handle the matter in a calm, detached, unaccusing way. Other societies, of course, also use go-betweens, but what is important to note is the frequency of such use among the Japanese, even in situations where it might strike a non-Japanese as involving people who shouldn't be brought into the matter.

(N)a. Both urúsài and yakámasìi may refer to being noisy, but urúsài emphasizes the accompanying annoyance. In extended meanings, urúsài is closer to indicating harassment, while yakámasìi implies strict, demanding, insistent on details. Both words refer to animate and inanimate items. Examples: urúsài seńsèe 'a teacher who is a nuisance'; urúsài moñdai 'a bothersome problem'; yakámasìi moñdai 'a much-discussed problem'; yakámasìi titioya 'a strict father.'
Sîzuka followed by na describes nominals; followed by the particle ni of manner, it describes predicates. Examples: sîzuka na matî 'a quiet town'; sîzuka na kôe 'a soft voice'; sîzuka na hito 'a quiet person' ; sîzuka ni hanâsu 'speak softly'; Sîzuka ni sité kudasài. 'Please be quiet.'

(J)a. Ñ.. : Mr. Suzuki hesitates as he considers what Smith has just said.
Iiwake: Note iiwake-suru or iiwake o iu 'provide an excuse'; umâi/mazûi iiwake 'a good/

poor excuse'; **iíwake ḡa zyoozù/hetà da** 'is good/poor at making excuses'; **hoóritu o siranai kotò wa, iíwake nì wa narânai** 'ignorance of the law is no excuse.' Note that **moosiwake↓**, introduced in the apology **moósiwake arimasèn**, is actually the polite equivalent of **iiwake**, with the stem **ii** (from **iu**) replaced by the humble equivalent **moosi** from **môosu**. The notion of apology is often incorporated in **iiwake**. **Koozitu**, another word meaning 'excuse,' is particularly common in situations in which an excuse is a pretext, a pretense, an alibi. Examples: **koózitu o tukùru** 'concoct an excuse'; **hoñ no koozitu** 'a mere pretext.'

(N)b. **Kâette**, despite its resemblance to the gerund of **kâeru**, is actually a nominal that occurs without a following particle as a pattern of manner. It describes the predicate that comes after it, when an event or a condition is different, a substitute for what was expected.

(J)b. Notice Mr. Suzuki's speech style at this point in the conversation. He is about to offer Smith important advice about what is done in situations like the one discussed. The use of |**ano nêe**| gives notice that what follows should be carefully heeded, and the breaking up of the following statement into two parts, the first ending in /neˁ/, signals an explicit speech style that again emphasizes the importance of close attention. At the end, Mr. Suzuki states what it is that one does, using an extended predicate: **Kañriniñ ni iù ñ desu yo.** The function of this statement is really to tell Smith what to do. Since this is what is done, he too will act accordingly if he intends to function acceptably in a society where conformity is of utmost importance. (Compare **Mîruku nômu no yo.** *lit.* 'It's that one drinks milk,' used in telling a child to do likewise!)

(J)c. In the sequence **aida ni hitó ni hàitte morau, aida ni** is linked to **hâiru**, and **hito ni** to **morau**.

(N)d. Smith's initial surprise (**Hêe↗**) is followed by his realization that what he has just heard makes perfect sense as he thinks about it (**Naruhodo nêe**).

Structural Patterns

1. **bâkari**

Bâkari (or emphatic **bâkkari**) 'only,' 'only just,' 'little else except for' occurs in a number of different patterns. Their variety reminds us of **dakê**, which sometimes behaves like a particle and at other times like a nominal. We should, in fact, think in terms of two **bâkari**, similar in meaning but different in patterning. Note the following patterns:

1. /Nominal X + **bâkari**/ = 'only X,' 'little else except for X,' or, when X is a quantity expression 'only about X.'[9] A combination ending in **bâkari** may constitute a quantity expression and occur before predicates without a following particle. It may also join with an immediately following form of the copula **dà** to form a nominal predicate. Examples:

> **beñkyoo bàkari suru** 'do nothing but study'
>
> **okâsi bâkari tabêru** 'eat little else but sweets'
>
> **yoósyoku bàkari sukî da** 'like only Western-style food'
>
> **sikêñ bâkari da** 'it's nothing but exams'
>
> **zip̀-puñ-bàkari mâtu** 'wait only about ten minutes'

Also possible is the occurrence of (a) **bâkari** following a /nominal + particle/ sequence, or

---

9. In such combinations, an accented quantity expression loses its accent and forms a compound with following **bâkari**.

(b) a particle following a /nominal X + **bâkari**/ sequence. (Compare English 'she works only for that company' and 'she works for only that company.') The particle in such cases depends, of course, on the relationship between the preceding nominal and the following predicate. Note that **bâkari** does not follow **o**, **ğa**, **wa**, or **mo**. Examples:

utí no nàka ni bâkari iru 'stay only inside the home' (a)

natú bàkari ğa isóğasìi 'only summers are busy' (b)

sonó kyookàsyo bâkari o yôñde (i)ru 'be reading little else but that textbook' (b)

2a. /Imperfective predicate X + nominal **bâkari** + **da**/ = 'it's just occurrences of X'; 'only X occurs'; 'little else happens but X.' Examples:

Hîdôku naru bâkari na ñ desu. '(It's that) all it does is get [more] severe.'

Naôsu tte iu bâkari de, nani mo sinai. 'All s/he does is say s/he'll fix it, and s/he does nothing.'

Kîree na bâkari de, yakû ni tatânai. 'It is (*lit.* being) only pretty; it serves no purpose.'

Note the contrast in meaning between:

koó iu zassi bàkari (o) yômu 'read nothing but this kind of magazine'

and

koó iu zassi o yòmu bâkari da 'do nothing but read this kind of magazine.'

2b. /Perfective predicate X + nominal **bâkari** + **da**/ = 'X only just occurred' (used regularly in a time sense). Examples:

Kû-zi no siñkàñseñ ğa dêta bâkari desu. 'The 9:00 siñkàñseñ just left.'

Tâtta bâkari no atárasìi mâñsyoñ ni hiḱkosi-simàsita. 'I moved to a new apartment that was just built.'

3. /Verbal gerund X + particle **bâkari**/ = 'only just doing X,' 'doing little but X.' This type of sequence may be followed by a predicate (specifically a form of **iru**) or may combine with the copula to form a predicate. Examples:

Saké o nòñde bâkari irárenài yo. 'You can't go on just drinking.'

Asóñde bàkari inâi de, sukôsi beñkyoo-sitàra? '[How would it be] if you studied a little instead of just fooling around?'

Yasúmì ni iťtà no ni, határaite bàkari desita. 'In spite of the fact that I went to take it easy, I was just working.'

How does **bâkari** compare with **-gùrai**, **hodo**, **dakê**, and **sika**? Following quantity expressions, **bâkari**, **-gùrai**, and **hodo** all express approximation, but **bâkari** suggests the low side ('only about'), **hodo** the high side ('about as much as'), and **-gùrai** a more neutral 'about.' **Dakê** and **sika**, on the other hand, do not express approximation: **X dakê** points to 'just X—no more, no less,' and **X sika**, with its requirement for a following negative, emphasizes the negative by indicating 'non-occurrence except for X.' Note that some combinations of these are possible (**dakê sika** and **daké bàkari**, for example) to combine the meanings of both items, provided that those meanings are not in contrast. The differences in meaning among these five carries over even when the item preceding them is not a quantity expression, except that **bâkari**, **-gùrai**, and **hodo** less strongly connote approximation. Compare now

Nihóñgo bàkari beñkyoo-site (i)ru. 'All I'm studying is Japanese.'

Nihóñgo-g̊ùrai omósiròi. 'It's interesting to the extent of Japanese'; 'It's as interesting as Japanese.'

Nihoñg̊o hodo omósìròku nâi. 'It's not interesting as much as Japanese is'; 'It's not so interesting as Japanese.'

Nihoñg̊o dake beñkyoo-site (i)ru. 'I'm studying just Japanese.'

Nihoñg̊o sika beñkyoo-site (i)nai. 'I'm not studying anything except for Japanese.'

2. THE REPRESENTATIVE

The patterns with **ya**, **nâñka**, and **nâdo** that have been introduced in connection with nominals indicate that the nominal(s) mentioned do not tell the whole story—that other similar items, though not explicitly identified, are also under consideration. Thus we find phrases like: **isya ya beñ́g̊òsi** 'doctors and lawyers and the like'; **siñ́rìg̊aku, ziñ́ruìg̊aku nado** 'psychology, anthropology, etc.'; **otôtosi nañka** 'the year before last, for example.'

Japanese also has a special form for predicates that parallels the meanings of **ya**, **nânka**, and **nâdo**. We call this form the REPRESENTATIVE, to suggest that each occurrence is representative of more—either more kinds of occurrences or more occurrences of the same kind.

The representative is formed by adding **-tari** to the roots of verbals (with the usual changes that occur in verbal roots before endings beginning with *t*), **-kattari** to the roots of adjectivals, and **-tari** to **dàt-** for the copula. For anyone familiar with the conditional, the easiest way to form the representative is simply to change the final *a* to *i*: for example, conditional **káttàra** > representative **káttàri**. All statements about accent of the conditional apply to the representative as well.

In its most typical usage, two representative forms X and Y (which occur in sequence with or without preceding modifiers) are immediately followed by a form of **suru**. The combination indicates 'the occurrence [often the repeated occurrence] of X and Y and the like,' or 'repeated alternation between the occurrence of X and Y.' When the topic of discussion is plural, another possible meaning is that each representative form refers to different members of the group. Examples:

têepu o kiítàri, kyoókàsyo o yôñdari suru 'do things like listening to tapes, reading textbooks, and the like'

kurúma de kìtàri, arûite kîtâri suru 'come by car and walk here, among other ways of getting here'

or 'some come by car, and some walk here'

dêtari hâittari suru 'keep leaving and entering, leaving and entering'

sâmûkattari âtûkattari suru 'it's cold and hot, cold and hot'

zyoózù dattari hetâ dattari suru '[s/he] goes back and forth between being good at it and poor at it'

It is also possible for three (rarely more) representative forms or a single representative form to occur with **suru**, again indicating other related occurrences that are not explicitly mentioned and/or the repeated occurrence of what is mentioned:

hôñ o yôñdari, teg̊ámi o kàitari, têrebi o mîtari suru 'read books, write letters, watch television, and so on'

osóku kìtàri suru 'come late and do other things that are a problem,' *and/or* 'keep coming late'

The representative sequence may also be followed by the copula instead of **suru**: **âme dattari yukî dattari da** 'it's rain and snow, rain and snow.'

In occurrences of /representative(s) + **site**, + predicate/, **site** may be dropped without any great difference in meaning beyond becoming slightly more casual. Example:

Kâre wa, môñku o ìttàri koózitu o tukùttari (site), iyâ na hito desu nêe. 'What with his complaining and making up excuses, he's an unpleasant person, isn't he!'

An example of this occurs as a minor sentence in CC2(N)b, in which **site** could be added after **ìttàri**.

In situations involving non-occurrence, either the representative or the following form of **suru** can be negative: (a) /X-**sitàri** Y-**sitàri sinai**/, or (b) /X-**sinâkattari** Y-**sinâkattari suru**/. In (a), there is no occurrence of X and Y; (b) focuses on the fact that the non-occurrence of X and Y is actually experienced, as, for example, when the opposite is expected. Compare

Siñbuñ o yòñdari sinai. '[S/he] doesn't do things like reading newspapers.' *and*

Siñbuñ o yomânakattari suru. '[S/he] fails to read newspapers, among other things'; '[S/he] keeps failing to read newspapers.'

For the English speaker, the representative is not a difficult form to understand or to construct. The main problem is remembering to use it! An English stimulus like 'do such things as —' may immediately suggest the need for a representative in Japanese, but the student of Japanese who requires this kind of cue will not only be depending on English—which is bad enough—but on a pattern that is rare in everyday natural English. The most commonly occurring equivalent is the English intonation that signals repetition and/or etcetera: 'What do you do on Saturdays?' . . . 'I go shopping — and read —.'

3. bèki

Bèki is a holdover from an earlier period of Japanese—a kind of fossil. We have met it before in another of its forms, as part of **narubeku** 'to the extent possible.' It has more forms besides **beku** and **bèki**: their endings are different from those of present-day verbals, adjectivals, and copula.

This fossil, not surprisingly, fails to fit neatly into any of the word classes of contemporary Japanese. **Bèki** follows an imperfective verbal (and loses its accent if the verbal is accented) and is itself followed by a form of the copula or a nominal. /Imperfective verbal X + **bèki (da)**/ = '[one] ought to X'; '[one] should X'; '[one] must X.' Corresponding perfectives and negatives are indicated by changes in the copula, not in the verbal preceding **bèki**. Patterns with **bèki** are not as forceful in prescribing behavior as expressions like **sinâkute wa 'ikenai/ narânai**, but they are stronger than **-tara îi** combinations. Examples:

Zikáñ-dòori ni kûru beki desu yo. 'You ought to come on time.'

Señsèe to soódañ-site oku bèki desita. 'You ought to have consulted with the doctor in advance.'

Soó iu bèki zya nâi desu. 'One ought not say that.'

Surú bèki koto, sinâi ñ desu ka⌡ 'You're not going to do the things you ought to do?'

Notice the conflicts that arise when we try to fit **bèki** into the patterns of current Japanese. The fact that it occurs before **dà** and **dàtta** and forms a negative in **zya nâi** suggests that it is a nominal or particle, but the fact that it is inflected (occurs with different endings) makes this theory untenable. It follows the imperfective of the verbal rather than the stem, so that we cannot look at /verbal + **bèki**/ as a compound.[10] As a holdover from the Japanese of a different period, it is best placed in a special "fossil class" with its own special patterning.

Drills

A 1. **Sukôsi wa asóbemàsita ka⌣**
'Were you able to have fun a little, at least?'

Iya, asónde bàkari desita yo.
'Oh, all I did was have fun!'

2. **Sukôsi wa ryokóo-dekimàsita ka⌣**
'Were you able to travel a little, at least?'

Iya, ryokóo-site bàkari desita yo.
'Oh, all I did was travel!'

3. **neráremàsita**; 4. **tabéraremàsita**; 5. **dekákeraremàsita**; 6. **moráemàsita**

B 1. **Kono-ǧoro bûnǧaku o benkyoo-site (i)ru sòo desu ne!**
'I hear you are studying literature these days.'

Êe, bûnǧaku bâkari benkyoo-site (i)màsu.
'Yes, I'm studying nothing but literature.'

2. **Kono-ǧoro waápuro o tukatte (i)ru sòo desu ne!**
'I hear you are using a word processor these days.'

Êe, waápuro bàkari tukátte (i)màsu.
'Yes, I'm using nothing but a word processor.'

3. **senpai to tukiàtte (i)ru**; 4. **hurûi hôn o atûmete (i)ru**; 5. **uti ni iru**; 6. **kônpa ni itte (i)ru**; 7. **wahuku o kite (i)ru**

C 1. **Kono hen no bukka wa, tasyoo yâsûku nâtta n desu ka⌣**
'(Is it that) prices around here have gone down (*lit.* become cheap) slightly?'

Tónde mo nài. Tâkâku naru bâkari desu yo.
'Heavens no! They do nothing but go up!'

2. **Konó daiǧaku no sikèn wa, tasyoo yasásiku nàtta n desu ka⌣**
'(Is it that) the examinations at this university have become slightly easier?'

Tónde mo nài. Muzúkasiku nàru bâkari desu yo.
'Heavens no! They do nothing but get [more] difficult!'

3. **otáku karà no tuúkin-zìkan/mizíkaku nàtta**; 4. **kono hen/sîzuka ni natta**; 5. **kosi no guai/yôku natta**; 6. **kono-ǧoro/himá ni nàtta**; 7. **taíhùu no kaze/yôwâku natta**

10. On the other hand, **narubeku** *is* analyzed as a single word, since it is not representative of a pattern that permits substitution of other items in place of **naru**, and its present meaning is totally unpredictable from its component parts.

D 1. **Atárasìi mâñsyoñ ni môo hikkosimàsita ka**   **Êe, hikkòsita bâkari desu.**
'Did you move to the new apartment yet?'   'Yes, I just moved.'

2. **Osatoo môo mazémàsita ka**   **Êe, mâzeta bâkari desu.**
'Did you mix [in] the sugar yet?'   'Yes, I just mixed [it] in.'

3. **kânozyo no zyûusyo/omóidasimàsita**; 4. **asóko karà no kyôri/ wakárimàsita**; 5. **asóko ni òtite (i)ta kippu/hiróimàsita**; 6. **siñrìgaku no señsèe ni/soódañ-simà-sita**; 7. **saḡásitè (i)ta kâsa/mitúkarimàsita**

E 1. **Koó iu kotò dattara, mâiniti sitâi desu nêe.**   **Dê mo, koó iu koto bàkari sitê (i)tyaa, yôku nâi desyoo?**
'If it's something like this, we want to do [it] every day, don't we!'   'But it wouldn't be good doing nothing but this kind of thing every day, would it?'

2. **Soó iu hanasì dattara, mâiniti kikítài desu nêe.**   **Dê mo, soó iu hanasi bàkari kiítè (i)tyaa, yôku nâi desyoo?**
'If it's stories like those, we want to listen to [them] every day, don't we!'   'But it wouldn't be good listening to nothing but those kinds of stories every day, would it?'

3. **koó iu monò/tabétài**; 4. **koo iu yoohuku/kitai**; 5. **koó iu monò/moraitai**; 6. **aá iu zyùḡyoo/sitai**; 7. **soo iu siḡoto/tetúdaitài**

F 1. **Kinóo no tèñki wa, saíkoo dèsita nêe.**   **Îtu mo aá iu tèñki dattara, îi no ni nêe.**
'The weather yesterday was tops, wasn't it!'   'I wish it were always weather like that, don't you!'

2. **Konáida no tùuyaku wa, saíkoo dèsita nêe.**   **Îtu mo aá iu tùuyaku dattara, îi no ni nêe.**
'The interpreter yesterday was tops, wasn't s/he!'   'I wish it were always an interpreter like that, don't you!'

3. **kyôo no aságòhañ**; 4. **señsyuu no kòñpa**; 5. **kyôneñ no ryokoo**; 6. **mâe no yânusi**; 7. **yuube no kooeñ**

G 1. **Soó iu hitò ni wa aítàku nâi nâa.**   **Zyâa, dôo iu hitô dattara âtte kudásaimàsu ka**
'People like that I don't want to meet!'

   'Then what kind of people (*lit.* if it is what kind of people) will you meet (for me)?'

2. **Soó iu sikèñ wa tukáitaku nài nâa.**   **Zyâa, dôo iu sikêñ dattara tukátte kudasaimàsu ka**
'Tests like that I don't want to use!'   'Then what kind of tests (*lit.* if it is what kind of tests) will you use (for me)?'

3. **hudoosañya ni/tanómitàku nâi**; 4. **sêminaa ni/detâku nâi**; 5. **mâñsyoñ ni/sumítàku**

nâi; 6. siḡoto/tuzúketaku nài; 7. tokórò de/asóbitaku nài; 8. mizûumi de/oyóḡitàku nâi

H 1. **Seńpai ni tukiàu koto mo âru ñ desyoo?**

'It's probably the case that there are also times when you associate with your seniors—right?'

Êe, mâa, seńpai ni tukiàttari . .

'Well, yes, I do things like associating with my seniors . . .'

  2. **Tûuyaku o surú kotò mo âru ñ desyoo?**

'It's probably the case that there are also times when you interpret—right?'

Êe, mâa, tûuyaku o sitàri . .

'Well, yes, I do things like interpreting . . .'

  3. otókò no ko ḡa tetúdàtte kureru; 4. bûñḡaku no gakusee ḡa kûru; 5. yamâ e iku; 6. waapuro o tukau; 7. kańriniñ ḡa site kureru

I 1. **Sumûuzu ni îkú koto bàkari zya nâi desyoo.**

'It's not that [things] just go smoothly, I suppose.'

Êe, baai ni yotte, sumûuzu ni íttàri, ikánàkattari . .

'That's right. Depending on circumstances, sometimes they go smoothly, sometimes not . . .'

  2. **Kimátta zikañ ni owaru koto bàkari zya nâi desyoo.**

'It's not that [things] just end at the predetermined time, I suppose.'

Êe, baai ni yotte, kimátta zikañ ni owattàri, owáranàkattari . .

'That's right. Depending on circumstances, sometimes they end at the predetermined time, sometimes not . . .'

  3. sonó tòori no; 4. otêñki no îi; 5. seńpai-ràsìku suru

J 1. **Teḡámi o dasimàsita neʕ**

'You mailed some letters, didn't you?'

Êe, teḡámi dàsitari, deńwa kàketari site . .

'Yes, I mailed letters, made telephone calls . . .'

  2. **Âtte iímàsita neʕ**

'You saw [him/her] and told [him/her], didn't you?'

Êe, âtte íttàri, deńwa kàketari site . .

'Yes, I saw [her/him] and told [her/him], made telephone calls . . .'

  3. kańriniñ kara itte moraimàsita; 4. seńsèe ni soódañ-simàsita; 5. âtte hanásimàsita; 6. têepu o okúrimàsita; 7. mêsseezi o todókemàsita

K 1. **Bukka wa, takâi desu ka⤸**

'Are prices high?'

Mâa, hi ni yotte, tâkâkattari yâsûkattari desu nêe.

'Well, depending on the day, they alternate between being high and low.'

  2. **Inû wa, îtu mo sôto desu ka⤸**

'Is the dog always outside?'

Mâa, hi ni yotte, sôto dattari nâka dattari desu nêe.

'Well, depending on the day, it alternates between being outside and inside.'

3. **ano heñ/yakámasìi desu**; 4. **Mîtiko-sañ/kono zikañ ni ôkite (i)masu**; 5. **suíyòobi no bañgumi/omósiròi desu**; 6. **kono miti/zuíto komimàsu**; 7. **tuúkiñ no deñsya no nàka de/tâtte (i)masu**

L 1. **Koó iu tokì wa, môñku iítè mo îi ñ desyoo ka.**
'(Is it that) it's all right to complain at times like this?'

Êe, motîroñ môñku iú bèki desu yo—soó iu tokì wa.
'Yes, of course you ought to complain—at times like that.'

2. **Koó iu tokì wa, koózitu o tukùtte mo îi ñ desyoo ka.**
'(Is it that) it's all right to make excuses at times like this?'

Êe, motîroñ 'koózitu o tukûru beki desu yo—soó iu tokì wa.
'Yes, of course you ought to make excuses—at times like that.'

3. **señpai ni aída ni hàitte moratte**; 4. **sigoto o yamete**; 5. **ni-sâñ-niti yasûñde**; 6. **gôhañ o nokôsite**; 7. **hoñtoo no kotò o hanâsite**

M 1. **Konó wañrùumu wa, kitá-muki dèsu nêe.**
'This studio apartment faces north, doesn't it.'

Âa, minámi-muki dà to îi no ni nêe.
'Oh, it would be nice if it faced south, wouldn't it!'

2. **Atúmàru no wa, usíro dèsu nêe.**
'The place where [they] gather is in the back, isn't it.'

Âa, mâe da to îi no ni nêe.
'Oh, it would be nice if it were in the front, wouldn't it!'

3. **koítì/dêguti**; 4. **señmeñzyò/ue**; 5. **konó kèeki/syatyoo ga kirai**; 6. **atárasìi arúbàito/zyosee**; 7. **tugî no ryokoo/samûi kisêtu**

N 1. **Kâre wa, asita sikêñ ga âru tte iítà kedo . .**
'He said there would be an examination tomorrow, but . . .' (is that true?)

Êe, kâre no iítà tòori desu yo
'Yes, it's just as he said.'

2. **Señsèe wa, asâtte zyûgoo ga âru tte óssyàtta kedo . .**
'The teacher said there would be classes the day after tomorrow, but . . .' (is that true?)

Êe, señsèe no óssyàtta tôori desu yo
'Yes, it's just as the teacher said.'

3. **Yamamoto-sañ/kono miti ga Kyôoto made tuzuite (i)ru/iu**; 4. **watasi/kono heñ no bukka ga hizyóo ni takài/omôtta**; 5. **Tâkano-kyoozyu/âki ga itíbañ kìree da/óssyàru**

O 1. **Têñki ga warúi to, komárimasèñ ka**
'Aren't you bothered when the weather is bad?'

Iya, kâette warûi hoo ga komárànai ñ desu yo
'No, on the contrary, (it's that) bad weather is less bothersome (*lit.* the bad alternative isn't bothersome).'

2. **Kooeñ ğa tuzuku to, tukáremasèñ
ka**↙

   'Don't you get tired when the lectures
run back to back?'

**Iya, kâette tuzúita hòo ğa tukárènai ñ
desu yo**↙

   'No, on the contrary, (it's that) it's less
tiresome when they continue back to back
(*lit.* the continued-back-to-back alternative
isn't tiresome).'

3. **wasyóku bàkari da/iyâ zya arímasèñ**; 4. **takúsañ nokòru/komárimasèñ**; 5. **tuúkiñ
no kyòri ğa nağâi/tukáremasèñ**; 6. **señpai ğa kònai/ki ní simasèñ**

Application Exercises

A1. Practice asking whether or not it is all right to do (or not do) certain things; the answers
should state that, on the contrary, one *ought* to do (or not do) the activity in question.
Choose situations in which question—and answer—might really be apt to occur. Examples
include questions relating to listening to tapes before coming to class; consulting directly
with the teacher when there are problems; not using English during class; speaking Japanese with one's Japanese teacher even at parties and the like; complaining in cases involving
the classroom's being cold; giving an excuse when one does not attend Japanese language
class.

2. Practice asking fellow students questions about their activities last summer; on weekends; after class is over; on vacation; when they are free; before coming to Japanese class.
Have the students responding to the questions use representative forms in their replies.

3a. Have members of the group perform activities possible in a classroom setting—
opening and closing windows and doors, turning lights on and off, throwing away old
newspapers, putting tapes into and taking them out of a box, and so on. In reply to questions
whether or not someone has already performed the activity in question, reply that s/he just
did it, using **bâkari**.

3b. In reference to public figures or mutual acquaintances who are associated with a
particular activity (one that you are able to express in Japanese!), make an appropriate
comment that includes **bâkari**. Be sure to distinguish between /nominal + **bâkari** + pred-
icate/ and /nominal + predicate + **bâkari**/.

4. Have paired members of your group engage in conversations involving a polite difference of opinion, using the patterns of CC1. Following the conversation, have other members of the group ask and answer questions about the content of the conversation.
Suggestions for topics: living in the center of a city versus living in a place slightly removed
from it; attending a large university versus a small college; attending college immediately
after graduating from high school versus taking a year off and working and traveling and
the like.

5. Reversing the thrust of CC2, suggest to a Japanese that s/he speak directly to the
people involved, instead of dealing with a go-between.

B. Core Conversations: Substitution

Practice the Core Conversations, changing the participants to close friends—two males,
two females, a male and a female. Next, ask and answer questions about content, including
both questions referring to small details and broader questions that require longer answers.

SECTION C

Eavesdropping

(Answer the following questions on the basis of the accompanying audiotape. A = the first speaker and B the second speaker in each conversation.)

1. What university does B plan to attend? Assuming what condition?
2a. What is A's problem?
 b. What is B's advice?
3a. What problem does A comment on?
 b. What has B been doing in connection with this?
4a. Comment on A's current mood.
 b. How does B react?
5a. What is A trying to learn from B?
 b. What information does B provide?
6a. Who is the topic of conversation?
 b. Where does that person work? In what capacity?
 c. What is A's mistaken assumption?
7a. Where does this conversation probably take place?
 b. Who are A and B?
 c. What is A's problem?
 d. What does A request?
8a. What is the probable setting of this conversation?
 b. What does B offer A, with what condition?
 c. What does A actually want?
 d. Why does B apologize?
9a. Initially, what is B instructed to do, under what circumstances?
 b. What further guidance does B ask for?
 c. In response, what instructions does A give?
10a. At what stage is the current project?
 b. What does A wish?
11a. What is the topic of discussion?
 b. Describe current conditions.
 c. What is A's complaint?
 d. What is B's wish?
12a. Why does B express thanks to A?
 b. What problem relating to the topic of discussion does A mention?
 c. How is B instructed to handle the problem?
13a. What is A's hope?
 b. What is B's reaction? Why?
 c. Comment on the relationship of A, B, and Mizuno.
14a. Describe the weather. Give details.
 b. What is A wondering?
 c. In what connection does B mention an umbrella?
15a. What does A think about the coffee? Give details.
 b. Describe B's reactions to A's comments.
16a. Why is A complaining about Keiko? Give details.
 b. How does B defend Keiko?
 c. What is A's reaction to this defense?
 d. How is B going to handle the situation?
 e. What is the probable relationship among A, B, and Keiko?

17a. In general terms, what are A and B complaining about?
  b. In what connection is tennis mentioned?
  c. What specific activities does B mention in connection with tennis?
  d. How does B describe the senior colleagues?
18a. What is A about to do?
  b. What is B told to do?
  c. What does B want A to do? Why?
  d. Why does A apologize?
  e. Why does B say thank you?
19a. What does A apologize for?
  b. What had B already done?
  c. How does A begin offering an excuse?
  d. What excuse does A offer?
  e. Why is A so annoyed?
20a. What does A comment on?
  b. What is B's explanation?
  c. Where did this happen?
  d. What is B certain of?
  e. What does A first suggest?
  f. What is B's response to this?
  g. What is B's subsequent question?
  h. According to B, what ought A to do?
21a. What is the topic of conversation?
  b. Why is A upset?
  c. According to A, what ought B to do?
  d. What is B's reaction?
  e. What does A think will happen?
  f. What does B predict?
22a. What information does A first ask for?
  b. What information does B actually provide? Give details.
  c. What does A ask for next?
  d. How does B suggest obtaining that information?
  e. What alternate way will A take, under what conditions?
23a. What is the probable relationship between A and B?
  b. What does A want B to do?
  c. Why does B refuse?
  d. What is A's reaction?
  e. What does A warn B about?
  f. What is B's reaction?
  g. Given what conditions would school be enjoyable, according to B?
24a. What does A ask B to do?
  b. What two things must A do first?
  c. What must A do with the red button? Give details.
  d. What makes this difficult?
  e. What will happen if A fails to follow what instruction?
  f. At what point is B to let go?
25a. Identify A and B.
  b. What is A's concern? Give details.
  c. What is B's present plan? Give details.
  d. Why does A tell B to be careful?
26a. Who moved recently? Into what kind of quarters?

b. Describe how those quarters are working out.

c. What does B think ought to be done?

d. What has A already done, with what results?

e. How has A's impression of the building superintendent changed?

f. What does B feel is going to be troublesome?

27a. Who is B?

b. What information is A checking on?

c. What mistaken impression did A have?

d. Who has been in Germany since last year?

e. Why didn't B go to Germany last year?

f. What are B's parents strongly recommending against?

g. How are B's parents described?

h. What surprises A?

i. What is B's explanation? Give the two reasons B mentions.

j. How does A reply?

k. What is B's hope?

l. How do you account for the difference in speech styles used by A and B?

28a. Who is coming to Japan? When? For how long?

b. Describe the plans B has made for the visit.

c. Give two reasons for the choice of location B has made.

d. What two concerns does A mention?

e. What is B's response?

Utilization

Follow the instructions given for Utilization in lesson 25. Be sure to aim at natural Japanese appropriate to the situation using patterns you have studied rather than trying to make literal translations of the English stimuli. Remember to use sentence-particles—**ne**, **nêe**, **yo**—and minor sentences whenever appropriate.

1a. Comment to a friend how late **Kee-tyañ** is, when you told her to come by 7:15. It's already almost 8:00.

b. Your friend offers as an explanation that **Kee-tyañ** is coming here for the first time, and besides, in coming from her home to this place, she must transfer several times.

2a. Inform a colleague that since Mr. Nakamura of Oriental Trade studied English from morning till night for eight months before going to America, he became very proficient.

b. Your colleague replies that even so, he's very good.

3a. You are organizing a small meeting. Ask a colleague what you should do if the **katyoo** isn't able to come by 10:00.

b. Your colleague replies that it will probably be all right if you wait until about 10:15 and begin then, even if he doesn't come.

4a. Ask a friend what she is going to do if she's free next Saturday.

b. Your friend replies that there's work she must do next Saturday, so unfortunately she won't be free.

5a. You have to telephone your professor tomorrow. Ask him (politely!) what time it would be good for you to call.

b. Your professor replies that he'll be at the university from about 10:30 on, so . . .

6a. You are going to Mejiro tomorrow. Ask a friend which train you should take.

b. Your friend replies that she has never been there, so she doesn't know, but she thinks that if you ask Kato, he will.

7a. Comment to a friend that just when you thought you'd reached the point where you could speak French a little, you again have the feeling you are unable to say anything.

b. Your friend replies that foreign languages are like that. You go back and forth between being good [at them] and being poor [at them].

8a. Complain to a friend that you are tired, and what is more, you have a headache.

b. Your friend replies by suggesting that you have some tea or something and rest for a bit.

9a. Ask a friend whether you push the red button on this machine or pull it.

b. Your friend replies that if you pull it the electricity goes on, but if you push it, it goes off.

10a. Ask an acquaintance if his colleague Ito (of equal status) is still in the U.S.

b. Your acquaintance replies that he is: he went (or came) as a student, but he now is employed as a Japanese-language teacher at an American college.

11a. Tell a colleague that last night you went home late. When you entered the house, the electricity suddenly went out.

b. Your colleague replies that it gets to be frightening when there is no electricity and you can't see anything.

12a. Comment to a colleague that somehow you have the feeling that Ms. Tanaka's (the secretary) manner is strange these days.

b. Your colleague agrees and points out that it's been that way ever since she came back from America.

13a. Comment to a friend that you wish the rain would stop.

b. Your friend agrees, saying that even for rain in the rainy season, it's too much.

14a. A friend has just returned from a year in Europe. Ask her how it was.

b. Your friend replies that it wasn't much fun. She had no close friends, she didn't understand the language, and so she did little else but work.

15a. Ask a friend how her vacation was.

b. Your friend replies that even though she went to the mountains to rest, all she did was study because she will be taking exams soon.

16a. Ask a stranger how to get to the Mizuno Building.

b. The stranger replies that if you go straight along this street, you'll see a bank, post-office, department store, and the like. It's a little beyond those buildings.

17a. Ask a colleague the distance from here to Kyoto.

b. Your colleague replies that he has no idea; he wishes you had asked Yamamoto, because he knows such things, but he just went home.

18a. Ask a classmate if he heard Professor Morimoto's lecture about Japanese law yesterday.

b. Your classmate replies that unfortunately he didn't know that Professor Morimoto was here; if he had known, he would of course have attended the lecture.

19a. Comment to an acquaintance that nothing but the same kind of weather goes on and on here.

b. Your acquaintance agrees and proceeds to ask if you don't think it's more interesting to have variation between hot and cold weather, depending on the season.

20a. Complain to a classmate that all you're doing is studying Japanese, but you're still poor at it.

b. Your classmate reassures you that you are doing well; that your test score (**sukoa**) this week was tops.

21a. Tell a friend that you've reached the point where you can speak Japanese a little, but you still don't understand the Japanese you hear when walking on the street and standing in stations and trains and such.

b. Your friend replies that you ought to listen to tapes more; if you listen to tapes, you'll certainly get to be able to understand.

22a. Complain to a classmate that when you do nothing but read books like this textbook, your eyes get to hurt.

b. Your classmate points out that you may need glasses, and suggests that you have an eye doctor check.

23a. Ask a colleague about her English-language study.

b. Your colleague replies that what with listening to tapes, reading the textbook, consulting with the teacher, and so on, it takes a lot of time, but it is very enjoyable. She adds that she ought to listen to tapes more, but . . .

24a. Ask a friend how his vacation was.

  b. Your friend replies that he had a wonderful time—swimming, taking walks, reading . . .

25a. Comment to a colleague that when you work in a place like this, all you (have to) concern yourself about is the heat.

  b. Your colleague agrees that it is just as you said.

26a. Ask a colleague if he fixed the typewriter.

  b. Your colleague replies that he tried to fix it, but instead it does nothing but get worse.

27a. Ask your senior colleague if he is going to attend the conference tomorrow even if it snows.

  b. The answer is no; your colleague informs you that if it snows, he plans to stay at home.

28a. You are having a problem with your landlord. Ask a friend which she thinks would be better— to speak directly to him, or to have someone act as a go-between.

  b. Your friend replies that things will go more smoothly having someone serve as a go-between.

29a. Point out to a colleague that the part-time worker keeps complaining —— and making excuses ——.

  b. Your colleague agrees and suggests that it would be great if he would quit.

30a. Ask an acquaintance how the people who are employed at his company come to work.

  b. Your acquaintance says that they come on buses and trains ——, and walk —— . . .

31a. Comment to a friend how pleasant (lonely; scary) it is when no one is here.

  b. Your friend agrees that it is indeed that way.

32a. Comment to a classmate on how happy you are that Professor Mizuno is going to continue this seminar until next year.

  b. Your classmate is happy, too. She remarks on his wonderful lectures.

33a. Ask the part-time worker to pick that up (bend that; mix that in; tie that up; hit that; pass that to the right; push that; pull that).

  b. In each case, the part-time worker asks about doing the same 'to this, too.'

34a. Tell a friend that you tried to bend (mix; open; attach) this, but it wouldn't.

  b. Your friend suggests that you try bending (mixing; opening; attaching) it once more.

35a. Tell a friend that you didn't know that your senior colleague, Mr. Watanabe, was going to come to this reception. You wish you had known.

  b. Your friend apologizes, saying he ought to have told you in advance.

36a. Tell a Japanese acquaintance that you have the feeling that Japanese has suddenly become very difficult.

  b. Your acquaintance asks if it isn't because you have reached the point where you know more about the Japanese language. She points out that you are very good at it; you ought not complain.

Check-up

1. Describe two very different English equivalents that /predicate + **no ni**/ may have depending on context. In which case is the predicate before **ni** always an imperfective verbal? In which case is the pattern regularly followed by **wa**? Compare **no ni** with **kedo** and **ḡa**. Why do we classify **no ni** as /noun + particle/ but **kedo** and **ḡa** as particles?   (A-SP1)

2. Describe how the conditional of verbals, of adjectivals, and of the copula are formed. What is the basic meaning of the conditional? In terms of its closest English equivalents, what problem does it present for native speakers of English? Describe its use in providing background.   (A-SP2)

3. In the Japanese equivalents of:

  'When I arrived home, I telephoned my parents.' *and*

  'When I arrived home, a call came in from my parents.'

only one would ordinarily include a conditional form. Which of the two is it, and what semantic feature accounts for this difference between the two sentences?   (A-SP2)

4. Describe the difference in usage between pairs like **Dôo sitara îi?** and **Koó sitàra dôo?** How is the conditional used as an indirect form of request? How does it contrast with /gerund + **mo**/? (A-SP2)

5. Compare

    Utí ni itàra îi.

    Utí ni ita hòo ǧa îi.

    Utí ni iru hazu dà.

All of these might have 's/he should be at home' as an English equivalent. (A-SP2)

6. Describe the use of the particle **to** of accompaniment following a predicate. In what form does this predicate occur? (A-SP3)

7. Describe the use of minor sentences ending in **no ni** to express contrary-to-fact wishes (examples: **Iru to îi no ni . .** ; **Môtto hâyâku hazímetàra yôkatta no ni . .**). (A-SP2, SP3)

8. What is the basic meaning of /**X to site**/? Compare the use of /**X to site**/, /**X to sitê wa**/, and /**X to sitê mo**/. What is the difference in meaning between /**X to site**/ and /**X ni site**/? What does X stand for in all these combinations? (A-SP4)

9. What is the meaning of **nàñka** following a nominal or series of nominals? What is its more formal equivalent? (A-SP5)

10. What is the basic meaning of **bâkari**? What problem does it pose when we try to assign it to a word class? Give an example of its use following (a) a general nominal; (b) a nominal of quantity; (c) an imperfective; (d) a perfective; and (e) a gerund. Compare **bâkari**, **hodo**, **-ǧùrai**, **dakê**, and **sika**. (B-SP1)

11. Describe how the representatives of verbals, of adjectivals, and of the copula are formed. What is the basic meaning of the representative? Give an example of its use (a) before a form of **suru**; (b) before a form of **dà**; (c) before a pause, hooking up with a following predicate. (B-SP2)

12. Why do we refer to **bèki** as a fossil? In current Japanese, what may precede it? What follows it? What does it mean? (B-SP3)

Lesson 27

SECTION A

Core Conversations

1(J)a. **Syuúsyoku kimatta sòo de, omédetoo gozaimàsu.**

    (N)a. **Dôo mo. Sûǧu goréñraku-siyoo to omoinàǧara, tûi sitûree-site simatte . .**

  b. **Iêie. Anâta mo, iroiro sinâkereba narânai koto ǧa oári desyòo kara . .**

    b. **Sumímasèñ.**

2(N)a. **Kodómo o sodatenàǧara siǧóto o tuzukerù no wa, taiheñ desyoo?**

    (J)a. **Mâa, oyâ to site no sekíniñ mo àru si, siǧoto mo tyañto sinàkereba narânai si, isóǧasìi koto wa isóǧasìi desu yo**

  b. **Môsi 'siǧoto ka 'katee no dôtira ka o erábànakereba narânaku nattara, dôo simasu?**

    b. **Sâa. Sonó tokì ni nâtte mînakereba, wakárimasèñ ne!**

3(N)a. |**Anoo . .**|

    (J)a. **Ñ?**

  b. **Tanáka-sañ ǧa tukùtta konó yoteehyoo nà ñ desu kedo neʕ Zêñbu yarínaòsite morau hitúyoo ǧa arimàsu ne!**

    b. **Sôo nêe. Sikâsi, soó nàru to, mata Tanáka-sañ ni tanomànakya ikénài wa nêe.**

c. Hâi. Sakamoto-sañ ka 'butyoo
   kara tanôñde mite itádakemasèñ
   ka⤹

d. Sôo desu ka nêe. Sakámoto-sañ
   ǧa soo ossyàru no nara, sikáta
   arimasèñ nêe.

c. Iyâa, kore wa yáppàri tañtòosya
   no Mîraa-sañ ǧa tanômu beki yo.

d. Mâa, otyá dè mo nomínàǧara,
   zizyoo o yôku setúmee-surèba,
   nattoku-site kurerù wa yo⤹

ENGLISH EQUIVALENTS

1(J)a. I hear (*lit.* having heard) your
       employment has been decided;
       congratulations.

(N)a. Thanks. While thinking I'd get in
      touch with you right away, in the
      end I unintentionally failed to (*lit.*
      committed a rudeness) and . . . (it
      was inexcusable).

b. No, no. You, too, must have all
   kinds of things you have to do
   so . . . (it's understandable).

2(N)a. Continuing work and bringing up
       children at the same time is
       difficult, isn't it?

b. I'm sorry.

b. Suppose it becomes necessary to
   choose one of the two—work or
   home; what will you do?

(J)a. Well, you have both responsibility as
      a parent, and you must also do your
      work properly; you *are busy*!

3(N)a. Uh . . .

b. It's about this schedule that Ms.
   Tanaka made, you know? There's
   a need to have it all redone, isn't
   there!

b. Hm. Unless I look at [the situation]
   when that time comes, I can't tell.

(J)a. Yeah?

b. That's right. But in that case (*lit.*
   with it coming to that), you'll have
   to ask Ms. Tanaka again, won't you!

c. Yes. Could (*lit.* can't) I have you,
   Ms. Sakamoto, or the division
   chief make the request?

c. No, this—you, Ms. Miller (who are)
   the person in charge, ought to
   request, all things considered.

d. Oh . . . As long as you say so, Ms.
   Sakamoto, there's nothing more to
   be said about it.

d. Well, provided you explain the

circumstances carefully—and, while doing that, have tea or something—s/he'll be persuaded.

BREAKDOWNS
(AND SUPPLEMENTARY VOCABULARY)

1. **medétài /-katta/**   is auspicious
   omédetoo gozaimàsu +   congratulations /neutral-polite/
   + **sotuğyoo-suru**   graduate
   omóinàğara (SP1)   while thinking
   tûi   unintentionally; carelessly; by accident;
                                            involuntarily

   sinâkereba *or*
   sinâkerya(a) *or*
   sinâkya(a) (SP2)   unless [someone] does
   sinâkereba narânai (SP3)   must do
   oári desyòo↑   probably have /honorific-polite/

2. **sodátèru/-ru; sodâteta/**   bring up, raise
   + **sodâtu/-u; sodâtta/**   grow up, be raised
   sodátenàğara . . . tuzukeru (SP1)   continue . . and, while doing that, bring up
   + **kyooiku**   education
   + **ukêru/-ru; ûketa/**   undergo; take (of courses, exams, etc.)
   + **kyoóiku o ukèru**   receive an education, be(come) educated
   sekiniñ   responsibility
   oyâ to site no 'sekiniñ   responsibility as a parent
   môsi   supposing
   katee   household, the home
   siğoto ka 'katee (SP4)   work or home
   siğoto ka ' katee no dôtira ka   either one—i.e., work or home
   erâbu/-u; erâñda/   choose, select; elect
   erábànakereba *or*
   erábànakerya(a) *or*
   erábànakya(a)   unless [someone] chooses
   erábànakereba narânai   must choose
   erábànakereba narânaku naru   become necessary to choose
   erábànakereba narânaku nâttara   if/when it has become necessary to choose
   mînakereba *or*
   mînakerya(a) *or*
   mînakya(a)   unless [someone] looks at [it]
   sonó tokì ni nâtte mînakereba   unless [someone] looks at [it] when that
                                           time has come

3. **ñ?**   yeah?

   yotee   plan, program, schedule

   yoteehyoo   (written) schedule

   yarínaòsite morau 'hituyoo   necessity for having [it] redone

   soó nàru to   (*lit.* with its becoming that)

   tanómànakereba *or*

   tanómànakerya(a) *or*

   tanómànakya(a)   unless [someone] asks for

   tanómànakya ikenai   must ask for

   Sakamoto   (family name)

   Sakamoto-sañ ka 'butyoo   Mr/s. Sakamoto or the division chief

   tañtòosya   person in charge

   tañtòosya no Mîraa-sañ   Mr/s. Miller who is the person in charge

   ośsyàru ↑ no nara   as long as [someone] says /honorific-polite/

   nomínàgara 'setumee-suru   explain and, while doing that, drink

   zizyoo   circumstances, conditions; the situation

   setúmee-surèba *or*

   setúmee-suryà(a)   provided [someone] explains

   nattoku-suru   become persuaded or convinced; consent to

   nattoku-site kureru   become persuaded (for the benefit of the in-group)

MISCELLANEOUS NOTES

1. In CC1, Smith, who has just found employment after finishing his graduate studies, is congratulated by his sponsor, Mr. Suzuki. As Smith apologizes for his failure to inform Mr. Suzuki about this himself, Mr. Suzuki politely reassures him by supplying a reasonable explanation for the lapse. Note that Mr. Suzuki undoubtedly *is* annoyed by Smith's failure to inform him, since he is Smith's sponsor in Japan.

The style of this conversation is careful, as is usual between these two men. Mr. Suzuki uses polite, distal-style forms as he offers congratulations and the likely explanation for Smith's not getting in touch with him, but notice that he can use **anâta** in reference to Smith, given the age difference between them and the fact that he is Smith's sponsor. Smith's polite apology progresses to the point of **sitûree-site simatte** (not contracted in this setting), is interrupted by Mr. Suzuki's ritualistic dismissal of the need for it, and concludes with a ritualistic **sumímaseñ**.

(J)a. **Sotugyoo-suru**: Note **daigaku o sotugyoo-suru** 'graduate from college'; **sotúgyòosee** 'a graduate.' The polite equivalent of **sotugyoo** is **gosotugyoo**.

The use of the intransitive **kimaru**, indicating that a job 'gets to be decided,' contrasts with the usual active pattern used in English, 'decide on a job,' the literal translation of which would include **kimeru** 'decide.'

Omédetoo gozaimàsu, the polite, distal-style equivalent of the adjectival **medétài** 'is auspicious,' is a ritualistic expression of congratulation, used for births, marriages, graduations, employment, promotions, and so on—in other words, for auspicious occasions. The patterning is identical with that of **oháyoo gozaimàsu**, from **hayâi** and, except for the absence of the polite prefix **o-** and the shift in accent, with that of **arîgatoo gozaimasu** from **arígatài** 'is obliged,' 'is grateful.' All three may occur without **gozáimàsu** as direct-style—but still polite—utterances.

(N)a. **Tûi** is a nominal that links up directly with a predicate and refers to actions performed (or not performed) 'carelessly,' 'unintentionally,' 'thoughtlessly.' **Tûi** also frequently ends a minor sentence when the context makes clear what happened 'unintentionally.'

(J)b. **Anâta mo** refers to 'you, too,' that is, like so many other people, suggesting that Mr. Suzuki is perfectly justified in making this assumption.

Compare **oári dèsu**↑ '[you] have,' the honorific-polite equivalent of **arímàsu**, and **gozáimàsu**＋ 'there exists,' 'there is,' 'have,' its neutral-polite equivalent. Either can be used in this context, but **oári dèsu** is personalized, emphasizing the connection with **anâta**.
Iroiro connects directly with the final predicate as a pattern of manner: 'variously,' i.e, 'of various kinds.'

2. In CC2, Sue Brown discusses with her Japanese colleague the problems encountered by women who are working and raising a family at the same time. We learn one way of avoiding a direct answer to a hypothetical question: one can say that there's no telling unless the situation described is actually experienced.

As usual, these two women use generally careful-style, with distal-style final predicates. However, the use of direct-style before particle **si**, and **simâsu?** (without question-particle **ka**), indicates an intermediate point on the casual-careful continuum.
Kyooiku: Note also **kyoóikùgaku** '(study of) education'; **kyoóiku no àru/nài hito** 'an educated/uneducated person'; **kyoóiku-màma** 'an "education mother,"' one who is aggressively—even excessively—involved in the education of her children.
Ukêru, a transitive, operational vowel verbal, implies undergoing or being given from the recipient's point of view. This is the verbal used for everything from *taking* tests, *undergoing* medical exams and surgery, and *suffering* losses to *receiving* a phone call, *having* an impression, and *earning* esteem.

(J)a. The **no** following **oyâ to site** is the special pre-nominal form of **dà**: 'it-is-as-a-parent responsibility,' i.e., 'responsibility (which is) as a parent.'
Sekinin is an extremely important concept for the Japanese. The identification and acknowledgment of responsibility by a party in all activities and events in which humans engage have enormous significance. In many situations, only when responsibility has been openly acknowledged can a matter be considered closed. What often surprises the Westerner is the fact that that "responsible party" may in fact not have been directly involved (as, for example, when the president of a major airline publicly assumes responsibility for the crash of one of the airline's planes and resigns his position). Note: **sekínin ga àru** 'have responsibility'; **sekínin o tòru** (*or* **mòtu**) 'take or assume responsibility'; **sekínìnsya** 'responsible person.'

(N)b. Note the use of particle **o** following **dôtira ka**, emphasizing the operand relationship with the following predicate.

3. In CC3, Deborah Miller is discussing with her supervisor, Ms. Sakamoto, an unsatisfactory schedule that was drawn up for her by Ms. Tanaka, the consultant. Ms. Miller hopes that either Ms. Sakamoto or the division chief can be persuaded to ask Ms. Tanaka to redo it, but Ms. Sakamoto points out the accepted Japanese procedure, which assumes that the person in charge, who is the **sekínìnsya**, will fulfill his/her responsibility on a continuing

basis and deal with difficulties until the project is completed. Ms. Miller, the foreigner, is clearly unhappy about what her role requires, but recognizing her position and what is expected of her, she complies.

In speaking to her supervisor, Deborah Miller uses careful-style, with distal-style final predicates. Her request for assistance is polite (gerund + **itádakemasèñ ka**), as is her use of **ośsyàru** in reference to Ms. Sakamoto. In contrast, Ms. Sakamoto uses feminine, gentle casual-style in talking to her employee, with direct-style final predicates (including gentle-style /**bèki + yo**/), contracted forms, and feminine sentence-particle combinations /**wa nêe**/ and /**wa yo**/. This is an indication of Ms. Sakamoto's solicitude and empathy in a situation that is clearly troublesome for Ms. Miller. Ms. Sakamoto is demonstrating closeness, concern, and feminine bonding.

(N)b. **Yotee**: Note also **yotée o tatèru** 'set up a plan'; **yotée-dòori** 'according to plan'; **yotée yòri hâyâku/osoku** 'ahead of/behind schedule.' **Yoteehyoo** is a chart of a plan, i.e., a written schedule.

(N)c. Note the polite use of **Sakamoto-sañ** in a situation in which she is actually being addressed. **Anâta** would be inappropriate, given the relationship between these two people.

Particle **kara** occurs here in a context in which its alternative **ni** would be ambiguous: **X ni tanôñde mîte itadaku** can mean either 'have X try asking [someone]' or 'have [someone] try asking X.' When **ni** is replaced by **kara**, only the former meaning is possible.

(J)c. **Tañtòosya no Mîraa-sañ**: **no** is again the special pre-nominal form of **dà**: 'Ms. Miller, (who is) the person in charge' (cf. CC2-[J]3, above). Note: **X o tañtoo-suru** 'take charge of X.'

(N)d. The reflective use of **nêe** following **sôo desu ka** shows that Ms. Miller is thinking over the new information she has received.

(J)d. Ms. Sakamoto suggests that the awkwardness of the upcoming situation can be reduced by making the atmosphere more relaxed, with a cup of tea, for example (perhaps at a **kissateñ**). Much Japanese business is conducted in this fashion.

Zizyoo: Note **zizyoo ga tiḡau** 'circumstances are different'; **zizyóo ni yòtte** 'depending on circumstances'; **katee no zizyoo** 'household situation.'

Nattoku-suru: **X o nattoku-suru** 'become convinced or persuaded of X.' In such cases, X is frequently /modifier + **kotô**/. Compare: **yotéehyoo o tukau kotò o nattoku-suru** 'be persuaded to use a schedule'; **kono yoteehyoo ni nattoku-suru** 'consent to this schedule'; **konó yoteehyoo o tukattà to wa nattoku-dekìnai** '[I] can't be persuaded that [s/he] used this schedule.' (In this last example, the claim—in contrast with fact [= **kotô**]—is followed by quotative **to**).

Note the use of **kureru**, which bonds Ms. Miller to Ms. Sakamoto as the in-group and places Ms. Tanaka in the out-group: 'she (out-group) will do that for you (in my in-group).'

Structural Patterns

1. -nàḡara

-Nàḡara occurs in patterns having to do with several activities or states that take place at the same time. We can divide its uses into two types

a. Compounded with a preceding stem of an operational verbal, it indicates that the action of the verbal occurs at the same time as that of the following verbal. *Both activities are performed by the same person(s).* The **X-nàḡara** compound is preceded by whatever can regularly precede verbal X, and it links up directly with a predicate, without any particle. For some speakers of Japanese, all **-nàgara** compounds are accented on /**na**/; for others, only those that include the stem of an accented verbal are accented—again, on /**na**/. Examples:

> **Râzio o kikínàgara, teḡámi o yomimàsita.** 'I read letters and, while doing that, listened to the radio.'

> **Otyá o nominàgara, sikêñ ni tuite soódañ-simasyòo.** 'Let's talk over the exam and, while doing that, have some tea.'

These examples immediately suggest the use of English 'while.' However, English 'do Y while X-ing' usually implies that X is the primary activity. In Japanese, the **X-nàgara** activity is the subordinate one.

> **Ano gaiziñ wa, koko de arúbàito o sinàgara, eéḡo no señsèe to site tutômete (i)masu.** 'That foreigner is doing part-time work here while being employed as an English teacher.'

The principal activity is employment as an English teacher; part-time employment here is a secondary activity.

If the principal activity has previously been mentioned or made clear by the context, a **-nàgara** sequence, indicating something that went on at the same time, may be followed by a form of the copula **dà**: **X-nàgara datta** 'X occurred at the same time' (as the other activity we already know about).

b. Compounded with a verbal stem, or as an adjunct to an imperfective adjectival or a nominal, **-nàgara** links the first activity or condition with a second one occurring at the same time, but in this case, the two contrast, and the **-nàgara** sequence and the following predicate need not have the same referent (although they often do). Again, English 'while' comes to mind:

> **Wakâru to iínàgara, hoñtoo wa wakárànai.** 'While saying s/he understands, actually s/he doesn't (understand).'

Here, the 'while' sequence in English and the **-nàgara** sequence in Japanese are parallel, both subordinate to the predicate they are linked to. In this type of contrastive use, **-nàgara** is often followed by particle **mo**, emphasizing the contrast. Accentuation is like that described above. Examples:

> **Otáku no kaisya no tokorò made ikínàgara, oyóri-dekìnakute sumímaseñ de-sita.** 'While I went all the way to (the place where) your company (is), I couldn't stop in; I'm sorry.'

> **Tyuúḡokuḡo o beñkyoo-site inàgara, hotôñdo dekínai-rasìi desu nêe.** 'While s/he is studying Chinese, s/he apparently is almost incapable of handling it.'

> **Okáne ḡa arinàgara, atárasìi koñpyùutaa wa kaʼte kuremaseñ.** 'While there is money, they're not going to buy new computers for us.'

> **Anó màñsyoñ wa, hirói-nàgara hûbeñ desu yo.** 'While that apartment is big, it's inconvenient.'

> **Zañnen-nàgara, asitâ wa oái-dekimasèñ.** 'While it's unfortunate, I can't meet you tomorrow.'

2. THE PROVISIONAL

In 26A-SP2, we were introduced to the conditional: **X-tara** 'if or when X has been realized,' 'assuming X has been realized,' 'supposing X has been realized.' The following predicate was called *the outcome,* and it expressed an event or situation that would occur or occurred, assuming the realization of X *by that time.* Thus: **Tomódati ğa yametàra, watási mo yameru tumori dèsu.** 'If or when my friend quits, I plan to quit, too.'

We noted that a **-tara** form was by no means always the equivalent of 'if' in English, and it should not have been surprising to learn that the reverse was also not true, given the fact that English and Japanese so rarely coincide: an 'if' sequence in English is not always equivalent to a **-tara** form in Japanese. For example, we have already learned that 'if ——' in English may also correspond to /imperfective + **to**/ in Japanese. We now introduce another possibility, the PROVISIONAL.

Like the conditional, the provisional is a specially inflected form of verbals, adjectivals, and the copula. First, we will examine how it is formed. For verbals, we add **-reba** to the root of vowel verbals (= imperfective minus **-ru**) and **-eba** to the root of consonant verbals (= imperfective minus **-u**).[1] All provisional forms are accented: for accented verbals, the accent is on the same mora as in the imperfective; for unaccented verbals, it is on the first mora of the ending. Examples:

	Imperfective	Provisional	English Equivalent
Vowel verbals	**tabê-ru**	**tabê-reba**	'eat'
	ake-ru	**aké-rèba**	'open [it]'
	i-ru	**i-rêba**	'be located (animate)'
	kari-ru	**karí-rèba**	'borrow'
	kae-ru	**kaé-rèba**	'can buy'
Consonant verbals	**ik-u**	**ik-êba**	'go'
	isôğ-u	**isôğ-eba**	'hurry'
	hanâs-u	**hanâs-eba**	'talk'
	mât-u	**mât-eba**	'wait'
	yob-u	**yob-êba**	'call'
	yôm-u	**yôm-eba**	'read'
	kâer-u	**kâer-eba**	'return'
	ir-u	**ir-êba**	'need'
	ka-u (< *kaw-u)	**ka-êba** (< *kaw-eba)[a]	'buy'
Special polite verbals	**irássyàr-u**	**irássyàr-eba**	'go'; 'come'; 'be located' (animate)
	nasâr-u	**nasâr-eba**	'do'

1. We could describe the provisional of *all* verbals as /imperfective minus final **-u** + **-eba**/, but /imperfective of vowel verbals minus final **-u**/ yields a form (e.g., *taber for **tabêru**) that is nowhere else in the language the basis for other forms.

	Imperfective	Provisional	English Equivalent
Irregular verbals	**kûr-u**	**kûr-eba**	'come'
	sur-u	**sur-êba**	'do'

*The /**w**/ of **w**-consonant verbals is lost before the **-eba** ending. Remember that /**w**/ occurs only before /**a**/ in modern Japanese.

In rapid, contracted speech, the **-(r)eba** ending may be contracted to **-(r)ya(a)**.

For adjectivals, **-kereba** is added to the root (= imperfective minus final **-i**). All provisional forms are accented: for accented adjectivals, the accent is on the same mora as for the **-ku** form;[2] for unaccented adjectivals, it is on the mora immediately preceding the ending. Examples:

takâ-i > **tâkâ-kereba**	'is expensive'; 'is high'
aka-i > **akâ-kereba**	'is red'
oókì-i > **ôókì-kereba**	'is big'
tabétà-i > **tabétà-kereba**	'wants to eat'
tabêna-i > **tabênakereba**	'doesn't eat'
nâ-i > **nâ-kereba**	'isn't located' (inanimate)
sâmûku nâ-i > **sâmûku nâ-kereba**	'isn't cold'
sôo zya nâ-i > **sôo zya** (or **de**)[3] **nâ-kereba**	'isn't like that'

In rapid, contracted speech, the **-kereba** ending frequently reduces to **-kerya(a)** or (**kya(a)**.

The provisional of the copula **dà** is **nàra** (*or* **nàraba**), reminding us of the **na** form of **dà** (**kìree na syasiñ, kîree na ñ desu**, etc.). Thus: **soré dà** > **soré nàra** 'is that.' But what do provisional forms mean, and how are they used???

In utterances like **Tomódati ḡa yametàra, watási mo yameru tumori dèsu**, I am stating that, assuming a situation in which my friend has quit, then my plan is to quit, too. The important point to note is that I am *not* posing a requirement for my quitting, nor am I stating the only thing that will necessarily follow my friend's quitting. I am simply stating that if or when my friend quits, I, too, intend to quit.

Now consider a different kind of situation: Suppose that I wish to state what, of a number of possibilities, will definitely bring about my quitting. Provided *what*, will I quit? This, in Japanese, is expressed as: **Tomódati ḡa yamerèba, watási mo yameru tumori dèsu**. 'Provided my friend quits, I plan to quit, too.'

The sequence /provisional X, Y/ emphasizes a close relationship between X and Y: X is the event or situation that will surely lead to Y. The provisional lacks the perfective notion incorporated in **-tara** forms, which says 'supposing X has (or will have) been realized, then what? Instead, it focuses on how one will get to the outcome.

Negative provisionals are often closely equivalent to 'unless' in English. Compare:

Ano gakusee, konó hòñ o yôñde (i)nâkattara, kyôo no kooeñ wa, wakárànai to omoimasu. 'If (we assume that) that student hasn't read this book, (then) I don't think he'll understand today's lecture.' *and*

Ano gakusee, konó hòñ o yôñde (i)nâkereba, kyôo no kooeñ wa, wakárànai to

2. Those adjectivals which presently have alternate accentuation for the **-ku** form have similar alternation for the provisional.
3. Cf. 22B-SP1.

omoimasu. 'I don't think that student will understand today's lecture unless s/he has read this book.'

In the first example, the implication is that if I assume that that student hasn't read this book, then I believe s/he will not understand today's lecture. There may be other reasons for not understanding it, and I might even mention other results of not having read the book. But in the second example, I am stating that I believe that student will not understand today's lecture *unless* s/he has read this book. I select, from a number of possibilities, one that will definitely lead to non-understanding.

If we return to the numerous patterns in which **-tara** forms occur, we find that in many cases there are corresponding sequences that use **-(r)eba** forms:

(a) **Dôo surêba îi desyoo ka.** 'What should I do?'

(b) **Konó miti o ikèba îi desyoo?** 'I should go along this street—right?'

(c) **Asita âme ğa hurânakereba îi desu ğa nêe.** 'I hope it doesn't rain tomorrow.'

In (a), the question asks for advice in more specific terms than the corresponding **-tara** question. The speaker is asking: '*provided* I choose to do what will it be all right?' Similarly, in (b), the suggestion is that all will be well *provided* the speaker takes this street.

Again in (c), the speaker is selecting the kind of situation that will definitely lead to all being well, not the result of its not happening to rain tomorrow. It is impossible to replace final **ğa** with **no ni** here, since a future, uncertain event is involved; the occurrence of /—— **no ni**/ 'in spite of ——' expresses contrast with a known situation.

Note the difference that results when a sentence-final conditional of suggestion is replaced by the corresponding provisional form: **Koré o kaèba?** In place of a rather gentle suggestion to buy this one, we now have a proposal that chooses the particular activity assumed to bring about the desired result. This alternative would rarely, if ever, be used in talking to a superior.

Just as there is a conditional of the extended predicate, there is also a corresponding provisional, combining the meanings of the component parts: /predicate X + **ñ** ~ **no** + **nàra**/ 'provided it's a situation described as X'; 'as long as X is the case.' Compare:

Kurúma de ikù ñ nara, watasi mo iku. 'As long as it's a matter of going by car, I'll go, too.' *and*

Anâta ğa kurúma de ikèba, watasi mo kuruma de iku. 'If (= provided) you go by car, I will, too.'

The first example implies that there is shared information to the effect that in fact transportation by car for those involved in the present situation has already been decided on or at least suggested.

Notice how /nominal X + **nàra**/ resembles—but contrasts with— /nominal X + **wa**/. The phrase-particle **wa** indicates that the item preceding it *at least* is a member of a set that applies to the following predicate; other members may or may not apply, but what is mentioned in the **wa**-phrase does apply (cf. 4A-SP2). When **nàra** follows a nominal X, the specification of X is absolute: there is no suggestion that X is the member of a set. The outcome is guaranteed, provided X has been selected as the item under consideration. Compare these pairs:

Tañtòosya wa, Tanáka-kuñ dèsu. '(Of the positions involved in the project) the person in charge (at least) is Tanaka.' (Tanaka may fill other roles as well, but they are unspecified.)

Taṅtòosya nara, Tanáka-kuñ dèsu. 'Provided it's the person in charge (that we're talking about), it's Tanaka.'

Watási wa simasèñ. '(Of the people involved) I (at least) am not going to do it.' (Others may not do it either, but this is not specified.)

Watási nàra simásèñ. 'Provided we're talking about *me*, there will be no doing it.'

In each case the alternative with **nàra** is a much stronger utterance, implying the selection of X as something that will definitely lead to the stated outcome. In some contexts, **watási nàra** closely resembles English 'if I were you.'

Provisional forms also occur frequently in contrary-to-fact statements. In those that end in /—— **no ni**/, the occurrence of **no ni** makes it absolutely clear that there is some kind of contrast with the actual situation. Examples:

Âme ğa hâyâku yamêba yôkatta no ni . . 'I wish the rain had ended early' (*lit.* 'in spite of the fact that it was fine provided the rain ended early, [it didn't]').

Utí ni irèba îi no ni . . 'It would be great provided s/he were home, but . . .' [s/he isn't].

Hâyâku kurêba îi no ni . . 'I wish s/he would come early, but . . .' [s/he doesn't].

Isôide kurêba ma ní àtta no ni . . 'Provided I had come in a hurry, I would have been on time, but . . .' [I didn't].

It is possible to create countless pairs of utterances differing only in including a provisional instead of the corresponding conditional form. Both may be standard, commonly occurring Japanese utterances, but the difference in focus is always present, and in many contexts, only one of the pair may be appropriate.

Consider now the uses of the conditional that do *not* have parallel uses in the provisional. The conditional, with its **-ta-** (in **-tara**), always introduces the perfective (= already realized) aspect, which does not mean realized *now*, but realized by the time of the outcome. This notion of sequence is crucial in Japanese. What is important is not absolute past, present, and future time, but which of two things is realized first (and both may be future events). Compare English 'I'll call you when I arrive' and Japanese **Tûita toki ni deñwa-simàsu** (the perfective **tûita**, since the arriving will precede the calling). The provisional, on the other hand, which selects a provision that will bring about the outcome, occurs without the notion of sequencing that the conditional stresses. Thus the provisional does *not* occur in utterances like **Heyâ ni hâittara, dêñki ğa kiémàsita.** 'When I entered the room, the lights went out,' which describes something known to have occurred. Except in **no ni** patterns and in the cases described in SP3 following, a /**-(r)eba** + perfective/ sequence can only be contrary-to-fact or (depending on context) express something that did happen provided something else occurred—but the speaker does not know. Example: **Anó hòñ o yôñde (i)rêba, koóeñ ğa wakàtta to omoimasu.** 'Provided s/he had read that book, I think s/he understood (*or* would have understood) the lecture.'

3. -(a)nakereba naránai ~ ikenai

In 22B-SP2, we introduced sequences like **ikánàkute wa ikémasèñ** 'you must go,' **kikánàkutya(a) 'ikenai** 'you must ask,' **tabênakute wa naránai** 'you must eat it,' etc. These expressions of necessity are double negatives: they express the fact that *not* doing something will *not* do, i.e., 'must do it.'

We now introduce a second pattern for expressing necessity, one that includes the negative of the provisional: /X-(a)nakereba + **narânai** ~ **ikenai**/ 'X must occur' (*lit.* 'unless X occurs, it won't do'). **Ikenai** is slightly more forceful and direct than **narânai**. The contracted forms of the negative provisional, **-(a)nakerya(a)** and **-(a)nakya(a)**, also occur in this pattern, particularly in direct-style.

Like the pattern that includes **-(a)nakute wa**, this pattern represents true necessity ('it *must be*—it *has to be*—X') and should not be used as an equivalent of the casual 'must' that occurs so commonly in English in sentences like: 'That must be Mr. Jones'; 'We must get together sometime soon'; 'You must come for dinner'; 'I must be out of my mind.' Not one of these examples has anything to do with necessity. It is important for native speakers of English not to fall into the trap of overusing this pattern when speaking Japanese. It should be identified as an exact opposite of the **X-(a)nakute (mo) îi/** pattern, which expresses acceptance of *not* doing or being X: **ikânakute (mo) îi** 'you don't have to go'; **âtûku nâkute (mo) îi** 'it doesn't have to be hot'; **îma zya nâkute (mo) îi** 'it doesn't have to be now' (cf. drill I, below). Examples:

Doó sitè mo konó siĝoto o sinàkereba narímasèñ. 'No matter what, I have to do this work.'

Kono kusuri, tumétaku nàkerya(a) 'ikenai. 'This medicine has to be cold.'

Nihóñzìñ de (*or* **zya**) **nâkereba narânai.** 'It has to be a Japanese.'

Kyoó-zyuu ni sinàkereba narânai koto wa, nâñ desyoo. 'What are the things I must do (within) today?'

Kêsa made ni 'kore o owári màde yomânakereba narímasèñ desita. 'I had to read this all (*lit.* as far as the end) by this morning.'

Yaménàkereba narânaku nattara, sûĝu soó itte kudasài. 'If it becomes necessary to quit, please say so right away.'

Kono kusuri, zut́to nomànakya ikénài no? . . . Iya, asítà kara môo nomânakute mo îi tte. 'Is it that you have to take this medicine indefinitely?' . . . 'No, they say I don't have to take it anymore, from tomorrow on.'

The occurrence of a negative provisional at the end of a minor sentence may imply necessity even though a following **narânai** or **ikenai** is unexpressed. Thus:

Kôñbañ kônakyaa . . 'Unless you come tonight . . .' (you're in trouble!) = 'You must come tonight.'

Tyañ́to sinàkereba . . 'Unless you do it properly . . .' (it won't do!) = 'You must do it properly.'

This pattern of necessity formed with the provisional has no parallel in the conditional. Given the difference in focus of these two forms, this should not be surprising. In the necessity pattern, we are stating that 'it won't do *unless* a particular action or state occurs.' **-Tara** forms, which deal with suppositions, are inappropriate here.

4. siĝoto ka 'katee 'WORK OR HOME'

In combinations like **mîruku to satôo**, **kore to 'sore**, and **titî to hâha**, nominals are joined as coordinates; both are to be included in the given context. We now add a new **ka**-particle (obviously related at a deep level to all the other **ka** we have learned, but differing from them in specific usage), which connects a pair of nominals when *either* one *or* the other of the nominals applies: **mîruku ka satôo** 'milk or sugar,' **kore ka 'sore** 'this or that,' **titî ka hâha** 'my father or my mother.' Like /**X to Y**/, the combination occurs in the same kinds of patterns as a single nominal:

> **Kore ka soré dèsu.**
>
> **Pâi ka kêeki o onéǧai-simàsu.**
>
> **Titî ka hâha ǧa kûru to omoimasu.**
>
> **Kôobe ka Oósaka ni ikimasyòo.**

☠●WARNING: Be sure to distinguish this pattern, which may occur within a question, from the alternate question pattern introduced in 12A-SP4. Compare:

> **Bâsu ka dêñsya de ikímasyòo ka.** . . . **Êe, soó simasyòo. Bâsu de ikímasyòo.** *or* **Iie, tâkusii de ikímasyòo.** 'Shall we go by bus or train?' . . . 'Yes, let's do that. Let's go by bus.' *or* 'No, let's go by taxi.' *and*
>
> **Bâsu de ikímasyòo ka, dêñsya de ikímasyòo ka.** . . . **Bâsu de ikímasyòo.** 'Shall we go by bus, or (shall we go by) train?' . . . 'Let's go by bus.'

The first example includes a choice *within a yes-no question*. In the second pattern, the person addressed is asked to *choose one of two alternatives*. Note the very different intonations of the English equivalents of these two patterns.

Drills

A 1. **Señsèe to reñraku-simàsita?**
'Did you get in touch with the professor?'

Iya, zitû wa, sûǧu reñraku-siyoo to omoinàǧara, tûi 'wasuretyatte . .
'No, as a matter of fact, while thinking I'd get in touch [with her/him] right away, unintentionally forgetting all about it . . .' (I didn't).

2. **Iránai monò sutémàsita?**
'Did you throw out the things that aren't needed?'

Iya, zitû wa, sûǧu sutéyoo to omoinàǧara, tûi 'wasuretyatte . .
'No, as a matter of fact, while thinking I'd throw them out right away, unintentionally forgetting all about it . . .' (I didn't).

3. **niwá no hanà taórènai yoo ni sibárimàsita**; 4. **koñǧetu no yàtiñ haráimàsita**; 5. **waapuro no tukaikata osíete aǧemàsita**; 6. **ryuúǧakusee no tame no apâato saǧásimàsita**; 7. **sibai no kippu tôri ni ikímàsita**

B 1. **Îtu ka konó kotò ni tuite Nakámura-señsèe ni gosóodañ-sitài ñ desu ǧa . .**

Sôo desu nêe. Zyâa, îtu ka otyá dè mo nomínàǧara gosóodañ-simasyòo.
'Fine! Then let's consult [with her/him]

'(It's that) I would like to consult with Professor Nakamura some time concerning this matter, but . . .' (do you think it's possible?)

sometime and, while doing that, have tea or something.'

2. **Râiḡetu no tûaa no kotô o 'butyoo ni gosétumee-sitài ñ desu ḡa . .**
'(It's that) I would like to explain to the division chief about the tour next month, but . . .' (do you think it's possible?)

Sôo desu nêe. Zyâa, îtu ka otyá dè mo nomínàḡara gosétumee-simasyòo.
'Fine! Then let's explain [to him/her] sometime and, while doing that, have tea or something.'

3. **anó utì made no tîzu o Suḡîura-sañ ni misétài**; 4. **raíneñ no sikèñ ni tuite señsèe to 'ohanasi-sitai**; 5. **hôteru no hirôoeñ no kotô o kañḡaetài**; 6. **raísyuu no zadàñkai ni dête morau hito o 'kimetai**; 7. **ryokoo no omiyaḡe o 'Oota-sañ ni 'owatasi-sitai**

C 1. **Syatyóo ni setumee-surù desyoo?**
'You're going to explain to the company president, aren't you?'

Êe, mâa, syatyoo ka Ôono-sañ ni 'setumee-siyoo to omôtte (i)ru ñ desu kedo nêe.
'Yes, well, I've been thinking of explaining to the president or Mr/s. Ono, but, you know . . .' (I can't decide).

2. **Butyóo kara hanàsite morau desyoo?**
'You're going to have the division chief talk, aren't you?'

Êe, mâa, butyoo ka Ôono-sañ kara hanâsite moraoo to omôtte (i)ru ñ desu kedo nêe.
'Yes, well, I've been thinking of having the division chief or Mr/s. Ono talk, but, you know . . .' (I can't decide).

3. **kâre o turete iku**; 4. **Hayasi-sañ ni kimeru**; 5. **doóryoo ni tanòmu**; 6. **katyoo ni syookai-suru**; 7. **Kodáma-sañ dakè ni wa hanâsu**

D 1. **Dâre ḡa tuzúkerù no?—kono siḡoto.**
'Who is it that's going to continue it—this work?'

Sâtoo-sañ ka Kimúra-sañ ḡa tuzukeru to omoimàsu kedo . .
'I think Mr/s. Sato or Mr/s. Kimura will continue it, but . . .' (I'm not sure).

2. **Dâre ḡa nokôtta no?—zimûsyo ni.**
'Who is it that stayed behind—in the office?'

Sâtoo-sañ ka Kimúra-sañ ḡa nokòtta to omóimàsu kedo . .
'I think Mr/s. Sato or Mr/s. Kimura stayed behind, but . . .' (I'm not sure).

3. **dâre to asobi ni iku/Kêe-tyañ**; 4. **dâre ḡa ôtita/señ̄getu no sikèñ**; 5. **dâre ḡa tukíàtte kureru/kaimono**; 6. **dâre kara naràtta/yarikata**; 7. **dâre ni soodañ-suru/syuúsyoku no kotò**

E 1. **Bûñḡaku mo geñ̄gòḡaku mo osíerù ñ desu ka**

Toñde mo nài. Bûñḡaku ka geñ̄gòḡaku, dôtira ka hitô-tu desu yo.

'(Is it that) one teaches both literature and linguistics?'

    'Heavens no! It's literature or linguistics, one of the two.'

2. **Nakamura-sañ mo 'Yosida-sañ mo sikêñ ukêru ñ desu ka**

    Toñde mo nài. Nakamura-sañ ka Yosida-sañ, dôtira ka hitô-ri desu yo.

'(Is it that) both Mr/s. Nakamùra and Mr/s. Yoshida are to take the examination?'

    'Heavens no! It's Mr/s. Nakamura or Mr/s. Yoshida, one of the two.'

3. **sebiro wa aôi no mo kurôi no mo 'motte iku;** 4. **zyûḡyoo wa siñrìḡaku mo tetûḡaku mo ukêru;** 5. **susîya ni mo teñpuraya nì mo 'yoru;** 6. **doyôo mo nitíyòo mo yasûmu;** 7. **kêeki mo pâi mo tâbete ii**

F 1. **Kore, sibâru ñ desu neʕ**

    Êe, sôo na ñ desu kedo, dôo yatte sibâreba ii desyoo nêe.

'This—we're to tie up, right?'

    'Yes, that's what's to be done, but (doing) how do you suppose we should tie it up?'

2. **Kore, yarínaòsu ñ desu neʕ**

    Êe, sôo na ñ desu kedo, dôo yatte yarínaòseba ii desyoo nêe.

'This—we're to do over, right?'

    'Yes, that's what's to be done, but (doing) how do you suppose we should do it over?'

3. **erâbu;** 4. **hakobu;** 5. **maḡeru;** 6. **nattoku-site morau;** 7. **todókèru;** 8. **tabêru**

G 1. **Môñku ittè mo naôsite kurénài ka sira.**

    Iya, môñku iêba kitto naôsite kurémàsu yo.

'Won't they fix [it] for me even if I complain, I wonder.'

    'No, I'm sure they'll fix [it] for you, provided you complain.'

2. **Mûri de mo yaménài ka sira.**

    Iya, mûri nara kitto yamemàsu yo.

'Won't they quit even if it's a strain, I wonder.'

    'No, I'm sure they'll quit, provided it's a strain.'

3. **harâ ḡa tâtte mo môñku 'iwanai;** 4. **urêsìkute mo 'soo itte kurenai;** 5. **sabîsìkute mo 'teḡami kakânai;** 6. **asóñdè (i)te mo tanôsiku nâi;** 7. **kañḡaete mo ii âidea wa dête kônai;** 8. **sûḡôku sêmâkute mo iyâ da tte 'iwanai**

H 1. **Tyañto sotuḡyoo-sitài ñ dattara, anó sikêñ o ûketa hoo ḡa îi desu yo**

    Zyâa, yáppàri anó sikêñ o ûkete okánàkereba, tyañto sotúḡyoo-dekìnai desyoo ka.

'If it's the case that you want to graduate (properly), you'd better take that exam!'

    'Then do you suppose that, in the end, I won't be able to graduate (properly) unless I take that exam (in advance)?'

2. **Yotéehyoo o tukuritài ñ dattara, señpai ni soodañ-sita hòo ḡa îi desu yo**

    Zyâa, yáppàri señpai ni soodañ-site okánàkereba, yoteehyoo o tukúrènai desyoo ka.

'If it's the case that you want to draw up the schedule, you'd better consult your seniors!'

    'Then, do you suppose that, in the end, I won't be able to make the schedule unless I consult my seniors (in advance)?'

3. îi iê o erábitài/iti-do mî ni itta; 4. ûmi de oyóḡitài/natú no iè o 'karita; 5. tônai kara 'hakobitai/karûi

I 1. **Asítà wa határakanàkute mo îi ñ desyoo?**
'(It's that) you don't have to work tomorrow (at least)—right?'

Ie, határakanàkereba narânai-mitai desu.
'No, it looks as if I do have to work.'

2. **Sikêñ wa tukúrinaosànakute mo îi ñ desyoo?**
'(It's that) you don't have to remake the examination (at least)—right?'

Ie, tukúrinaosànakereba narânai-mitai desu.
'No, it looks as if I do have to make it over again.'

3. tañtòosya o kiménàkute; 4. zyûusyo o kiíte okanàkute; 5. zuʹto onazi siḡoto o tuzukenàkute; 6. kañriniñ ni reñraku-sinàkute; 7. h(u)ôomaru na monô o kité ikanàkute

J 1. **Señsèe ni omíse-sinàkerya ne!**
'We have to show it to the professor, don't we.' (*lit.* 'Unless we show to the professor . . .')

Dê mo, îma omíse-sinàkute mo îi yo.
'But we don't have to show it now.'

2. **Katyoo ni gosétumee-sinàkerya ne!**
'We have to explain to the section chief, don't we.'

Dê mo, îma gosétumee-sinàkute mo îi yo.
'But we don't have to explain now.'

3. oyaḡosañ ni otódoke-sinàkerya; 4. waapuro no tukaikata o oósie-sinàkerya; 5. Watánabe-syòtyoo ni omé ni kakarànakerya; 6. otaku ni ukáḡawanàkerya; 7. señsèe no onîmotu o oázukari-sinàkerya

K 1. **Señsèe ḡa zizyóo o setumee-nasàru soo desu kara . .**
'They say the professor is going to explain the circumstances, so . . .' (don't worry).

Âa, señsèe ḡa setúmee-site kudasàru ñ nara, watási wa setumee-suru hituyoo arímasèñ ne!
'Oh, as long as the professor is going to explain (for us), then I (at least) have no need to explain, do I.'

2. **Señsèe ḡa hôñ o oérabi ni nàru soo desu kara . .**
'They say the professor is going to select the book, so . . .' (don't worry).

Âa, señsèe ḡa erâñde kudásàru ñ nara, watási wa eràbu hituyoo arímasèñ ne!
'Oh, as long as the professor is going to select [it] (for us), then I (at least) have no need to select [it], do I.'

3. koózitu o okañḡae ni nàru; 4. tañtòosya ni oái ni nàru; 5. okyákusañ ni otukiai ni nàru; 6. yotéehyoo o okasi ni nàru; 7. konó mòñdai no sekiniñ o otori ni nàru

L 1. **Getúyòo ni mo mokúyòo ni mo reñsyuu-site (i)màsu.**
'I am practicing both on Mondays and on Thursdays.'

Môsi getúyòo ka mokúyòo no dôtira ka o erábànakereba narânaku nattara, dôo simasu ka�
'Supposing it becomes necessary to choose

2. **Morimoto-san mo Kêe-tyan mo**
   yoǹde (i)màsu.
   'I'm inviting both Mr/s. Morimoto and
   Kei.'

one of the two—Mondays or Thursdays—
what will you do?'

Môsi 'Morimoto-san ka Kêe-tyan no
dôtira ka o erábànakereba narânaku
nattara, dôo simasu ka
'Supposing it becomes necessary to choose
one of the two—Mr/s. Morimoto or Kei—
what will you do?'

3. **nêko/inû/sodâtete;** 4. **hâru ni/âki ni/Yoóròppa o 'mawatte;** 5. **otókò no ko/oǹnà no**
   ko/arúbàito to site 'tukatte; 6. **hîrosa/yâtiǹ/îi apâato o 'saǵasite;** 7. **koóǵakù-bu de/**
   buǹǵakù-bu de/zyûǵyoo o ûkete

M1. **Oyâ to site no seikiniǹ o kaǹǵaèzu**
    ni sûmeba îi desu nêe.
    'I hope we get by (*lit.* it ends up)
    without deliberating about one's
    responsibility as a parent, don't you!'

Môsi kaǹǵaènakereba narânaku nâttara,
dôo simasyoo.
'Supposing it becomes necessary to
deliberate about it, what shall we do?'

2. **Iiwake o iwázu ni sùmeba îi desu**
   nêe.
   'I hope we get by (*lit.* it ends up)
   without making (*lit.* saying) excuses,
   don't you!'

Môsi iwánàkereba narânaku nattara, dôo
simasyoo.
'Supposing it becomes necessary to make
(*lit.* say) them, what shall we do?'

3. **iroiro na kusúri o nomàzu ni;** 4. **katée no kotò o siǹpai-sèzu ni;** 5. **komákài naiyoo**
   o setúmee-sèzu ni

Application Exercises

A1. Practice asking about the occurrence of particular events, and answer in terms of the provision that will guarantee the occurrence of that event. For example: **Asita pîkunikku ni ikû desyoo?** . . . **Êe, âme ǵa hurânakereba . .** 'You're going to the picnic tomorrow—right?' . . . 'Yes, unless it rains.' Suggested topics: continuing the study of Japanese; consulting with your professor; going home early today; going to see a movie tonight; taking it easy this weekend; going to bed late; getting up early; speaking Japanese with Japanese people; watching television in the evenings; buying a word processor; going to Japan after graduating.

2. Practice asking and answering questions that involve being required and not being required to do certain things, using the pattern of necessity that includes the provisional. For example: **Asita kônakute (mo) îi?** . . . **Iie, kônak(er)ya(a) ikénài yo.** 'Will it be all right (even/also) if I don't come tomorrow?' . . . 'No, you have to come.' Practice various levels of politeness and formality, making them appropriate to identities that members of the group assume. Suggested topics: listening to tapes; learning the CCs (= **siísìi**); attending class; handing in (= **dâsu**); eavesdropping (= **iíbuzudoròppiǹǵu**) on the assigned (= **kimatta**) day; reading the textbook; practicing the CCs before coming to class; con-

sulting with the instructor about things you don't understand; studying on days when there is no class; practicing the drills (= **dôriru**).

3. Practice asking questions about experiences ('have you ever ——?' or 'do you ever ——?') or enjoyment ('do you like to ——?') that involve two concurrent activities. Remember that in Japanese the verbal representing the accompanying, less focused activity is the one to which **-nàḡara** is attached. Suggested topics: attending school and working part-time; eating and watching television; going to work by car and listening to Japanese tapes; reading the paper and listening to the radio; consulting with your teacher and having coffee.

4. In response to yes-no questions about various occurrences, respond with a contrary condition using a **-nàḡara** pattern. Examples:

> **Tanaka-sañ ni môo teḡámi o kakimàsita? ... Iya, kakôo to omóinàḡara, tûi 'wasuretyatte ..** 'Have you written a letter to Mr/s. Tanaka yet?' ... No, while I was thinking of writing, I unintentionally forgot...'

> **Anó kàiḡi ni demâsita ka✓ ... Zañneñnàḡara, deráremasèñ desita.** 'Did you attend that meeting?' ... 'It was too bad, but I wasn't able to (attend).'

5. Practice asking questions involving two items ('both X and Y'), to which the responses offer an 'either X or Y' correction (cf. Drill E of this lesson section). Make up questions that are appropriate to the person(s) addressed or referred to, and answer on the basis of reality. Include discussions of groups like students at this school, people who work for this company, instructors at this university, doctors in this town, Japanese, etc., as topics of your discussions.

B. Core Conversations: Substitution

The Core Conversations of this lesson are important as models. Use them in their original form except for the substitution of a few situational elements. For example:

> 1(J)a. Change the situation to: graduation; becoming a **katyoo**, **butyoo**, or head of an institute.

> (N)a. Change the intention to: writing a letter; telephoning. Change what actually happened to: forgetting; failing to be in touch.

> 2(N)a. Change the activity to: working and going to school; appearing on television and teaching at a university; teaching foreign languages and writing textbooks. Revise the remainder of the conversation as required.

> 3(N)a. Have the conversation involve explanations/tests/drills that Ms. Sato, the new instructor, made up. Change all following minor details as required, but keep strictly to the basic sequencing of the original.

Continue this kind of practice until the underlying conversational patterning of these samples becomes internalized to the point of becoming automatic. Make sure that your intonations and facial expressions are appropriate to what you are saying!!!

SECTION B

Core Conversations

1(J)a. **Môo rokû-neñ mo Nihôñ ni irássyàru ñ da soo desu nêe.**

(N)a. **Êe. Nâḡâku sûmeba sûmu hodo, Nihôñ ḡa ki ní irimàsite nêe.**

b. Sôo desu ka. Nihoñ no seekatu
ǧa osúki nà ñ desu ne!

c. Goryôosiñ wa, kâette kite hosîi
tte ośsyaimasèñ?

d. Sore wa, sitûree-simasita.

e. Âa, sôo na ñ desu ka.

2(N)a. Kôñdo no atúmàri no koto, dôo
simasyoo.

b. Râiǧetu nara îi no ni nêe.
Nobâsu wake ni wa ikímasèñ ka
nêe.

c. Sôo desu nêe. Zyâa, tônikaku
basyó dakè de mo
kiménàkereba . .

3(J) Taíheñ dàtta desyoo? Mûri na
kotô o onéǧai-sità no ni,
isóǧàsìkute otêtudai ni ikú wàke
ni mo ikánàkute, moósiwake
arimasèñ desita.

b. Êe. Dekîreba, zuťto koko ni itai to
omòtte (i)ru ñ desu yo.

c. Zitû wa, huta-ri to mo nâñ-neñ mo
mâe ni nakúnarimàsite nêe.[4]

d. Sore ni, kyôodai mo hitó-ri mo
inài kara . .

(J)a. Ñ. Âto iś-syuukañ mo nài no ni,
mâda naní mo kimatte (i)nài ñ
desyoo?

b. Sâa. Osóku nàreba nàru hodo,
korárènai hito ǧa huémàsu yo⤳

c. Mâa, basyó sàe kimárèba, âto wa
nâñ to ka nâru desyoo.

(N) Iie. Yaťte mìtara, hañ-nitì mo
kakárimasèñ desita yo⤳

 English Equivalents

1(J)a. They say that (it's that) you've
been in Japan all of six years
already.

b. Oh. (It's that) you like life in
Japan, don't you!

c. Don't your parents say that they'd
like you to come home?

(N)a. Yes. The longer I live here, the
more Japan appeals to me, and . . .
(that's why I stay).

b. Yes. You know, I've been thinking
I'd like to stay here indefinitely, if
it's possible.

c. Actually, both of them (having) died
a number of years ago . . .

4. The accompanying video has **nakúnattà ñ desu**.

d Forgive me for bringing that up.

e. Oh, is that how it is!

2(N)a. What shall we do about this next meeting?

b. If only it were next month! We couldn't really postpone it?

c. That's right. Well, in any case, we must decide the place or something, at least.

3(J) That was awful, wasn't it? Even though I asked you to do something unreasonable, I was busy and couldn't really even give you a hand; I'm terribly sorry.

d. What's more, I don't have any brothers or sisters, so . . . (there's no one wanting me to return home).

(J)a. Yeah—even though there isn't even a week left [before it begins], (it's that) nothing has been decided yet—right?

b. Oh, the later it gets, the more [the number of] people who can't come will increase.

c. Well, the rest will probably work out, if only the place is decided.

(N) No problem. When I tried doing it, it didn't take even half a day!

BREAKDOWNS
(AND SUPPLEMENTARY VOCABULARY)

1. **rokû-neñ mo** (SP1)   even six years, as much as six years
   sûmeba sûmu hodo (SP2)   the more I reside (*lit.* provided I reside, to the extent I reside)
   seekatu   daily life, living
   huta-ri to mo (SP3)   both people
   nâñ-neñ mo mâe ni   any number of years ago
   nakunaru /-u; nakunatta/ *or*
   + **sinu /-u; siñda/**   die
   + **umareru /-ru; umareta/**   be born
   + **ikîru /-ru; îkita/**   live, be alive
   hito-ri mo /+ negative/   (not) even one person
2. **kôñdo**   this time, this next time
   atúmàrì   a meeting, a gathering
   iś-syùukañ mo   even one week, as much as one week
   nobâsu /-u; nobâsita/   lengthen, extend; postpone; prolong
   nobîru /-ru; nôbita/   [something] extends, stretches; is postponed, is prolonged

wâke	reason, cause, grounds
nobâsu wake ni wa 'ikanai (SP4)	can't really postpone
osóku nàreba nâru hodo	the later it becomes (*lit.* provided it becomes late, to the extent it becomes [late])
huêru /-ru; hûeta/	[something] increases
+ huyâsu /-u; huyâsita/	increase [something]
tônikaku	at any rate, in any case
basyo	place, spot, location, site
basyó dakè de mo 'kimeru	decide just the place or something
basyó sàe (SP5)	even the place
basyó sàe kimárèba	if only the place is decided
nâñ to ka nâru	become something, i.e., things will work out somehow
3. tetúdài/otêtudai	help, assistance
otêtudai ni 'iku	go to help (you), give (you) a hand
ikú wàke ni mo 'ikanai	can't really even go, can't really go, either
hań-nitì	half a day
+ hań-tukì	half a month
+ hań-tosi	half a year
+ hań-zìkañ	half an hour
hań-nitì mo	even half a day, as much as half a day

MISCELLANEOUS NOTES

1. In CC1, Mr. Suzuki and his colleague Mr. Carter discuss Mr. Carter's plans to stay on in Japan indefinitely. Mr. Suzuki, who raises the subject of Mr. Carter's parents, apologizes when he learns that they are no longer living. Note that Mr. Carter continues the conversation as if nothing of a delicate, personal nature had come up, the most considerate way of handling a situation like this in a Japanese context.

As usual, Mr. Suzuki and Mr. Carter use careful-style in speaking with each other, with distal-style final predicates. Mr. Suzuki, who is asking very personal questions of Mr. Carter, uses honorific-polite **irássyàru** (in reference to Mr. Carter) and **ossyaimasèñ** (in reference to Mr. Carter's parents). Mr. Carter, who is speaking about himself and his own family, uses plain distal-style. Note that his use of distal-style gerunds **irímàsite** and **nakúnarimàsite** as the final predicates of minor sentences is markedly careful, but later in the conversation, his use of **inai** before **kara** is a bit more casual.

(J)b. **Seekatu**: Note also **seekatu-suru** 'pursue daily life,' 'make a living'; **seékatu no tamè ni hataraku** 'work to make a living'; **kekkoñ-sèekatu** 'married life'; **syakài-sèekatu** 'social life.'

(J)c. **Kâette kite hosîi** 'they want you to *come* back' (i.e., to where they are).

(N)c. **Nâñ-neñ mo** 'a (large) number of years' links up with **mâe**, indicating how far (the extent to which) in the past the deaths occurred: 'a (large) number of years before or ago.' **Nakunaru**, in reference to humans, is a more indirect, softer equivalent of **sinu**. (Compare

English 'pass on' or 'pass away' to 'die.') Note the contrast of: **Ryôosiñ g̃a nakúnarimàsita.** 'My parents died' to **Tokée g̃a nakunarimàsita (nâi + nâru > nakunaru).**[5] 'My watch disappeared' and **Kodómo g̃a inaku narimàsita (inai + nâru > ináku nàru).** 'A child disappeared.' **Sin-u**, a consonant verbal, is the only verbal whose root ends in /n/. Its derivative forms parallel those of verbals whose root ends in /m/: **siní(màsu), sinêba, sinda, sinde, sindàra, sindàri.** This verbal is used of humans and animals, but not of plant life. **Ikîru**: compare **îkite (i)ru** 's/he's living' (= is alive); **seekatu-site (i)ru** 's/he's living' (= is pursuing daily life, making a living); and **sûñde (i)ru** 's/he's living' (= is residing).

Kyôodai g̃a iru 'there are brothers and sisters' not surprisingly uses **iru**, the verbal of location regularly used with animate referents. Also possible, particularly with family members, is the verbal **âru**, indicating that one 'has' family members in the given category. In other words, the meaning focuses not on their animate existence in a location, but rather that they exist, in a passive kind of way, for the referent. Particularly common is **kodómo g̃a àru** 'I have children.'

2. In CC2, Deborah Miller and her colleague Mr. Yamada are expressing concern about the fact that few arrangements for an upcoming meeting have been completed. The two are in total agreement, each supporting the other's comments with utterances ending in **desyoo? nêe**, and **ne**.

The style is careful, with distal-style final predicates, as is usual in conversations between these two colleagues.

(N)a. The **-do** of **kôñdo** has already occurred in **maido** 'every time' and as the classifier for counting times or occurrences.

Atúmàri is a nominal derivative of the verbal **atúmàru** 'come together.'

(J)a. The occurrence of **ñ** as a response to an information question indicates agreement that asking the question is indeed to the point. **Âto** in this context refers to the time that remains before the meeting.

(N)b. Here we encounter another example of a provisional in a contrary-to-fact statement ending in **no ni**: 'it would be great, provided it were next month, but . . .' [it isn't].

In her utterance ending in **ka nêe**, Deborah Miller signals her assumption that Mr. Yamada would be apt to ask the same question.

(J)b. Mr. Yamada's response warns what will happen if any inclination to postpone the meeting is followed.

Huêru and **huyâsu** are another intransitive/transitive pair: '[X] increases' and 'increase [X].' On the basis of patterning we have observed in other pairs and what we know about the occurrence of /y/ in current Japanese (it occurs only before /a/, /u/, and /o/), we can assume that **huêru** comes from an earlier ***huyêru.**

(N)c. Deborah Miller readily agrees with Mr. Yamada's warning and then retreats to the very least that must be done: 'in any case . . .' The minor sentence ending in the negative provisional **kiménàkereba** 'unless we decide . . .' implies a following 'it won't do': i.e., 'we must decide.'

Basyo in some of its uses overlaps with **tokórò**, but unlike **tokórò**, it frequently occurs without a preceding modifier. (When **tokórò** does occur without modification, it usually refers to one's place of residence, as in the phrase **onamae to 'otokoro**, which **basyo** never does.) What is more, **basyo** never alternates with **tokórò** in the structural patterns in which **tokórò** refers to location in time (see 25B-SP1). Note: **basyó o tòtte oku** 'hold or reserve a

---

5. Given the shift in accent, **nakunaru** is considered a single word rather than a phrase.

place'; **basyo o akeru** 'open up a place'; **basyó o eràbu** 'choose a site'; **basyó o tòru** 'take up space.'

(J)c. **Âto wa** refers to what is left after the matter of deciding the place has been taken care of, that is, the remainder, the rest, in contrast to the decision on location.

Nâñ to ka nâru: /nominal + **to** + **nâru**/ is an alternate goal pattern, another example of particle **to** alternating with particle **ni** (see 26A-SP4 for the difference in meaning between these two particles). The occurrence of **ka** makes the interrogative **nâñ** indefinite: 'get to be (as if) something.'

3. In CC3, Sue Brown's colleague apologizes for what she has made Sue Brown do, but the apology is politely turned aside on the grounds that the task didn't take even half a day. This kind of reaction is more polite than a simple **dôo itasimasite**. As is usual in conversation between these two women, the style is careful, with distal-style final predicates. The apology includes a humble-polite form (**oneḡai-sita**).

(J) Note that **isógàsìkute** 'being busy' accounts for **ikú wàke ni mo ikánàkute** 'not really even being able to go,' which in turn accounts for the apology.

Otêtudai is a polite nominal derived from the verbal **tetúdàu**, referring to 'help for you.'

(N) Note the use of the conditional in a sentence referring to a past event *which we know actually occurred*. This knowledge determines the appropriate English equivalent: *'when* I tried doing it . . .' In a different context, the same Japanese sequence could have different English equivalents that included an if-clause.

Hañ-nitì: As our vocabulary grows, we find more and more examples of alternatives that cover similar meanings, reflecting native Japanese forms alternating with forms that were originally borrowed from Chinese. For example, **-niti** (from Chinese), as in **hañ-nitì, koñ-niti wa**, and **ití-nitì**, and **-ka** (native Japanese), as in **hutu-ka, mik-ka**, etc., both mean 'day'; in addition, **hi** (native Japanese) occurs as an independent word meaning 'sun' or 'day.' In reference to months, we find **-ḡatu** (from Chinese), as in **ití-ḡatù, ni-ḡátù**, etc., **ḡetu** (from Chinese), as in **koñ-ḡetu, ik-kàḡetu**, etc.; and **-tuki** (native Japanese), as in **hañ-tukì**. **Tukî** also occurs as an independent word meaning 'moon' or 'month.' Note that **-tuki** may occur as a classifier that forms compounds with the Japanese series of numerals—**hito-, huta-**, etc. This leads to alternate forms for counting months: **hitô-tuki** and **ik̇-kàḡetu** both mean 'one month' (never 'January'). **-Tuki** as a classifier is common only with the very low numerals.

Structural Patterns

1. /QUANTITY EXPRESSION + **mo**/

As the particle **mo** is introduced in more and more patterns, its range of usage from neutral "additionalness" ('X, also,' 'X, too'), to emphatic "additionalness" as an extreme ('even X'), to all-inclusiveness (as in **îtu mo** 'always,' **dôtira mo** 'both,' **nâni o sitê mo** 'whatever [you] do') becomes clear.

We now meet **mo** following a quantity expression X (which may or may not be a number). Here, **X mo** emphasizes X as an extreme quantity: 'even X,' 'as much/many as X,' 'all of X.' With a negative predicate, the combination is equivalent to '(not) even X,' 'not to the extreme of X.' Examples:

Hyakû-niñ mo miémàsita. 'As many as 100 people came.'

Utí no kaisya nì wa, końpyùutaa ga nizyûu-dai mo arimasu. 'In our company, we have all of twenty computers.'

Kamî wa itî-mai mo nâi. 'I don't have a single sheet of paper.'

Ano kooeñ wa sukôsi mo wakáránakatta. 'I didn't understand that lecture at all' (*lit.* even a little).

With this addition of /quantity expression + **mo**/, we can now complete the following chart:

	Neutral amount 'just X'	Amount on the low side 'only X'	Extreme amount 'as much as X'
Definite	**X dakê**	**X sika**	**X mo**
Approximate	**X-gùrai**	**X-bàkari**	**X-hodo**

☠WARNING: /Quantity X + **mo**/ does *not* express the *addition* of X, i.e., 'X, also,' 'X, too.' Compare:

Zassi (o) gô-satu mo katta. 'I bought as many as five magazines.'

Zassi mo gô-satu katta. 'I bought five magazines, too.'

Zassi mo gô-satu mo katta. 'I bought as many as five magazines, too.'

Zassi (o) moó gò-satu katta. 'I bought five more magazines.'

Zassi (o) moó gò-satu mo katta. 'I bought as many as five more magazines.'

Zassi mo moó gò-satu mo katta. 'I bought as many as five more magazines, too.'

Zassi wa iś-satu mo nài. 'I don't have a single magazine.'

Zassi mo iś-satu mo nài. 'I don't have a single magazine, either.'

Môo 'already,' or (with a negative predicate) 'not any more' (note accent difference) can also be added to the above examples!

On the other hand, /number + **mo**/ *does* express the addition of X provided the number names rather than counts. Compare: **ni-gátù mo** 'February, too' and **ni-kâgetu mo** 'all of two months.' Depending on context, **ni-kai mo** can mean either 'the second floor, too' or 'as many as 2 floors,' 'even two floors.'

2. sûmeba sûmu hodo

We continue our study of the provisional with the introduction of a special combination. All of its parts are already familiar. Consider the examples that occur in the Core Conversations:

Nâgâku sûmeba sûmu hodo, Nihôñ ga ki ní irimàsu.

Osóku nàreba nâru hodo, korárènai hito ga huémàsu.

The pattern that describes these two examples can be formulated as: /provisional X + imperfective X + **hodo**/. Linked to a following predicate Y it means 'provided it's X, to the extent that it's X, it's Y.' In other words, X must occur to begin with, and to the extent that it does occur, Y occurs (or occurred). This is a very complicated way of expressing the usual English pattern, 'the more X, the more Y.' Examples:

Ôókìkereba oókìi hodo îi. 'The bigger, the better.'

Keńkyuu-surèba 'suru hodo, omósìroku narimasu nêe. 'The more one does research, the more interesting it becomes, doesn't it.'

Soré o mìreba mîru hodo, hôsîku nâtta ñ desu. 'The more I saw it, the more I wanted it.'

Tônai ni tîkâkereba tikâi hodo, yâtiñ ğa takâi desu yo⌐ 'The closer it is to the center of town, the higher the rent.'

Sîzuka nara sîzuka na hodo, keñkyuu ni ìi to omoimasu. 'The quieter it is, the better for research, I believe.'

In this pattern **hodo** is classified as a nominal, since **na**, the alternate of the copula **dà** that occurs *only before nominals,* may precede it, as in the last example above.

3. /NUMBER + to mo/

The particle combination **to mo**, following a number that expresses a total quantity, indicates that the total quantity is included in the given context. Examples:

Uti no kodomo, sañ-niñ to mo, Yoóròppa ni sûñde (i)masu. 'Our children—all three of them—are living in Europe.'

Utí no koñpyùutaa, ni-dai to mo, kowârete (i)ru soo desu. 'They say that our computers—both of them (*or* the two of them)—are out of order.'

The occurrence of **mo** in this pattern is a reminder both of the emphatic 'even' meaning of **mo** and of its all-inclusive meaning (as in /interrogative + **mo**/: **îtu mo, dôre mo, dôtira mo**, etc.). **Dôtira mo** 'both alternatives' is an alternate of /two + classifier + **to mo**/. As an alternate of **ni-dai to mo** above, **dôtira mo** is also possible.

4. /—— wâke ni wa 'ikanai/

The basic meaning of **wâke** is 'reason,' 'cause,' 'grounds.' This may extend to 'meaning'— 'significance'—and 'circumstances' that are explanatory. Following an accented word, **wâke** usually loses its accent. Examples:

Wâke no wakárànai kotô o iťtè (i)ta. 'S/he was saying things that were meaningless.'

Môñku o iú wàke ğa âru to omôu. 'I think there is cause for complaining.'

Dôo iu wâke de okôtta ñ desu ka⌐ 'For what reason is it that you got angry?'

Soó iu wàke nara, yaméta hòo ğa îi desu yo⌐ 'If it's [for] a reason like that, you'd better quit!'

Dekînai to iú wàke zya nâi kedo, tyôtto iyâ na siğóto dèsu yo. 'It's not that I can't do it, but it's unpleasant work.'

In the combination /**X** wâke ni wa 'ikanai/, a situation is described as not proceeding (= **ikanai**) at least (= **wa**) to a point where (= **ni**) X serves as a cause or reason (= X + **wâke**). This translates as a situation in which X, at least, is considered without reason, impossible to consider. A frequently cited English equivalent is 'can't really X,' which accurately suggests unreasonableness rather than lack of ability. In this pattern, X is usually a sentence modifier ending in (or consisting of) an imperfective affirmative verbal or a negative equivalent (an **-(a)nai** form). Note that **mo** can replace **wa** in this pattern, with the usual change in emphasis: 'can't really X, either' or 'can't really even X.'

🕮WARNING: Be sure to distinguish the **ikanai** of this pattern from the **ikenai** of **sitê wa 'ikenai, sinâkute wa 'ikenai,** and **sinâkereba 'ikenai.** Examples:

Iyâ de mo, mônku o iú wàke ni wa ikánài ñ zya nâi desu ka 'Isn't it the case that you can't really complain, even if it's unpleasant?'

Señsèe no kóóeñ nì wa dênai wake ni wa ikánài desyoo? 'You can't really not attend our professor's lecture—right?'

Soó iu baai nì wa, orée o aǧenai wàke ni wa ikánài to omoimasu. 'In such circumstances, I believe you can't really not give some expression of gratitude.'

5. *PHRASE-PARTICLE* **sàe**

The phrase-particle **sàe** 'even' is a particle of strong emphasis—more emphatic than **mo**. Like **mo**, it replaces **ǧa** and **o**, but follows other phrase-particles and gerund forms, particularly the gerund **dè**. It may itself also be followed by **mo**, resulting in an even more emphatic combination. Following an accented word or phrase, **sàe** usually loses its accent. Thus: **isú sàe nâi** 'there aren't even any chairs'; **tukî ni sae 'iku** 'go even to the moon'; **kodómo de sàe** 'even being a child'; **taípuràitaa sae mo 'tukaenai** 'can't use even a typewriter.'

The pattern we are particularly interested in here involves the occurrence of **sàe** in provisional sequences, expressing emphatically the single requirement that assures the stated outcome: 'if, only if . . . ,' [the outcome will be assured]. In this pattern several things happen.

1. **Sàe** may follow a nominal, placing exhaustive emphasis on the nominal, as in

Okáne sàe âreba, raineñ waápuro o kau tumori dèsu. 'If only I have the *money*, I plan to buy a word processor next year.'

2. A /nominal + **suru**/ compound becomes /nominal + **sàe** + **surêba**/, again placing exhaustive emphasis on the nominal, as in:

Beñkyoo sàe surêba, wakâru yoo ni narímàsu yo 'If only you'll *study*, you'll get to understand.'

3. A /gerund + **iru**/ pattern becomes /gerund + **sàe** + **irêba**/, placing exhaustive emphasis on the gerund. Example:

Soré o sitte sàe irêba, moñdai wa nài desu yo 'If only s/he *knows* that, there won't be a problem.'

4. A verbal receives exhaustive emphasis by being restated as /*verbal stem + **-suru**/ (thus **kau** 'buy' becomes *kai-suru 'do buying'), with **sàe** then following the stem and **suru** in the provisional. Examples:

Osí sàe surêba, sûǧu akímàsu yo 'If only you'll *push* it, it will open.'

Mî sae surêba, kaítaku nàru to omoimasu. 'If only you'll *look at* it, you'll get to want to buy it, I believe.'

5. An adjectival receives exhaustive emphasis by being restated as /*adjectival stem + **âru**/[6] (thus **oókìi** 'is big' becomes *ôókìku âru 'there is "being big" '), with **sàe** then following the stem and **âru** occurring in the provisional. Examples:

Omósìròku sae âreba, owári màde yômu kedo . . 'If only it's *interesting*, I'll read it to the end, but . . .' (otherwise I won't).

---

6. This is the affirmative equivalent of the actually occurring negative adjectival pattern /**-ku nâi**/.

Yâsûku sae âreba, takúsañ kau tumori dèsu. 'If only they're *cheap*, I plan to buy a lot of them.'

6. A /nominal + **dà**/ predicate receives exhaustive emphasis by being restated as /nominal + **de àru**/,[7] with **sàe** following /nominal + **de**/ and **âru** occurring in the provisional. Examples:

Yasásii nihoñḡo de sàe âreba, yomêru hazú dèsu. 'If only *it's easy Japanese,* s/he should be able to read it.'

Raísyuu de sàe âreba, nañyòobi de mo îi soo desu. 'If only *it's next week,* any day will be fine, they say.'

Kyôo de sae nâkereba ikéru to omoimàsu. 'If only *it's not today,* I think I can go.'

Drills

A 1. **Nañ-neñ-ḡùrai Nihôñ ni irássyaimàsu?**
'About how many years have you been in Japan?'

Môo rokû-meñ mo irû ñ desu yo↗
'(It's that) I've been here all of six years already.'

2. **Nañ-niñ-ḡùrai tûaa ni atúmarimàsita?**
'About how many people gathered for the tour?'

Môo rokû-niñ mo atúmàtta ñ desu yo↗
'(It's that) as many as six people have gathered already.'

3. **nañ-kaḡetu-ḡùrai arúbàito sité (i)màsu;** 4. **nañ-kai-ḡùrai hiḱkosimàsita;** 5. **nañ-neñ-ḡùrai sonó hanà sodâtete (i)masu;** 6. **nañ-dai-ḡùrai zitêñsya kowâsityaimasita;** 7. **nañ-ḡeñ-ḡùrai depâato mawátte (i)màsu**

B 1. **Nâñ-niti mo kakâru to taíheñ desyòo nêe.**
'It's probably a nuisance when it takes a (large) number of days, isn't it!'

Êe, dê mo, sûḡu hazímerèba hañ-nitì mo kakárimasèñ yo.
'Yes, but provided we start right away, it won't take even half a day.'

2. **Nâñ-neñ mo kakâru to taíheñ desyòo nêe.**
'It's probably a nuisance when it takes a (large) number of years, isn't it!'

Êe, dê mo, sûḡu hazímerèba hañ-tosì mo kakárimasèñ yo.
'Yes, but provided we start right away, it won't take even half a year.'

3. **nañ-zìkañ;** 4. **nañ-kàḡetu**

C 1. **Señpai, oózee mìeta?**
'Did many senior members show up?'

Hitó-ri mo miemasèñ desita.
'Not even one showed up.'

2. **Sebiro, takúsañ mòtte (i)ru?**
'Do you have many suits?'

Iḱ-tyaku mo mòtte (i)masèñ.
'I don't have even one.'

3. **mise, iroiro yotta;**[8] 4. **osake, kânari mesiaḡatta;** 5. **señèñsatu, sukôsi âru;** 6. **kâsa, iróiro mìsete moratta**

---

7. Actually **dà** is a contraction of **de âru**, which still occurs in impersonal written Japanese.
8. Particle **ni** is absent following the goal of **yoru** in this example of casual direct-style.

D 1. **Mîyazi-sañ, otôosañ mo okâasañ mo beñ̃ǵòsi de (i)rássyaimàsu kara . .**
'About Mr/s. Miyaji—both his/her father and mother are lawyers, so . . .' (that explains the situation).

Hêe✓ Ohúta-ri to mo beñ̃ǵòsi de irássyàru ñ desu ka.
'Wow! You mean both of them are lawyers?'

2. **Kyoozyu wa, âsa mo hirû mo 'ban mo sôto de mesíaǵarimàsu kara . .**
'The professor eats breakfast, lunch, and dinner out so . . .' (that explains the situation).

Hêe✓ Sań-syoku to mo sòto de mesíaǵarù ñ desu ka.
'Wow! You mean s/he eats all three meals out?'

3. **Kyôoto de wa, getúyòo/kayôo/ryokáñ ni otomari ni narimàsu; 4. mâe ni iťta tokì/ sonó màe/señ̃sèe ni omé ni kakaremàsita**

E 1. **Ití-d(e)ii-kèe de mo, wań̃rùumu de mo, hirôi no ga îi desyoo?**
'Whether it's a 1-DK or a studio, a large one would be good, wouldn't it?'

Êe, hîrôkereba hirôi hodo îi desu nêe.
'Yes, the larger the better, don't you agree!'

2. **Seézi no kotò de mo, kêezai no kotô de mo, yôku siťte (i)rù no ga îi desyoo?**
'Whether it's about politics or about economics, being well informed would be good, wouldn't it?'

Êe, yôku siťte (i)rèba 'iru hodo îi desu nêe.
'Yes, the more you know the better, don't you agree!'

3. **siń̃guru-rùumu/tuîñ/sîzuka na no; 4. hirôoeñ/kôñpa/tanósìi no; 5. sakana/yasai/ atárasìi no; 6. mêgane/koñtàkuto/hâyâku narêru no; 7. tîzu/yoteehyoo/kuwásìi no**

F 1. **Yamanaka-sañ wa, tañ̃tòosya to site, ano yoteehyoo o yarínaòsu tumori wa nâi ñ desyoo ka nêe.**
'I wonder if (it's the case that) Mr/s. Yamanaka doesn't have any intention of redoing that schedule, as the person in charge.'

Mâa, watási ga yarinaòseba îi to wa omóimàsu kedo nêe.
'Well, I do think it would be good if *I* did it over, but, you know . . .' (it *is* his/her responsibility).

2. **Yamanaka-sañ wa, tañ̃tòosya to site, miñ̃nà ni setúmee-suru tumori wa nài ñ desyoo ka nêe.**
'I wonder if (it's the case that) Mr/s. Yamanaka doesn't have any intention of explaining it to everybody, as the person in charge.'

Mâa, watási ga setumee-surèba îi to wa omóimàsu kedo nêe.
'Well, I do think it would be good if *I* explained it, but, you know . . .' (it *is* his/her responsibility).

3. **îi no o erâbu; 4. tekitoo na zikañ o kimeru; 5. sekíniñ o tòru; 6. okyákusañ ni tukiàu; 7. kokó ni nokòru**

G 1. **Katyoo g̃a yotéehyoo o kakinaòsita soo desu.**
'I hear the section chief rewrote the schedule.'

Dôo iu wake de kakínaòsita ñ desu ka nêe.
'For what reason is it that s/he rewrote [it], I wonder!'

2. **Katyoo g̃a zikáñ o kaeta sòo desu.**
'I hear the section chief changed the time.'

Dôo iu wake de kaétà ñ desu ka nêe.
'For what reason is it that s/he changed [it], I wonder!'

3. **konó irò o erâñda**; 4. **zêñbu syabêttyatta**; 5. **mití o matig̃àeta**; 6. **basyo o 'koko ni kimeta**; 7. **eñkai o yameta**

H 1. **Anó apàato g̃a kirái ni nàtte hikkòsita ñ desu ka**
'Is it that you came to dislike that apartment and moved (*lit.* you moved having gotten to dislike that apartment)?'

Iêie, hikkòsu koto wa hikkosimàsita kedo neʃ Betu ni anó apàato g̃a kirái ni nàtta wake zya nâi ñ desu.
'No, no. I did move, but (the fact is) it is not particularly that I came to dislike that apartment.'

2. **Anó sèetaa g̃a ki ní iranàkute hitó ni ag̃età ñ desu ka**
'Is it that you did not like that sweater, and gave it away to somebody (*lit.* you gave it to a person not having liked that sweater)?'

Iêie, ag̃eru kotò wa ag̃émàsita kedo néʃ Betu ni anó sèetaa g̃a ki ní iranàkatta wake zya nâi ñ desu.
'No, no. I did give it [away], but (the fact is) it is not particularly that I did not like that sweater.'

3. **kâig̃i g̃a sumûuzu ni ikánàkute 'siñpai-sita**; 4. **kotóbà g̃a wakárànakute sîzuka datta**; 5. **zizyóo g̃a àtte kaísya o yasùñda**; 6. **nattoku-site sonó sig̃oto o tetudàtta**; 7. **zyûg̃yoo no naíyoo g̃a omosìròkute gakúsee g̃a hùeta**

I 1. **Atárasìi kyoókàsyo o erábitài desu ne!**
'We want to select the new textbook, don't we.'

Sôo desu ne! Sikâsi, îma sûgu erâbu wake ni wa ikánài desyoo.
'You're right. But we probably can't really select one right this minute.'

2. **Kono hoñyaku wa yarínaositài desu ne!**
'We want to do this translation over, don't we.'

Sôo desu ne! Sikâsi, îma sûgu yarínaòsu wake ni wa ikánài desyoo.
'You are right. But we probably can't really do it over right this minute.'

3. **kono inu no namae o kimetai**; 4. **konó kikài o tukaitai**; 5. **môtto îi râzio o kaitai**; 6. **kono niwa de asobitai**; 7. **demae o tyuumoñ-site moraitai**; 8. **konó mizuùmi de oyóg̃itài**

J 1. **Atúmari no hì wa nobásemasèñ ka**
'You can't postpone the date of the gathering?'

Hâa. Moósiwake gozaimasèñ g̃a, nobâsu wake ni wa maírimasèñ.
'Right. I'm terribly sorry, but I really cannot postpone it.'

2. **Kore to sore wa mazéraremasèñ ka**

Hâa. Moósiwake gozaimasèñ g̃a, mazêru wake ni wa maírimasèñ.

'You can't mix this and that?'

'Right. I'm terribly sorry but I really cannot mix them.'

3. **anó kì wa taósemasèñ**; 4. **koñpyùutaa ni iréraremasèñ**; 5. **Matúda-kuñ ni oneḡai-dekimasèñ**; 6. **tuiñ o hutâ-heya tôtte okémasèñ**

K 1. **Tônikaku basyó dakè wa kiménàkereba . .**

'Anyway, we must decide on just the place at least' (*lit.* Unless we decide . . .').

Sôo desu ne! Basyó sàe kimárèba, âto wa nâñ to ka nâru desyoo kara . .

'That's right. If only the place is decided, the rest will somehow resolve itself, I guess, so . . .' (let's decide on the place).

2. **Tônikaku hitó dakè wa atúmènakereba . .**

'Anyway, we must gather just the people at least' (*lit.* 'Unless we gather . . .').

Sôo desu ne! Hitó sàe atúmàreba, âto wa nâñ to ka nâru desyoo kara . .

'That's right. If only the people gather, the rest will somehow resolve itself, I guess, so . . .' (let's gather the people).

3. **kore/irénàkereba**; 4. **ano huta-ri/hanásànakereba**; 5. **kyôo no siḡoto/sumásèna-kereba**; 6. **zyûḡyoo/hazímenàkereba**; 7. **Morimoto-kuñ/okósànakereba**

L 1. **Añmari[9] hi o nobâsu to, daré mo korarènaku narímàsu yo**

'With postponing the date too much, it will get so that nobody will be able to come.'

Tâsika ni nobâseba nobâsu hodo korárènai hito ḡa huèru desyoo nêe.

'Certainly the more we postpone, the more [the number of] people who can't come will probably increase.'

2. **Añmari moñdai ḡa muzukasìi to, daré mo dekìnaku narímàsu yo**

'With the problems being too difficult, it will get so that nobody will be able to do them.'

Tâsika ni muzúkasìkereba 'muzukasii hodo dekînai hito ḡa huèru desyoo nêe.

'Certainly the more difficult they are, the more [the number of] people who can't do them will probably increase.'

3. **siô o ireru/tâbete kurenaku**; 4. **tuúkiñ ḡa hùbeñ da/kayoenaku**; 5. **kikâi o huyâsu/iranaku**; 6. **yâtiñ o tâkâku suru/karirarenaku**

M 1. **Yáppàri 'gakusee wa zyûḡoo ni dênakutyaa nêe.**

'After all, unless students attend class (it won't do), don't you agree!'

Êe, mâa, zyûḡyoo ni dê sae surêba îi to iú wàke zya nâi desu kedo . .

'Yes. It's not (the reason) that [everything] is fine if only they attend class, but, well . . .' (I do agree).

2. **Yáppàri apâato wa êki ni tikáku nàkeryaa nêe.**

'After all, unless apartments are close to the station (it won't do), don't you agree!'

Êe, mâa, êki ni tikáku sàe âreba îi to iú wàke zya nâi desu kedo . .

'Yes. It's not (the reason) that [everything] is fine if only they're near the station, but, well . . .' (I do agree).

9. Note the use of **a(ñ)mari** with an affirmative predicate in this drill, indicating excessive degree (i.e., 'too much,' 'so much [that]').

3. **nîmotu/karúku nàkutyaa**; 4. **hisyô/eég̃o g̃a yomènakutyaa**; 5. **atúmàri/nobâsite moráwanàkutyaa**; 6. **yasûmu tokoro/sîzuka zya nâkutyaa**; 7. **oṅna no hitò/oṅna-ràsìku nâkutyaa**; 8. **kuruma/Nihôṅ no zya nâkutyaa**

N 1. **Deñsya g̃a okureru to komárimàsu nêe.**

    'It's a nuisance when the train is late, isn't it!'

    Êe. Okúre sae sinàkereba daízyòobu desu kedo nêe.

    'Yes. It's fine if only it's not late, but you know how it is!'

  2. **Naíyoo g̃a señmoñ-teki dà to komárimàsu nêe.**

    'It's a nuisance when the content is specialized, isn't it!'

    Êe. Señmoñ-teki de sàe nâkereba daízyòobu desu nêe.

    'Yes. It's fine if only it's not specialized, isn't it!'

  3. **miti/kômu**; 4. **ue no kai/urúsài**; 5. **deṅwabàñg̃oo/kawaru**; 6. **kâig̃i/suíyòobi da**; 7. **sakana/hurûi**; 8. **atárasìi hito/Yosída-sañ-mìtai da**

Application Exercises

A1. Select one member of your group who will answer questions abut a particular family—his/her own or a fictional one. As other members of the group elicit information about this family, have them jointly construct a family tree that represents what they have learned. Include questions about current residence, employment, when and where individuals were born and raised, whether grandparents are living, etc. Wherever appropriate, incorporate /quantity + **mo**/ and /quantity number + **to mo**/ patterns, as well as **dakê** and **sika** patterns.

  2. In answer to comments or yes-or-no questions about activities or conditions that involve members of the group, reply in terms of what results, the more the given activity or condition occurs. Examples: **Têepu kikímàsu ne⌡ . . . Êe, kikêba 'kiku hodo, wakâru yoo ni narímàsu kara . .** 'You listen to tapes, right?' . . . 'Yes, because the more I listen, the more I understand.' **Tyôtto âtûku nâi desu ka⌐ . . . Iêie. Âtûkereba atûi hodo îi to omoimasu yo⌐** 'Isn't it a bit [too] hot?' . . . 'No, no. The hotter the better, I think.'

  3. Using the same kind of stimuli as in A2, reply by giving the required provision, using an /X sâe ——(r)eba/ pattern. Example: **Anó zadàñkai, owári màde kiku? . . . Omósìroku sae âreba, kikímàsu kedo . .** 'Are you going to listen to that round-table discussion all the way to the end?' . . . 'I will (listen) if only it's interesting, but . . .' (otherwise not).

  4. Using the same kind of stimuli as in A2, reply in the negative with an explanation for why it is out of the question to expect the occurrence of the matter that has been brought up, using the /—— wâke ni wa 'ikanai/ pattern. Example: **Kôñdo no atúmàri, nobási-maseñ ka⌐ . . . Korárènai hito g̃a huêru soo desu kara, nobâsu wake ni wa ikímaseñ.** 'Won't you postpone this next meeting?' . . . 'They say that the [number of] people unable to come will increase, so we can't really postpone it.'

  5. Conduct personal history interviews, covering name, address, where the interviewee was born and raised, educational background, marital status, and employment history. Again, group members may answer with fact or fiction.

B. Core Conversations: Substitution

  Again practice the Core Conversations with appropriate substitutions, retaining the original overall structure. Follow the practice with questions and answers on the content.

SECTION C

Eavesdropping

(Answer the following questions on the basis of the accompanying tape. For each conversation, A = the first speaker and B the second.)

1a. What does A offer?
 b. How does B react?
2a. What is A's concern?
 b. What provision does B mention, in order for it to come about?
3a. Who is the topic of discussion?
 b. What hasn't yet been decided?
 c. What does A wish would happen that isn't happening yet?
4a. What does A want?
 b. What does B suggest?
5a. Why does B thank A?
 b. What has A heard about B?
 c. In what connection does B use **gosiñpai**?
6a. How is the work under discussion described?
 b. What does B want?
 c. Whom did B talk to about this?
 d. What was that person's reaction to B's request? On what grounds?
7a. What is B inquiring about? Where is it located?
 b. Why is A annoyed?
 c. What does B wish would happen that isn't happening?
 d. At what times is the situation bothersome?
 e. What is the relationship between A and B, as indicated by their speech styles?
8a. Who is B? Affiliation?
 b. To what place does B make a call?
 c. To whom does B want to speak?
 d. Why does A apologize?
 e. What information does A ask for?
 f. What is B going to do?
9a. Who is B?
 b. Where does this conversation take place?
 c. How long has B been there?
 d. Compare B's comments on foreign countries and on Japan.
 e. How many children does B have? Where are they now?
 f. What is B's plan? What led him to that decision?
 g. What is A's reaction?
10a. What has happened that was unexpected?
 b. Who is A?
 c. Where did A plan to go? When?
 d. How was the plan changed?
 e. Why did A stop in?
 f. Describe B's reaction.
 g. According to B, what will be possible?
11a. How does B look to A?
 b. What is the work situation these days?
 c. What does A wish would happen?
 d. What is B's reaction? Why?

e. What is A's final warning?

12a. Who has just met with A?
 b. What has B unintentionally failed to do?
 c. Whose health does A inquire about?
 d. What didn't A know until now?
 e. In what two connections is half a year mentioned?
 f. What occurred at the hospital?

13a. Who is scheduled to meet with whom? When?
 b. What is A wondering about?
 c. What is required for B to answer A's question positively?
 d. What does B assume?
 e. What language will be used at the meeting?
 f. Comment on the relationship between A and B, as indicated by their speech styles.

14a. What is the problem?
 b. How much time is left?
 c. What does B suggest?
 d. How does A react to the suggestion?

15a. Who is B?
 b. Why is B upset?
 c. What does A assume about B's reaction to the situation?
 d. Describe the problem from B's point of view.
 e. What is out of the question, according to A?
 f. What is B going to do?

16a. What is the situation?
 b. What happened? When? Give details.
 c. How is B reacting to the situation?

17a. What request does A make of B?
 b. Why does the request surprise B?
 c. What explanation does A offer?
 d. Why does A apologize?
 e. How does B turn the apology aside?
 f. Comment on the difference in styles used by A and B.

18a. What is the topic of discussion?
 b. What is causing problems for B?
 c. What is B's field of specialization?
 d. What is B's only requirement for choosing a line of work?

19a. Who is being discussed?
 b. What is that person's position?
 c. Contrast that person at home and at the office.
 d. How does B explain the difference?
 e. Give details pertaining to B's child(ren).

20a. Who is A?
 b. What is A's mistaken impression?
 c. Why didn't A know the correct facts?
 d. What change has occurred? Give details.
 e. How far in the future is the date mentioned?
 f. Where will the scheduled event take place?

21a. What is being examined?
 b. What is strange about it? Give details.
 c. Who is in charge?
 d. What does A tell B to do?

   e. How is the relationship between A and B made clear by the language styles they use?

22a. What is the relationship between A and B, as indicated by their language styles?

   b. Who is in charge of the item being discussed?

   c. Where is that person assumed to be?

   d. What specifically is A trying to find out?

   e. Who has that information?

   f. What does B offer to do?

   g. What else does A require?

23a. Who is B?

   b. Initially, what information does A seek from B?

   c. What information does B provide in response?

   d. What did B study in college?

   e. What connection is there between B's present job and B's upperclassman?

   f. What kind of work is B doing, and how does B feel about it?

   g. In what connection is graduate school mentioned?

24a. Who is the topic of discussion?

   b. Where is that person? Since when?

   c. How long does that person expect to stay there?

   d. How does that person feel about that place?

   e. When does that person return to Japan? Give details.

   f. What is that person's marital status? Give details.

Utilization

Follow the directions given for the utilization section in lesson 25. Use the English stimuli that follow not for direct translation but rather as suggestions that will elicit the Japanese patterns and conversational style that have been introduced.

   1a. You've just run into an acquaintance you haven't seen for a long while. Apologize for not having been in touch.

   b. Your acquaintance turns aside your apology by replying that you, too, have been busy.

   2a. Comment to a colleague that while that part-timer always says she understands, actually she doesn't.

   b. Your colleague agrees, and adds that if she would say that she didn't understand, he would explain, but . . . [she doesn't].

   3a. Check with your supervisor on whether there are things that must be done today.

   b. Your supervisor replies that there *are* things that must be done, but they don't have to be done today.

   4a. You are interviewing a prospective instructor. Find out where she was born and where she grew up.

   b. The prospective instructor replied that she was born in America, but grew up in Japan.

   5a. Congratulate an acquaintance on his graduation. Ask if his employment has been settled.

   b. Your acquaintance replies that instead of taking a position this year, he plans to enter graduate school in America in order to study physics.

   6a. Congratulate Mr. Tanaka on becoming a **butyoo**.

   b. Mr. Tanaka expresses his thanks but points out that one's responsibility as a **butyoo** is something of a concern.

   7a. Ask a colleague by when you must choose the textbook you will use next year.

   b. Your colleague replies that the decision has already been made. It will be the textbook you are using this year.

   8a. Tell the secretary to call Mr. Yamada or Mr. Nakamura.

   b. The secretary informs you that they are both away from their desks.

9a. You are discussing next year's schedules with a fellow student. Ask him which he will choose—science or mathematics—if it becomes necessary to choose one.

b. The student replies that he won't know until the time comes.

10a. Ask Mr. Sakamoto to tell Ms. Kato that she has to redo the entire schedule.

b. Mr. Sakamoto asks if someone else can't tell her. He points out that he is always asking her to do unreasonable things.

11a. Suggest to a fellow student that you discuss the schedule and, while doing that, have some coffee or something.

b. Your fellow student thinks it's a great idea and suggests tomorrow or the next day.

12a. Complain to a colleague that no matter what time you telephone Ms. Sato's house, nobody seems to be at home.

b. Your colleague says that he thinks she will be at home, provided you call before 8:30 A.M.

13a. Complain to a fellow student that in spite of studying Japanese for all of two years, you don't seem able to understand very well yet.

b. Your fellow student replies that you'll understand better, provided you listen to tapes more.

14a. Find out from a colleague who will be responsible if it becomes necessary to have the schedule redone.

b. Your colleague replies that since Ms. Yamada is the person in charge . . .

15a. Tell a fellow student that this year you have to study French or English.

b. Your fellow student replies that if he were you, he'd take English, because there are more people who know English.

16a. Tell a friend that you're going to take a cab to the station today because it's raining. Invite her to go along.

b. Your friend replies that as long as you're going by cab, she'll be glad to go with you.

17a. Tell an acquaintance that you have heard her children are in Europe.

b. Your acquaintance says that that is true, that all three are there. One is married and is living in Germany, and the other two are studying in graduate school in England.

18a. Tell a colleague that you have heard he's been working here all of ten years already.

b. Your colleague replies that that is true and adds that the more he does work like this, the more he likes it. If possible, he'd like to be here indefinitely.

19a. Ask your fellow student if Professor Ito doesn't say he wants her to attend the seminar on economics.

b. Your fellow student replies that he does say that, but she thinks that seminar is too difficult for her. She can't be persuaded that it will be of use.

20a. Tell a colleague that Professor Yamamoto wants him to translate this.

b. Your colleague agrees to do it. He points out that as long as the professor asked for it, he can't really not do it.

21a. Confirm with your colleague that the next gathering is next week.

b. Your colleague agrees. She adds that you can't really postpone it, but she wishes it were next month.

22a. Tell an acquaintance that you have heard that [the number of] people studying Japanese as a foreign language has increased.

b. Your acquaintance agrees, saying that they have increased a great deal. However, she points out that unfortunately many quit without continuing for even one year, so [the number of] people who are really proficient hasn't increased that much.

23a. Tell a friend that you bought *three* calculators recently, but all three of them are out of order already.

b. Your friend says that that shouldn't be and wonders why it is. He points out that in the case of his calculator, he has dropped it any number of times, but it is still OK.

24a. Ask a friend if he has seen the movie at the Japan Theater.

b. Your friend replies that she hasn't seen it yet, but she has heard that it's interesting. She adds that if only she has free time, she plans to go to see it.

25a. Ask an acquaintance if Mr. Matsuda is bringing his wife to the Yamamoto reception.

b. Your acquaintance replies that Mrs. Matsuda died all of five years ago.

26a. Tell a colleague that while you thought this work would probably take as long as two months, it actually didn't take even one month.

b. Your colleague thinks this is great and expresses the hope that the work that began yesterday is finished quickly, too.

27a. Tell a close friend that you've heard that Ms. Watanabe is living with her grandparents.

b. Your friend expresses amazement that they are still living.

28a. Tell a colleague that while you thought using a word processor would be difficult, when you tried using it, it was simple.

b. Your colleague indicates that she had the same experience.

29a. Ask a colleague where the next meeting is.

b. Your colleague replies that it hasn't been decided yet. He adds that if only they decide the day, they can choose the place.

30a. Comment to a friend (assuming agreement) that you've heard that Sugiura has bought an expensive sportscar.

b. Your friend says that it's true. He thinks that if only you look at it, you'll surely understand why Sugiura got to want to buy one, too.

31a. Tell a colleague that you've heard that Mr. Yamamori is still opposed to moving.

b. Your colleague replies that if only the person in charge will talk it over with him, he'll probably be persuaded.

32a. You're looking at some maps in a shop. Check with the salesperson on your assumption that the bigger they are, the more expensive.

b. The salesperson replies that both the big ones and the small ones are the same price.

33a. You are looking for an apartment. Tell a friend that if only it's quiet/large/convenient/near the station/cheap, the rest can be handled.

b. Your friend says he knows a good real estate broker, so he'll try asking him.

34a. Tell a colleague that you are looking for someone who knows (things about) Hokkaido.

b. Your colleague replies that if it's (things about) Hokkaido, you should ask Ms. Nakamura. She lived there for all of ten years, so she knows it well.

35a. Your friend has been complaining about his English studies. Suggest that he quit and go to another school next year.

b. Your friend explains that he can't really quit the school he is attending now because his teacher is a close friend of his father's.

36a. Your friend points out (assuming agreement) that the place where you are going to gather must be quiet.

b. You agree, with the reservation that it's not (for the reason) that it will be fine if only it's quiet.

Check-up

1. How does Japanese express two activities going on at the same time, performed by the same person(s)? Which activity is primary? (A-SP1)

2. When **-nagara** expresses contrast, what forms immediately precede it? What particle may follow it, when contrast is being emphasized? (A-SP1)

3. How is the provisional of verbals, adjectivals, and the copula formed? What are its contracted equivalents? What is the basic meaning of the provisional? How does this contrast with the conditional? (A-SP2)

4. Compare the pairs:

Otyá wa nomimàsu. *and* **Otyá nàra nomímàsu.**

Watási wa simasèñ. *and* **Watási nàra simásèñ.**   (A-SP2)

5. How is the provisional used in expressions of hope (i.e., 'I hope it doesn't rain,' 'I hope s/he's in,' etc.)? In contrary-to-fact wishes (i.e., I wish it hadn't rained,' 'I wish s/he were in,' etc.)?   (A-SP2)

6. Describe a pattern expressing necessity or requirement that includes the provisional. What are its contracted equivalents? Compare the use of this pattern with that of 'must' in English. What pattern serves as its exact opposite?   (A-SP3)

7. Compare the Japanese equivalents of 'Japanese and Chinese (language)' and 'Japanese or Chinese (language)'; of 'Are you studying Japanese or Chinese?' (yes or no) and 'Are you studying Japanese, or Chinese?' (which one).   (A-SP4)

8. What is the basic meaning of /quantity expression + **mo**/? Compare the meanings of /**ití-gatù mo**/ and /**ik̇-kàĝetu mo**/. Compare the meanings of **zyûu-doru dake**, **zyûu-doru sika**, and **zyûu-doru mo**. What are the corresponding patterns indicating approximate amounts?   (B-SP1)

9. Describe the Japanese pattern that corresponds to English 'the more X, the more Y.' What is the literal meaning of the Japanese pattern? Why is **hodo** classified as a nominal in this pattern?   (B-SP2)

10. What is the meaning of the pattern /quantity number + **to mo**/? When the quantity number refers to two items, what alternate is possible?   (B-SP3)

11. What is the basic meaning of **wâke**? Describe its use in the combination /——**wâke ni wa** ′**ikanai**/. What may precede **wâke**? What warning was given in reference to **ikanai**?   (B-SP4)

12. What is the basic meaning of the phrase-particle **sàe**? What does the combination /**X sàe** + **-(r)eba**/ express? Describe how one puts focus on a verbal /adjectival/nominal + **dà** within this pattern. What else may be focused within a sequence ending in a provisional?   (B-SP5)

Lesson 28

SECTION A

Core Conversations

1(N) Watási de oyaku ni tàtu koto ḡa
      âttara, oŝyàtte kudasai.

(J)   Ariḡatoo gozaimasu. Seŕkakù desu
      ḡa, utí no monò ni
      tetúdawasemàsu kara . .

2(N)a. Kyôo wa, watasi ḡa . .

(J)a. Tońde mo nài. Kyôo wa, watási ḡa
       osasoi-sità ñ desu kara . .

   b. Ie. Kyôo wa, watási ni
      harawàsete kudasai. Îtu mo îtu
      mo gotísoo ni nàtte bâkari desu
      kara . .

   b. Soñna koto, ki ní sinài de.

   c. Ie, kyôo wa, hoñtoo ni sonó
      tumori de kimàsita kara,
      dasâsete kudasai.

   c. Sôo desu ka⌐ Zyâa, okotoba ni
      amaete, gotísoo ni narimàsu. Dôo
      mo gotísoosama dèsita.

   d. Iie.

3(N)a. Kâtoo-sañ. Kinóo no kòoḡi dêta?

(J)a. Mînami-sañ no syakâiḡaku? Ñ.
       Dêta kedo . .

   b. Warûi kedo, sonó nòoto kôpii-
      sasete[1] kurénài ka nâa.

   b. Iya, bôku no zi, kitânàkute
      yomênai to omôu yo⌐

   c. Daízyòobu daízyòobu. Kâeru[2]
      made ni kanárazu kàesu kara . .

   c. Wakáránakute mo 'siranai yo⌐

   d. Ariḡatoo. . . . Kîree ni kâite âru
      zya nai ka.

   d. Sôo? Yomésòo?

   e. Ñ. Sûḡôku tasúkàtta. Ariḡatoo.

---

1. The video has **kôpii-site**, resulting in a different meaning.
2. The video has the derivative nominal **kaérì** 'a return.'

ENGLISH EQUIVALENTS

1(N) If I can be of any use to you, please say [the word].

(J) Thank you. It's very kind of you, but I'm going to have my people help me, so . . . (there's no need for you to take the trouble).

2(N)a. Today it's on me.

(J)a. Certainly not! Today (it's that) *I* did the inviting, so . . . (*I* will pay).

b. No. Today, please let *me* pay. I'm constantly being treated by you, so . . . (it's my turn).

b. Don't be concerned about that kind of thing.

c. No, today I honestly came with that intention, so let me pay.

c. Really? Well, then, I'll take you at your word and be your guest. It was delicious. [Thank you.]

d. Not at all.

3(N)a. (Mr.) Kato! Did you attend yesterday's lecture?

(J)a. Mr/s. Minami's sociology? Yeah. I attended, but . . . (why do you ask?)

b. I'm sorry to ask this, but I wonder if you'd let me copy those notes.

b. Oh, no, my writing is a mess; I don't think you can read it.

c. Don't worry about that! I'll positively return [the notes] by the time you go home, so . . . (please lend them to me).

c. It won't be my problem when you can't make them out.

d. (Receiving the notes) Thanks. . . . (Looking at the notes) C'mon, they're written neatly!

d. They are? You think you'll be able to read them?

e. Yeah. You saved my life. Thanks.

BREAKDOWNS
(AND SUPPLEMENTARY VOCABULARY)

1. **watási de oyaku ni tàtu koto**

things that will be of use to you because of me

   monô
   utí no monò
   tetúdawasèru /-ru; tetúdawàseta/ (SP1, 2)
   utí no monò ni tetúdawasèru

person(s) (in my in-group)
person(s) in my home or in-group
cause to help

have my people help

2. **sasou /-u; sasotta/**

invite (to do something)

osasoi-suru ↓   invite /humble-polite/

+ syôotai-suru   invite (to an event)

haráwasèru /-ru; haráwàseta/   cause to pay

(watasi ni) haráwàsete kudasai   please let me pay

gotísoo ni nàru   receive hospitality; be treated to food and/or drink

+ gotisoo-suru   entertain, treat a person to food and/or drink

gotísoo ni nàtte bâkari da   all it is is being treated

sonó tumori de kùru   come with that intention

dâsu   pay, put up the money; *also* put out

dasásèru /-ru; dasâseta/   cause to pay

(watasi ni) dasâsete kudasai   please let me pay

amaeru /-ru; amaeta/   presume upon; take advantage of someone's kindness or affection; behave like a (spoiled) child

okotoba ni amaeru   take advantage of your (kind) words

3.koóènkai   lecture meeting

+ meñsetu   job interview

nôoto   notes

kôpii-suru   copy

kôpii-saseru /-ru; kôpii-saseta/   cause to copy

(watasi ni) kôpii-sasete kurénài ka   won't you let me copy?

zi   written symbol; letter; character

+ roómàzi   romanization

+ kañzi   Chinese character

+ kana   Japanese written syllabary

+ hirâgànà   the hiragana syllabary

+ katâkàna   the katakana syllabary

+ keeĝo   Japanese polite language

kitánài /-katta/   is dirty; is squalid, obscene, sordid; is stingy

kâeru made (SP3)   until [someone] returns

kâeru made ni   by the time [someone] returns

kanarazu   surely, positively, without fail

kâesu /-u; kâesita/   give back, return [something]

siru   give heed to, be(come) concerned with; *also* find out

wakárànakute mo 'siranai   [I]'ll pay no attention even if [you] don't understand

+têenee /na/   polite; careful, conscientious, thorough
  kîree ni kâku   write neatly or beautifully
  kîree ni kâite âru zya nai ka (SP4)   isn't it written neatly? surely you agree that it's written neatly!

MISCELLANEOUS NOTES

1. In CC1, Smith offers his assistance to his sponsor, Mr. Suzuki, but he is assured politely that the task will be handled within Mr. Suzuki's in-group. Smith's utterance is polite (he uses **oyaku** and the honorific-polite verbal **ośsyàru** before **kudásài**). His use of **watakusi** is typical of careful-style. Mr. Suzuki's polite thank you and his use of distal-style before **kara** are also signals of polite, careful-style speech. The language reflects these speakers' relationship and the situation.

(N) **Watakusi de** links with **oyáku ni tàtu**, and the combined sequence describes **koto**: 'things (described as) "they are of use to you, if it's [*lit.* being] me or by means of me."'

(J) **Seḱkakù desu ga**, as usual, begins a polite refusal of an offer, with the implication that the speaker is reluctantly turning down something that was proposed with special kindness and consideration (see lesson 15A).

Monô meaning 'person(s)' refers to members of the in-group—family, work group, club, and so on—in talking politely to the out-group. It is a humble-polite term. Compare **utí no monò** with **otáku no katà**, an honorific-polite phrase. **Monô** is frequently used in business-related self-introductions: **Watasi, Oríeñtaru-bòoeki no monô de gozaimasu.** 'I'm an employee (*lit.* person) of Oriental Trade.'

2. In CC2, Deborah Miller, lunching with her colleague, Mr. Yamada, succeeds in finally persuading him to let her pay the check. This conversation represents a recurring problem that is particularly difficult for foreign professional women in Japan. Traditional Japanese culture does not dictate appropriate behavior for this kind of nontraditional situation. The foreign woman is torn, on the one hand, between trying to behave in a manner considered appropriate for a woman and to reflect her understanding that Japanese tend to be extremely solicitous to foreign guests; on the other hand, she wants to repay mounting obligations of the kind that are expected to be repaid within Japanese society. On this occasion, Ms. Miller decides to insist that she be permitted to take the check. She is dealing with a colleague who works closely with her, and she can assume that there will be many future occasions for mutual repayment.

Ms. Miller's speech is essentially careful-style, with a distal-style predicate occurring before sentence-final **kara**, and request patterns ending in polite **kudásài**. Her first utterance is a fragment that is a bit more casual in style, but polite in sense in implying what it is she wants to do (i.e., pay) without actually stating it. Mr. Yamada also uses careful-style, with distal-style predicates in final position and before **kara**. However, note his initial direct-style utterance, **toñde mo nài**, which reflects his startled reaction to Deborah Miller's first indication that she wants to take the check. His direct-style request J(b) reflects a friendly reassurance. Once he decides to give in to Ms. Miller, he immediately moves into ritual language J(c), in distal-style.

(J)c. Note the /◝/ intonation ending **Sôo desu ka**, indicating the polite reluctance Mr. Yamada feels in yielding to Ms. Miller's insistence that she pay the bill.

Amaeru is an important concept in Japanese culture. It covers not only behavior typical of a spoiled child, but also a kind of dependence on another (by adults as well as children) that calls for nurturing and care. The result is a special kind of interdependence. The student who exhibits dependence in interacting with a teacher can expect solicitous behavior on the part of the teacher in return. Similar relationships exist between employees and employers. Entire books have been written about **amaeru** and its ramifications, and examples of it are frequent in Japanese society. Note: /nominal of person + **ni amaeru**/ 'establish dependency on (a person).' In its extended meaning, **amaeru** can refer simply to taking advantage of something. Thus **okotoba ni amaeru** 'take advantage of your offer (*lit.* your words).'

3. In CC3, Smith is asking his fellow graduate student, Kato, to lend him notes that Kato took during yesterday's sociology lecture. Kato's objection, on the grounds that Smith will not be able to read his writing, is countered by Smith's assurances that Kato's notes have been written very neatly. If the relationship between the speakers were one that required politeness, deference, and indirectness, an objection of the kind raised by Kato would probably be interpreted as a clear indication that he did not want to lend his notes, and Smith would not press on.

The style used by these two male students, who are good friends, is very casual, with direct-style final predicates and a number of minor sentences and fragments. The sentence endings **kurénài ka nâa, siranai yo**, and **âru zya nai ka** are blunt-style and typical of masculine casual-style.

(N)a. Note that while **kôogi**, representing the goal of the verbal **dêta**, would regularly be followed by phrase-particle **ni** (or, less commonly, **e**), it occurs without a following particle in this casual-style conversation. This Japanese utterance might be compared to English 'Yesterday's lecture—'d'ja go?'

Meñsetu: Note **meñsetu o ukèru** 'have an interview,' 'be interviewed.'

(J)b. For the different systems of romanization in use in Japan today, see Part 1, introduction. The native writing system is a mixture of **kañzi** and **kana**: generally speaking, **kañzi**—the characters borrowed from Chinese—are used to represent nominals and the roots of verbals and adjectivals, i.e., individually they represent sound + meaning.

Hirâğànà (one type of **kana**) is used principally to represent particles, verbal and adjectival endings, and the copula in all its forms. It is also used for Japanese words or roots for which there are no **kañzi** or no **kañzi** in currently accepted usage.

Katâkànà (the second type of **kana**) is used mainly to represent words recently borrowed into Japanese from foreign languages, as well as onomatopoetic expressions. Both systems of **kana** are syllabaries (each symbol represents a mora without reference to meaning) developed through simplification of Chinese characters (**kañzi**). In the written representation of **Kâataa-sañ wa ití-zi-ğòro hôteru kara kûru to omóimàsu**, the seven mora of **Kâataa** and **hôteru** would be written with a total of seven **katâkana** symbols; **itî, zi, ku** (of **kûru**) and **omo** (of **omóimàsu**) with four **kañzi**; and the remaining twelve mora, with a total of twelve **hirâğànà** symbols.[3]

(N)c. When the speaker promises to do something 'positively,' 'without fail,' **kanarazu** is regularly used. In contrast, when something is 'surely,' 'undoubtedly' going to occur (not through the direct action of the speaker), that meaning is usually expressed by **kitto**.

Kâesu 'give back,' 'send back' is the transitive partner of **kâeru** 'go back,' 'return (home).' Both are operational consonant verbals. Note: **X o Y ni kâesu** 'return X to Y.'

(J)c. **Siru** occurred previously in its more general sense of 'find out,' 'get to know' (cf.

---

3. For a more complete description of the writing system, see *Japanese: The Written Language* or *Reading Japanese*.

sitte (i)ru, siranai). It is important to remember that, unlike **wakâru**, it is an operational verbal. In the context of this lesson, it expresses getting to know in the sense of deliberate, personally motivated paying attention, giving heed to, granting recognition to. Kato's direct-style warning to Smith is similar in tone to English 'Don't blame me if you don't understand!'

Structural Patterns

1. THE CAUSATIVE

We know by now that many grammatical signals in the Japanese language come through elements attached to verbal, adjectival, and copula roots, resulting in complex inflectional forms. A form like **kakênakattara** 'if [someone] can't write' includes the notions represented in English by 'can,' 'not,' and 'if,' as well as the root, 'write,' all in a single complex word.

Japanese has three word classes that take endings (i.e., are "inflected"): verbals, adjectivals, and the copula. Every inflected word consists of /root + ending/, but the root may be (a) simple (like **kak-**), or compound (like **kakinaos-**);[4] and (b) it may also be complex, in cases where the root (simple or compound) is expanded through the addition of one or more root-extenders—meaningful elements attached directly to the root, to which an ending is then added. (Examples are the negative root-extender **-(a)na-** and the potential root-extender **-(ra)re/e-**.)

We now add another verbal set that is formed in a way similar to the potentials. The citation form for this set of verbals again consists of /complex root (= root + root-extender) + vowel verbal ending **-ru**/. The root-extender is **-sase-** for vowel verbals and **-ase-** for consonant verbals. These new verbals will be called CAUSATIVES.

tabé-sasè-ru		**tabê-ru** 'eat'
ake-sase-ru		**ake-ru** 'open [it]'
nom-ásè-ru		**nôm-u** 'drink'
sir-ase-ru		**sir-u** 'get to know'
tukúr-asè-ru	is the causative of	**tukûr-u** 'make'
tukaw-ase-ru		**tuka-u < *tukaw-u** 'use'
hanás-asè-ru		**hanâs-u** 'talk'
s-ase-ru		**su-ru** 'do'
ko-sásè-ru		**kû-ru** 'come'

Causative verbals have their own inflectional and derivative forms that follow the regular patterning of vowel verbals. For example:

> Imperfective: **ake-sase-ru**
>
> Perfective: **ake-sase-ta**
>
> Stem: **ake-sase**
>
> Gerund: **ake-sase-te**
>
> Conditional: **aké-sase-tàra**
>
> Provisional: **aké-sase-rèba**
>
> Representative: **aké-sase-tàri**

---

4. The nonfinal member of a compound root is a verbal stem, an adjectival root, or a nominal.

Imperfective negative: **ake-sase-na-i** (and all inflected forms)

-**tai** form: **ake-sase-ta-i** (and all inflected forms)

One causative form was introduced earlier (lesson 12B) as a ritual expression: **omátase-itasimàsita** 'I have made you wait.' This is the perfective (**-ta**), distal (**-masi**), humble-polite (**o-** + verbal stem + **-suru** or **-itasu**) form of the causative **mat-ásè-ru**, derived from **mât-u**. The list below gives more information about the causative.

1. Special polite **-aru** verbals do not have causative equivalents, nor do regularly formed polite verbal patterns like **omáti ni nàru**.

2. All **w**-consonant verbals retain the /**w**/ in causative forms, as in **tukaw-ase-ru**, since the root-extender begins with an /**a**/, the one vowel before which /**w**/ occurs in modern Japanese. Additional examples are **kaw-ase-ru** (< **kau**), **iw-ase-ru** (< **iu**), **ukaĝaw-ase-ru** (< **ukaĝau**), and **kayow-ase-ru** (< **kayou**).

3. Causatives of accented verbals are also accented, and their accentuation follows the regular patterning of accented vowel verbals; the citation form is accented on the next-to-last mora.

4. Causatives are regularly derivatives of operational verbals and are themselves operational verbals.

5. In the speech of some Japanese, there are alternate forms for the causative that imply a citation form **-(s)as-u** in contrast to the standard, **-(s)ase-ru**. For example, one often hears causative gerunds ending in **-(s)asi-te** as alternates of forms in **-(s)ase-te**. The use and acceptance of such forms depends on the speaker. The standard forms described are always acceptable, but only some speakers accept the alternate forms.

Causatives, as the name implies, express the bringing about of an activity performed by someone else, i.e., having someone do something. The meaning ranges from 'making' people do things, perhaps even against their will, to 'letting' them perform activities in accordance with their desires. **Ikásemàsita** '[I] brought about a going by someone' can be equivalent to English '[I] *had* someone go,' '[I] *made* someone go,' or '[I] *let* someone go.' Here again, Japanese and English do not agree in the range of meaning that roughly equivalent forms in the two languages represent.

Whether the causative represents 'making' or 'letting' someone do something, the implication is that the 'causer' is in a position of power. Accordingly, the form is never under ordinary circumstances used in situations in which a superior is made or allowed to do something.

The 'let' range of the causative can be made more explicit by linking a causative gerund to a following verbal of giving or receiving. Compare **Nihóñĝo de hanasasemàsita.** 'I had *or* made *or* let someone speak in Japanese' with **Nihóñĝo de hanasàsete aĝémàsita.** 'I let someone speak (*lit.* I granted having someone speak) in Japanese.' But even this example with **aĝémàsita** may have a 'make' kind of meaning in a different context as it can also mean 'I had *or* made someone speak in Japanese for the benefit of someone else.'

Combinations of /causative gerund + verbal of giving or receiving/ occur commonly as permission patterns. Compare **Harâtte kudasai.** 'Please pay' and **Haráwàsete kudasai.** 'Please let me pay' (*lit.* 'please grant to me having me pay'); also **Yóñde itádakemasèñ ka↙** 'Can('t) I please have you read [this]?' and **Yomâsete itádakemasèñ ka↙** 'Can('t) I please have you let me read [this]?' (*lit.* 'Can't I have you grant to me having me read?') Note that this last example represents a very polite equivalent of **Yôñde (mo) îi desu ka↙** 'May I read [this]?' since it puts the permission-giver in a position of power as the potential "causer" of the activity.

The combination /causative gerund + **itádakimàsu**/ occurs commonly as a ritualistic, humble-polite statement of the speaker's intention to do something that reflects or assumes the permission (and power) of the person addressed, comparable to English 'I'm going to take the liberty of doing so-and-so' ('I'm going to accept [your] letting me do so-and-so'). This is the manner in which a building superintendent might inform tenants that he was going to turn off their water during repairs to the plumbing system. Examples:

> **Osáki ni kaeràsete itadakimasu.** 'I'm going to take the liberty of going home before you.'

> **Myôoniti 'otaku ni ukáğawasete itadakimàsu.** 'I'm going to take the liberty of coming to your place tomorrow.'

> **Kore o yomâsete itadakimàsu.** 'I'm going to take the liberty of reading this.'

This Japanese pattern occurs much more frequently than its closest English equivalents.

Not all operational verbals have commonly occurring causative derivatives. In some cases, the meaning of the basic verbal does not lend itself to the causative concept. In others a separate verbal usually fills the role of a causative. For example, the verbal **misêru** 'show' in many contexts assumes the role a causative of **mîru** might be expected to fill. The causative **misáseru** does, however, occur in expressing the concepts 'make someone look at' or 'let someone look at.'

2. ADDITIONAL CAUSATIVE PATTERNS

The person who brings about the activity of a causative (the "causer"), if expressed, is followed by phrase-particle **ğa** (or **wa** or **mo**). The person made or allowed to perform the underlying activity, again if expressed, is usually followed by phrase-particle **ni**. Other phrase-particles occur in accordance with what is required by the underlying verbal of the derived causative. Examples:

> **Dâre ğa 'ano gakusee ni koré o kakinaosàseta ñ desu ka⤸** 'Who is it who made that student rewrite this?'

> **Itóo-señsèe ni konó teğami o yomàsete itádakimàsita.** 'I received permission from Professor Ito to read this letter.' (*lit.* 'I received from Professor Ito the letting me read this letter.')

In many cases, phrase-particle **o** may also follow the person made or allowed to perform the underlying activity. Thus **kodomo o ikaseru** alternates with **kodomo ni ikaseru**, both meaning 'I have/make/let the child go.' Such alternation is common only when: (1) there is no resulting ambiguity (i.e., **tomodati o yobaseta** regularly means only 'I had [someone] call my friend,' NOT 'I had my friend call [someone]'); and (2) no other /nominal + **o**/ operand phrase links up with the given causative. When the person made or allowed to do something is followed by particle **o**, that personal nominal becomes the operand of the causative functioning as a unit. The alternate with **ni** implies stronger emphasis on the causation of a particular event, often implying that someone was made to perform an activity in place of the speaker. Compare:

> (a) **Kodómo o tabesàseta.** 'I fed the children' *and*

(b) **Kodomo ni 'yasai o takúsañ tabesàseta.** 'I made the children eat lots of vegetables.'[5]

(c) **Arúbàito o yamésasemàsita.** 'I fired the part-timer' *and*

(d) **Arúbàito ni koó iu siḡoto o yamesasemàsita.** 'I made the part-timer quit this kind of work.'

(e) **Kodomo o hâyâku gaḱkoo e ikasetàra?** 'How about having the children go to school early?' *and*

(f) **Watási ḡa sono mèsseezi o tôri ni ikénàkatta kara, kodómo ni ikasemàsita.** 'Since I couldn't go to pick up that message, I had my child go.'

In other words, in (a), (c), and (e), the causatives operate as units. But in (b), the causation operates on /**yasai o takúsañ tàbe**/ in reference to the children; in (d), it operates on /**koo iu siḡoto o yame**/ in reference to the part-timer; and in (f), the causation operates on /**ik**/ in reference to the child who will perform the action in place of the speaker. In (a), (c), and (e), particle **ni** is also possible, with a change of emphasis.

When the representative and the causative are brought together, either the representative(s) or the following **suru** may occur in the causative form.

> **têepu o kikásetàri, kyoókàsyo o yomâsetari suru** 'do things like having someone listen to tapes, (having someone) read the textbook . . .' *or*

> **têepu o kiítàri, kyoókàsyo o yôñdari saseru** 'have someone do things like listening to tapes, reading the textbook . . .'

In expressing ability to have someone do something, the /**kotô ḡa dekîru**/ pattern is used:

> **Aǹna gakusee nì wa koó iu beñkyoo o tuzukesaseru kotò wa dekînai.** 'I can't let a student like that continue this kind of study.'

Now compare pairs like:

(a) **Gakusee ni asíta hàyàku kitê moráttàra?** *and*

(b) **Gakusee ni asíta hàyàku kosâsetara?** 'How about having the students come early tomorrow?'

In both examples having the students come early is being proposed, but in (a), the event is being described in terms of benefit to the receiver, while in (b), the occurrence is viewed from the point of view of causation, with power over the students—either making or letting them come early.

Finally, consider these examples:

> **Tomáttè wa 'ikenai.** 'You mustn't stop.'

> **Tométè wa 'ikenai.** 'You mustn't stop [it—e.g., the car].'

> **Tomárasetè wa 'ikenai.** 'You mustn't make/let [them] stop.'

> **Tomésasetè wa 'ikenai.** 'You mustn't make/let [them] stop [it—e.g., the car].'

☠WARNING: When both members of a transitive-intransitive pair are operational, the corresponding causatives may be very similar in form although markedly different in meaning. Beware!

---

5. Note the difference in relationship between the noun and verb in English, too, depending on context. Compare 'he fed the children' and 'he fed the children to the lions'!

3. /IMPERFECTIVE VERBAL + màde (ni)/

We are already familiar with the phrase-particle **màde** following a nominal X which represents an extreme point: 'as far as X,' 'all the way to X,' 'until X.' Thus: **koóeñ màde 'iku** 'go as far as the park'; **kokó màde zyoózù ni nâru** 'become skillful to this point'; **sitî-zi made mâtu** 'wait until 7 o'clock.'

We have also learned that when **X màde** is followed by the phrase-particle **ni**, X represents the extreme time or point *by which* the predicate applies. That is, something happens within (= **ni**) the range that has X as its limit (= **X màde**).

As an extension of these patterns, we now add /imperfective verbal X + **màde**/ 'until X occurs' and /imperfective verbal X + **mâde ni**/ 'by (the time) X occurs.' Note that, as before **mâe**, *only the imperfective can occur before* **màde**. In the combination /predicate X **màde (ni)**/ followed by predicate Y (perfective or imperfective), predicate Y occurs during the time when X *is going to occur*, never when it already has been realized (cf. 19A-SP3 for a parallel discussion of **mâe**). Examples:

> **Beñ́ġòsi ġa kûru made matímàsita.** 'I waited until the lawyer came.' (i.e., I waited through the period when the lawyer was going to [but had not yet] come.)

> **Nakámura-sañ ġa kàette kûru made ni, kanárazu kore o zèñbu yôñde simaimasu.** 'By the time Mr/s. Nakamura comes back, I'll finish reading all of this without fail.'

The same kind of particle contrast occurs within **màde** sequences as within **kara** sequences. Compare

> **Tâkasi ġa sotúġyoo-suru màde Toókyoo ni imàsita.** 'Until Takashi graduated, I was in Tokyo' *and*

> **Tâkasi wa sotúġyoo-suru màde Toókyoo ni imàsita.** 'Takashi was in Tokyo until he graduated.'

4. Kîree ni kâite âru zya nai ka.

The combination **zya nâi ka** (and its distal-style equivalents) was introduced as a way of negating /nominal (+ particle) + **dà**/ predicates:

> **Sôo zya nâi ka✓** 'Isn't it like that?' (direct-style, blunt)

> **Yô-zi made zya arímasèñ ka✓** 'Doesn't it last until 4 o'clock?'

The corresponding verbal and adjectival negative patterns were very different. For example,

> **Ikímasèñ ka✓** 'Won't you go?' *and*

> **Omósìròku nâi desu ka✓** 'Isn't it interesting?'

We now introduce a new pattern, /predicate X + **zya nai (ka)**./, in which X is a direct-style verbal, adjectival, or nominal predicate, perfective or imperfective. Once again, the **dà** form of the copula is dropped. The /**zya nai (ka)**./ sequence, which may be replaced by its distal-style equivalent, is special in three respects: (1) it is unaccented; (2) it ends in period intonation; and (3) preceding it, a normally unaccented verbal or nominal predicate acquires an accent on its final mora and an adjectival on the mora preceding the final **-i**.

This conversational pattern, clearly signaled by accent and intonation, is very different in meaning from the negative patterns cited above. It indicates that the preceding predicate is assumed by the speaker to represent something that the person(s) addressed must surely agree with: 'Surely you agree that X is true!' 'Don't you agree that X is true?' Examples:

Dekîru zya nai ka. 'Surely you can do it!'

Yasásìi zya nai. 'Don't you agree it's easy?'

Muzúkasiku nài zya nai. 'Surely you agree it's not hard!'

Mońdaì zya nai desu ka. 'Don't you agree it's a problem?'

Nihóńzìń datta zya arimaseń ka. 'Surely you agree it was a Japanese!'

Drills

A 1. **Otêtudai-simasyoo ka**
'Shall I help you?'

Seḱkakù desu ḡa, utí no monò ni tetúdawasemàsu kara . .
'That's very kind of you, but I'll have one of my people (my in-group) help, so . . .' (please don't worry about it).

2. **Suútukèesu omóti-simasyòo ka**
'Shall I take (lit. hold) your suitcase?'

Seḱkakù desu ḡa, utí no monò ni motásemàsu kara . .
'That's very kind of you, but I'll have someone from the house (my in-group) take it, so . . .' (please don't worry about it).

3. **tâkusii oyóbi-simasyòo**; 4. **otya oíre-simasyòo**; 5. **teeburu no ue okátazuke-sima-syòo**; 6. **kosyoo onáosi-simasyòo**; 7. **deńwabàńgoo osírabe-simasyòo**; 8. **yoteehyoo otúkuri-simasyòo**

B 1. **Apâato saḡásitaku nài ń da kedo . .**
'(It's that) I don't want to look for an apartment, but . . .' (is there a good way out?)

Zyâa, dâre ka ni saḡásasetàra?
'Then how about having someone [else] look?'

2. **Nîmotu hakóbitaku nài ń da kedo . .**
'(It's that) I don't want to carry the luggage, but . . .' (is there a good way out?)

Zyâa, dâre ka ni hakóbasetàra?
'Then how about having someone [else] carry [it]?'

3. **teḡami kakítàku nâi**; 4. **deńwa kakétàku nâi**; 5. **syasiń torítàku nâi**; 6. **kinoo no siḡoto yarínaositàku nâi**

C 1. **Anâta ḡa erâńda ń desu ka**
'Is it that *you* chose it?'

Iie, zikáń ḡa nàkatta kara, kodómo ni erabàseta ń desu.
'No, since there wasn't time, (it's that) I had my child choose it.'

2. **Anâta ḡa sutétà ń desu ka**
'Is it that *you* threw them out?'

Iie, zikáń ḡa nàkatta kara, kodómo ni sutesasetà ń desu.
'No, since there wasn't time, (it's that) I had my child throw them out.'

3. **todôketa**; 4. **yoyaku-sita**; 5. **kaʔtè kita**; 6. **mukae ni itta**

D 1. **Dâre ka yamésaseta sòo desu nêe.**
'I hear you fired someone (*lit.* made someone quit)!'

Êe, sikáta ḡa nài kara, rêe no Nakámura o yamesasetà ñ desu kedo . .
'Yes, there's no way out, so (the fact is) I fired that Nakamura, but . . .' (maybe it was a mistake).

2. **Dâre ka 'Oosaka ni syuttyoo-saseta sòo desu nêe.**
'I hear you made someone go to Osaka on business!'

Êe, sikáta ḡa nài kara, rêe no Nakámura o syuttyoo-sasetà ñ desu kedo . .
'Yes, there's no way out, so I made that Nakamura go (on business), but . . .' (maybe it was a mistake).

3. **kaéràseta**; 4. **gakkai ni 'ikaseta**; 5. **kosâseta**; 6. **osókù made 'hatarakaseta**

E 1. **Kyôo wa, watási ḡa haràu kara . .**
'Today *I* will pay, so . . .' (don't you pay).

Iêie. Watási ni harawàsete kudasai.
'No, no. Please let *me* pay.'

2. **Kyôo wa, watási ḡa kaù kara . .**
'Today *I* will buy [them], so . . .' (don't you buy [them]).

Iêie. Watási ni kawasete kudasài.
'No, no. Please let *me* buy [them].'

3. **katázukèru**; 4. **nokôru**; 5. **motte iku**; 6. **syôotai-suru**; 7. **atúmèru**; 8. **tukûru**

• Repeat the preceding drill, replacing the **-(s)ase-te** forms in the responses with the corresponding **-sasi-te** forms.

F 1. **Atumari no basyo kaétà ñ desu ka⌇**
'(Is it that) you changed the place of the gathering?'

Êe, señpai ḡa kaésàsete kurétà ñ desu yo⌇
'Yes, (it's that) my senior colleague let me (change).'

2. **Hâyâku kâetta ñ desu ka⌇**
'(Is it that) you went home early?'

Êe, señpai ḡa kaéràsete kurétà ñ desu yo⌇
'Yes, (it's that) my senior colleague let me (go home).'

3. **sêminaa 'hazimeta**; 4. **kono dooḡu 'tukatta**; 5. **tañtòosya ni nâtta**; 6. **gakkai ni itta**; 7. **ano siḡoto hañtosì mo tuzuketa**

G 1. **Atumari no zikañ, kimesasete kurenai?**
'Would (*lit.* won't) you let me decide the time of the gathering?'

Motîroñ kimétè mo îi desu yo⌇
'Of course, it's all right [for you] to decide.'

2. **Kono deñwa, tukawasete kurenai?**
'Would (*lit.* won't) you let me use this telephone?'

Motîroñ tukáttè mo îi desu yo⌇
'Of course, it's all right [for you] to use it.'

3. **konó tèepu, kikasete**; 4. **atumari, nobásàsete**; 5. **moo iti-do yarínaosàsete**; 6. **tyokusetu setumee-sasete**; 7. **tyôtto 'sore, nomâsete**; 8. **kore, soko ni okasete**

• Repeat the preceding drill, replacing **kurenai?** in the stimuli with its humble-polite, distal-style equivalent, **itádakemasèñ ka⌇**

H 1. **Zizyoo, moó sùg̃u kawáru to**
   omoimàsu yo⌇
   'You know, I think the circumstances will change soon now.'

   Zyâa, kawáru màde matímàsu kara . .
   'Then I'll wait until they change, so . . .'
   (don't be concerned about me).

2. **Yamanaka-sañ, moó sùg̃u kâette**
   kuru to omóimàsu yo⌇
   'You know, I think Mr/s. Yamanaka will come back soon now.'

   Zyâa, kâette kuru made matímàsu kara . .
   'Then I'll wait until s/he comes back, so . . .'
   (don't be concerned about me).

3. yoteehyoo/dekîru; 4. tañtòosya/kimaru; 5. syakâig̃aku no kôog̃i/owaru

I 1. **Râig̃etu hik̃kosi-suru sòo desu nêe.**
   'I hear you are going to move next month, aren't you!'

   Êe. Dê mo, hik̃kosi-suru màde ni ʼkono
   sig̃oto sumásetài ñ desu g̃a . .
   'Yes, but (it's that) I'd like to finish this job by the time I move, but . . .' (I'm not certain I can).

2. **Râig̃etu yaméru sòo desu nêe.**
   'I hear you are going to quit next month, aren't you!'

   Êe. Dê mo, yaméru màde ni ʼkono sig̃oto
   sumásetài ñ desu g̃a . .
   'Yes, but (it's that) I'd like to finish this job by the time I quit, but . . .' (I'm not certain I can).

3. **butyóo ni nàru**; 4. **Oosaka e iku**; 5. **atárasìi sig̃oto o ʼhazimeru**; 6. **końpyùutaa o**
   ʼkaeru; 7. **gak̃kai ni dèru**; 8. **yasúmì o tôru**

J 1. **Kono teg̃ami, kitânàkute**
   sumímasèñ.
   'I'm sorry that this letter is a mess.'

   Iya, kîree zya arimaseñ ka.
   'No, c'mon! It's neat!'

2. **Koko, hûbeñ de sumímasèñ.**
   'I'm sorry that this place is inconvenient.'

   Iya, bêñri zya arimaseñ ka.
   'No, c'mon! It's convenient!'

3. **eeg̃o/hetâ de**; 4. **konó kudàmono/sûp̃pàkute**; 5. **nîmotu/omôkute**; 6. **zî/yomínìkù-**
   kute; 7. **konó nikù/katâkute**; 8. **uti/sêmâkute**; 9. **kono kañzi/muzúkasìkute**

K 1. **Atúmarì o nobásànakattara, ma ní**
   awànai to omôu.
   'If we don't postpone the gathering, I don't think we'll make it in time.'

   Nobâsite mo, ma ní awànai zya nai.
   'Even if we postpone it, don't you agree we won't make it in time?'

2. **Końpyùutaa o tukáwanàkattara, ma**
   ní awànai to omôu.
   'If we don't use the computer, I don't think we'll make it in time.'

   Tukáttè mo, ma ní awànai zya nai.
   'Even if we use it, don't you agree we won't make it in time?'

3. **isóg̃ànakattara**; 4. **hitó o huyasànakattara**; 5. **uñteñ g̃a hàyàku nâkattara**; 6. **gô-zi**
   made ni owáranàkattara; 7. **tok̃kyuu zya nàkattara**; 8. **âsa zya nâkattara**

L 1. **Kinoo no kooeñ, kiki ni itta?**
   'Did you go to hear yesterday's

   Êe, arîg̃atoo. Okotoba ni amaete, kikí ni
   ikimàsita.

lecture?'

'Yes, thanks. I took advantage of your kind offer (*lit.* words) and went to hear it.'

2. **Gokâzoku ni 'reñraku-sita?**
'Did you get in touch with your family?'

Êe, arîĝatoo. Okotoba ni amaete, reñraku-simàsita.
'Yes, thanks. I took advantage of your kind offer (*lit.* words) and got in touch.'

3. **uti no kuruma, tukatta**; 4. **bîiru mo, tyuumoñ-sita**; 5. **siñrìĝaku no kyoókàsyo, karita**; 6. **tomodati, okuri ni itta**

Application Exercises

A1. Using the new patterns that include the causative, ask permission of your instructor to do certain things. Have the instructor agree to the request or refuse politely, in each case giving a reason. Examples of requests: to let you (a) use this computer; (b) listen to these new tapes; (c) speak in English; (d) write in romanization; (e) read the letter that came from Ms. Nakamura this morning; (f) go home early; (g) take the day off tomorrow; (h) attend Professor Watanabe's lecture tomorrow.

2. Practice asking questions involving duration (**îtu made**) and answering in terms of occurrences (verbal + **màde**). For example, in reply to a question as to how long (i.e., until when) you studied French, you might reply that you studied it until you entered college.

3. Using CC3 as a model, practice situations in which speaker A makes a request *of a close friend B,* speaker B raises an objection, and speaker A offers a solution to the objection. For example: ask permission to (a) use B's dictionary this evening; (b) read the letter from Yamada; (c) listen to this tape; (d) copy B's psychology notes; (e) pay in dollars.

B. Core Conversations: Substitution

Practice the Core Conversations, making substitutions that do not alter the basic framework of the conversations. Practice asking and answering questions about content.

SECTION B

Core Conversations

1(N) |**Anoo**| **Sumímasèñ. Señsèe no gohôñ, tyôtto haísyaku-sasete itadakenài desyoo ka.**

(J) **Îi desu to mo. Dôozo dôozo. Siñĝàkki ĝa hazímaru màde tukáimasèñ kara, dôozo goyúkkùri.**

2(J)a. **Mîraa-sañ. Sûmu tokórò ĝa mitúkaru màde, zutto hôteru desu ka⌐**

(N)a. **Iie. Îma Oóhasi-sañ no tokorò ni tomárasete moratte (i)rù ñ desu.**

b. **Nî-sañ-niti utí no hòo e
irássyaimasèñ ka**✓ **Utí no monò
ğa anâta ni aítağàtte (i)ru ñ desu
yo.**

b. **Arîğatoo gozaimasu.**[6] **Dê mo,
Oohasi-sañ ğa ki ó wàrùku
nasárànai desyoo ka.**

c. **Âa, daízyòobu desu yo. Oóhasi-
sañ nì wa, tyañto hanâsite
okímàsu kara, konó bòku ni
makâsete kudasai.**

c. **Dê mo, gomêewaku zya arímasèñ
ka**✓

d. **Iie, títtò mo.**

3(J)a. **Noo ya kabuki o môsi goráñ ni
naritàkereba, îtu de mo goáñnai-
itasimàsu kedo . .**

(N)a. **Gosîñsetu ni dôo mo. Matá ìtu ka
onéğai-surù ka mo siremaseñ.**

b. **Tyoodo doyôobi no kiṕpu ğa àru
ñ desu ğa, ikâğa desu ka**✓

b. **Seḱkakù desu ğa; doyôobi wa,
zaṅneñ-nàğara seṅyaku ğa
arimàsu no de . .**

ENGLISH EQUIVALENTS

1(N)   Uh, excuse me. Would I be able
to (have you let me) borrow a
book of yours for a little while?

(J)   Of course. Please go ahead. I won't
use [that book] until the new term
begins, so take your time.

2(J)a. Ms. Miller. Will you be [in] a hotel
all the time until you find a place
to live?

(N)a. No. (The situation is that) I'm now
staying (*lit.* accepting [someone's]
letting me stay) at Mr/s. Ohashi's
place.

b. Won't you come to my place for
two or three days? (It's that) my
family would like to meet you.

b. Thank you, but wouldn't Mr/s.
Ohashi be offended?

c. Oh, it'll be all right. I'll speak to
Mr/s. Ohashi in advance
(properly) so leave it up to me.

c. But isn't that a nuisance for you?

d. No, not a bit.

6. The accompanying video has **ğa** following **arîğatoo gozaimasu**.

3(J)a. If you would like to see no(h) and kabuki and the like, I'll take you any time, but . . . (are you interested?)

b. The fact is I just [happen to] have tickets for Saturday. How about it?

(N)a. Thanks for being so kind. I may ask you [to do that] some time (again).

b. Oh, thank you, but Saturday, unfortunately, (being that) I have a previous engagement . . .

BREAKDOWNS
(AND SUPPLEMENTARY VOCABULARY)

1. **gohôñ**	/polite equivalent of **hôñ**/
haisyaku-suru↓ (SP1)	borrow /humble-polite/
haisyaku-sasete↓ **itadaku**↓	accept [your] letting me borrow; take the liberty of borrowing /humble-polite/
îi to mo (SP2)	of course [it's] good
+**gakki**	term (of the school year)
siñgàkki	new term
+**koñgàkki**	this term
+**señgàkki**	last term
+**raígàkki**	next term
+**ití-gàkki**	one term
2. **Oohasi**	(family name)
tomarasete morau	have [someone] let me stay
aítagàru /-u; aítagàtta/ (SP3)	want to meet/see; be eager or anxious to meet/see
ki ó wàrùku suru	be(come) displeased, offended; have one's feelings hurt
Oohasi-sañ ga ki ó wàrùku suru/ nasâru↑	Mr/s. Ohashi will become offended; hurt Mr/s. Ohashi's feelings
konó bòku	this me right here
makásèru /-ru; makâseta/	trust [someone] with [a matter]; leave [a matter] to [someone]
bôku ni makásèru	leave [a matter] to me
(go)mêewaku	nuisance
títtò mo /+ negative/	not even a little
3. **noo**	no(h) (traditional Japanese theater)
kabuki	kabuki (traditional Japanese theater)
goráñ ni nàru↑	look at; see /honorific-polite/
haikeñ-suru↓	look at; see /humble-polite/

añnài-suru	guide, show the way
goaññai-suru ↓	guide, show the way /humble-polite/
(go)sîñsetu /na/	kind, considerate
zañneñ-nàg̃ara	while regrettable
señyaku	previous appointment

Supplementary Theater Vocabulary

mañzài	cross-talk comedy
bûñraku	traditional Japanese puppet theater
ôñgaku	music
oñg̃àk(ù)kai	concert
rakug̃o	traditional Japanese comedy monologue

MISCELLANEOUS NOTES

1. In CC1, a 'permission dialogue,' Mr. Carter requests permission from Professor Ono to borrow a book, and Professor Ono agrees to the request. Mr. Carter's language is extremely careful and polite: note the initial hesitation noise (**anoo**), polite **gohôñ**, inclusion of **tyôtto**, and the very polite request form that includes two humble-polite verbals. Professor Ono's willingness to lend his book to Mr. Carter is enthusiastic, with three occurrences of **dôozo** and an invitation not to hurry to return it (**goyúkkùri**). Professor Ono uses plain careful-style, with distal-style predicates.

The Japanese school year begins on April first, and its academic calendar causes considerable difficulty for most foreign students matriculating in Japan and for Japanese students entering schools in foreign countries. Japanese colleges use a semester system, but elementary and high schools are on trimester.

2. In CC2, an "invitation dialogue," Mr. Yamada is trying to arrange for Ms. Miller to spend a few days at his home with his family. She is currently staying with someone else from the office while she looks for permanent housing. Ms. Miller's concern that she may hurt the feelings of her current benefactors is turned aside by Mr. Yamada, who assures her he will take care of the matter.

As usual, Mr. Yamada and Ms. Miller converse in careful-style, with distal-style final predicates, but Mr. Yamada's use of **anâta** and **bôku** suggests some relaxation. In extending his invitation, however, Mr. Yamada uses an honorific-polite form (**irássyaimasèñ ka**). Ms. Miller's use of a similar level in referring to Mr/s. Ohashi (**nasárànai desyoo**) suggests either that she and Mr. Yamada are outranked by him/her, or that Ms. Miller categorizes both of them as out-group in relation to herself.

(N)a. Note the difference in connotation between **tomatte (i)ru** and **tomarasete moratte (i)ru**. The first expression means simply 'I am staying,' while the second indicates that 'I am being allowed to stay, for my benefit.'

(J)c. **Kono** preceding the self-referent **bôku** emphasizes the closeness of the person to the immediate situation.

Makásèru looks as if it might be a derivative causative verbal, but actually it is the basic form of a transitive, operational verbal. Note: **X o Y ni makásèru** 'entrust X to (person) Y.' When X refers to the doing of a particular action, the nominal **no** is preceded by an appropriate verbal modifier, as in **Señsèe to soódañ-surù no o 'watasi ni makâsete ku-**

dasai. 'Leave the consulting with the doctor to me.' Even though **makâsete kudasai** alone would regularly assume the meaning 'leave it *to me,*' **konó bòku ni** is included to make the shift from Mr/s. Ohashi, who was mentioned earlier in the sentence, clear, and to emphasize the fact that Mr. Yamada will handle the matter himself.

(N)c. **Meewaku** (polite **gomêewaku**) refers to 'trouble' in the sense of 'nuisance,' 'annoyance.' It appears frequently in **mêewaku-suru** 'be(come) troubled, annoyed'; **mêewaku o kakêru** 'cause trouble,' 'annoy (someone)'; **mêewaku ni nâru** 'become a nuisance.'

(J)d. **Tiťtò** is an alternate of **tyôtto** that occurs only before particle **mo.**

3. In CC3, a "refusal-of-offer dialogue," Smith's landlady offers to take him to see no(h) and kabuki any time at all at his convenience. Smith turns down her offer of tickets for Saturday because of a previous engagement. We don't know whether Smith actually does have an engagement or simply has no interest in going to the Saturday performance, or *any* performance of traditional theater, or *any* performance with his landlady. His refusal is polite, and the reason he cites is a plausible one, thereby avoiding any unpleasantness.

The conversation is careful, with distal-style predicates in sentence-final position and before particles **kedo** and **ḡa,** and before **no de.** The landlady's speech is markedly polite (**goráñ ni naritàkereba; goáññai-itasimàsu; ikâḡa**). Smith's only polite-style verbal form is **onegai-suru,** but he uses a number of ritual expressions that are definitely considered polite: **gosîñsetu ni dôo mo; seḱkakù desu ḡa; zaññeñ-nàḡara.**

No(h), a very old form of Japanese traditional theater in which all the players are male, is unusual in that masks are worn by the players throughout a performance. In kabuki, a newer form of theater than no(h), the players continue the all-male tradition but do not wear masks.

(J)a. **Aññài-suru:** The area through which guidance takes place is followed by particle **o** (or **wa** or **mo**), as is the person who is guided; however, the verbal does not link up with two **o**-phrases at once. Examples: **mití o aññài-suru** 'guide along the road'; **Toókyoo o aññài-suru** 'show around Tokyo'; **okyáku o aññài-suru** 'show a guest around'; **tomodati o annai-site 'Tookyoo o mawaru** 'go around Tokyo, acting as a guide for a friend,' i.e., 'show a friend around Tokyo.' Compare /place + **ni** + **aññài-suru**/ 'lead to X.' Note also: **aññaizyò** 'information desk' (*lit.* place); **aññàiniñ** 'guide,' 'usher.'

(N)a. **Sîñsetu: sîñsetu ni suru** 'act kindly'; **gosîñsetu ni amaete** 'taking advantage of your kindness.'

Mata refers here to a situation in which this matter is discussed again.

Structural Patterns

1. POLITE VERBAL-NOMINALS

We have already learned that in the regularly formed honorific-polite equivalent of verbals, the simple verbal is replaced by /**o-** + stem + **ni nâru**/ (10A-SP3) or /**o** + stem + **dà**/ (23A-SP1). Examples: **oáke ni nàru** from **akeru; oyóbi ni nàru** from **yobu; otúkai ni nàru** from **tukau; odékake dà** from **dekakeru; oyóbi dà** from **yobu.** In the humble-polite equivalent, however, the simple verbal is replaced by /**o-** + stem + **-suru** (or **-itasu**)/ (7B-SP3). Examples: **oake-suru** from **akeru; oyobi-suru** from **yobu; otukai-suru** from **tukau.** In each case, the /**o-** + stem/ is A POLITE VERBAL-NOMINAL. It expresses politeness either to the operator or primary affect (honorific-polite patterns) or to the target of the activity (humble-polite patterns). We have also encountered this form compounded with **kudásài** in honorific-polite requests (one example is **omáti-kudasài** from **mâtu**).

As the unpredictable replacement for /o- + stem/ of the verbals **iku**, **kuru**, and **iru**, we learned the special polite verbal-nominal **oide** (10A-SP3).[7] This word occurs in honorific-polite patterns (**oíde ni nàru**, **oíde dà**, **oíde-kudasài**), but not in humble-polite ones. In contrast, **tyoodai** occurs compounded with **-suru** as a humble-polite equivalent of **morau**, but it is never found in honorific-polite patterns. The honorific-polite equivalent of **morau** is a regular form, **omórai ni nàru**.

Now we add three more unpredictable polite verbal-nominals that occur only in honorific-polite or only in humble-polite patterns. **Gorañ** is an honorific-polite verbal-nominal that replaces an expected /o + mi/ (from **mîru** 'look at') in honorific-polite patterns. **Goráñ ni narimàsita ka** 'Did you see it?' **Goráñ-kudasài.** 'Please look at it.'

Haisyaku and **haikeñ** are humble-polite verbal-nominals: **haisyaku-suru** (or **-itasu**) is the humble-polite equivalent of **kariru** 'borrow' (for which the regular, slightly less formal equivalent **okari-suru/-itasu** also occurs). **Haikeñ-suru/-itasu** is the humble-polite of **mírû** 'look at' (for which a regularly formed humble-polite does NOT occur).

Polite verbal-nominals may occur at the end of sentences as casual (but polite) request forms. The ones that are humble-polite words continue to reflect their reference to the speaker. Thus:

Tyôtto 'omati. 'Wait a minute.'

Kotira e oide. 'Come here.'

Kore gorañ. 'Look at this.'

Koré haikeñ. 'Let me look at this.'

Eñpitu haisyaku. 'Let me borrow a pencil.'

Mizu tyoodai. 'Let me have some water.'

Polite verbal-nominals—both those that are regularly formed and those unpredictable ones that may enter into honorific-polite patterns—occur in another casual but polite request pattern by combining with **-nasài**:

Onómi-nasài. 'Drink [it].'

Kotíra e oide-nasài. 'Come over here.'

Tyôtto goráñ-nasài. 'Take a look.'

The ritual expression **Oyásumi-nasài** is another example of this pattern. Equally casual, but less polite, are regularly formed imperatives consisting of /verbal stem + **-nasài**/, without the polite **o-** prefix. (Examples: **nomí-nasài**, **tabé-nasài**, **yamé-nasài**). Such forms are less polite and more familiar than /gerund + **kudasai**/.

2. SENTENCE-FINAL PARTICLE SEQUENCE **to mo**

The particle sequence **to mo** following predicates—perfective or imperfective, direct or distal—occurs at the end of responses that confirm what was asked. The meaning is strong emphasis: 'certainly,' 'of course,' 'definitely.' Before **to mo**, **dà** (the copula) is NOT dropped. Examples:

Dekímàsu ka . . . **Dekímàsu to mo.** 'Is it possible?' . . . 'Of course it's possible.'

Konó hòñ wa daré ni mo kasanài desyoo? . . . **Kasímasèñ to mo.** 'You don't lend this book to anyone—right?' . . . 'Of course I don't (lend).'

---

7. For the verbal **iku**, there is a regularly formed polite verbal-nominal **oiki** in addition to the irregular **oide**.

Tukatte îi? . . . Îi to mo. 'Is it all right to use it?' . . . 'Certainly it's all right.'

Seńsèe no zêmi ni demâsita ka⁄ . . . Demâsita to mo. 'Did you attend the professor's lecture?' . . . 'Of course I attended.'

Kaĝî kakênakute mo daízyòobu? . . . Daízyòobu da to mo. 'Will it be safe even if I don't lock it?' . . . 'Of course it will be safe.'

☠WARNING: Generally speaking, definiteness is avoided in Japanese except where the context makes it nonthreatening (as in CC1, above). More common are occurrences of **kitto**, **kanarazu**, and **hotôńdo**, especially in combination with **to omôu** and **daròo**. Among young people, sentence-particle **yo** is more common than **to mo**.

3. THE VERBAL SUFFIX **-ĝàru**

The suffix **-ĝàru** is attached to adjectival roots and **na**-nominals to form verbals that indicate the showing of feelings and emotions expressed by the initial element (the part of the word that precedes **-ĝàru**), usually by third person(s). In other words, adjectivals and **na**-nominals that occur with **-ĝàru** are those like **hazúkasìi**, **urésìi**, **kowâi**, **mêewaku**, and so on. They have emotive connotations and unless qualified usually refer to the speaker or the person addressed. Whereas the basic adjectivals and nominals are affective, the derivative verbals in **-ĝàru** are regularly operational. Accent is on the **-ĝa-** mora. Examples:

zisíń o kowaĝàru 'show fear of earthquakes'

huyû o samúĝàru 'find the winter cold (and show that reaction)'

syoókai o meewakuĝàru '(show that) [one] finds introductions a nuisance.'

In many cases, the 'showing' notion simply means that the speaker has been made aware of the fact that a third person has certain feelings, and normal English equivalents often do not reflect the **-ĝàru** suffix at all. Culturally we are much less reluctant than the Japanese to describe the feelings of others in definite statements ('she is happy,' 'he is sad,' etc.).

-Ĝàru occurs commonly in combination with **-tai** forms. Whereas the **-tai** form, like emotive adjectivals and nominals in general, regularly refers to the speaker, the derivative **-taĝàru** verbals almost never do. Insofar as **-ĝàru** verbals *are* used in reference to the speaker, they usually refer to past situations, often (a) conditions extending over a period of time or (b) conditions contrary to which something occurred, particularly when looked at from the perspective of another person (see the last two examples below). Predictably, **-ĝàru** verbals frequently appear in the **-te (i)ru** pattern, indicating a state existing over time.

For some speakers, **-taĝàru** verbals are accented only if the underlying **-tai** form is accented. For others, they are always accented verbals. Remember that an accented **-ĝàru** verbal is always accented on the **-ĝa-** mora.

We have already encountered the particle alternation reflected by pairs like: **zîsyo ĝa kaitai** 'I want to buy / a dictionary' and **zîsyo o kaitai** 'I want / to buy a dictionary' (see 7B-SP4). The **-taĝàru** verbals, even though they incorporate **-tai**, are operational and never occur in double-**ĝa** patterns.

These verbals often occur in the causative, describing a situation in which one causes someone to have certain feelings. It is also possible to derive a **-taĝàru** verbal from the **-tai** form of a causative. Thus: **kowáĝaraseru** 'make [someone] be afraid'; **yorókobasetaĝàru** '[someone] wants to make [someone else] enjoy.' Examples:

Koo iu waapuro wa, mińnà ga hosígaru daroo to omóimàsu. 'I think that everyone will probably want this kind of word processor.'

Otóotò wa, iyágari-nàgara, kêezai no beñkyoo o tuzúkeru tte itte (i)màsu. 'My (younger) brother has been saying he's going to continue studying economics, while at the same time (showing) he dislikes it.'

Nihoñgo o beñkyoo-site (i)ru gakusee wa, miñna Nihôñ e ikítagàtte (i)masu nêe. 'All the students studying Japanese want to go to Japan, don't they!'

Zibuñ no kodomo o Toódai ni hairasetagàru oyâ wa, oôi desu nêe. 'There are lots of parents who want to have their children enter Tokyo University, aren't there!'

Kodómo no tokì wa, amái mono bàkari tabétagàtta soo desu. 'When I was a child, they say (I showed the feeling that) I wanted to eat nothing but sweet things.'

Watasi zuíto màe kara arúbàito o yamétagàtte (i)ta no ni, titioya wa yamésasete kurenàkatta. 'Even though I had (been showing that I) wanted to quit part-time work for a long time, my father wouldn't let me (quit).'

Drills

A 1. **Nôoto, kôpii = sitâ[8] no?**
'(Is it that) you copied the notes?'

Ñ, Hayasi-sañ ni kôpii-sasete moráttà ñ da yo.
'Yeah, (it's that) I had Mr/s. Hayashi let me copy them.'

2. **Keésàñki, tukáttà no?**
'(Is it that) you used a calculator?'

Ñ, Hayasi-sañ ni tukáwasete morattà ñ da yo.
'Yeah, (it's that) I had Mr/s. Hayashi let me use one.'

3. **kyoókàsyo/yôñda**; 4. **anó kòogi no têepu/kiita**; 5. **syasiñ/tôtta**; 6. **îñtabyuu/yatta**; 7. **nâni ka oísii monò/tâbeta**

B 1. **Dôozo, atíra no hòo ni oháiri-kudasài.**
'Please go in over there.'

Arîgatoo gozaimasu. Haíràsete itadakimasu.
'Thank you. I will (accept your letting me go in).'

2. **Dôozo, kotíra ni oagari-kudasài.**
'Please come in (*lit.* up) this way.'

Arîgatoo gozaimasu. Agárasete itadakimàsu.
'Thank you. I will (accept your letting me come in).'

3. **kotira de omati-**; 4. **ohanasi otuzuke-**; 5. **kono deñwa otukai-**; 6. **osyokuzi ohazime-**; 7. **osúki na monò oerabi-**

---

8. Occasionally the derived **suru**-form of compounds consisting of /accented nominal + **suru**/ has an accent of its own or becomes part of a following accent phrase. In such cases, the /nominal + **suru**/ is connected by /=/ to point up the special accentuation.

C 1. **Dâre ğa tukáttà ñ desu ka⌐**
    'Who is it that used it?'

    Daré mo tukawanai yòo desita kara, watási ğa tukawasete moraimàsita.
    'It seemed as if no one was going to use it, so I took the liberty (of using).'

  2. **Dâre ğa syôotai = sitâ ñ desu ka⌐**
    'Who is it that invited them?'

    Daré mo syòotai-sinái yòo desita kara, watási ğa syòotai-sasete moráimàsita.
    'It seemed as if no one was going to invite them, so I took the liberty (of inviting).'

  3. **kimeta**; 4. **aṅnài-sita**; 5. **erânda**; 6. **kita** ('wore'); 7. **notta**; 8. **tukûtta**; 9. **yarínaòsita**

D 1. **Sakámoto-kyoozyu no kòoği, kikítai no?**[9]
    '(Is it that) you'd like to listen to Professor Sakamoto's lecture?'

    Êe, kikásete itadakenài desyoo ka.
    'Yes, could(n't) I be allowed to listen?'

  2. **Suğîura-sañ ni aítài no?**
    '(Is it that) you'd like to meet Mr/s. Sugiura?'

    Êe, awâsete itádakenài desyoo ka.
    'Yes, could(n't) I be allowed to meet her/ him?'

  3. **konó zèmi ni haíritài**; 4. **hâyâku kaéritài**; 5. **konó koñpyùutaa ğa tukaitai**

E 1. **Kono zikokuhyoo tukatta?**
    'Did you use this timetable?'

    Êe, ariĝatoo gozaimasu. Seḱkaku soo itte kudasàtta no de, tukáwasete itadakimàsita.
    'Yes, thank you. Since you kindly told me to (*lit.* took the trouble to say so), I took the liberty (of using).'

  2. **Raíğàkki no 'yoteehyoo 'kôpii-sita?**
    'Did you copy the schedule for next term?'

    Êe, ariĝatoo gozaimasu. Seḱkaku soo itte kudasàtta no de, kôpii-sasete itádakimàsita.
    'Yes, thank you. Since you kindly told me to (*lit.* took the trouble to say so), I took the liberty (of copying).'

  3. **Saítoo-kyoozyu**[10] **ni ome ni kakàtta**; 4. **ohûro ni hâitta**; 5. **syasiñ tôtta**; 6. **sukî na no erâñda**; 7. **kinoo hâyâku kâetta**

F 1. **Roómàzi yomêru?**
    'Can you read romanization?'

    Yomémàsu to mo. Kokó no hitò wa, miṅna yomèru hazu desu yo⌐
    'Of course I can (read). I expect that the people here are all able to read it.'

  2. **Kabuki suki?**
    'Do you like kabuki?

    Sukî desu to mo. Kokó no hitò wa, miṅna sukì na hazu desu yo⌐

---

9. The **-tai** questions of the stimuli indicate interest in what the addressees' actual wishes are. They are NOT invitations, for which negative questions are the regular Japanese pattern.
10. **Saitoo** is a family name.

'Of course I do (like). I expect that the people here all like it.'

3. **asuko no zizyoo ni kuwásìi;** 4. **môo noó o mìta;** 5. **yôku 'nattoku-saseta;** 6. **gokâzoku natúkasìi;** 7. **sikêñ siñpai dàtta;** 8. **kôñpa tanôsìkatta**

G 1. **Zêhi konó atumari no tañtòosya ni aítài ñ desu kedo . .**
'(It's that) I would really like to meet the person in charge of this gathering, but . . .' (do you think it's possible?)

Kotira no katyoo mo aítagàtte (i)ru soo desu yo⤸
'I hear that our section chief is also anxious to meet her/him.'

2. **Narubeku 'koo iu siǧoto o kâre ni yarásetài ñ desu kedo . .**
'(It's that) I would like to have him do this kind of work as much as possible, but . . .' (do you think it's possible?)

Kotira no katyoo mo yarásetagàtte (i)ru soo desu yo⤸
'I hear that our section chief is also anxious to have him do it.'

3. **dekîreba, Hasímoto-señpai ni sekiniñ o torasetài;** 4. **tyokusetu zizyoo o setumee-site moraitai;** 5. **nâñ to ka Sakámoto-sañ to sitàsìku narítài;** 6. **môo rêe no meñsetu no kotò wa 'wasuretai**

H 1. **Señpai ǧa nakunatte, sabísìi desu nêe.**
'It's sad that our senior colleague passed away, isn't it!'

Sabísiǧàtte (i)ru hito wa oôi-mitai da kedo, sikáta ǧa nài wa yo.[11]
'There seem to be many people who (show that they) are feeling sad, but there's nothing we can do.'

2. **Ano rakúǧo no tèepu ǧa hosîi desu nêe.**
'How I want that **rakugo** tape!'

Hosíǧàtte (i)ru hito wa oôi-mitai da kedo, sikáta ǧa nài wa yo.[11]
'There seem to be many people who (show that they) want it, but there's nothing we can do.'

3. **asoko no kañriniñ ǧa urúsài desu;** 2. **katyóo ni àu no wa hazúkasìi desu;** 5. **boósi o kabùru no wa iyâ desu;** 6. **ano sîñsetu na hisyô ǧa yamete, zañnèñ desu**

I 1. **Siñǧàkki ǧa hazímaru màde, konó koñpyùutaa tukáwanàkatta ñ desu ka⤸**
'(Is it that) you didn't use this computer until the new school term started?'

Iya, hazímaru màe ni mo tukáimàsita yo⤸
'Oh, no. I used it even before it started.'

2. **Atárasìi zimûsyo ni hiḱkòsu made, konó koñpyùutaa tukáwanàkatta ñ desu ka⤸**

Iya, hiḱkòsu mâe ni mo tukáimàsita yo⤸
'Oh, no. I used it even before we moved.'

---

11. Sentence-final **wa yo** is feminine.

'(Is it that) you didn't use this computer until you moved to the new office?'

3. dâre ka ni kuwâsìku 'setumee-site morau; 4. sikêñ ĝa 'owaru; 5. señmoñ no hitò ni sirábesasèru; 6. syotyóo ĝa kàette (i)rássyàru

J 1. **Watasi ĝa yorókòñde konó nòoto kâesite aĝeru kara, makâsete kudasai.**
'I will gladly return these notes (for them), so please leave it up to me.'

Seḱkakù desu ĝa, watasi ĝa zibúñ de kàesite aĝénàkereba naránài ñ desu.
'It's kind of you [to offer], but (the fact is) I have to return them (for them) myself.'

2. **Watasi ĝa yorókòñde 'zizyoo setúmee-site aĝerù kara, makâsete kudasai.**
'I will gladly explain the circumstances (for them), so please leave it up to me.'

Seḱkakù desu ĝa, watasi ĝa zibúñ de setumee-site aĝénàkereba naránài ñ desu.
'It's kind of you [to offer], but (the fact is) I have to explain it (for them) myself.'

3. nîmotu todókèru; 4. heyâ katázùket(e) oku; 5. kono teĝami kâite simau; 6. okane azúkete kuru; 7. kodomo kiĝáesasèru

K 1. **Konó kyookàsyo o tukáù no wa, siñ-ĝàkki ĝa hazímattè kara desu ka⁄**
'Will you begin using this textbook after the new term starts?' (*lit.* 'Will the using of this textbook be after the new term has started?')

Êe, hazímaru màde tukáwanai to omoimàsu.
'Yes, I don't think we'll use it until [the term] starts.'

2. **Konó kyookàsyo o tukáù no wa, koñpyùutaa o narâtte kara desu ka⁄**
'Will you start using this textbook after having instruction in the computer?' (*lit.* 'Will the using of this textbook be after learning the computer?')

Êe, narâu made tukáwanai to omoimàsu.
'Yes, I don't think we'll use it until [we] have instruction.'

3. **Saitoo-kyoozyu ĝa goráñ ni nâtte;** 4. **kañzi ĝa yôku yomêru yoo ni nâtte;** 5. **kôñdo no sikêñ ĝa 'owatte;** 6. **señĝàkki no o yôñde simatte;** 7. **kyoozyu ĝa Nyuúyòoku kara okáeri ni nàtte**

L 1. **Watási nàra, haḱkìri iû kedo . .**
'If I were you (*lit.* provided it's me), I'd lay it on the line (*lit.* say it clearly), but . . .' (you may not want to).

Dê mo, haḱkìri iṫtàra, kâre no ki o wârûku surû ñ zya nâi desyoo ka.
'But if I lay it on the line, isn't it the case that I'll hurt his feelings?'

2. **Watási nàra, hoká no hitò o erâbu kedo . .**

'If I were you (*lit.* provided it's me), I'd choose somebody else, but . . .' (you may not want to).

Dê mo, hoká no hitò o erâñdara, kâre no ki o wârûku surû ñ zya nâi desyoo ka.

'But if I choose somebody else, isn't it the case that I'll hurt his feelings?'

3. **omiyaĝe kâesu**; 4. **nâñ-do mo yarínaosasèru**; 5. **tyokusetu môñku iu**; 6. **atárasìi hito mo mazêru**

Application Exercises

A1. Using CC1 as a model, practice making extremely polite requests and having the person who was asked reply with either an emphatic affirmative answer or a reluctant refusal. Sample requests: (a) to use this telephone; (b) to go home early; (c) to speak in English; (d) to borrow a Japanese-English dictionary; (e) to look at the pictures the person addressed took in France; (f) to write in romanization; (g) to write in kana when you don't know the Chinese character; (h) for the person addressed to look at the letter you wrote in Japanese. In each case, include a reason for your making the request.

2. Following the general outline of appropriate portions of CC2, practice situations for which speaker B volunteers to handle difficulties raised by speaker A. For example:

a. A has so many books she wants to return to Professor Ito that she can't carry them; B offers to call a cab.

b. A wants to invite Ms. Watanabe to the student party, but he doesn't know her telephone number; B has a friend who knows the number, so s/he'll check on it for A.

c. A wants to use a word processor to write a letter but doesn't know how to use this one; B offers to call the part-time worker, because s/he knows a good deal about word processors.

d. A has a friend who wants to come here for a rest next month for about a week, but s/he doesn't know where to stay; B knows a pretty inn a bit removed from the center of town and offers to make a reservation.

e. A's (older) brother has been wanting to study English in England for a long time, but he doesn't know which schools are good; B offers to consult with a friend who has been to England any number of times.

3. Using CC3 as a basic model, practice making polite offers and having the person to whom the offer is made either accept gratefully and enthusiastically or turn down the offer politely, giving a reason (real or made up). Examples of offers: (a) to take the addressee to the new tempura restaurant near the station; (b) to show the addressee the pictures you took when you were in New York; (c) to buy some wine for the addressee when you go to Australia next month; (d) to return these books for the addressee when you go to the library tomorrow.

B. Core Conversations

Practice the Core Conversations, making substitutions that do not alter the basic structure. Include changes in the participants' relations that require a shift in style. Ask and answer content questions.

SECTION C

Eavesdropping

(Answer the following on the basis of the accompanying tape. A = the first speaker; B = the second speaker.)

1a. What does A suggest?
 b. What does B request?
2a. Describe A's invitation.
 b. What request does B make in response?
3a. How is A's typing, as described by A?
 b. What does B tell A to do?
 c. What is the result?
4a. What suggestion does A make? Why?
 b. What is B's reaction? Why?
 c. Who is B?
5a. What is A trying to find out?
 b. What does A learn from B?
6a. What request does A make?
 b. What does A promise to do?
 c. How does B respond? Why?
7a. Who is being discussed?
 b. What is A wondering about, in regard to that person?
 c. What information does B provide?
 d. Why has A brought up this topic?
 e. What is B's reaction?
8a. What is the probable relationship of A to the individuals being discussed?
 b. How does A describe them?
 c. Give one negative and one positive comment made by B about them.
 d. What comment does A make about their behavior?
 e. In what connection does B mention **manzai**?
9a. What is about to start?
 b. What is going to happen at that time?
 c. What is causing problems for B?
10a. What is the topic of discussion?
 b. What description of it does B provide?
 c. What suggestion does B make?
 d. What is A's response?
 e. Why wasn't A involved this semester?
 f. What explanation does B offer?
11a. When is the party?
 b. What is A checking on?
 c. What is B's problem?
 d. Why does B apologize?
 e. How does A react to the apology?
12a. What does A want to know about the word processor?
 b. Describe how the word processor works.
 c. What about katakana?
 d. What request does A make?
13a. Describe the problem encountered by both A and B.
 b. What solution is arrived at?

14a. Why is the professor busy at this time?
  b. What does A want to do?
  c. When can this be arranged?
  d. How will A handle the arrangements?
15a. What does A request? Why?
  b. What does B note about A?
  c. What advice does B give to A?
  d. What suggestion does B make? Why?
  e. What does A plan to do?
  f. What is the probable relationship between A and B?
16a. Who is in charge of the meeting next month?
  b. Who did A think was in charge?
  c. What change was made? Why was it made?
  d. How can A find out things like the time of the meeting?
17a. Where is B thinking of going on Sunday?
  b. What is A's reaction?
  c. What alternative does A suggest?
  d. How does B react to this suggestion?
18a. When are the guests coming? From where?
  b. Why is A concerned?
  c. What is B's response? Give details.
19a. What request does A make?
  b. What is B's reservation in granting it? Why?
  c. What does B do, in the end?
  d. What does A promise to do?
  e. Comment on the style used by A and B.
20a. What does A apologize for?
  b. What is B's response?
  c. What actually happened? Contrary to what intention on A's part?
  d. What does B express thanks/apologies for?
  e. What is described by B as something that might have happened? Under what circumstances?
21a. What request does A make of B?
  b. What is B's reaction?
  c. What request does B make?
  d. What explanation does A offer for giving assignments to B?
  e. What problem does B anticipate?
  f. What assurances does A offer?
  g. Given the style and tone of the conversation, what is the probable relationship between A and B?
22a. What is the setting?
  b. What does A suggest?
  c. What does A offer to do?
  d. In contrast, what does B want to do? Why? Give two reasons.
  e. Who wins out?
23a. Who makes the call, and who answers the phone?
  b. What was apparently discussed by A and B before the call?
  c. What is the purpose of the call?
  d. What is B planning to do for A?
24a. In what connection is "18" mentioned?
  b. What question does B raise regarding Ms. Yamanaka?
  c. What is A's response?

d. In what connection is "25" mentioned?

e. What does A want B to do?

f. Comment on the style of language used by A and B.

25a. Where is B planning to go? When?

b. What offer does A make? Why?

c. What is B's reaction to the offer?

d. How does A reassure B? On what basis?

26a. What is the topic of conversation?

b. What activities contributed to B's enjoyment?

c. What was the result of the kindness with which B was treated?

d. How does A turn aside the thanks B expresses?

27a. What does A want to do?

b. Why is B pleased?

c. What is B going to do now?

d. How does A respond?

28a. Who is being discussed?

b. How is that person's Japanese? Give complete details, covering both speaking and writing.

c. What is B's reaction?

Utilization

Use the following as bases for short (or long, if you prefer!) conversations. Remember that the appropriate procedure is not to try to translate literally, but to provide the Japanese that would be situationally appropriate.

1a. Ask your supervisor to let you know if you can be of any assistance (i.e., use).

b. Your supervisor thanks you, but tells you he is having the secretary help.

2a. As you fumble through your pockets looking for money to pay for a newspaper you just bought, tell your colleague that you *should* have some small change, but . . .

b. Your colleague replies that he has some and tells you to let him pay.

3a. Ask your supervisor (very politely!) for permission to leave early today. Explain that you have caught a cold and don't feel well.

b. Your supervisor agrees to your leaving and tells you to take care of yourself.

4a. Ask a classmate to let you read her notes from Professor Noguchi's lecture.

b. As your classmate hands them over, she warns that you may not be able to read them because her writing is sloppy.

5a. Ask a German classmate if she can read Japanese.

b. Your classmate replies that of course she knows hiragana and katakana, but since she knows only a few kanji, she can't read anything of the kind she wants to read.

6a. Ask a colleague about what time he will arrive in Nagoya tomorrow.

b. Your colleague replies that he doesn't know for sure, but he will arrive by the time the manager returns from Osaka, without fail.

7a. Tell an acquaintance that you've taken advantage of his offer and come to consult with him.

b. Your acquaintance invites you to sit down and offers you coffee.

8a. Confess to a friend that you've reached the point where you can speak Japanese a little, but no matter what you do, polite language doesn't come out naturally.

b. Your friend indicates that surely you must agree that you *can* use it skillfully. She adds that, in any case, the more you practice, the better you'll get to be.

9a. Tell a colleague that you went to the station and waited until the 9:00 **sińkàńseń** left, but Mr. Watanabe apparently didn't take that train.

b. Your colleague suggests that perhaps he was late and took the next train.

10a. You've just finished a meal at a restaurant with a colleague. Offer to pay the check.

b. Your colleague emphatically refuses your offer, pointing out that *he* invited *you*.

11a. Tell an acquaintance that you are constantly obliged to him (*lit.* coming under his helpful service).

b. Your acquaintance replies that it is *he* who is obliged to *you*.

12a. You've been asked to give a talk in Japanese. Explain to a colleague that you don't know whether you are able to do it or not.

b. Your colleague indicates that surely you must agree that you *can* do it.

13a. Suggest to a colleague that you both go to eat at the new sushi shop near the station.

b. Your colleague suggests that, since it's still early, you wait until Mr. Yamamoto returns and go together.

14a. Apologize to a Japanese classmate for always borrowing his notes.

b. The classmate tells you not to be concerned about that kind of thing. He points out that if they were English notes, *he* would be borrowing.

15a. A close friend of yours has a book written in extremely difficult Japanese. Ask him to let you borrow it.

b. Your friend agrees but points out that it won't be his problem if you can't read it.

16a. Comment to a friend on the fact that Mr. Ono is always speaking terribly politely.

b. Your friend wonders if it isn't explained by the fact that he has worked in hotels ever since he graduated from college and is used to a very polite way of speaking.

17a. Tell your colleague that you don't want to make next month's schedule.

b. Your colleague suggests that you have someone [else] make it.

18a. Your group is having an office party at a restaurant. Ask your colleague if he was the one who made the reservations.

b. Your colleague replies that since he didn't have time, he had the secretary do it.

19a. Tell a colleague that you've heard he fired his part-time worker.

b. Your colleague says that it's true. The part-timer kept coming late, not coming at all . . . Nothing could be done.

20a. A meeting has just ended. Tell your colleague that *you* will straighten up.

b. Your colleague tells you to let *her* straighten up.

21a. You and a friend are on your way to a class. Tell him that if you don't take a special express, you don't think you'll be on time.

b. Your friend's reaction is that you surely must agree that you won't be on time even if you do take a special express.

22a. Ask your professor (very politely!) if you may borrow next semester's schedule. You would like to make a copy of it.

b. Your professor replies that next semester's schedule hasn't been completed yet. It's supposed to be finished by next Friday.

23a. Ask your professor (very politely!) for permission to look at the pictures he took the other day.

b. Your professor agrees enthusiastically.

24a. Ask a fellow student if he is doing research only in Japan.

b. Your fellow student replies that he is also being allowed to do research at an American university.

25a. Tell a close friend that you think Kei will be offended if Takashi doesn't come to the student party.

b. Your friend reassures you by saying he'll speak to her beforehand. He tells you to leave it up to him.

26a. Tell a friend that you have tickets for this Saturday for a concert. Invite her to go with you.

b. Your friend refuses politely on the grounds of a previous engagement.

27a. Tell a stranger in the hallway that you are looking for Mr. Takashi Ono's office.

b. The stranger explains that it is on the fourth floor. He offers to show you the way.

28a. Tell your professor that these are pictures you took recently of temples and shrines in Kyoto. Invite him (politely) to look at them.

b. Your professor compliments you on how skillfully they've been taken.

29a. You are parking your car. Ask a friend if it's all right not to lock it.

b. Your friend assures you that of course it's all right. He adds that in this town, nobody locks cars.

30a. Ask a colleague if she took pictures of Professor Watanabe yesterday.

b. Your colleague says that she did; the professor let her take them.

31a. Invite your guest, who is looking at a menu, to choose things that he likes.

b. Your guest thanks you and assures you politely that he will take the liberty of doing that.

32a. Ask a friend if Kei is homesick for her family.

b. Your friend replies that she probably is; she hasn't been home for all of three years.

33a. Comment to a colleague that it's too bad the part-timer who was good in English quit.

b. Your colleague comments that there seem to be many part-timers who want to quit work these days.

34a. Tell your professor (very politely) that you are going to take advantage of his kindness and borrow his tape.

b. Your professor tells you to go ahead. He adds that he won't use it until the next semester begins, so you should use it without any rush.

35a. A colleague has just handed over a book he bought at your request. Tell him you're sorry for having caused him this trouble [i.e., annoyance, nuisance].

b. Your colleague indicates that it wasn't a bit of trouble; he adds that he was also able to buy a book that his wife had been wanting to read for a long time (since a long time ago).

36a. Ask your friend, who has scheduled a job interview, when he will have it.

b. Your friend replies that he has already had it. He expects to join (*lit.* enter) the company next month.

Check-up

1. What is the basic meaning of a causative verbal? Give the causative derivative of **tukûru; mâtu; akeru; harâu; iu; kûru; suru**. Describe, in general terms, how the causative is formed. What alternate form is used by some speakers of Japanese? (A-SP1)

2. Give an example of a simple verbal root; a compound verbal root; a simple-complex verbal root; a compound-complex verbal root. What is a root-extender? (A-SP1)

3. Describe the use of particles **ni** and **o** linked to a causative and following the person who is made or allowed to do something. (A-SP2)

3. Contrast the meaning of a causative alone with /causative + verbal of giving or receiving/. What is the difference between the causative and /verbal gerund + **morau**/? Give an example of a polite permission pattern that includes the causative. (A-SP1, 2)

5. In the pattern /verbal + **màde**/, what form of the verbal occurs? How does this resemble /verbal + **mâe**/? What is the difference in meaning between /verbal + **màde**/ and /verbal + **màde ni**/? (A-SP3)

6. What is the meaning of /predicate X + **zya nai [ka]**./? In what forms may predicate X occur? (A-SP4)

7. How are regular polite verbal-nominals formed? Give examples. In what patterns do they occur? (B-SP1)

8. The polite verbal-nominals **oide, tyoodai, gorañ, haisyaku**, and **haikeñ** are unpredictable forms. How does their usage differ from that of most of the regularly formed polite verbal-nominals? What is the meaning of a polite verbal-nominal, regular or irregular, at the end of a sentence? (B-SP1)

9. Describe the formation of request patterns ending in **-kudasài** and **-nasài**. (B-SP1)

10. Describe the occurrence of the sentence-final particle sequence **to mo**. What may precede it? (B-SP2)

11. What is the meaning of the **-g̈àru** suffix? To what form of words of what word classes may it be attached? In general, what do these words have in common, in terms of their meaning? (B-SP3)

12. Compare a basic **-tai** form like **kaitai** with a **-g̈àru** derivative like **kaítag̈àru**: how do their basic meaning, their usage, and the phrase-particles with which they can be linked differ? (B-SP3)

Lesson 29

SECTION A

Core Conversations

1(N)   Kêsa 'kaisya no erâi hito ni
zûibuñ têenee na âisatu sarétà
kedo, naní mo wakarimasèñ
desita.

           (J)   Muzúkasìi desyoo neſ Kimátta
iikata suru monò desu kara . .

2(N)a.   Anó kodomò-tati, nâñ to ka
narímasèñ ka nêe. Oyâ wa
tyûui = sinâi ñ desyoo ka.

           (J)a.   Sukósi-ğùrai tyûui = sarétè mo
heéki nà ñ desu yo. Oyâ mo
kibîsìku wa 'iwánài si . .

    b.   Watási ğa kodomo no kòro wa,
zûibuñ kibîsìku sitúkeràreta
mono desu kedo nêe.

           b.   Mâa, końna tokorò de wa, kodómo
dè mo sîzuka ni surú monò da to
wa omóimàsu ğa nêe.

                  . . .

    c.   Tyôtto ukáğaimàsu ğa, atíra no
okosañ-ğàta no 'oyağosañ wa,
dôtira desyoo ka.

           (J')a.   Sâa.

    d.   Minâsañ mêewaku-site orárèru
yoo desu no de nêe.

           b.   Hâa. Moósiwake gozaimasèñ.
Tyûui-site moráu yòo ni itásimàsu
kara . .

    e.   Onéğai-simàsu.

3(N)a. |Anoo| Tyôtto yokée na kotò ka
mo sirémasèñ kedo neſ Koko no
tokoro neſ Tyôtto naósàreta hoo
ğa îi ka mo siremaseñ nêe.

           (J)a.   Hâa. Koó iu hùu ni wa iwánai
monò desyoo ka.

b. **Mâa, iú hitò mo irû ka mo siremaseñ kedo; konó mamà da to, îmi o gokái-sareru kanoosee mo arimàsu kara . .**

c. **Iie. Dôo mo sitûree-itasimasita.**

b. **Sôo desu ka. Dôo mo gotêenee ni arîgatoo gozaimasita.**

ENGLISH EQUIVALENTS

1(N)   This morning I was greeted awfully politely by one of the bigwigs in the company, but I didn't understand a thing.

(J)   I guess it's difficult, isn't it? You use set ways of saying things, so . . . (they may be very difficult).

2(N)a. Can't anything be done about those children, I wonder. Don't their parents warn them?

(J)a. Even if they're warned (a little), they couldn't care less. The parents don't say anything strictly, and . . .

b. When I was a child, we used to be strictly disciplined, but . . . you know.

b. At a place like this, I think that even children ought to be quiet, but . . . (they don't seem to be).

. . .

c. Excuse me. Where would the parent(s) of the children over there be?

d. Since everyone seems to be annoyed . . . you know.

(J')a. Hmmm.

b. Yes, I'm sorry. I'll try to have them warn them, so . . . (leave it to me).

e. Would you, please?

3(N)a. Uh, this may be something unnecessary [to bring up], but this place here—you know? Perhaps you ought to correct it a bit.

b. Well, there may (also) be people who do (say), but if it's left this way, there's the possibility of having the meaning misunderstood, so . . . (it's better to correct it).

(J)a. Yes. Shouldn't you say it this way?

b. Really. Thank you for being so conscientious.

c. Not at all. Forgive my rudeness (for pointing out an error).

BREAKDOWNS
(AND SUPPLEMENTARY VOCABULARY)

1. **erâi /-katta/**   is great, eminent, superior
   âisatu   greeting, salutation
   âisatu (o) suru   greet
   âisatu (o) sareru /-ru; sareta/ (SP1)   be greeted
   + **situmoñ-suru**   ask a question
   têenee na âisatu   polite greeting
   + **hukuzatu /na/**   complicated
   + **kañtañ /na/**   simple
   têenee na̧ âisatu (o) sareru   be greeted politely; (lit. be affected by a
                                                              polite greeting

   kimatta iikata   a set way of saying
   surú monò da (SP3)   [one] is to do; the regular procedure is to
                                                              do

2. + **-tati ~-g̈ata ~-ra** (SP4)   /pluralizing suffixes/
   kodómò-tati   children
   tyûui-suru   pay attention, be careful of; advise, warn
   tyûui-sareru   be advised or warned
   + **sikaru /-u; sikatta/**   scold
   heeki /na/   calm, cool; indifferent, unconcerned
   kibísìi /-katta/   is strict, stern, rigorous
   kibîsìku wa 'iwanai (SP5)   does not speak *sternly* (at least)
   + **otónasìi /-katta/**   is gentle, mild, obedient
   kôro   approximate time
   watási g̈a kodomo no kòro   around the time when I was a child
   sitúkèru /-ru; sitûketa/   train, discipline; teach manners
   sitúkerarèru /-ru; sitúkeràreta/   be brought up or trained or disciplined
   kibîsìku sitúkeràreta mono da   used to be brought up strictly
   sîzuka ni suru   be quiet; act in a quiet way
   sîzuka ni surú monò da   [one] is to be quiet; the regular procedure
                                                              is to be quiet

   sîzuka ni surú monò da to wa omôu   think that one is to be quiet (at least)
   okósañ-g̈àta   children /polite/
   + **omôtya**   toy
   + **niñg̈yoo**   doll
   mêewaku-suru   be(come) troubled or annoyed
   mêewaku-sareru↑ (SP2)   be(come) troubled or annoyed /honorific-
                                                              polite/

   mêewaku-sité orarèru↑ /-ru; orâreta/   be troubled or annoyed /honorific-polite/

tyûui-site morau	have [someone] pay attention; have [someone] advise or warn
tyûui-site moráu yòo ni suru	act so as to have [someone] pay attention, advise, or warn
3. **yokee** /na/	excessive, unnecessary, uncalled for
naósarèru↑ /ru; naósàreta/	repair /honorific-polite/
hûu /na~no/	manner, style
koó iu hùu ni wa 'iwanai	does not say *in this way* (at least)
iwánai monò da	[one] is not to say; the regular procedure is not to say
mamà (SP6)	condition just as it is
konó mamà da to	when it is like this without being changed
gokai-suru	misunderstand
îmi o 'gokai-sareru	have the meaning misunderstood
kanoosee	possibility
îmi o 'gokai-sareru kanoosee	possibility of having the meaning misunderstood

MISCELLANEOUS NOTES

1. In CC1, Sue Brown is expressing her concern about not having understood when one of the senior staff members of her company greeted her in very polite language. Her colleague is sympathetic, pointing out that the difficulty comes about because of the ritualized way of talking one is supposed to use in Japanese. As usual, these two people use careful-style, with distal-style final predicates. Ms. Brown's colleague also uses distal-style before **kara**.

In addition to its regular uses, expressing a quality of eminence, superiority, and high rank, **erâi** is frequently used to praise small children for doing something well.

Âisatu refers to all the ritualized expressions used in greeting people and saying farewell, inquiring about the well-being of someone's family, apologizing for not having been in contact, etc. They are, as we have noted on many occasions, very important in Japanese society. Not only is the form of the **âisatu** extremely important; the occasions that require **âisatu** are strictly prescribed, and to ignore the rules is to commit a serious social blunder. It is not surprising that Sue Brown would be worried if she fears she may not have replied appropriately to the incomprehensible (to her) greeting of one of her bosses.

+**Situmoñ-suru**: Note also the nominal **situmoñ** 'question.'

2. In CC2, Sue Brown and Mrs. Carter are having difficulty conducting a conversation in a restaurant because of the noise being made by some unruly children. On the accompanying video, part of the commotion is a noisy rendition of **zyâñ·kêñ·pôñ**, the Japanese equivalent of "rock, paper, scissors." Sue Brown is sufficiently annoyed to call the waiter and ask him to speak to the children's parent(s). She appropriately chooses to use a go-between (in this case, the waiter) instead of talking to the parent(s) directly. The Japanese practice of being extremely permissive with small children and strict with older children results in some foreigners' being annoyed at the behavior of very young Japanese and favorably impressed when the children get a bit older.

As usual, Sue Brown and Mrs. Carter address each other in careful-style, with distal-style final predicates. Sue Brown also uses distal-style before **kedo**, whereas Mrs. Carter's negative before **si** is direct-style. When Ms. Brown addresses the waiter on a subject that she is hesitant to bring up, she shifts to polite careful-style, using honorific terms both in reference to the children (**okósañ-ğàta**) and to their parents (**oyağosañ**), and an honorific-polite verbal (**orárèru**; cf. SP2, following) in reference to the parents. Note also her use of distal-style before **no de**. Predictably the waiter is also polite in speaking to Ms. Brown: cf. **gozáimasèñ** and **itásimàsu**, the latter preceding **kara**.

(N)a. The meaning of **tyûui** covers carefulness as well as advice and warning: **tyûui-suru** 'be(come) careful,' 'pay attention,' or, depending on context, 'advise' or 'warn.' Note also **tyûui o harâu** 'pay attention'; **keñkoo ni tyûui-suru** 'pay attention to one's health'; **kuruma ni tyûui-suru** 'be careful of the cars'; **soó sinai yòo ni tyûui-suru** 'warn not to do that'; **tyûui o hiku** 'attract [someone's] attention'; **komákài tyûui** 'meticulous attention.'

(N)b. **Kòro** has already occurred in its alternate form, **-ğoro**. In the sequence **watási ğa kodomo no kòro, watasi ğa** occurs as the affect of the nominal predicate **kodómo dà**, which occurs here in its pre-nominal form **kodomo no**: 'the (approximate) time described by saying, "I am a child".'

Sitúkèru: Note also **situke** 'training,' 'discipline,' 'upbringing.'

3. In CC3, Sue Brown is in the difficult position of correcting her Japanese colleague's English. We can assume that before deciding to do this she gave the matter serious thought and in the end came to the conclusion that it was advisable to go ahead. (In many situations it is clearly better *not* to bring up a matter like this at all, particularly if the person needing correction is a superior.) Here we can imagine a context in which the company may lose face if the document is sent out in its present form, and Ms. Brown is looking at the situation as a company employee and in-group member.

As usual, Ms. Brown and her colleague use careful-style in speaking with each other. Ms. Brown conveys the politeness, hesitation, and tact required by the situation by her initial **anoo**; the suggestion that what she is about to say may be extraneous; the use of an honorific-polite verbal form (**naósàreta** [cf. SP2, following]) in reference to her colleague; the giving of advice in terms of what *may* be the better procedure; the suggestion that there may be those who *would* say what her colleague has written (undoubtedly untrue but a tactful thing to say); the mention of a possible problem arising from not correcting the mistakes; and a final very polite apology for what she has said. The polite thanks given to Ms. Brown is meant to reassure her that what she did was appropriate and appreciated.

(J)a. **Hûu** 'manner,' 'way,' 'style' can be preceded by a modifier of the kinds that regularly precede nominals, or it may form a compound with a preceding nominal. When describing a following nominal, it may occur with either **no** or **na**; if it describes a predicate (in a pattern of manner), it is followed by particle **ni**. Examples: **añna** (or **aá iu**) **hùu na erâi katâ** 'an eminent person of that kind'; **koñna** (or **koó iu**) **hùu ni suru** 'do it in this way': **Nihóñ-huu na** (or **no**) **àisatu** 'a Japan-style greeting'; **gakúsee-huu ni hanàsu** 'talk in student-style.'

Structural Patterns

1. THE PASSIVE: INVOLUNTARY AND ADVERSATIVE

In this lesson, we add another class of derivative verbals that involve root-extenders: the PASSIVE. How we form the passive can be described in a number of ways. Two of these are:

(1) the formation entails adding the root-extender **-rare-** to the root of vowel verbals and **-are-** to the root of consonant verbals, and then adding **-ru** to form the imperfective. For vowel verbals, the passive is identical with the long form of the potential; (2) another way to arrive at the passive is to change every **-s-** in the root-extenders used in the causative to an **-r-**. Thus, causative **tabé-sasè-ru** becomes passive **tabé-rarè-ru**; **nom-ásè-ru** becomes **nom-árè-ru**; **kaw-ase-ru** becomes **kaw-are-ru**; **ko-sásè-ru** becomes **ko-rárè-ru**; and **s-ase-ru** becomes **s-are-ru**. Even the accentuation is parallel. Additional examples:

Imperfective	*Passive*
ake-ru 'open [something]'	**ake-rare-ru**
dê-ru 'go/come out'	**de-rárè-ru**
i-ru 'be located (animate)'	**i-rare-ru**
mî-ru 'look at'	**mi-rárè-ru**
ût-u 'strike'	**ut-árè-ru**
hik-u 'pull'	**hik-are-ru**
os-u 'push'	**os-are-ru**
yob-u 'call'	**yob-are-ru**
hâir-u 'enter'	**haír-arè-ru**
i-u 'say' (<*iw-u)	**iw-are-ru**
omô-u 'think' (<*omow-u)	**omów-arè-ru**

The special polite **-aru** verbals do not have passive derivatives.

These passive verbals occur in the many forms in which verbals usually occur. Using **yob-are-ru** as an example, we find **yob-are-ta, yob-are-te, yob-áre-màs-u, yob-are-na-i, yob-áre-tàra, yob-áre-nà-kattara, yob-áre-tàri, yob-áre-rèba**, etc. However, there is no passive of a potential. The passive of the causative (you can anticipate the form!) is introduced and discussed in lesson 30.

In examining now how the Japanese passive is used, the first requirement is to cast aside any notion that it coincides with the English passive, even though they are occasionally similar. As always, it is better to examine the form as part of the Japanese system, not as a translation of English. In particular, it must be pointed out (note the English passive in that sequence!) that the passive is *much* more common in English than in Japanese.

WARNING: Using English passives as triggers for Japanese passives is very dangerous indeed.

The first meaning of the passive that we will take up is that the referent (the person to whom the form refers) '*is affected* by an occurrence of the verbal root which happens outside his/her control.' We call this type of passive the INVOLUNTARY PASSIVE. If I say in reference to myself, **Ikáremàsita**, the meaning is that *someone else* went somewhere and *I* was the one affected: 'I was affected by someone's going.' The implication in this type of example is that I reacted unfavorably to the event—that it was contrary to my wishes.

If the basic verbal is an operational verbal that can occur with a *personal operand* (= **o**-phrase; examples: **yobu** 'call,' **sasou** 'invite (to do something),' **syôotai-suru** 'invite (to an event),' **syookai-suru** 'introduce,' **okôsu** 'awaken'), its involuntary passive implies that the referent and the operand are the same, if no operand is mentioned. In this usage, there is usually no implied unfavorable reaction.

Yobáremàsita. 'I was called.' (i.e., '*I* was affected by the calling of *me*.')

Syoókai-saremàsita. 'I was introduced.' (i.e., *'I was affected by the introducing of me.'*)

Only examples of this kind regularly parallel the corresponding English passives in meaning.

We actually encountered a passive of this kind in lesson 28. **Umareru** 'be(come) born' is the passive of the verbal **umu,** used most commonly in reference to the laying of eggs and giving birth (**kodomo o umu** 'give birth to a child'). We assume no implied unfavorable reaction!

But now consider this example: **Kodómo o okosaremàsita.** English is of little help here. The meaning of this Japanese sentence is that someone else awakened *the children,* but *I* was the person affected: 'I was affected by the waking of the children.' Here again, the implication is that I was adversely affected—I would have preferred that this hadn't happened, but the event was out of my control. We call this use of the involuntary passive the ADVERSATIVE PASSIVE. The connotation is the opposite of that of **kodomo o okôsite moraimasita,** which indicates that someone woke the children and I was the beneficiary.

Since not all examples of the passive have an adversative implication, some claim that the implication is dependent on context, not expressed by the passive form itself. Whichever interpretation is accurate, the important thing is that in examples like **ikáremàsita,** and **kodómo o okosaremàsita,** and others of this kind, something happened that *affected* the person to whom the passive refers, even though that person did not participate directly in the occurrence. Almost invariably the affect is unfavorable.

The person to whom the passive refers (i.e., the person who is affected), if expressed, is followed by particle **g̃a** (or **wa** or **mo**). When the operator of the underlying verbal from which the passive is derived is expressed, that personal nominal is followed by particle **ni** (or, less commonly, **kara**).[1] Examples:

Tomodati wa, señsèe ni yobáremàsita. 'My friend was called by the teacher.' (*lit.* 'My friend was affected by calling done by the teacher'; since no one else is mentioned, the assumption is that it was my friend who was called).

This may or may not imply an adverse reaction on my friend's part, but unlike **Señsèe wa, tomódati o yobimàsita.** 'The teacher called my friend,' it emphasizes the fact that the occurrence was outside my friend's control and that my friend was affected by it.

Kodomo ni okósaremàsita. 'I was awakened by the children.' (*lit.* 'I was affected by awakening done by the children.')

Again, this may or may not imply an adverse reaction.

Dâre ka ni kodómo o okosaremàsita. 'Somebody woke the children, damn it!' (*lit.* 'I was [adversely] affected by the waking of the children by somebody.'

In this pattern, in which the person affected and the person[s] awakened are different, the implication is almost invariably adversative.

Arúbàito ni osóku koràrete, ano sig̃oto wa sumásemasèñ desita. 'With the part-timer coming late (not something I wanted to happen), I didn't finish that work.' (*lit.* 'Being unfavorably affected by the part-timer's coming late . . .')

---

1. Compare: **Tomódati ni kikaremàsita.** 'I was asked by a friend' *or* 'Unfortunately for me [someone] asked my friend.'

Again, the meaning is adversative.

An inanimate cause of a passive, if expressed, is usually followed by particle **de**: **tuyôi kaze de 'kowasareru** 'be(come) destroyed by a strong wind.' A common exception to this is **âme ni hurárèru** 'get rained on' (*lit.* 'be affected by falling by rain').

When the representative and passive are brought together, either the representative(s) or the following **suru** may occur in the passive (cf. the causative [28A-2]).

> **dêtari hâittari sareru** *or* **derâretari haíràretari suru** '[someone] keeps going out and coming in (and I am affected unfavorably)'

Pay attention to the following important points about the passive:

a. /person X **ğa** (**wa, mo**) + person Y **o** (**wa, mo**) + operational verbal/ is converted to /person Y **ğa** (**wa, mo**) + person X **ni** + passive verbal/. Passives in this pattern are not necessarily adversative: **Tomodati wa señsèe ni yobáremàsita.** 'My friend was called by the teacher.'

b. In spoken Japanese, the referent of a passive is regularly animate. In those rare instances in which it is inanimate, the conversion to the passive follows the pattern of (a) above and does not have an adversative implication. Example: **Kore wa nâni ni tukáwarete (i)màsu ka** 'What is this being used for?' This type of usage is rather stiff and is more common in written Japanese. It is not to be confused with the **-te âru** pattern, which refers to an *existing state* resulting from a previous activity (**konó kikài ğa tukátte àru** 'this machine has been used'). For an explanation of that pattern, refer to lesson 16A-SP2).

c. When /person X **ğa** (**wa, mo**) + person or thing Y **o** (**wa, mo**) + operational verbal/ is converted to /person X **ğa** (**wa, mo**) + person or thing Y **o** (**wa, mo**) + passive verbal/, person X shifts from being the operator (the doer) to being the person involuntarily affected, usually with adversative implications: **Kânai ğa dâre ka ni kodómo o okosaremàsita kara . .** 'Someone woke the children (and my wife didn't like it, so . . .).'

d. In Japanese, passives of both operational and affective verbals, of both transitive and intransitive verbals are possible. Not every verbal commonly occurs in the passive, but some members of each class are represented among the passives.

Compare now the following examples:

Kû-zi no kawari ni sitî-zi ni {

kitê moraimasita. 'I had him/her come at 7:00 instead of 9:00—just what I wanted!'

kosásemàsita. 'I had him/her come at 7:00 instead of 9:00—utilizing my position of power, I brought it about.'

koráremàsita. 'S/he came at 7:00 instead of 9:00—what I did *not* want!'

Some English patterns that use passives *do* seem to parallel the Japanese pattern that includes an operand, but they do not imply an adversative connotation, and they occur with only a few English verbs. Examples are 'be awarded a prize,' 'be given a present,' 'be handed an ultimatum,' and 'be told a story.'

2. *THE HONORIFIC PASSIVE*

We now take up an entirely different use of the passive. Far from implying notions of involuntary affect or of adverse reactions, this use expresses politeness! A passive may be used as an honorific-polite equivalent of the basic verbal from which it is derived. In such cases, particle usage is the same as with the basic verbal. We refer to this type of passive as the HONORIFIC PASSIVE. It is an alternative to the other honorific-polite patterns we already know. When the Emperor Showa died in 1989, the verbal form used most commonly on television and radio in reference to his dying was **nakúnararemàsita**. Other examples of the honorific passive follow.

> **Asita nâṅ-zi ni koráremàsu ka** 'What time are you coming tomorrow?'
>
> **Anó màdo wa seṅsèe ḡa akéraremàsita.** 'That window the teacher opened.'
>
> **Asita oṅgàkkai ḡa arímàsu ḡa, ikáremasèṅ ka** 'There's a concert tomorrow; won't you go?'

The verbal **ôru** was originally introduced as a humble-polite (↓) verbal. Later, its use as a neutral-polite (+) following gerunds was added (example: **âme ḡa hûtte orimasu**). We now find a most unusual switch: it occurs in the passive form **orárèru** as an honorific-polite (↑) form! (Cf. CC2[N]d.)

Assignment of passive verbals to the operational or affective category presents special problems. Clearly the polite passives belong to the same category as the verbals from which they are derived. We would assume that the involuntary passives, which express lack of control, would all be affective verbals, but many of them occur linked to /nominal + **o**/ phrases, regularly the sign of an operational verbal. In every such case, however, the /nominal + **o**/ phrase actually hooks up specifically with the root of the basic verbal, not with the derived passive, so we can assign involuntary passives to the affective category, allowing for the incorporation of a subordinate operational pattern that includes an operand. Example: **Êki no mâe de [haṅdobàggu o tor]áremàsita.** 'I had my handbag taken in front of the station.' The affective passive verbal incorporates the operational root **tor-**, which has as *its* operand the nominal **haṅdobàggu**.

Depending on context, a sequence like **Zyûḡyoo ḡa hazímaru màe ni koráremàsita.** can mean

> 'I was able to come before the class began.' (potential) *or*
>
> '(Somebody) came before the class began.' (honorific passive) *or*
>
> '(Somebody) came before the class began, damn it!' (adversative passive)

This is a striking reminder of the importance of context!

3. /PREDICATE + monò da/

A /predicate + **monò da**/ denotes regularly recurring activities and states. This nominal **monò** (the contracted form is **mòṅ**) is not to be confused with **monô** 'thing' or 'person' (humble). When the predicate preceding **monò** is imperfective, the pattern refers to 'the thing to do,' i.e., what is expected as a regular occurrence, what one regularly does. Examples:

> **Âisatu surú tokì ni wa, kimátta iikata o suru monò desu yo.** 'When you greet someone, the idea is to use fixed ways of saying things.'
>
> **Soṅna tokì ni wa, omíyaḡe o motte ikanai monò desu.** 'At times like that, you don't take a souvenir (according to regular practice).'
>
> **Nihôṅ no iê ni hâiru toki ni wa, kutû o nûḡu mono desu.** '(At times) when you enter a Japanese home, you take off your shoes (as a regular procedure).'

When the predicate preceding **monò** is perfective, the pattern describes an activity or state that used to occur on a regular basis. Thus:

Kodómo no tokì wa, okâsi o yôku tâbeta mono desu. 'When I was a child, I used to eat lots of sweets.'

Kyôoto ni itá tokì ni wa, otéra ya zìnzya o mî ni iṫta monò desu. 'When I was in Kyoto, I used to go to see the temples and shrines.'

Mâe wa, sakána ga kirai dàtta mono desu ga, kokó e kitè kara wa, sukî ni nâtte kimasita. 'In the past I used to dislike fish, but since coming here, I've come to like it.'

4. PLURALIZING SUFFIXES

With few exceptions, Japanese nominals do not distinguish between singular and plural. However, there are a few that refer to the singular only. For example, the personal nominals **wata(ku)si, bôku, anâta**, and **kimi**, and proper names with or without titles (**-san, -kun, -tyan**) are always singular.

Several pluralizing suffixes are affixed to personal nominals to form compounds meaning 'nominal X + another or others' or 'nominal X within a group (with X the focus).' The suffixes introduced in this lesson are **-tati, -ra**, and the polite **-gata**.[2] Examples:

watá(ku)sì-tati 'we' (i.e., 'I + other[s]')

bôkú-tàti or **bôku-ra** 'we' (masculine)

anâta-tàti or **anáta-gàta** ~ **anata-gata** 'you' (plural)

Nakámura-sàn-tati 'Mr/s. Nakamura and his/her group'

Some other nominals—usually those denoting persons[3]—which in their basic form refer to singular or plural number without distinction, may also occur with these suffixes to refer to plural number only. Thus:

hito 'person' or 'persons'; but **hitô-tati** 'persons'

katâ 'person' or 'persons' (polite); but **katâ-gata** 'persons' (polite)

gakusee 'student' or 'students'; but **gakúseè-tati** 'students'

Which suffix(es) occur with which nominals must be checked for each nominal, but generally speaking, **-tati** is the most widely used.

5. /ADJECTIVAL STEM + wa/

We have already been introduced to the stem of the adjectival (the **-ku** form) hooking up to a predicate (a) as a pattern of manner: **hâyâku hanâsu** 'speak fast'; (b) as a goal pattern: **ôókìku suru** 'make [it] big'; and (c) in the negative adjectival pattern: **tâkâku nâi** 'is not high.'

The particle **wa**, with its usual function of indicating that the following predicate applies to what precedes it "at least" (whatever else it may or may not apply to), also occurs following

---

2. Many /nominal + pluralizer/ combinations have alternate accents. Those noted above are not necessarily exhaustive listings.

3. Pluralizers may be affixed to a very limited group of nominals denoting inanimates. In their basic form such nominals refer to one or more than one item. **Kore** is 'this thing' or 'these things'; but **korêra** can mean only 'these things.'

an adjectival stem. A normally unaccented adjectival stem acquires an accent on its final mora when followed by particle **wa.**

Hâyâku wa hanásimàsu. 'S/he does talk *fast* (at least).'

Ôókìku wa simâsita kedo, amari kîree zya nâi desu nêe. 'S/he did make it *big,* but it isn't very pretty, is it!'

Kibîsìku wa sitúkènai si . . 'They don't bring [them] up *strictly* (at least) and . . .'

Muzúkasikù wa nâi desyoo? 'It's not difficult (whatever else it may be)—right?'

Predictably, **mo** may replace **wa** in this pattern, with the usual change of focus. Example: **tâkâku mo nâi** 'it isn't even expensive *or* expensive, either.'

6. mamà

The nominal **mamà** refers to an existing condition without a change that has been suggested or might be anticipated. The existing condition is expressed by the modifier that precedes **mamà.** The sequence ending in **mamà** is frequently followed by the gerund of the copula (**dè**), although in a goal pattern, particle **ni** may also follow it. When **mamà** connects with a predicate as a pattern of manner, it occurs without a phrase-particle. After an accented word or phrase, **mamà** loses its accent. Examples:

Sonó mamà de kêkkoo desu. 'It's fine as it is, like that.'

Âtûku simásyòo ka. . . . Iie, tumétai mamà de îi desu. 'Shall I heat it? . . . No, it's fine as it is, cold.' (*lit.* 'Being a continuing cold condition is fine.')

Okane wa, ańna tokorò ni iréta mamà ni suru? 'Are you going (to decide) to leave the money as it is (inserted) in that kind of place?'

Kutû o nuĝânai mama hâitte mo kamáimasèñ ka 'Will it be all right (even) if I come in as I am, without taking my shoes off?'

Konó kikài nara, tâtta mama tukáeru sòo desu. 'They say that if it's this machine, you can use it as you are, standing up (*lit.* in a having stood up condition).'

An affirmative verbal preceding **mamà** is regularly perfective or /gerund + (i)ru/, because the existing condition (**mamà**) results from an activity that has already taken place.

Drills

A 1. **Yamâĝuti-sañ o syôotai-sita ñ desu ka**
'(Is it that) you invited Mr/s. Yamaguchi (to an event)?'

Iya, anô hito ni syóotai = sarétà ñ desu.
'No, (the fact is that) I was invited by him/her.'

2. **Yamâĝuti-sañ o sasóttà ñ desu ka**
'(Is it that) you invited Mr/s. Yamaguchi (to do something with you)?'

Iya, anô hito ni sasówaretà ñ desu.
'No, (the fact is that) I was invited (to do something together) by him/her.'

3. **osita**; 4. **okôsita**; 5. **tasúkèta**; 6. **okutta**; 7. **sirâbèta**; 8. **syookai-sita**; 9. **yoñda**

B 1. **Hisyô ĝa osóku kimàsita nêe.**
'The secretary came late, didn't s/he!'

Êe, isóĝasìi toki ni osóku koràrete komárimàsita.

2. **Hisyô ǧa kawárimàsita nêe.**
'The secretaries changed, didn't they!'

'Yes. It was a nuisance, having her/him come late at a time when we were busy.'

Êe, isóǧasìi toki ni 'kawararete komárimàsita.
'Yes. It was a nuisance having them change at a time when we were busy.'

3. **byoóki ni narimàsita;** 4. **hâyâku kaérimàsita;** 5. **syokúzi ni ikimàsita;** 6. **dekákemàsita;** 7. **gokái-simàsita**

C 1. **Kâre, okosaň o okôsita ň desu ka✔**
'(Is it that) he woke up your child?'

Êe, mâiniti no yoo ni kâre ni kodómo o okosàrete, iyâ ni nattyaimasita.
'Yes, I'm fed up, having him wake up our child almost every day.'

2. **Kaňriniň, môňku o iťtà ň desu ka✔**
'(Is it that) the superintendent complained?'

Êe, mâiniti no yoo ni 'kaňriniň ni môňku o iwarete, iyâ ni nattyaimasita.
'Yes, I'm fed up, having the superintendent complain almost every day.'

3. **taňtòosya/atumari no zikaň o kaeta;** 4. **hudoosaňya/heyâ o mî ni kitâ;** 5. **hisyô/siǧoto o nokosite kâetta;** 6. **kâkari no hito/namáe o matiǧàeta;** 7. **okosaň/keésàňki o hosíǧatta;** 8. **kânozyo/katée no hanasì o sita;** 9. **okosaň/omôtya o kowâsita;** 10. **tomodati/deňwa o kàketa**

D 1. **Nihoňǧo, raíǧakki mo beňkyoo-saremàsu ka✔**
'Are you going to study Japanese next term, too?'

Êe, beňkyoo-suru tumori dèsu kedo . .
'Yes, I intend to (study), but . . .' (I'm not sure).

2. **Okosaň, kibîsìku sitúkeraremàsu ka✔**
'Are you going to discipline your children strictly?'

Êe, sitúkèru tumóri dèsu kedo . .
'Yes, I intend to (discipline), but . . .' (what do you think?)

3. **karíta hòň/sûǧu kaésaremàsu;** 4. **Suzuki-saň/kôňdo mo sasówaremàsu;** 5. **kono hoňyaku/moo iti-do yarínaosaremàsu;** 6. **Yoóroppa-ryòkoo/haňtosi nobásare-màsu;** 7. **anó oňǧàkkai no kippu/nî-mai kawáremàsu;** 8. **obeňtoo/asítà mo motte koraremàsu**

E 1. **Koko no tokoro, naósimasyòo ka.**
'Shall I correct this place here (on the manuscript)?'

Êe, naósàreta hoo ǧa îi ka mo siremaseň nêe.
'Yes, maybe you had better fix it.'

2. **Uwaǧi, kimásyòo ka.**
'Shall I wear a jacket?'

Êe, kiráreta hòo ǧa îi ka mo siremaseň nêe.
'Yes, maybe you had better wear one.'

3. **seňmoň no hito/huyásimasyòo;** 4. **môtto hirôi apâato/saǧásimasyòo;** 5. **kâre ni tanômu no/yamémasyòo;** 6. **hurûi no/tukátte simaimasyòo;** 7. **siǧoto/tetúdàtte mo-ráimasyòo;** 8. **isya/yoňde kimàsyoo;** 9. **kabuki no kippu/tôri ni ikímasyòo**

F 1. **Sońna tokì ni wa, kimátta iikata simàsu ka✓**
'Do you use fixed expressions on occasions like that?'

    Êe, kimatta iikata surú monò desu yo✓
'Yes, the idea is to use fixed expressions.'

  2. **Sońna tokì ni wa, ziípañ hakimasèñ ka✓**
'You don't wear jeans on occasions like that?'

    Êe, ziipañ hakánai monò desu yo✓
'That's right, you should not wear jeans.'

  3. omíyağe motte ikimàsu; 4. kimóno kimàsu; 5. keéğo tukaimàsu; 6. okáne moraimasèñ; 7. kusúri nomasemàsu; 8. namáe yobaremàsu; 9. meési watasimàsu; 10. sekíniñ tòtte moraimasu; 11. kuwásìi hanasi kikímasèñ

G 1. **Arúbàito suru gakusee wa, oôi desu ka✓**
'Are there many students who work part time?'

    Êe, watasi mo gakusee no toki, arúbàito sitá monò desu nêe.
'Yes, when I was a student, I too used to work part time, I recall.'

  2. **Oyâ ni zêñbu harâtte morau gakusee wa, oôi desu ka✓**
'Are there many students who have their parents pay everything?'

    Êe, watasi mo gakusee no toki, oyâ ni zêñbu harâtte morátta monò desu nêe.
'Yes, when I was a student, I too used to have my parents pay everything, I recall.'

  3. rakuğo o kiki ni iku gakusee; 4. yasai ğa kirai na kodomo; 5. tyañto âisatu dekînai kodomo; 6. ziipañ sika hakanai gakusee; 7. eéğa o mì ni 'ikasete moraenai kodomo; 8. âsa zibúñ de okirarènai kodomo; 9. gaíziñ no tomodati ğa oòi gakusee

H 1. **Kabúki o gorañ ni naritài kata, irássyaimàsu ka✓**
'Is there anybody who would like to see kabuki?'

    Hâi, orímàsu. Watásì-tati, zêhi mitâi ñ desu kedo . .
'Yes, here we are. We would very much like to see it, but . . .' (is it possible?)

  2. **Yoteehyoo o kôpii = nasáritài kata, irássyaimàsu ka✓**
'Is there anybody who would like to copy the schedule?'

    Hâi, orímàsu. Watásì-tati, zêhi kôpii = sitâi ñ desu kedo . .
'Yes, here we are. We would very much like to copy it, but . . .' (is it possible?)

  3. kû-zi no tokkyuu ni onóri ni naritài; 4. konó dooğù o otúkai ni naritài; 5. tañtòosya ni oái ni naritài; 6. yuuğata odékake ni naritài; 7. wasyóku o mesiağaritài; 8. natú no aida kokó ni otutome ni naritài

I 1. **Yasúmì o nobâsita soo desu ğa, hoñtoo dèsu ka✓**
'I hear you extended your vacation, but is it true?'

    Êe. Anáta-ğàta mo nobásimasèñ ka✓
'Yes. Won't you (all) extend yours, too?'

  2. **Tabáko o yameta sòo desu ğa, hoñtoo dèsu ka✓**
'I hear you quit smoking, but is it true?'

    Êe. Anáta-ğàta mo yamémasèñ ka✓
'Yes. Won't you (all) quit, too?'

3. gakúsee o huyàsita; 4. rêe no 'gakkai ni hâitta; 5. hudoosañya ni zêñbu makâseta; 6. okosañ ni anó omòtya o 'katte ağeta; 7. okosañ ni tênisu o naráwàseta; 8. mezúrasìi kî o sodâteta

J 1. **Anó señsèe kibísìi to omówànai?**
'Don't you think that teacher is strict?'

Sôo desu nêe . . . Betu ni kibîsìku wa nâi kedo . .
Hmm . . . S/he *isn't* particularly *strict,* but . . .'

2. **Anó kodomò-tati yakámasìi to omówànai?**
'Don't you think those children are noisy?'

Sôo desu nêe . . . Betu ni yakámàsìku wa nâi kedo . .
'Hmm . . . They *aren't* particularly *noisy,* but . . .'

3. zisiñ kowâi; 4. konó hòñ kâita hito ni aítài; 5. zibuñ no señmoñ ikásitài; 6. âkatyañ hosîi; 7. gaikoku ni ikasete moraitai; 8. hâyâku határakeru yòo ni narítài; 9. gosyûziñ ni êráku natte hosîi

K 1. **Konó koohìi, usúku simasyòo ka⤹**
'Shall I make this coffee weak[er]?'

Iya, kôi mama de kêkkoo desu yo⤹
'No, it's all right strong (as it is).'

2. **Dêñki, kesímasyòo ka⤹**
'Shall I turn off the light?'

Iya, tûkêta mama de kêkkoo desu yo⤹
'No, it's all right turned on (as it is).'

3. râzio no kôe/ôókìku simasyoo; 4. tuğî no atumari/nâğâku simasyoo; 5. mâdo/akémasyòo; 6. osake/âtûku simasyoo; 7. teğami/hikidasi kara dasímasyoo; 8. raísyuu no sikèñ/yasásiku simasyòo

L 1. **Kutû o haítè (i)te mo, haíremàsu ka⤹**
'Can we come/go in (even) with our shoes on?'

Motîroñ. Haíta mama hàitte mo kamáimasèñ yo⤹
'Of course! It's all right to come/go in with your shoes on (as you are).'

2. **Wakárànakute mo, hazímeraremàsu ka⤹**
'Can we start even if we don't understand?'

Motîroñ. Wakárànai mama hazímetè mo kamáimasèñ yo⤹
Of course! It's all right to start, not understanding (as you are).'

3. sukôsi kowârete (i)te mo/kaésemàsu; 4. owáranàkute mo/kaéremàsu; 5. tuğî no hito o matâsete (i)te mo/tuzúkeraremàsu; 6. nîmotu o môtte (i)te mo/deráremàsu; 7. tâtte (i)te mo/tukáemàsu; 8. kurôi mono ğa mazîtte (i)te mo/nomémàsu; 9. dêñki ğa kiétè (i)te mo/syasiñ torémàsu; 10. kutû o nuğânakute mo/ağáremàsu

Application Exercises

A1. Using the passive as an honorific-polite form, practice asking questions to be answered by the respondent on the basis of reality. For example, find out when X first studied Japanese; how (i.e., by what means) X comes here; where X bought his/her textbook; where X listens to tapes; whether X reads Japanese newspapers; whether X uses a computer; whether X has ever been to Europe. Answers to these questions should be expanded beyond the minimal, direct answer to the question.

2. In response to questions about current activities, indicate that you did these things regularly when you were a child, but . . . For example, ask about eating sweets, drinking milk, listening to the radio, watching television, going to see movies.

3. In response to offers to change something to an opposite condition, indicate that things are fine in their present condition. For example, offer to close the window, turn on the light, heat the milk, turn up the radio, make the coffee weak[er], slice (i.e., cut) this meat thin[ner], make this [more] spicy, make the test [more] difficult, make the message long[er].

4. Using your instructor as a go-between, complain about a current situation that is causing problems for you. Examples: you are embarrassed by the fact that your colleague is putting out letters from your company in weird English; you are annoyed by the irregular attendance of your colleague (i.e., he keeps coming and not coming), resulting in your having to do his work as well as your own; your colleague keeps coming late, so you have to answer her phone all morning long; your colleague smokes from morning till night— which is bad for your health as well as his; the bicycles belonging to your apartment neighbors' children, which they leave in the hallway every night, have become a nuisance.

5. *Very tactfully and politely and hesitantly and apologetically,* offer a Japanese colleague advice about conduct abroad that implies criticism of his/her current practice. For example, suggest correction of a commonly made mistake in English ("we say 'discuss X,' not 'discuss about X'"); suggest a change in his style of dressing ("you don't have to wear a coat and tie to English class"); suggest that he not smoke in English class; suggest that he speak in more polite English to the American secretary; suggest that he not ask the American secretary to make coffee and tea; suggest that she not bring her children to Mr. Smith's wedding reception. In every case, avoid being confrontational and avoid suggesting that any *serious* mistake has been made.

B. Core Conversations: Substitution

In practicing the Core Conversations with appropriate, very limited substitutions, follow each version with questions on the contents.

SECTION B

Core Conversations

1(N)a. **Osóku nàtte gomén-nasài.**
   Mâtta?

    b. **Deyôo to sitá tokorò o 'syotyoo ni yobarete neʕ**

    c. **Meńdòo na kotô o tanómàretyatta.**

    d. **Gaíkoku kara mièru 'okyakusañ o ańnài-site kure tte iû no.**

    e. **Ñ.**

(J)a. **Îi yo. Nàrete (i)ru kara ..**

    b. **Ñ.**

    c. **Nâni?**

    d. **Mata? Konáidà kara sońna koto bàkari zya nai.**

    e. **Kotówàttyae yo—sońnà no.**

f. **Soó iu wàke ni mo ikánài no
yo—asoko ni osêwa ni nâtte
(i)ru aida wa ne˥**

2(N)a. **Yasuda-sañ wa, waréware g̃a
nòñde (i)ru aida mo, sig̃oto
'sig̃oto de kinódòku desu ne!**

b. **Ñ.**

c. **Zyâa, yamérò tte íttè mo,
yaméru wàke ni mo ikánài
desyoo nêe!**

3(J) **Okyákusañ g̃a kaeràretara kitê
kure tte, butyóo g̃a itte (i)màsita
yo⤳**

f. **Mûri surû-na yo—amari.**

(J)a. **Nân da ka ne˥**

b. **Kóttì ni iru aida ni, atárasìi
koñpyuutaa-purogùramu o mít-tù
mo kâke tte iwárete (i)ru-rasìi ñ
desu yo.**

c. **Mâa, anô hito wa mazíme dà kara
ne˥**

(N) **Sôo. Zyâa, bôku g̃a 'inai aida ni
deñwa àttara, mêsseezi kiít(e) òite
ne˥**

ENGLISH EQUIVALENTS

1(N)a. Excuse me for being late. Did you
wait [long]?

b. I was called by the head of the
institute just as I was about to
leave, and . . .

c. I was asked [to do] something
that's a bother.

d. (It's that) s/he says I'm to act as a
guide for some visitors who are
coming from abroad.

e. Yeah.

f. (It's that) I can't really do
anything like that—while I depend on that place, you know?

2(N)a. [For] Mr/s. Yasuda, even while
we're drinking, it's work, work,
and that's too bad, isn't it.

b. Yeah . . .

(J)a. It's O.K. (Because) I'm used to it.

b. Yeah.

c. What?

d. Again? (You must agree that) it's
been nothing but that kind of thing
(since) recently.

e. Refuse!—that kind of thing.

f. Don't overdo!—too much.

(J)a. [It's] something or other, you know?

b. (It's that) apparently s/he's been told
to write all of three new computer
programs while s/he's here.

c. Then even if we tell him/her to (quit), s/he probably can't really quit, can s/he.

3(J)   The division chief was saying you were to come when the visitors left.

c. Well, since s/he's conscientious, you know.

(N)   Right. Then if there are any phone calls while I'm gone (*lit.* not here), take a message, will you?

BREAKDOWNS
(AND SUPPLEMENTARY VOCABULARY)

1. **goméñ-nasài** (SP1)	excuse me, pardon me
deyôo to sita tokoro	the moment when [I] was about to leave
deyôo to sitá tokorò o 'yobareru	be called when [I] was about to leave
+**sihâiniñ**	manager
+**X-g̃àkari**	person in charge of X
meńdòo /na/	bothersome, troublesome, annoying
tanómàrete simau *or*	
tanómàretyau	end up being asked
kure (SP1)	give (to me/us) /command/
ańnài-site kure	show around (for me/us) /command/
ańnài-site kure tte iu	tell to show around (for me/us)
konáidà kara	starting recently
kotówàru /-u; **kotówàtta**/	refuse
kotówàtte simau *or*	
kotówàttyau	end up refusing; absolutely refuse
kotówàttyae	refuse /command/
osêwa ni nâtte (i)ru aida (SP2)	while being under obligation, while being dependent
mûri surû-na (SP1)	don't strain /command/
+**warau** /-u; **waratta**/	laugh
+**naku** /-u; **naita**/	cry
2. **Yasuda**	/family name/
wareware	we
nôñde (i)ru aida	while drinking
+**sawâg̃u** /-u; **sawâida**/	make a noise; raise a racket; revel
+**utâ o utau** /-u; **utatta**/	sing songs
kinódòkù	pitiable, unfortunate
nâñ da ka	something or other
iru aida	while being present (animate)

koṅpyuutaa-purogùramu	computer program
kâke	write /command/
kâke tte iwareru	be told to write
yamero	quit /command/
yamérò to iu	tell to quit
+homêru /-ru; hômeta/	praise
+kiboo-suru	hope
+susumeru /-ru; susumeta/	recommend; encourage; urge
mazime /na/	serious, steady, conscientious
3. kitê kure	come (for me/us) /command/
kitê kure tte iu	tell to come (for me/us)
inai aida	while not present (animate)

MISCELLANEOUS NOTES

1. In CC1, Sue Brown is complaining to Kato, her fellow graduate student, about the after-hour requirements that are placed on her to act as a guide for foreign guests. Her feeling of obligation to her employers, even though she is only a part-time worker, is strong: she realizes that she cannot refuse even though she is annoyed by the request. Kato expresses sympathy for her complaint and even encourages her to say no in an effort to make her feel better, but she shows her understanding of what is expected of any loyal employee in Japan. She handles her frustration by expressing her anger only to her friend, and then will knuckle under and conform.

Requirements of this kind are common in Japan. The notion of a strict nine-to-five day is rarely encountered, and after-hour duties are freely imposed on employees at all levels.

The conversation between these two close friends is casual-style: in the entire conversation there isn't a single distal-style predicate. Other features of casual-style are: contracted **tanómàretyatta**; the affirmation alternate **ṅ** 'yeah'; and the sentence-final rough imperatives **kotówàttyae** (also a contracted form) and **surû-na** (cf. SP1, following).

(J)a. Kato's slightly teasing **nârete (i)ru kara** indicates that he feels very relaxed in his conversation with Sue Brown.

(N)b. Note the use of **tokorò o** with the passive **yobarete**, indicating that Sue Brown was summoned when she was about to leave (*lit.* 'was affected by summoning through the time period when [she] was about to leave.')

+**-Ĝakari** is the form of **kâkari** (cf. **kâkari no hito** 'person in charge') that occurs in compounds. Examples: **aṅnai-ĝàkari** 'person in charge of ushering or information,' 'tour guide'; **reṅraku-ĝàkari** 'person in charge of liaison.'

(N)c. **Meṅdòo**: Note **meṅdòo ni nâru** 'become a nuisance'; **meṅdòo o kakêru** 'cause trouble (for someone)'; **meṅdòo o mîru** 'care (for someone)'; **goméṅdoo-nàĝara** 'while it's a bother for you.'

(J)e. **Kotówàru** is a transitive, operational consonant verbal covering refusing and declining of both requests and invitations. Note **nâṅ to ka itte kotówàru** 'fabricate an excuse' (*lit.* 'refuse, saying something or other').

+**Warau** and +**naku** are both operational consonant verbals. Note **warai-naĝara/naki-**

naĝara teĝámi o yòñda '[I] laughed/cried as [I] read the letter'; itâkute 'naku 'cry in pain'; mîruku ĝa hôsîkute 'naku 'cry for milk.'

2. In CC2, Mr. Yamada and Deborah Miller are pitying the hard-working, conscientious Mr/s. Yasuda, who is creating new computer programs at the office even while they are enjoying themselves, having a drink after work. Mr/s. Yasuda is apparently on temporary duty at their office and must finish a specific task while s/he is there. As usual, these two individuals use careful-style, with distal-style final predicates, in talking to each other. However, the use of ñ 'yeah' and of the direct-style before kara indicates some degree of relaxation.

(N)a. **Wareware** is a slightly more businesslike, stiff alternate for watá(ku)sì-tati. It is particularly common in the combination waréware-nihoñzìñ 'we Japanese.' The frequency of the use of this expression is a reminder of how Japanese tend to look on themselves as a cohesive group in reference to which general statements can often be made. It also reminds us that 'we Japanese' form a group that excludes all non-Japanese, particularly when talking to foreigners. In comparison, consider how much less frequently we speak of 'we Americans.'

+ **Sawâĝu**, an operational consonant verbal, covers making a noise in the literal sense as well as raising a fuss over something.

+ **Utau**, a transitive, operational w-consonant verbal, appears commonly with the nominal utâ 'song.' Japanese, generally speaking, are very fond of singing. It is not at all unusual for a group of men at a party to take turns, each singing a solo, with no self-consciousness about the quality of their voices. Even at bars individual customers will often take the floor and offer a song. Musical accompaniments without singers (the singing being provided by nonprofessionals on the spot) are called **karaoke**. In addition to **karaoke** bars, there are **karaoke** tapes and records for practice and enjoyment at home.

Siĝoto 'siĝoto: The repetition is for emphasis.

Kinódòkù: Note kinódokuĝàru 'feel sorry (for someone)'; **Okínodòkù desu nêe.** and **Okinodokusama.** 'That's too bad, unfortunate; I'm sorry.' The situations for which pity is expressed can cover everything from an unreasonable workload to poverty, a death in the family, unemployment, and so on.

(J)a. This utterance is connected with (J)b: Mr. Yamada is indicating that he isn't exactly clear on Mr/s. Yasuda's situation, so he prefaces what explanation he can give by stating that it's 'something or other' (*lit.* 'what is it, huh').

(J)b. **Iwarete (i)ru** 's/he is in a state of having been told.'

The supplementary verbals **homêru**, **susumeru**, and **kiboo-suru** are all transitive, operational verbals. The first two, which may have personal operands, occur frequently in the passive.

3. In CC3, Mr. Carter, who has just walked into the office, is given a message from the division head by the secretary. Since he will be going to see his boss, he asks the secretary to take messages during his absence.

In speaking to Mr. Carter, the secretary uses careful-style with a distal-style final predicate. She conveys the request from the **butyoo** as a **kureru**-type instruction, and **ítte (i)màsita** is used in reference to their in-group superior who is not present. In speaking of Mr. Carter's out-group visitor(s), she uses an honorific passive (**kaéràretara**). Mr. Carter, on the other hand, gives his own instructions to the secretary in an informal request form, a sentence-final gerund.

(J) Note that **kaéràretara** in reference to the visitor(s) must refer to their returning to their own base of operations—their home(s) or their own office(s)—not to coming back to where Mr. Carter and the secretary are. That meaning would be expressed as **modôtte korâretara**.

(N) **Kiít(e) òite**: Mr. Carter is instructing the secretary to ask for messages 'in advance,' to be passed on to him later.

Structural Patterns

1. MORE ON REQUESTS: DIRECT-STYLE IMPERATIVES

It is not surprising that a language that places as much emphasis on interpersonal connections and relative rank as does Japanese—a reflection of the workings of the society—should have an elaborately developed set of request forms. Which form is used on any occasion depends on the relationship of the person making the request to the person to whom it is addressed and on the nature of the request. We have already introduced a sizable number of such patterns, ranging from casual requests like **Mâtte neʃ Mâtte tyoodai.** and **Omati.** to very polite, distal-style combinations like **Mâtte kudásaimasèñ ka⌣** and **Omáti ni nàtte itádakenài desyoo ka**. These patterns may be direct-style or distal, plain or polite, but the surprising thing is that most of them do not include an imperative form. They are not direct orders, using a special form of the verbal, but roundabout requests that use regular imperfective forms, gerunds, or honorific- or humble-polite verbal-nominals. This is a clear reflection of the Japanese dislike of direct confrontation. Instead of ordering people to do things—setting up 'you' versus 'me'—the preference is for approaching such situations as concerted efforts ('let's do so-and-so'), or suggestions ('how would it be if you did so-and-so?'), or invitations to perform an action as a benefit to the speaker ('won't you grant me [or can't I receive] your doing so-and-so?').

The only exceptions we have encountered are **kudásài**, **irássyài**, and **nasâi**. At a very early stage in our study of Japanese (lesson 4A-SP6) we learned that **kudásài** is, in fact, a direct-style imperative of the verbal **kudásàru**. Similarly, **irássyài** is the direct-style imperative of **irássyàru**, **nasâi** of **nasâru**, and **oʃsyài** of **oʃsyàru**. These are all honorific-polite verbals, and their politeness counteracts the usual confrontational, aggressive quality of the direct imperative form. Request forms like **onómi ni nàtte kudasai, onómi-kudásài, nôñde kudasai, onómi-nasài,** and **nomí-nasài** all include direct-style imperatives, but their politeness softens the abruptness implied by their form. Framing a request as something that will be 'given to the in-group' (using **kudásài**) is another softening device.

Which of these patterns is used in which kind of social encounter is a question of extreme complexity that requires direct observation of actual situational use, since native speakers use these forms automatically, totally without awareness. They *are* aware, of course, of which forms are more polite than others, but the sweeping generalizations native speakers like to make about their language and the claims about what they say in it—whatever that native language may be—often do not reflect reality. All the careful research that has been done in this area indicates that we are much more apt to base our statements on how we think we *should* talk!

Of the forms listed above, a note on the last two examples, **onómi-nasài** and **nomí-nasài**, is in order. These two patterns—/honorific-polite verbal nominal + **-nasài**/ and /stem + **-nasài**/, occur most commonly in addressing children, close relatives, subordinates, service personnel, and so forth. They are *never* used in addressing superiors.

But if there is a direct-style imperative of the special **-aru** polite verbals, we might reasonably suspect that there are other direct-style imperatives, used in circumstances when politeness and indirection are abandoned. This turns out to be true. We introduce these forms only *after* countless other request patterns. They have more constrained uses, and for foreigners are markedly limited in application.

A. AFFIRMATIVE DIRECT-STYLE IMPERATIVE

The affirmative direct-style imperative of verbals is made by adding **-e** to the root of consonant verbals and **-ro** to the root of vowel verbals; the corresponding form of **kûru** is **kôi** and of **suru** is **siro**. (The imperative of an accented verbal is accented on the same mora as the imperfective; the imperative of an unaccented verbal is unaccented, but it acquires an accent on its final mora in some contexts—for example, preceding sentence-particle **yo**.) Another way of describing the form (except for that of the two irregular verbals) is to say that the final **-u** of the imperfective of vowel verbals is changed to **-o**, and the final **-u** of consonant verbals to **-e**. All these imperatives may be followed by sentence-particle **yo**. Examples:

> **tabêro** 'eat!'
>
> **okîro** 'get up!'
>
> **nôme** 'drink!'
>
> **tomare** 'halt!'
>
> **harâe** 'pay!'

Note that the special verbal **-màsu** (which never occurs initially and has no meaning beyond signaling distal-style) also has a direct-style imperative. This appears only with the polite **-aru** verbals, and we have already encountered it in such forms as **irássyaimàse** and **kudásaimàse**. We must identify these as direct-style imperatives of distal-style honorific-polite verbals! The usual abrupt tone of the direct-style is completely counteracted in such forms.

When we say that the Japanese avoid direct confrontation, this certainly does not mean that it never occurs. When two really close friends talk to each other, polite patterns may be thrown to the wind. Japanese bosses may speak to their employees in a manner that shocks even generally plain-spoken Americans. Lack of politeness is also evident when people become angry: when someone in a crowd is pushing to the point of endangering the safety of those in the area, even in Japan one does not politely request, 'I wonder if I would be able to be the recipient of your not pushing.'

The direct-style imperatives listed above occur as final predicates only in very rough, familiar style, much more commonly in the speech of men. Some may claim that these are used exclusively by males, but there is good evidence that, at least within the family, orders that children are not to ignore may come, even from their mother, as direct-style imperatives. (This depends on the individual mother and the type of family.) Foreigners would be well advised to avoid such orders unless the situation and the addressee clearly make it appropriate. In CC1, it is only the male, Kato, who uses the form. He uses it in speaking to his close friend Sue Brown in a context supportive of her position.

One special direct-style imperative must now be added: less polite than a **kudásâi** imperative is a corresponding **kureru** imperative. However, the direct-style imperative of **kureru** is irregular: it is the root alone, without following **ro**. Thus we find: **Kurê yo**. 'Give it to me.' and **Mâtte kure**. 'Wait!' (Also possible and slightly more polite, although less common in current Japanese, is **Mâtte okure**, an example of an honorific-polite verbal nominal in sentence-final position used as a request. Cf. 28B-SP1.)

But the direct-style imperatives have another use which is not confrontational and which occurs commonly in the speech of both men and women. In this use the direct-style imperative is embedded and reports on a request made by someone else.

Kag̃î kakêro tte iímàsita yo 'S/he said to lock the door.'

Hâha ni, mâiniti no yoo ni, môtto beñkyoo-sirò tte iwarete, iyâ ni nâttyatta. 'I'm sick of being told by my mother almost every day to study more.'

This embedded use of the direct-style imperative does not imply that the original request necessarily occurred in this form. It alternates with such patterns as found in:

Kag̃î kàkete (kudasai *or* **kure) tte iímàsita yo** 'S/he said to lock the door [for him/ her].' *and*

Kag̃î kakêru yoo ni iímàsita yo 'S/he told him/her to lock the door.'

B. Negative Direct-Style Imperative

For most affirmative patterns there is a corresponding negative. Thus far, negative imperative requests have involved the use of /negative + gerund **dè**/ or /negative + **yòo ni**/ followed by an affirmative request pattern with **kudasài**. Examples: **Matânai de kudasai.** and **Matânai yoo ni sité kudasài.** In more casual equivalents, the **kudasài** and **sité kudasài** can be dropped. We can now add to these: **Matânai de kure. Matânai yoo ni 'site kure.** All of these are requests that someone not wait. The regular pattern for forming the negative direct-style imperative, comparable in tone to the affirmative forms introduced above, consists of /verbal imperfective + **-na**/. An unaccented verbal acquires a final-mora accent. Examples:

Mâtu-na. 'Don't wait!'

Mîru-na. 'Don't look!'

Soó iù-na yo. 'Don't say that!'

Everything we have said about the affirmative applies equally to the negative. As final predicates, these negative imperatives are extremely direct, aggressive, and not at all polite, but when they are embedded in a sentence, the following predicate sets the tone. Thus:

Surû-na tte iwáretà kara, môo sinâi. 'Since I was told not to do it, I won't do it any more.'

Nakamura-kuñ wa, kore nômu-na tte iítà kedo, dôo site desyoo ka nêe. 'Nakamura said not to drink this, but I wonder why!'

☠WARNING: The difference between long and short consonants can be the difference between a friendly informal request and a direct order. Be careful! **Mâtte.** is very different in tone from **Mâte.**

2. /PREDICATE + **aida**/

The nominal **aida** was originally introduced as a place word indicating an interval of space in sequences like **giñkoo to yuúbìñkyoku no aida** 'between the bank and the post office' and later as an interval of time in the combination **kon(o)aida** 'recently' ('this time interval close to us'). **Aida** may also be preceded by a sentence modifier indicating the interval during which something occurs.

We have already learned another pattern that described the occurrence of one activity while another occurs: For example, **Nakinaḡara teḡámi o yomimàsita.** 'I cried and read the letter at the same time'; 'I cried while I read the letter.' Compare now **Tomodati ḡa naite (i)ru aida ni, teḡámi o yomimàsita.** 'While my friend was crying, I read the letter.'

Naḡara is used when two activities are concurrent and performed by the same person(s) (e.g., I whistle while I work). **Aida**, on the other hand, is used (a) when the two predicates are linked to different operators or affects (*I'll* whistle while *you* work); or (b) when one activity occurs intermittently during an uninterrupted **aida** interval (while I worked, I *often* whistled); or (c) when at least one of the predicates refers to a state rather than an activity (while I was *here*, I was always whistling).

/**Aida + ni**/ tells the time *at* which something occurs; **aida** without a following particle (or, with a change of focus, followed by **wa** or **mo**), describes the *extent* of the interval during which the following predicate occurs. Since **aida** is a nominal, the operator or affect of the final predicate of the sentence modifier that precedes it may be followed by **ḡa** or **no**. A final verbal in that modifier is either a non-action verbal like **âru** or **iru** (or a more polite equivalent) or a verbal gerund + **(i)ru** (or a more polite equivalent). Even in reference to a past event, the predicate preceding **aida** may be imperfective, but the perfective also occurs commonly.

> **Anâta ḡa têepu o 'kiite (i)ru aida ni, watasi tyôtto deńwa site kimàsu.** 'While you are listening to tapes, I'll just go and make a phone call.'

> **Anó kaisya ni tutòmete (i)ta aida, yôku tyuúka-ryòori o tâbeta mono desu.** 'All the while I was working for that company, I used to eat Chinese food a lot.'

> **Nihôñ ni ita aida, zutto tomódati no utì ni tomárasete moratte (i)màsita.** 'All the while I was in Japan, I stayed (i.e., I was being permitted to stay) at a friend's house.'

> **Hâha ḡa rûsu no aida wa, utî o derárènai.** 'For as long as my mother is out, I can't leave the house.'

> **Kodomo no 'nete (i)ru aida mo, dekákerarenàkatta.** 'Also/even while the children were sleeping, I couldn't go out.'

Drills

A 1. **Kâre ni tyûui = sinâkatta ñ desu ka⤸**

'You mean you didn't warn him?'

Êe, tyûui-siyoo to sitá tokorò o 'syotyoo ni yobarete nêe.

'That's right. Just as I was about to warn him, I was called by the institute director, and—you know.'

2. **Soñna meńdòo na siḡoto kotówaranakatta ñ desu ka⤸**

'You mean you didn't turn down that kind of bothersome work?'

Êe, kotówaròo to sitá tokorò o 'syotyoo ni yobarete nêe.

'That's right. Just as I was about to turn it down, I was called by the institute director, and—you know.'

3. atárasìi sihâiniñ ni âisatu sinâkatta; 4. Yasuda-sañ mo sasówanàkatta; 5. hîsyo ni môñku iwánàkatta; 6. kânozyo ni 'ano siḡoto yarínaosasènakatta; 7. ohírugòhañ

tâbe ni ikánàkatta; 8. koóhìi kaŕte kònakatta; 9. sonó kikài tukáwasete morawanàkatta

B 1. **Koóhai g̃a koñpyùutaa tukáttà ñ**
   desu ka⤸
   'You mean the junior members used
   the computer?'

   Êe, tukátte (i)rù no o mimâsita yo⤸
   'Yes, I saw them using it.'

2. **Mazíme na Sakamoto-sañ-tati g̃a utâ**
   utáttà ñ desu ka⤸
   'You mean the serious Sakamoto
   group sang songs?'

   Êe, utátte (i)rù no o mimâsita yo⤸
   'Yes, I saw them singing.'

3. kyoózyu g̃a kono nòoto goráñ ni nàtta; 4. kaǹriniñ g̃a gomì ʹhirowaseta;
   5. Yamâg̃uti-sañ g̃a kâre no namáe to zyùusyo ʹosiete moratta; 6. kânozyo g̃a sihâiniñ ni ʹsikarareta; 7. hîsyo g̃a ʹnaita

● Repeat the preceding drill, replacing **no** with **tokoro** in the responses.

C 1. **Señpai no ʹSakamoto-sañ ni, deńwa**
   kakemàsita ka⤸
   'Did you call Mr/s. Sakamoto (who is
   senior to us)?'

   Zitû wa, kakéyòo to sitá tokorò e, daízi
   na deñwa g̃a hàitta no de . .
   'Actually, just as I was about to (call), an
   important phone call came in, so . . .' (I
   didn't).

2. **Tanôñd(e) oita mono, kôpii-simasita**
   ka⤸
   'Did you copy the thing I requested
   (in advance)?'

   Zitû wa, kôpii-siyoo to sitá tokorò e,
   daízi na deñwa g̃a hàitta no de . .
   'Actually, just as I was about to (copy), an
   important phone call came in, so . . .' (I
   didn't).

3. ano teg̃ami/kâite simaimasita; 4. kinoo no kabuki/mî ni ikímàsita; 5. syasiñ/tôtte
   moraimasita; 6. matíg̃àtta tokoro/yarínaosasemàsita; 7. ano utá no tèepu/kikásete
   moraimàsita

D 1. **Kôñdo no atumari, nobâsu ñ desu**
   ka⤸
   'Are we to postpone the next
   gathering?'

   Êe. Butyoo ni nobâse to iwáretà kara,
   sikáta arimasèñ yo.
   'Yes. We were told by the division chief to
   postpone it, so that's it!'

2. **Rêe no hanasi, kotówàru ñ desu**
   ka⤸
   'Are we to turn down that thing we
   talked about?'

   Êe. Butyoo ni kotówàre to iwáretà kara,
   sikáta arimasèñ yo.
   'Yes. We were told by the division chief to
   turn it down, so that's it!'

3. **wáreware g̃a okyakusañ añnài-suru**; 4. **zêñbu kimáru màde mâtu**; 5. **matíg̃àtte (i)te**
   mo ʹtuzukeru; 6. **añna îi sig̃oto akíramèru**; 7. **kyoó-zyuu ni tukùtte simau**; 8. **zêñbu**
   hitô-ri de sekíniñ tòru; 9. **aǹna tookù made todôke ni iku**; 10. **atárasìi tañtòosya**
   ni âtte kuru; 11. **ano mazíme na hisyò o ʹyamesaseru**

E 1. **Konó tèepu de sibâtte kure.**
   'Tie it with this tape.'

   A, sibâru no? Siránàkatta wa⤸ Goméñ-
   nasài.

'Oh, are we to tie it? I didn't know. Sorry.'

2. **Kotíra no hòo o 'susumete kure.**
'Recommend this one.'

A, susúmerù no? SD̀ránàkatta wa⤸
Gomén-nasài.
'Oh, are we to recommend it? I didn't know. Sorry.'

3. **môtto zyosée o huyàsite**; 4. **ki ní sinài de 'tuzukete**; 5. **môtto mizú o màzete**; 6. **îi to ìttàra, hanâsite**; 7. **nokôttara, zêñbu 'sutete simatte**; 8. **môtto kîree ni kâite moratte**; 9. **Yasúda-kuñ ni tukuràsete**

F 1. **Koóhai to tukiawànai?**
'Don't you associate with your juniors?'

Ñ. Zañnèñ da kedo, tukíawànai de tte, señsèe ni iwáretà kara . .
'Right. It's too bad, but I was told not to (associate) by the professor, so . . .'

2. **Koñgàkki mo arúbàito sinai?**
'Aren't you going to do part-time work this term, either?'

Ñ. Zañnèñ da kedo, sinâi de tte señsèe ni iwáretà kara . .
'Right. It's too bad, but I was told not to (do any) by the professor, so . . .'

3. **tôru zyûḡyoo huyásànai**; 4. **zêmi no atumari nobásànai**; 5. **yasúmì ni 'asobi ni ikanai**; 6. **hurûi sikêñ kôpii-sasete 'morawanai**; 7. **dâre ka ni 'hoñyaku-sasenai**; 8. **Yosida-sañ tetúdàtte aḡenai**

G 1. **Môo osû-na yo.**[4]
'Don't push any more!'

Osánàkatta wa yo.
'I didn't push!'

2. **Môñku bâkari iû-na yo.**
'Don't just complain!'

Iwánàkatta wa yo.
'I didn't complain!'

3. **matíḡàtta toki waráu-na**; 4. **añna hitò no sewâ ni nâru-na**; 5. **señsèe no ozyama surû-na**; 6. **sukôsi sika nâi ñ da kara, tôtte simáu-na**; 7. **goryôosiñ ni siñpai-saserù-na**; 8. **sekkaku syòotai-site kurétà ñ da kara, kotówàru-na**

G'1. **Môo osánài de yo.**[5]
'Don't push any more!'

Osánàkatta yo.
'I didn't push!'

2. **Môñku bâkari iwánài de yo.**
'Don't just complain!'

Iwánàkatta yo.
'I didn't complain!'

● Continue with corresponding examples 3–8 from G.

H 1. **Kâre ni, ano siḡoto yaméru yòo ni ìttà desyoo?**
'You told him to quit that work, didn't you?'

Êe. Sikâsi, yamérò tte ìttè mo, yaméru wàke ni wa ikánài desyoo.
'Yes. But even if I tell him to (quit), he probably can't really quit.'

2. **Kâre ni, anó kotò ki ní sinai yòo ni ìttà desyoo?**

Êe. Sikâsi, ki ní surù-na tte ìttè mo, ki ní sinai wàke ni wa ikánài desyoo.

4. The stimuli of this drill are extremely blunt and the responses feminine.
5. The stimuli of this drill are gentle and the responses blunt.

'You told him not to be concerned about that matter, didn't you?'

'Yes. But even if I tell him not to (be concerned), he probably can't really not be concerned.'

3. kôñdo no ryokoo nobâsu; 4. yôku naítoku-surù made 'kimenai; 5. yokee na siñpai sinâi de 'beñkyoo tuzukeru; 6. añmari 'amai mono 'kodomo ni tabésasènai; 7. zêñbu 'watasi ni makáseru; 8. iyâ nara, hoká no hitò ni 'yaraseru

I 1. **Kore kara, kono hoñyaku yarínaosòo to omôu ñ desu ḡa . .**
'(It's that) I think I'll do this translation over (from) now, but . . .' (is that all right?)

Zyâa, yarínaòsite (i)ru aida ni, watasi wa tyôtto deñwa-site kimàsu kara . .
'Then while you're doing it over, I'm just going to go and make a phone call, so . . .' (take your time).

2. **Kore kara, sûutu ni kiḡáeyòo to omôu ñ desu ḡa . .**
'(It's that) I think I'll change into a suit (from) now, but . . .' (is that all right?)

Zyâa, kiḡâete (i)ru aida ni, watasi wa tyôtto deñwa-site kimàsu kara . .
'Then while you're changing, I'm just going to go and make a phone call, so . . .' (take your time).

3. rêe no siḡóto ni tùite 'butyoo to soódañ-siyòo; 4. atárasìi koñpyùutaa no tukáikata ni tùite osíete moraòo; 5. hituyoo na mono hakóbaseyòo; 6. nîmotu azûke ni ikôo; 7. zikokuhyoo sirábeyòo; 8. mîdori no madôḡuti ni narábòo

J 1. **Yosída-sañ-tati wa, dooryoo ḡa siḡoto-site (i)ru aida, naní mo yaranàkatta wa nêe.**[6]
'Mr/s. Yosida and his/her group didn't do anything while their peers were working, did they!'

Ñ. Wareware ḡa site (i)ru aida mo, yaránàkatta daro(o)?
'That's right. They didn't do anything while *we* were working either, did they?'

2. **Yosída-sañ-tati wa, dooryoo ḡa siḡoto-site (i)ru aida, iítàri kitâri sitê (i)ta wa nêe.**
'Mr/s. Yosida and his/her group were going back and forth while their peers were working, weren't they!'

Ñ. Wareware ḡa site (i)ru aida mo, iítàri kitâri sitê (i)ta daro(o)?
'Yeah. They were going back and forth while *we* were working, too, weren't they?'

3. zeñzeñ tetudawànakatta; 4. zaśśi nàñka yôñde (i)ta; 5. gôruhu no reñsyuu sitê (i)ta; 6. sêki o hazúsitè (i)ta; 7. otyá o nòñde bâkari datta; 8. butyoo ni sikáraretè (i)ta

K 1. **Tanómàretara, kotówàru desyoo?**
'If you are asked, you'll refuse, won't you?'

Iya, kotówàru wake ni wa ikímasèñ yo— koko ni iru aida wa.
'That's not right. I can't really refuse—for as long as I stay here.'

---

6. The stimuli of this drill are feminine and the responses blunt.

2. **Hasimoto-sañ, sasówanài desyoo?**
'You won't ask Mr/s. Hashimoto along, will you?'

Iya, sasówanai wàke ni wa ikímasèñ yo— koko ni iru aida wa.
'That's not right. I can't really not ask her/him along—for as long as I stay here.'

3. **zisá-syùkkiñ ni 'kaesaseru**; 4. **syotyoo ni 'soodañ-sinai**; 5. **môtto bêñ no îi tokoro ni híkkòsu**; 6. **ki ní iranàkattara, hañtai-suru**; 7. **môo asóko nì wa 'syuttyoo-sasenai**; 8. **konó sìgoto ğa owattàra, yasúmàsete ağeru**

L 1. **Tyûuğoku de rekísi beñkyoo-surù ñ desu ka⤸**
'So you are going to study history in China?'

Êe, Tyûuğoku ni iru aida, zuʱto beñkyoo-suru tumori dèsu.
'Yes, the whole time I'm in China, I intend to study it.'

2. **Uti de tetúdàu ñ desu ka⤸**
'So you are going to help in the house?'

Êe, uti ni iru aida, zuʱto tetudàu tumori desu.
'Yes. The whole time I'm at home, I intend to help.'

3. **Amerika/tênisu 'reñsyuu-suru**; 4. **hôteru/azúkèru**; 5. **Tookyoo/kabúki mì ni iku**; 6. **daiğaku/rekísi no zyùğyoo tôru**; 7. **Amerika/kodomo ni eéğo narawasèru**

M 1. **Kotówàtte gomeñ-nasai⤸**
'Forgive me for having turned it down.'

Iêie. Anâta mo kotówarànai wake ni wa ikánàkatta ñ desyoo?
'No, no. (It's probably that) you, too, couldn't really not turn it down—right?'

2. **Daré ni mo soodañ-sinàkute gomeñ-nasai⤸**
'Forgive me for not having consulted with anybody.'

Iêie. Anâta mo soódañ-suru wàke ni wa ikánàkatta ñ desyoo?
'No, no. (It's probably that) you, too, couldn't really not consult [with anybody]—right?'

3. **soódañ-sèzu ni 'kimete**; 4. **zizyoo hanásànakute**; 5. **mińna atumàru mâe ni 'hazimete**; 6. **yokée na kotò itte**; 7. **añmari reñsyuu-sasenàkute**; 8. **rêe no sìgoto isóğàsete**; 9. **arúbàito no hito 'yamesasete**

Application Exercises

A1. Practice a relay exercise in which student A tells student B to have student C perform some activity that can easily be done in the classroom. In relaying this request to student C, have student B use the new pattern that incorporates the direct-style imperative of the appropriate verbal. Example:

A to B: **B-sañ/-kuñ: C-sañ/-kuñ ni mâdo o akéru yòo ni itte neʕ**

B to C: **C-sañ/-kuñ: A-sañ/-kuñ ğa mâdo o akérò tte itte (i)rù kara, onéğai-simàsu.**

Examples of tasks: close the door; turn on/off the lights, return this textbook to the teacher; lock the door; take these magazines to the next room; throw away those old newspapers; give this message to the teacher; listen to this tape; translate this letter; write your name and address on this paper; write your telephone number on the back of this paper.

2. Repeat the preceding drill, in each case relaying a negative request—i.e., a request *not* to do the activity in question.

3. Repeat the preceding two drills, this time replacing the direct-style imperative with (a) the corresponding gerund pattern; and (b) the corresponding gerund + direct-style imperative of **kureru**.

4. Prepare verbal cards, using pictures or line drawings, with one activity clearly represented on each card (for example, telephoning, reading a newspaper, writing a letter, making sushi, using the word processor, talking with a friend, cleaning a room, washing dishes, eating a meal, listening to tapes, watching television, taking a bath). Using appropriate pairs of cards in turn, explain that while your friend is engaged in the activity shown on one card, you will perform the activity shown on the other.

5. In the style of CC1, complain to a friend about tasks you are being made to perform that you really cannot refuse even though you find them a burden. Examples: the translation into Japanese of all the English-language letters coming into the company; the correction of all the incomprehensible English written by the section chief; working on Saturday and Sunday even though you were told, when you entered the company, that your weekends would be free.

B. Core Conversations: Substitution

Practice the Core Conversations, changing the casual conversations to careful-style and vice versa. Make any other changes that become appropriate. Follow the practice with questions and answers on the contents.

SECTION C

Eavesdropping

(Answer the following on the basis of the accompanying tape. A = the first speaker, and B = the second speaker, in each conversation.)
  1a. What is B's problem?
   b. What is the reason?
  2a. What is A's fear?
   b. What is B's reaction?
  3a. What is A's complaint? Describe the conditions.
   b. What is B's explanation?
  4a. What is A checking on?
   b. Why can't B answer?
  5a. What is A's command? Explain the reason for it.
   b. What is B's reaction?
   c. Comment on the tone of the exchange.
  6a. What is B's relationship to A?
   b. What does A want to know?
   c. What does A learn?
   d. What is A's reaction?
   e. How does B feel about the situation?
  7a. What is B's current involvement in golf?
   b. How does this compare with the past?
   c. When did the change occur?

  d. In what connection is Sunday mentioned?
8a. Who is B?
  b. What is B's probable relationship to A?
  c. What three things does B tell A to do?
9a. Who is described as cute?
  b. What has that individual just done?
  c. What is thought to be difficult?
  d. What evidence is offered?
  e. What is assumed to be a source of happiness? For whom?
  f. What is B told to do? Why?
10a. What does A want to know about the things under discussion?
  b. What does A learn, and what is A told to do?
  c. What is A's reaction?
  d. What is B's description of the task and explanation for the request?
  e. What is A's alternate suggestion?
  f. What is B's reaction to the suggestion?
11a. Why is A asking to be forgiven?
  b. What is B's reaction?
  c. Why is A relieved?
12a. What comment does A make about B?
  b. What is B's explanation?
  c. What did B study at college?
  d. What connection does this have with B's future?
13a. What did A hear about B?
  b. Where and under what circumstances did this event occur?
  c. What does B suggest was not a good idea?
  d. Who did what together with B, and what was the result?
14a. What does A want to do?
  b. What is causing the delay?
  c. What alternative does A suggest?
  d. Why does B reject it?
  e. What comment does A make? About whom?
15a. Why is Akio upset?
  b. Why does A think this happened?
  c. What is Akio's explanation?
  d. What is A's reaction?
16a. What has A seen?
  b. What is A's reaction?
  c. How does B react to A's comments?
  d. Why is A pleased?
17a. What group is being discussed?
  b. How does A feel about this group?
  c. According to B, how is this group being handled?
  d. What comparison does A make?
  e. What contradiction does B offer, and on what grounds?
18a. Who is B?
  b. What does A tell B to do? Following whose instructions?
  c. What is A going to do at the same time?
  d. What does B want to do?
  e. Why doesn't A proceed according to B's wishes?
  f. What will B do?

19a. What has impressed A? Give details.
  b. What does A want to know?
  c. What explanation does B offer?
  d. What general statement does A make?
20a. What is the general topic of conversation?
  b. Who is B?
  c. What is the problem this year? For whom?
  d. What comparison is made by B?
  e. According to A, what is it that teachers can't really do?
  f. Why is this, according to B?
21a. In what connection does B mention three days?
  b. What is B not yet doing?
  c. What activities are currently going on?
  d. What is A's attitude toward such activities?
22a. What has the division chief ordered?
  b. What is the reason for the order?
  c. What kind of person is the division chief? Give details.
  d. What guidance that B would like to have is not forthcoming from the division chief?
23a. Who is B?
  b. What advice does A offer B?
  c. What is B's reaction?
  d. What is A's concern in regard to the item of discussion?
24a. Who is B?
  b. Why is A angry? Give details.
  c. What is the relative rank of A and B?
25a. Who is the topic of discussion?
  b. Why is that person not at work?
  c. How do A and B describe that person's general condition?
  d. What is A's concern?
  e. What general concurrence does B offer?
  f. What reassurance does B offer A?
26a. When is the conference?
  b. Who will attend?
  c. How many copies of the conference materials does A think will be sufficient?
  d. How many copies are decided on?
  e. Who will make the copies? When?
  f. What is the relative ranking of A and B?
27a. Who is telephoning whom?
  b. What is the purpose of the call?
  c. How does A react to the news of B's decision?
  d. What was the basis of B's decision?
  e. Why is B apologetic?
  f. What does A plan to do in the future?
  g. What is B's reaction?
28a. What good news is A bringing to B? Give details.
  b. Who is B?
  c. What are the division chief's instructions for the future?
  d. What is B's reaction?
  e. What would B like to do that is out of the question?
  f. What does A say in jest?
  g. How does B react?

Utilization

Again, follow the directions given in lesson 25. Remember *not* to attempt to translate directly. Be sure to use sentence particles, minor sentences ending in **kara**, **kedo**, etc., as appropriate. Speak Japanese, not translated English!

1a. Comment to a friend that when you were introduced to Professor Watanabe, unfortunately you didn't have a name card with you.

b. Your friend suggests that you give him one the next time (i.e., this [next] time) you see him.

2a. Confess to a friend that you are always upset when you are introduced to distinguished people, because your Japanese isn't good.

b. Your friend agrees that it's difficult because the idea is to use fixed expressions, but he reassures you that you are very good at it.

3a. Complain to an acquaintance about how noisy those children are.

b. Your acquaintance agrees and points out that since their parents don't pay attention (to what the children are doing), everyone is annoyed.

4a. In speaking to a fellow instructor, express wonder as to whether something can't be done about those Japanese language students. Recently they don't listen to tapes, they don't read the textbook . . .

b. Your fellow instructor points out that they are also studying Japanese history. Since there's a history exam tomorrow . . .

5a. Comment to a friend that when you were a child you didn't study very much, so you used to make your mother angry.

b. Your friend is surprised, pointing out that all you do these days is study.

6a. Comment to a friend that Mr. Carter must be concerned about his inability to understand Japanese.

b. Your friend disagrees, pointing out that even if he misunderstands, Mr. Carter seems unconcerned. It's the Japanese who is speaking who seems to be concerned.

7a. Show a friend something you've written in Japanese and (pointing) ask if it's all right to use this kanji here.

b. Your friend replies that there may also be people who write this way, but it would probably be better to use this kanji (demonstrating).

8a. Ask a friend about the fish in the shops around here.

b. Your friend replies that it's not *expensive*, but since it's not too fresh, she doesn't buy it very much.

9a. Speaking to a colleague, offer to make this explanation (on the paper you are holding) simpler; longer; shorter.

b. Your colleague replies that it is fine as it is—complicated; short; long.

10a. Comment to a friend that one is supposed to be quiet in a place like this, but those students are very noisy.

b. Your friend agrees and expresses the wish that they'd be quiet. She adds that when it's this noisy, work is impossible.

11a. Suggest tactfully to a colleague that this may be uncalled for, but point out that he should probably correct this English.

b. After commenting, "You mean you don't say it like this?" your colleague thanks you for your kindness.

12a. At a department store, tell your Japanese guide that you'd like to buy a doll as a souvenir.

b. Your guide replies (politely) that if you go to the third floor, there should be every kind of toy.

13a. Complain to a colleague that it was a nuisance having the part-timer go home early yesterday.

b. Your colleague points out that since he keeps coming late, going home early, and leaving behind work to be done, perhaps you should fire him.

14a. Complain to a fellow student about having the professor change the time for class any number of times.

b. Your fellow student agrees, pointing out that it's particularly troublesome since it's the teacher who repeatedly doesn't show up for class.

15a. Ask a colleague what you should do about this English translation the section chief wrote.

b. Your colleague replies that you had probably better correct it, because as it is, there's the possibility of having the meaning misunderstood.

16a. Tell a colleague you've been invited to Mr. Yasuda's home for dinner. Ask if you should take something.

b. Your colleague replies that the thing to do on such occasions is to take something like candy or flowers or wine.

17a. Find out from a colleague if there are any Japanese children who are not allowed to watch television.

b. Your colleague replies that it depends on the parents. There are probably quite a few children who are allowed to watch only certain (fixed) programs, but there are almost none who aren't allowed to watch at all. He adds that when he was a small child, he used to watch television every night from 6:00 to 8:00, no matter what kind of program it was.

18a. Ask a fellow student if she doesn't think the teacher is strict.

b. Your fellow student replies that she doesn't think he's *strict,* but his way of teaching isn't at all skillful.

19a. Comment to a close friend on what strange people Ueda and Tanaka are.

b. Your friend agrees, adding that no matter how they are thought of, they seem unconcerned.

20a. At the entry to a traditional-style shop, ask the proprietor if you should take off your shoes.

b. The proprietor replies that it's all right to come in as you are, with your shoes on.

21a. Ask a group of colleagues if they were the ones who bought these concert tickets.

b. One of the colleagues replies that they were not the ones. It was the secretary who bought them.

22a. Ask a fellow student if she knows whether the professor has listened to the new tape you made yesterday.

b. Your fellow student replies that he has—that she saw him listening to it.

23a. Ask a colleague if he has paid his respects to the new English instructor yet.

b. Your colleague replies that just as she was about to greet him, she was summoned by the division chief, so . . .

24a. Ask a friend if she has practiced that new song yet.

b. Your friend replies that just as she was about to practice, a friend came to talk over some things, so . . .

25a. Ask a friend if he is going to tie; bend; mix; remove; return; carry these things.

b. Your friend replies that he was told by the manager to tie; bend; mix, remove; return; carry them, so . . .

26a. (Repeat 25, in the negative: [a] Aren't you going to tie. . . ? [b] I was told by the manager not to tie . . .)

27a. Shout to a crowd of students in a station not to push.

b. The students shout back that they didn't push.

28a. As you leave the office, tell a colleague to tell Ms. Ueda not to overwork.

b. Your colleague replies that even if he tells her not to (overwork), she probably can't really not overwork since there is so much work that only she can do. He expresses pity for her.

29a. Tell your traveling companion that while he is checking the timetable, you'll just go and buy some souvenirs.

b. Your companion says that that is fine, he'll be waiting here.

30a. Tell a friend you assume he'll refuse if asked to do things that are uncalled for.

b. Your friend replies that he can't really refuse as long as he works for that company.

31a. Your colleague is moving a number of heavy objects. Apologize for not helping. Explain that your back is hurting and you can't lift anything.

b. Your colleague turns aside your apology, saying that he is having the part-timer help, so . . .

32a. Tell a colleague that all the while you (are permitted to) stay at Mr. Hashimoto's home, you plan to use nothing but Japanese.

b. Your colleague replies that if you do that, surely you'll become very good at understanding Japanese.

33a. Tell a colleague that you went to Hokkaido and stayed in a **miñsyuku**. What with the singing and racket in the next room, you couldn't sleep at all.

b. Your colleague replies that you should have complained.

34a. Comment to a colleague on how serious Ms. Ono is.

b. Your colleague agrees and adds that she is a very capable person. She was praised by the manager yesterday for having made an excellent new computer program.

35a. Comment to an acquaintance that you were brought up strictly, and if you did anything bad you used to be scolded right away, but nowadays it's very different.

b. Your acquaintance replies that of course it depends on the family, but recently, no matter what children do, most parents seem unconcerned.

36a. Comment to a colleague that the secretary is crying. You wonder why.

b. Your colleague replies that it's probably because she was scolded by the manager again, and adds that he's always making her do things that are troublesome.

37a. Tell a friend that you assume Ms. Yasuda cried when she read that letter (you both know about).

b. Your friend contradicts you emphatically, saying that she read it and ended up laughing.

38a. Tell an acquaintance that you've heard he plans to go to England to study economics.

b. Your acquaintance replies that that is his hope, but whether it will be possible or not isn't clear yet.

39a. Ask a friend casually but politely to let you look at; borrow this magazine.

b. Your friend invites you to go ahead, pointing out that she already finished reading it and doesn't need it anymore.

40a. Ask your friend to forgive you for being late.

b. Your friend turns aside the apology, saying that he, too, just arrived.

41. You would like to have this Japanese letter read for you. How would you make the request of your teacher; a slight acquaintance; a colleague; a close friend; a teenager whom you know fairly well? (How many different patterns can you come up with?)

42. You do not want English used at today's gathering. How would you make the request of the same individuals as those mentioned in #41? (Again, furnish as many patterns as possible.)

Check-up

1. What is the passive derivative of **akeru, tabéru, mîru, okîru, hanásu, nômu, yobu, kau, iu, kûru, suru**? Describe, in general terms, how the passive is formed. (A-SP1)

2. What is meant by the involuntary passive? The adversative involuntary passive? The honorific passive? Depending on context, what three possible kinds of situations can a form like **yobáremàsita** cover? (A-SP1, 2)

3. In the Japanese equivalent of 'Ms. Watanabe's watch was taken by someone,' identify the affect (= the person affected), the operand (= the thing acted upon), and the agent (= the person by whom the action was done). What particles follow these items? What is unusual about a verbal's having both an affect and an operand? How can this be explained in the case of a passive? (A-SP1)

4. Give two honorific equivalents of **Matúmoto-señsèe ğa nakúnarimàsita.** (A-SP2)

5. Compare the meanings of **kono teğami o mîte moratta** and **kono teğami o mirâreta.** (A-SP1, 2)

6. What pattern is used: to describe an activity that is the thing to do, i.e., that is expected as a regular occurrence? An activity or state that used to occur on a regular basis? (A-SP3)

7. Name three pluralizing suffixes. Which one is polite? Give examples of their use (a) with nominals that refer to the singular only; and (b) with nominals which refer to singular or plural number without distinction. (A-SP4)

8. Compare the difference in meaning between **muzúkasiku nài** and **muzúkasikù wa nâi**; between **hâyâku hanâsu** and **hâyâku wa hanâsu**; between **oísiku nài** and **oísikù mo nâi**. (A-SP5)

9. How does one refer to an existing condition that is continuing without change? Give an example of the pattern with and without following **dè**. (A-SP6)

10. What is the direct-style imperative of **tabêru, nômu, okîru, oku, kaeru, kâeru, kûru, suru**? Their negative equivalents? Describe the use of these forms in sentence-final position (with or without a following sentence-particle). Describe a pattern in which these forms are used within a sentence. (B-SP1)

11. How do we analyze the **-màse** endings of such forms as **irássyaimàse** and **kudásaimàse**? (B-SP1)

12. What nominal is used to indicate the interval during which something occurs? Give an example of its use (a) without a following phrase-particle; (b) followed by particle **ni**; (c) followed by particle **wa**. How do such sequences differ from **-naĝara** patterns? (B-SP2)

Lesson 30

SECTION A

Core Conversations

1(J) **Kono hoñyaku, zêñbu anâta ǧa saséraretà ñ da soo desu ne!**

(N) **Êe. Anó señsèe ni wa kotówarènai girî ǧa âru kara, sikáta ǧa nàkatta ñ desu.**

2(J)a. **Gaíkokùziñ no supíiti-kòñtesuto tte, kiíta kotò arímàsu ka**

(N)a. **Êe. Zitû wa neʃ Señsèe ni dêro dêro tte 'susumerarete, komâtte (i)ru ñ desu.**

b. **Komâru koto wa nâi desyoo. Señsèe ǧa soó iwarerù ñ nara, dête mitara dôo desu ka.**

b. **Iya. Bôku, aá iù no ni wa muíte (i)nài ñ desu yo. Oózèe no mâe de syabéras(er)arèru no wa, nigátè na ñ desu.**

c. **Dê mo, sekkakù da kara, gañbàtte yaʹte mìtara?**

c. **Ie, hoñtoo ni, bôku nañka ǧa dêru to, kâette señsèe no kao o tubúsu yòo na koto ni narímàsu kara. .**

d. **Sôo desu ka nêe.**

3(N)a. **Dôo desu ka—eékàiwa no hôo wa.**

(J)a. **Okaǧesama de, mâe to wa kurábemono ni narimasèñ yo. Tâda siǧóto si-nàǧara da kara, tyôtto turâi desu kedo nêe.**

186

b. **Syukudai mo kânari dêru ñ desu ka**╱

    b. **Êe. Iti-niti 'heekiñ ni-zíkañ-g̃ùrai têepu kikû ñ desu yo. Kaíwàbuñ o 'tyañto obôete okanai to neʃ Kurâsu de iwás(er)areta tokì komâru kara . .**

ENGLISH EQUIVALENTS

1(J)   I hear that *you* were made to do all of this translation.

    (N)   Yes. (It's that) I have an obligation to that **seńsèe** not (to be able) to refuse, so there was no way out of it.

2(J)a. Have you ever heard of what's called "a speech contest for foreigners"?

    (N)a. Yes. As a matter of fact, you know? (It's that) I've been urged by my teacher to enter [one] and I'm really upset.

    b. Surely there's nothing to be upset about. As long as (it's that) your teacher is saying it, why don't you try entering?

        b. No, (it's that) I'm not suited for things like that. (It's that) being made to talk in front of a crowd is my weak point.

    c. But since you've been specially asked, why don't you give it your all and try doing it?

        c. No, really, when a person like me takes part, it ends up on the contrary disgracing the teacher so . . . (I'd better not do it).

    d. Oh?—I wonder . . .

3(N)a. How is it?—your English conversation [program].

    (J)a. (Thanks for asking.) There's no comparing it with before. Only I'm working at the same time so it's a bit hard, but—you know.

    b. Is (it that) there (is) quite a bit of homework?

        b. Yes. It involves listening to tapes for about two hours on the average per day. Unless you learn the conversation portion carefully in advance, you know, when you're made to say it in class, you're in trouble, so . . . (you must do your homework).

BREAKDOWNS
(AND SUPPLEMENTARY VOCABULARY)

1. **saserareru /-ru; saserareta/** (SP1)	be made to do
girî	obligation, duty
+**ôñ**	debt of gratitude
señsèe ni girî g̃a âru	have an obligation to a teacher
2. **supíiti-kòñtesuto**	speech contest
supíiti-kòñtesuto tte (SP2)	"speech contest"; what is called "a speech contest"
señsèe ni dêro tte 'susumerareru	be urged by a teacher to participate
komâru koto wa nâi (SP3)	there's nothing to be upset about
muku /-u; muita/	face, turn toward; look out on; suit, be inclined
+**mukau /-u; mukatta/**	face; confront; proceed to
+**mukeru /-ru; muketa/**	point [something] toward
aá iù no ni 'muku	be inclined toward that kind of thing
syabéraserarèru /-ru;	
syabéraseràreta/ *or*	
syabérasarèru /-ru; syabérasàreta/	be made to talk
nig̃átè/nig̃ate	weak point, one's downfall
+**tokûi/tokui**	one's specialty, one's forte
gañbàru /-u; gañbàtta/	exert special effort, give it one's all
gañbàtte 'yaru	give it one's all and do it
tubusu /-u; tubusita/	crush, smash, mash
+**tubureru /-ru; tubureta/**	become crushed; collapse
kao o tubusu	destroy face; disgrace
+**kao g̃a tubureru**	lose face; become disgraced
kao o tubúsu yòo na koto ni nâru	become a thing of the kind that destroys face
3. **kaiwa**	conversation
eékàiwa	English conversation
eékàiwa no hôo wa	regarding English conversation (at least)
+**kuraberu /-ru; kurabeta/**	compare
kurabemono	a comparable thing; a match
kurábemono ni narànai	is no match
tâda	only, merely; free (of charge)
turai /-i; turâkatta/	is hard; is a strain; is tough
syukudai	homework, outside assignment
syukúdai g̃a dèru	homework is assigned
heekiñ	average, the mean

kaíwàbuň   conversation text portion (e.g., the "CC")

kûrasu   class

iwaserareru /-ru; iwaserareta/ *or*

iwasareru /-ru; iwasareta/   be made to say

MISCELLANEOUS NOTES

1. In CC1, Mr. Suzuki is discussing some translation work that Smith was made to do. As usual, these two men use careful-style in talking with each other, with distal-style final predicates. Before **kara**, Smith uses a direct-style predicate.

Girî and **ôň** are extremely important concepts in Japanese interpersonal relationships. Japanese have obligations (**girî**) to their parents, teachers, and various members of the society, which they are taught never to ignore. When a Japanese points out **girî ğa âru** in reference to a particular situation, it is clear that s/he feels a necessity to pursue a prescribed course of action. In the case of CC1, since Smith has been told to do something by his **seňsèe**, to whom he is of course duty-bound, there is no way he can refuse. **Ôň**, on the other hand, refers to obligations that arise from past favors. Being a "good Japanese" involves functioning smoothly within the society, involving oneself reciprocally in the granting of and benefiting from favors, the giving and receiving of gifts, helping and being helped. To ignore one's obligations is to behave in a manner that gives rise to serious criticism. Note: **girî/ôň o 'siranai** 'ignore one's **girî/ôň**; **girî o tatêru** 'recognize an obligation'; **girî ni 'sibarareru** 'be bound in obligation'; **ôň ni nâru** 'become indebted'; **ôň o 'wasureru** 'forget a favor'; **ôň o kâesu** 'return a favor.'

2. In CC2, Mr. Suzuki and Smith discuss Smith's possible participation in a speech contest. Smith is reluctant to enter on the grounds of his inadequate ability, but Mr. Suzuki tries to persuade him to enter the competition.

As usual, the speech-style used by these two men in speaking with each other is careful, with distal-style final predicates. Note Mr. Suzuki's suggestion, ([J]c), expressed in a minor sentence ending with a conditional. Smith also uses one minor sentence, ending in **kara** ([N]c), in a situation in which the result of the **kara** sequence is clear from the context without being explicitly stated.

(J)a. Japanese are extremely fond of speech contests, which a good many foreigners view with significantly less enthusiasm. Participants deliver prepared (often memorized) speeches in a foreign language and are rated by a team of judges selected on the basis of widely divergent credentials. The advance preparation guarantees that a participant will be shown to best advantage. Contrast the debate format of the West, where contestants are judged on the basis of ability that must be demonstrated without advance preparation. What are the cultural implications? How does this tie in with questions of "face"? In which society can we expect surprises to be more generally enjoyed?

(N)a. Note the use of the quotative **tte** followed by the involuntary passive verbal **susumerarete**: 'having been urged [with the words] "participate! participate!".' That the passive here has an adversative connotation is made clear by **komâtte (i)ru**, which follows. In many circumstances, the involuntary passive **susumerareru** 'be urged,' 'be recommended' would definitely *not* have an unfavorable implication. The verbal **dêru** is used here to express 'going out as a participant.' Compare the use of English 'go out' in expressions like 'go out for basketball,' 'go out for the swimming team.'

(J)b. **Iwareru** occurs here as an honorific passive used in reference to **seńsèe**. Note the difference in meaning that would result from changing **seńsèe ḡa** to **seńsèe ni: seńsèe ni 'soo iwareru** 'be told that by the teacher,' 'have the teacher say that.' In this case, the verbal is an involuntary passive that may or may not have an adversative connotation depending on context. Do particles matter???

Iwárerù ń nara: The provisional of the extended predicate (i.e., /verbal + **ń nàra**/) implies that **iwareru** is to be taken as fact: 'as long as it is (actually) the case that **seńsèe** says . . .'

(N)b. **Muku**, obviously related to **mukoo**, is an affective intransitive verbal that we have already seen in its nominal derivative form in compounds like **minami-muki** 'facing south,' **gaiziń-muki** 'aimed at foreigners,' and others. From its literal meaning, 'look out on,' is derived a generalized meaning 'be(come) inclined toward,' 'tend toward.' Note: **X ni muku** 'look out on X,' 'be(come) suited for X.' Also related to **muku** are the operational intransitive verbal **mukau** 'face,' 'confront,' and the operational transitive verbal **mukeru** 'make [something] face [in a particular direction],' 'point [something] toward' (**X o Y ni mukeru** 'point X toward Y'). In its gerund form, **mukau** occurs frequently in giving directions: **Mukatte miḡí no hòo desu.** 'It's on the right as [you] face it.'

(J)c. **Gańbàru**: Given the importance of striving, doing one's best, struggling to achieve, "hanging in there" in Japanese society, it is not surprising that this verbal is very common.

(N)c. The transitive/intransitive pair **tubusu/tubureru** provides additional examples of verbals that have a basic, concrete meaning ('crush,' 'become crushed') along with a derived figurative meaning (as in **kao o tubusu/kao ḡa tubureru**). Losing face is an extremely painful experience for a Japanese, and causing this should be carefully avoided. A probing question whose answer may cause a Japanese to admit publicly that s/he made a mistake or caused a problem should not be asked unless aggressive confrontation is deliberate, with the questioner prepared to take the consequences. Loss of face and confrontation are often related, both having extremely negative connotations for the Japanese.

Dêru to 'with participating' links with **tubúsu yòo na koto ni narímàsu**, and the combination describes what other event will accompany participation.

(J)d. The **nêe** following **sôo desu ka** suggests that Mr. Suzuki remains unconvinced as he continues to deliberate about what he has just heard.

3. In CC3, Mr. Suzuki and Mr. Carter discuss Mr. Suzuki's new English conversation program. The style is careful, with distal-style final predicates, but there are a few features typical of casual-style: an inverted sentence ([N]a), minor sentences ending in **kedo nêe** ([J]a) and **kara** ([J]b), and the breaking up of a long sentence into two parts with the first part ending in **neʕ** ([J]b). Mr. Suzuki uses distal-style before **kedo**, but direct-style before **to** and **kara**.

(N)a. **Eékàiwa no hôo**: 'the English conversation alternative' as compared with other things—for example, what they have been talking about.

(J)a. **Okaḡesama de**, as usual, implies a favorable answer to a question that showed personal concern for the person addressed.

Tâda 'only,' 'merely' may qualify a following predicate: **tâda tetúdàu tamê ni sita** 'I did it only to help.' As a sentence connective, its use in this CC, it indicates a reservation: /**X. Tâda Y**/ 'X is true. Only Y is something that introduces a slightly contrary condition.' Thus, in (J)a, Mr. Suzuki follows his reply that his current English program is going extremely well with the reservation that it is tough because he is working at the same time. (Note the use of a **-nàgara** form before **dà**, in a situation in which the second of the coinciding activities [studying English conversation] is known from the context). **Tâda** also occurs with a very different meaning: 'free of charge.' Thus, **tâda da** 'it's free,' **tâda de morau** 'get [it] free.'

(J)b. **Heekiñ** occurs here as an expression of manner: 'average-ly,' 'from the point of view of the average.' Note the perfective preceding **tokî**: Mr. Suzuki becomes upset (**komâru**) at times when he *has been* made to recite the conversational text insufficiently prepared.

Structural Patterns

1. THE PASSIVE CAUSATIVE

We have already learned the passive and the causative, which are derived from basic verbals. These two derivatives may occur in combination to form the PASSIVE CAUSATIVE (the passive of a causative), consisting of /verbal root + **-(s)ase-** + **-rare-** + **-ru**/, i.e., /verbal root + two root-extenders + ending/. As usual, **-sase-** is attached to roots ending in a vowel, and **-ase-** is attached to roots ending in a consonant, to form the regular causative. In forming the passive of that causative, only the root-extender **-rare-** occurs, since all causatives are vowel verbals. The accentuation is the same as that of simple passives: only the derivative of an accented verbal is accented, and the accent occurs on the next-to-last mora of the imperfective.

In the passive causative of a consonant verbal, the root-extender combination **-ase-rare-** is sometimes abbreviated to **-asare-**. The irregular verbal **kûru** may also occur in an abbreviated form (see below). Examples:

Basic Verbal	*Passive Causative Derivative*
Vowel verbals	
tabê-ru 'eat'	**tabé-sase-rarè-ru**
ake-ru 'open [X]'	**ake-sase-rare-ru**
yame-ru 'quit'	**yame-sase-rare-ru**
i-ru 'be located (animate)'	**i-sase-rare-ru**
okî-ru 'wake up'	**okí-sase-rarè-ru**
kae-ru 'change [X]'	**kae-sase-rare-ru**
Consonant verbals	
kiku 'ask,' 'listen'	**kik-ase-rare-ru/kik-asare-ru**
nôm-u 'drink'	**nom-áse-rarè-ru/nom-ásarè-ru**
hâir-u 'enter'	**haír-ase-rarè-ru/haír-asarè-ru**
hanâs-u 'talk'; 'let go'	**hanás-ase-rarè-ru/hanás-asarè-ru**
mât-u 'wait'	**mat-áse-rarè-ru/mat-ásarè-ru**
ka-u (<*kaw-u**) 'buy'	**kaw-ase-rare-ru/kaw-asare-ru**
i-u (<*iw-u**) 'say'	**iw-ase-rare-ru/iw-asare-ru**
kâer-u 'return'	**kaér-ase-rarè-ru/kaér-asarè-ru**
Irregular Verbals	
kû-ru 'come'	**ko-sáse-rarè-ru/ko-sásarè-ru**
su-ru 'do'	**s-ase-rare-ru**

The special polite verbals in **-àru** do not occur in the passive causative.

The passive causative is usually an involuntary passive, indicating that X (followed by **g̃a** or **wa** or **mo**, if expressed) is affected by Y's making him/her do something. Y, if expressed, is followed by particle **ni**. Thus: **Kânozyo g̃a/wa/mo kâre ni kakás(er)àreta.** 'She (too) was made to write [it] by him.' This situation can also be expressed as: **Kâre g̃a/wa/mo kânozyo ni kakâseta.** 'He (too) made her write [it].' However, when the person made to do something is the speaker, the alternate with the passive causative is regularly used: **(Watasi g̃a/wa/mo) kâre ni kakás(er)àreta.** 'I (too) was made to write [it] by him'; 'He made me write [it].' A /nominal + o/ phrase added to this sequence would be linked to the underlying verbal root: **Teg̃ámi o kakas(er)aremàsita.** 'I was made to write a letter.' The causative portion of the passive causative, in combination with the involuntary passive, regularly indicates a notion of involuntary causation: someone is *made* to do something, rather than *allowed* to do it. This meaning often resembles, but is not identical with, that of **-(a)nakereba narânai** or **-(a)nakute wa 'ikenai** patterns, which express necessity based on any kind of situation, including a direct order. Unlike them, the passive causative implies that some person(s) are causing the action, even if they are not identified.

A passive causative is a regular vowel verbal, and has all the predictable forms of verbals in that category. What would the following mean? **yamesaserareta**; **yomáserarènakatta**; **kakásaretàra**; **iwásaretàri**; **tetúdawaserarènakereba.**[1] Additional examples:

>   **Zikáñ-doori ni tukimàsita kedo, señsèe ni ití-zìkañ mo matás(er)aremàsita.** 'I arrived on time, but the teacher made me wait (*lit.* I was made to wait by the teacher) all of an hour.'

>   **Ano kaisya de határakasete morattàra, nihóñg̃o de hanasas(er)arèru to omoi-masu.** 'If I am allowed to work at that company, I think I'll be made to speak in Japanese.'

>   **Anó arubàito wa, osóku kìtàri, hâyâku kâettari site, kêsa sihâiniñ ni yamésase-raremàsita.** 'That part-timer who has (*lit.* having) repeatedly come late and left early, was fired this morning by the manager.'

2. MORE ON THE QUOTATIVE (t)te

The quotative **(t)te** was originally introduced (18B-SP1) as an alternate of quotative **to** in the pattern /**X to** ~ **(t)te iu**/ 'be called or named X'; 'say "X".' In this pattern, X can be absolutely anything—any sequence of Japanese, a foreign language utterance, even some mistake-ridden Japanese of a foreigner. Verbals other than **iu** can, of course, occur in this pattern: **kiku, kâku, yômu, kotáèru, ukag̃au**, etc.

We also learned that **(t)te** frequently appears at the end of a sentence, again establishing what immediately precedes as a quotation, even though a verbal of saying, asking, writing, and so on is not explicit. In this pattern, the **to** alternative may also occur in the written language, but is rare in spoken Japanese.

(T)te can come at the end of a phrase or utterance as a more casual alternate of /**X to** ~ **(t)te iû no wa**/. Thus: **Koobañ te, nâñ desu ka⌐** 'What is (the thing called) a "koobañ"?' or **Koobañ te?** ' "Koobañ"?' Here we do not expect to find the **to** alternative.

---

1. English equivalents: '[I] was made to quit (*or* was fired)'; '[I] wasn't made to read'; 'if [I] am made to write'; 'being made to say . . .'; 'unless [I] am made to help.'

A most unusual pattern in which **(t)te** (but not **to**) is found is the casual-style /**X (t)te Y**/, especially in the combination **X (t)te kotô**, which alternates with the more usual **X to ~ (t)te iu Y**/ (cf. Drill E, following).

3. komâru koto wa nâi

In CC2, the sequence **komâru koto wa nâi** occurs with the gloss 'there's nothing to be upset about.' However, if we were to interpret this same sequence as an example of the pattern introduced in 25A-SP3 (/—— **kotô ḡa âru**/) it would mean something like 'there are no occasions when [someone] is upset.' This is yet another example of the fact that Japanese and English patterns—and vocabulary—do not coincide, *not* an indication that this Japanese sequence has 'two meanings.' It may have two—or five or ten—different English *equivalents,* but this variation points up the fact that the *ranges* of meaning of items in the two languages are not the same even though they may overlap.

Taking this particular sequence as an example, **kotô** refers to inanimate 'things' in Japanese. Those 'things' may be facts or situations or conditions or acts or activities. Determining a less general meaning of a particular **kotô** depends on the context. It seems important to English speakers to do this because we distinguish between facts and conditions and acts, but **kotô** is a broad term that covers the entire range. In some contexts, /verbal + **kotô wa nâi**/ refers to a non-occurrence of any occasions (acts) when the verbal takes place, but in a different context, the reference is to the non-existence of conditions described by the verbal.

Consider a reverse situation. In English, we have a single verbal covering the putting on of clothing. Imagine suggesting to a native speaker of English that *put on* has "different meanings" depending on what part of the body is involved! But this is exactly what a Japanese might say. This distinction is required by Japanese but absent in English. A more accurate description of the situation is to say that *put on* covers a range of meaning in English that is broken down more specifically in Japanese. In any single occurrence, only context determines which particular limited range(s) of meaning the item covers.

This is another reminder of how the filter of our native language can prejudice our view of a foreign language. Completely objective analysis is a very difficult—in fact, impossible—challenge.

Drills

A 1. **Arúbàito yamétà ñ desu ka↗**   **Êe, señsèe ni yamésaseraretà ñ desu yo.**
   '(Is it that) you've quit your part-time work?'   'Yes, (it's that) I was made to quit by the teacher.'

2. **Anó zyùḡyoo matá tòtta ñ desu ka↗**   **Êe, señsèe ni torás(er)àreta ñ desu yo.**
   '(Is it that) you took that class again?'   'Yes, (it's that) I was made to take it by the teacher.'

3. **siñriḡaku no kyoókàsyo zêñbu yôñda**; 4. **señsyuu no hoñyaku yarínaòsita**; 5. **ano buátui hòñ kôpii-sita**; 6. **Riñkàañ ni tuite kâita**; 7. **nitíyòobi ni mo gaḱkoo ni kità**; 8. **anó ryuuḡakùsee ni âtta**

● Repeat 2, 3, 4, 6, 7, and 8 of the preceding drill, giving the short form of the passive causative in the answers (Example 2: **torásàreta**).

B 1. **Hurañsuğo beñkyoo-sinàkute yôkatta ñ desyoo?**

'You probably didn't have to study French—right?'

Iyâa. Hâha ni beñkyoo-saserareta monò desu yo.

'No. I used to be made to study it by my mother.'

2. **Utí no kotò tetúdawànakute yôkatta ñ desyoo?**

'You probably didn't have to help with household things—right?

Iyâa. Hâha ni tetúdawas(er)àreta monô desu yo.

'No. I used to be made to help by my mother.'

3. **syokuzi tukúrànakute;** 4. **tênisu naráwànakute;** 5. **hâyàku kaérànakute;** 6. **omói monò hakóbanàkute;** 7. **deñsya de kayówanàkute;** 8. **kirái na monò tabênakute**

● Repeat 2, 3, 4, 5, 6, and 7 of the preceding drill, giving the short form of the passive causative in the answers (Example 2: **tetúdawasàreta**).

C 1. **Ano siğoto saséraretà ñ desu ka⌇**

'Is it that you were made to do that work?'

Iya, watási ğa sitài tte iťtà ñ desu yo.

'No, (it's that) I said I wanted to do it.'

2. **Kônpa de utáwas(er)aretà ñ desu ka⌇**

'Is it that you were made to sing at the party?'

Iya, watási ğa utaitài tte iťtà ñ desu yo.

'No, (it's that) I said I wanted to sing.'

3. **mañzài no kippu 'kawas(er)areta;** 4. **atûi no ni 'kimono kisaserareta;** 5. **kinoo no syokuzi zêñbu haráwas(er)àreta;** 6. **atárasìi yoteehyoo otáku màde todókesaseràreta;** 7. **hikkosi tetúdawas(er)àreta;** 8. **kuruma de otáku màde 'okuras(er)areta;** 9. **isóğasìi no ni nañ-zìkañ mo matás(er)àreta;** 10. **soñna omói monò o moťte kosas(er)àreta**

D 1. **Supíiti-kòñtesuto ni iťta kotò ğa arímàsu ka⌇**

'Have you ever gone to a speech contest?'

Supíiti-kòñtesuto tte, dôñna monô desu ka⌇

'What kind of thing is a "speech contest"?'

2. **Takkyuubiñ de okùreba îi no ni . .**

'If only they'd send it by **takkyuubiñ**' (but they won't)!

Takkyuubiñ te, dôñna monô desu ka⌇

'What kind of thing is "**takkyuubiñ**"?'

3. **Teésyoku no hòo ğa yâsûkute oísisòo desu yo⌇** 4. **Bûñraku o goráñ ni nàtta koto ğa arímàsu ka⌇** 5. **Siñkàñseñ de iku to hayâi desu yo⌇** 6. **Soñna tokì wa kiśsateñ ğa tyoodo îi desu yo⌇** 7. **Omósiròi hoómu-dòrama ğa kôñbañ âru kedo, mîru?**

E 1. **Utáenài tte iťtè mo, sukôsi wa utáerù desyoo?**

'Even if you say you can't sing, you can probably sing a little (at least)—right?'

Iyâa, zeñzeñ utaenài tte kotô desu yo.

'No, it's a fact that I can't sing at all.'

2. **Homêru tokoro wa nâi tte iťtè mo, sukôsi wa âru desyoo?**

Iyâa, zeñzeñ nài tte kotô desu yo.

'No, it's a fact that there aren't any at all.'

'Even if you say there aren't any
things (*lit.* places) to praise, there are
probably a few (at least)—right?'

3. **urêsîku nâi**; 4. **yomîkaki wa dekînakatta**; 5. **yakû ni tatânai**; 6. **tabétàku nâi**;
7. **tukátta kotò g̃a nâi**; 8. **yuube nenâkatta**; 9. **sawág̃ènakatta**; 10. **eég̃o syabérasènai**

F 1. **Kâre, seńsèe ni 'susumerarete,**
komâtte (i)ru ñ desu.

'(It's that) he's concerned about
having been recommended by his
teacher.'

Susúmeraretè mo, komâru koto wa nâi
desyoo?

'Even if he has been recommended, there's
nothing for him to be concerned about—
right?'

2. **Kâre, sikêñ g̃a tikázùite, sińpai-site**
(i)rù ñ desu.

'(It's that) he's worried about the
exams being near at hand.'

Tikázùite mo, sińpai-suru kotò wa nâi
desyoo?

'Even if they're near at hand, there's
nothing for him to worry about—right?'

3. **seńpai ni sikararete/ki ni site**; 4. **ano kaisya ni syuúsyoku kotowaràrete/akíràmete**;
5. **sikêñ ni ôtite/gaḱkàri-site**; 6. **tomodati g̃a sotug̃yoo-site/sabísig̃àtte**; 7. **syukúdai**
dasàrete/komâtte; 8. **kôñpa ni sasówarenàkute/ki ó wàrùku site**

G 1. **Kotówàtte mo, kañkee wa kawáranài**
desyoo?

'Even if you refuse, your relationship
probably won't change—right?'

Ie, kotówàru to, kañkee g̃a kawáru yòo
na koto ni narímàsu kara . .

'No, when you turn them down, it ends up
with (*lit.* gets to be a thing like) your
relationship changing, so . . .' (that is what
to expect).

2. **Setúmee-sinàkute mo, gokái-sarenài**
desyoo?

'Even if you don't explain, you
probably won't be misunderstood—
right?'

Ie, setumee-sinai to, gokái-sareru yòo na
koto ni narímàsu kara . .

'No, when you don't explain, it ends up
with (*lit.* gets to be a thing like) your being
misunderstood, so . . .' (that is what to
expect).

3. **arûite itte/okurenai**; 4. **îma kâre ni korârete/mêewaku-sinai**; 5. **yarikata naráwà-**
nakute/matíg̃aènai; 6. **matíg̃àtte/yarínaosas(er)arènai**; 7. **sawâide/tyûui-sarenai**;
8. **kôoto² kité ikanàkute/kaze 'hikanai**

H 1. **Mîyazi-kuñ o susúmetà desyoo?**
'You recommended Miyaji, right?'

Êe. Dê mo, watási nàñka g̃a susumeru to
nêe.

'Yes. But when someone like me
recommends him, you know how it is!'

2. **Sug̃îura-kuñ no sig̃oto hômeta**
desyoo?

'You praised Suigura's work, right?'

Êe. Dê mo, watási nàñka g̃a homêru to
nêe.

'Yes. But when someone like me praises it,
you know how it is!'

2. **Kôoto**, like **ôobaa**, is a borrowing based on English 'overcoat.' **Oóbaakòoto > ôobaa** *or* **kôoto**.

3. **Oosaka no gakkai ni 'ikas(er)areta**; 4. **syatyoo o kuúkoo màde 'mukae ni itta**;
5. **siḡoto no yarikata o tyûui-sita**; 6. **taṅtòosya ni narás(er)àreta**

I 1. **Kotówarànakatta ñ desu ka⌐**
'Do you mean you didn't refuse?'

Êe. Anó señsèe ni wa kotówarènai girî ḡa âru kara, sikáta ḡa nàkatta ñ desu.
'That's right. When it comes to that teacher, I'm duty bound not (to be able) to refuse, so (it's that) there was no way out.'

2. **Haḱkìri iwásete morawanàkatta ñ desu ka⌐**
'Do you mean you weren't allowed to state your position (*lit.* didn't receive letting [you] say) clearly?'

Êe. Anó señsèe ni wa haḱkìri iwásete moraenai girì ḡa âru kara, sikáta ḡa nàkatta ñ desu.
'That's right. When it comes to that teacher, I'm duty bound not (to be able) to be allowed to state my position clearly, so (it's that) there was no way out.'

3. **mâtte moráwanàkatta**; 4. **môñku iwánàkatta**; 5. **yoyaku kaénàkatta**; 6. **siḡoto yaménàkatta**

J 1. **Anó oñḡàkkai, dêru?**
'That concert—are you going?'

Ṅ. Señsèe ni, dêro dêro tte iwáretà kara . .
'Yeah. I kept being told to go by the teacher, so . . .' (I really have to).

2. **Eékàiwa, môtto 'tuzukeru?'**
'Your English conversation—are you continuing any longer?'

Ṅ. Señsèe ni, tuzukero tuzúkerò tte iwáretà kara . .
'Yeah. I kept being told to continue by the teacher, so . . .' (I really have to).

3. **arúbàito, yameru**; 4. **rekisi no syukudai, dâsu**; 5. **koohai ni koṅpyùutaa 'tukawaseru**; 6. **isya ni mîte morau**; 7. **ano atárasìku dêta eéwa-zìteñ, kau**

K 1. **Señsèe ni, raíḡàkki mo dêro tte iwáretà ñ desu yo⌐**
'(It's that) I was told by the teacher to attend next semester, too.'

Soó iwaretà ñ nara, dête mitara?
'As long as you were told [to do] that, [how would it be] if you tried attending?'

2. **Señsèe ni, syakâiḡaku no señsèe ni kikê tte iwáretà ñ desu yo⌐**
'(It's that) I was told by the teacher to ask the sociology professor.'

Soó iwaretà ñ nara, kiíte mìtara?'
'As long as you were told [to do] that, [how would it be] if you tried asking?'

3. **ano zassi ni kôpii 'okure**; 4. **hitúyoo dàttara îtu de mo 'reñraku-siro**; 5. **kâkari 'tuzukero**

L 1. **Kotíra no kyòosi, kibísìi desu ka⌐**
'Are the instructors here strict?'

Êe, mâa, hutúu no kyòosi ni kuraberu to, yaṕpàri kibísìi desu nêe.

'Yes, well, when you compare them to the usual instructors, they *are* strict.'

2. **Kâre no katee, moñdai oôi desu ka** 'Does his household have many problems?'

Êe, mâa, hutuu no katee ni kuraberu to, yáppàri 'moñdai oôi desu nêe.
'Yes, well, when you compare it to the usual household, it *does* have lots of problems.'

3. **atárasìi kikâi/yakû ni tatímàsu**; 4. **anó ryuuĝàkusee/yomîkaki dekímàsu**; 5. **kono kaisya/yôku syuĺtyoo-saseraremàsu**; 6. **êki no 'nisiĝuti no mâe ni dêkita mâñsyoñ/takâi desu**; 7. **kinoo mî ni itta apâato/sîzuka desu**

M Repeat the stimulus questions of Drill L, responding according to the following pattern:

1. **Êe, hutúu no kyòosi to wa, zeñzeñ kurabemono ni narimasèñ yo.**
'Yes, there's absolutely no comparison, with the usual instructor (at least).'

2. **Êe, hutúu no katee tò wa, zeñzeñ kurabemono ni narimasèñ yo.**
'Yes, there's absolutely no comparison, with the usual household (at least).'

Application Exercises

A1. Answer questions as to whether you performed certain activities by stating that you were made to (do so) by the manager. Examples of activities: translate the division chief's letter into English; correct the English in the letter the section chief wrote; use the old computer; change the computer program Mr. Ono made; straighten up the office; go to the station to meet Ms. Watanabe; go to Narita Airport to see the division chief off; listen to Professor Hashimoto's lecture; postpone the conference; speak in Japanese.

2. In response to questions involving general necessity (using **sinâkereba narânakatta ñ desu ka** *or* **sinâkute wa ikénàkatta ñ desu ka**), reply in terms of having been made to do the activity by a particular person, using the passive causative. Examples of activities: write in kanji; read Japanese-language newspapers; listen to tapes; stay in bed all day long; get up early; give up smoking (= cigarettes); line up; wait long; buy a new textbook; come early.

3. In response to questions involving quantities, answer factually on the basis of averages (cf. CC3[J]b). For example, ask about hours of tape listening per week, hours of television watching per day, hours of sleep per night, days of vacation per year, hours at work/school per day.

4. In generally favorable answers to questions, introduce a reservation, using **tâda** (cf. CC3[N]a and [J]a). For example, ask about thoughts on Japanese food, Japanese language study, kanji, kana, last year's vacation, etc.

5. Using CC2 as a general model, conduct role-playing exercises. Setting #1: A **gaiziñ** has been asked to make a speech (**supîiti**) in Japanese at the wedding of his closest Japanese friend. Setting #2: A **gaiziñ** has been asked to make sushi for an upcoming student party.

B. Core Conversations: Substitution

Practice the Core Conversations in the form in which they might occur if the participants were close friends. Follow this practice with questioning based on the content.

SECTION B

Core Conversations

1(J)a. **Butyoo to keńka-sityattà ñ da
     tte?**

        (N)a. **Ñ. D-âtte, koítì ḡa iśsyookèñmee
setúmee-site (i)rù no ni, zêñbu
iíowarànai uti ni hanásihazimèrù
kara . .**

   b. **Dê mo sa! Konó mamà zya,
     mazûi wa yo. Osóku narànai uti
     ni, ayámàtta hoo ḡa îi to omôu
     yo⌣**

        b. **Sońna kotò iít-àtte, warûi no wa
mukôo na ñ desu yo⌣ Dâ no ni,
dôo site bôku ḡa ayámarànakutya
narânai ñ desu ka.**

   c. **Syoó ḡa nài yo. Wârûkut-atte sa!
     Aítè wa butyóo dà kara neʕ**

        c. **Dâ kedo, yáppàri naítoku-
dekimasèñ nêe.**

   d. **Mâa, sońna mòñ yo.
     Gâmañ = sinâkyaa . . Dâ kara,
     hâyâku ayámàtte (i)rássyài yo.**

2(N)a. **Nâñ no kîzi desu ka⌣**

        (J)a. **Daítòkai no kûuki ḡa kîree ni
nâtte kitâ tte.**

   b. **Tyôtto haikeñ. . . . Âa, ûmi to ka
     mizúùmi ni mo, sakána ḡa
     modòtte kitâ tte iu ñ desu neʕ**

        b. **Sôo sôo. Sizeñ no kañkyoo mo,
sukósi-zùtu yôku narídàsità tte
(iu) kotô desu ne!**

3(N)a. **Komárimàsita neʕ—końna
     tokorò de końna ni
     matas(er)àrete.**

        (J) **Kuráku narànai uti ni tukítài no
ni ne!**

   b. **A, uḡókidàsita.**

ENGLISH EQUIVALENTS

1(J)a. You say (it's that) you ended up
     having an argument with the
     (division) chief?

        (N)a. Yeah. But even with me going out
of my way to explain, before I finish
saying everything, s/he starts talking
so . . . (the argument hasn't been
settled).

b. But listen! Leaving it this way is no good. I think you'd better apologize before it's [too] late.

b. Even if you say something like that, the fact remains that the one at fault is him/her (*lit.*, over there). In spite of that, why is it that *I* have to apologize?

c. That's life! Even if it's not fair, since the other side [of the argument] is the division chief . . . (knuckle under!)

d. Well, that's the way it is. You have to (*lit.*, unless you) put up with it; so go and apologize quickly.

c. But I really can't go along with this.

2(N)a. What is the article about?

b. Let me look at it for a bit. . . . Oh, (it's that) the fish have come back to the oceans and/or the lakes and the like, too—right?

(J)a. It says that the air in the big cities has begun to clear up (*lit.* become clean).

b. That's right. They say that the natural environment has also begun to improve, a little at a time.

3(N)a. This is annoying, isn't it?—being made to wait like this in this kind of place.

(J) When we want to arrive before it gets dark!

b. Oh, we've begun to move!

BREAKDOWNS
(AND SUPPLEMENTARY VOCABULARY)

1. **keñka-suru** — argue, quarrel; fight
   d-âtte (SP1) — but, however, even so
   iśsyookèñmee — with all one's might; wholeheartedly
   iíowàru /-u; iíowàtta/ — finish saying
   iíowarànai uti ni (SP2) — while one [still] hasn't finished saying; before one finishes saying

   hanásihazimèru/hanasihazimeru /-ru; hanásihazìmeta/hanasi-hazimeta/ — begin talking
   sa (SP3) — /sentence particle of assertion/
   konó mamà zya(a) — being this condition; as it is
   mazûi /-i; mâzûkatta/ — is inadvisable; is poor at; tastes bad
   osóku narànai uti ni — while it hasn't become late; before it gets (too) late

+ (o)wabi	apology
ayámàru /-u; ayamatta/ or	
+ (o)wabi o iu	apologize
iťt-àtte	even if [someone] says
dâ no ni	in spite of that, nevertheless
wârûkut-atte	even if it's bad
aítè	partner; the other party
sońna mòñ/monò	that kind of thing
gâmañ-suru	bear, endure, put up with, suffer in silence; "grin and bear it"; "knuckle under"
gâmañ = sinâkereba or	
gâmañ = sinâkerya(a) or	
gâmañ = sinâkya(a)	unless one puts up with
dâ kara	therefore
2. kîzi	news article
+ syasetu	editorial
+ kookoku	advertisement
+ syoosetu	a novel
+ si	poem, poetry
+ roñbuñ	article, essay; thesis
nâñ no kîzi	article about what?
tokai	city
daítòkai	large city, metropolis
+ inaka	the country
kûuki	air
+ sôra	sky
ûmi to ka mizúùmi (SP4)	oceans and/or lakes and the like
modôru /-u; modôtta/	return; back up
+ modôsu /-u; modôsita/	put back, send back; throw up
sizeñ	nature; natural
kañkyoo	environment
sizeñ no kañkyoo	natural environment
narídàsu/naridasu /-u; narídàsita/	
naridasita/	start to become
3. kurai /-i; kurâkatta/	is dark
+ akarui /-i; akárùkatta/	is light (not dark)
kuráku narànai uti ni	while it hasn't become dark, before it gets dark
uğôku /-u; uğôita/	[something] moves

uǧókàsu /-u; uǧókàsita/	move [something]
uǧókidàsu/uǧokidasu /-u; uǧóki- dàsita/uǧokidasita/	start to move

MISCELLANEOUS NOTES

1. In CC1, Mr. Carter pours out his troubles to Ms. Tanaka, the consultant, during a meeting at a local restaurant. He is angry with his boss, who won't even listen to his side of a disagreement they are having. Ms. Tanaka is firm in her insistence that it is Mr. Carter who must apologize, regardless of the circumstances, since he is the subordinate. Mr. Carter finds this very, very difficult to tolerate. This dialogue emphasizes the importance of hierarchy and the influence it exerts on determining appropriate behavior in Japan. It also indirectly makes reference to the treatment of subordinates by superiors within an in-group, which often shocks Westerners. What for the Japanese may be an indication of the closeness of members of the in-group may strike a foreigner as extremely rude and insensitive behavior. To reprimand one's subordinate or to criticize one's own children in the presence of a member of an out-group is meant to demonstrate the unity of the in-group, not—as in many societies—the denigration of an individual. Loss of face does not play a part here, in Japanese society.

Note carefully the style of this dialogue. The participants are away from the office, in a relaxed setting, and they are discussing a very personal matter. Ms. Tanaka, who outranks Mr. Carter, uses casual-style with direct-style predicates throughout, thus demonstrating a close relationship, with all signs of distance removed. In spite of the fact that she is a woman, her style is generally blunt, reflecting the fact that she is a business associate of Mr. Carter's; however, she does use one example of gentle-style (**môn yo**) and an example of feminine-style (sentence-final **wa yo**).

Mr. Carter, on the other hand, does not forget his position even in his angry state. While his utterances include a few casual-style features (**ñ, -àtte** [cf. SP1, following], **kotti, -anakutya**), his style is generally careful with distal-style final predicates.

(N)a. **Kotti:** Mr. Carter refers to himself as 'this side,' i.e., of the argument.
Iíowàru/hanasihazimeru: The verbal **owaru** 'end' occurs as the second part of verbal compounds, following the stem of another verbal. The combination indicates the ending of the action represented by the first verbal. Thus: **iíowàru** 'finish saying'; **yomiowaru** 'finish reading.' The opposite meaning is represented by /verbal stem + **-hazimeru**/, as in **hanasihazimeru** 'begin talking,' **siházimèru** 'begin doing,' or /verbal stem + **-dasu**/ (cf. CC2 and CC3), as in **naridasu** 'start to become,' **uǧokidasu** 'start to move,' **waráidàsu** 'burst out laughing.' Compounds in **-dasu** often imply more suddenness than those in **-hazimeru**.

Traditionally the accent of all such compound verbals has depended on the accent of the first verbal of the compound: if it was accented, the compound was unaccented; if it was unaccented, the compound was accented on the next-to-last mora of the dictionary form (the imperfective) of the verbal. The trend among younger Japanese is to accent all these verbals. Thus **yomíowàru, hanásihazimèru, narídàsu,** and **uǧókidàsu** are now frequently occurring alternates of the verbals cited above.

(J)b. **Konó mamà zya** (or **zyaa**): **Zyà(a)**, of course, is a contraction of **dè wa:** 'being this condition without change (at least).'
Mazûi is the opposite of **umâi**, covering all the same areas of meaning—taste, skill, and smoothness of operation—in a negative sense.

Note that even though she is being insistent, Ms. Tanaka follows her advice with **to omôu**.

(N)b. Mr. Carter contrasts himself (**koŕtì**) with **mukôo**, the other side of the argument. **(O)wabi** is a nominal meaning 'apology,' 'excuse.' The combination **(o)wabi o iu** is slightly more formal than **ayámàru**. Note: **owabi no teğami** 'letter of apology.'

Dâ no ni: Note the unusual occurrence of the **dà** form of the copula before a nominal. If optional **sore** were included, we would expect **soré nà no ni**,[3] but without **sore**, the **nà** form of the copula—which, after all, regularly occurs *only* following a nominal—may revert to its underlying form (**dà**).

(J)c. **Aítè** refers to the other party in encounters involving two sides.

(J)d. **Soñna mòñ yo**: **Môñ**, the contracted form of **monô**, refers to the way things should be (cf. 29A-SP2). Here **soñna** precedes the nominal **monô** instead of a verbal, as was the case in Lesson 29.

Gâmañ = sinâkya(a) is the contracted form of **-sinâkerya(a)**, which in turn is a contraction of **-sinâkereba**. This minor sentence suggests a following **narânai**, thus constituting a pattern of necessity, although all that Ms. Tanaka actually says is 'unless you knuckle under . . .' The conclusion is obvious.

2. In CC2, Sue Brown and her colleague are discussing a newspaper article about the environment. As is usual in conversations between these two women, the style is generally careful, with distal-style final predicates. In reporting on the contents of the article, however, Sue Brown's colleague uses a direct-style verbal before sentence-final **tte**, and Sue Brown's **Haikeñ.** is a polite but casual request form.

(J)a. **Nâtte kita**, as we learned previously (22A-SP3), indicates a gradual 'having come to be.' In general, a compound in **-dasu** or even **-hazimeru** expresses a more sudden start, but in combination with **sukósi-zùtu** ([J]b), **narídàsita** represents a situation virtually identical with that expressed by the **-te kûru** pattern.

3. In CC3, Deborah Miller and Mr. Yamada are caught in a traffic jam at a time when they are in a hurry. In this short conversation, Ms. Miller's first utterance is an inverted sentence with a distal-style predicate. Mr. Yamada's only utterance is a minor sentence, and Ms. Miller's final exclamation is a direct-style verbal. Overall the style of the conversation might be described as midway between casual and careful, indicating that these two individuals, who work closely together, are beginning to use a slightly more relaxed style—at least when they are stuck in a taxicab!

(J) Mr. Yamada's utterance ending in **no ni ne!** states a condition against which present circumstances are working. In other words, contrary to their wish to arrive at their destination before dark, they are being made to wait in traffic.

Kurai and **akarui**, in addition to their basic use in reference to things that are 'dark' and 'light,' also describe people who are gloomy and cheerful respectively.

(N)b. **Uğôku** and **uğókàsu** are an intransitive/transitive pair of operational verbals: **X ğa uğôku** 'X moves'; **X o uğókàsu** 'move X.' 'Move' here refers to shifting position, *not* to changing one's place of residence (**hiḱkòsu**).

Deborah Miller's final exclamation to the effect that she and Mr. Yamada are on their way reflects the position of all those who have persisted in their study of Japanese to this point: You, too, are on your way—to advanced proficiency!

---

3. The alternate with **sore** seems to occur more commonly in modern Japanese.

Structural Patterns

1. -àtte

We now introduce a pattern, common in the spoken language, consisting of /gerund with final -e dropped (a requirement!) + -àtte/, which occurs as an alternate of /gerund + mo/. Both patterns are found in the same contexts (except that -àtte is not used in requests for permission), but stylistically the new pattern is more casual. An accented gerund retains its accent before -àtte, which then loses its accent. If the gerund preceding -atte is unaccented, the compound is accented on the first mora of -àtte. Examples:

> yamétè mo alternates with yamét-àtte 'even if [I] quit'[4]
> wârûkute mo ~ wârûkut-atte 'even if it's bad'
> ikítàkute mo ~ ikítàkut-atte 'even if [I] want to go'
> dekînakute mo ~ dekînakut-atte 'even if it's impossible'
> oísiku nàkute mo ~ oísiku nàkut-atte 'even if it's not tasty'
> nihóñḡo zya nàkute mo ~ nihóñḡo zya nàkut-atte 'even if it's not Japanese'
> kîree de mo ~ kîree d-atte 'even if it's pretty'
> dê mo ~ d-âtte 'even so,' 'however'

Note that it is also possible to describe the pattern as a gerund with final -e changed to -a + tte, but to do this creates a special form of the gerund that occurs nowhere else and obscures the apparent connection with âtte, the gerund of âru. Quotative tte can precede sequences in -àtte. Note the accumulation of t's when a quotation and this new pattern occur in combination.

> Ittà tte (i)tt-àtte, hoñtoo wa ikánàkatta nêe. 'Even if s/he says s/he went, actually s/he didn't go, did s/he!'
> Ittà tte (i)tt-àtte, hoñtoo wa iwánàkatta nêe. 'Even if s/he says s/he said it, actually s/he didn't say it, did/she!'
> Itâ tte (i)tt-àtte, hoñtoo wa inâkatta nêe. 'Even if s/he says s/he was there, actually s/he wasn't there, was s/he!'

Additional examples of -àtte are

> Yamétàkut-atte, yaméru wàke ni wa ikánài. 'Even if I want to quit, I really can't (quit).'
> Mâzûkut-atte, nomí-nasài. 'Drink it [e.g., medicine] even if it tastes bad!'
> Dôno daiḡaku ni kimét-àtte, sirásete kudasài. 'Whichever college you decide on, please let me know.'
> Nâñ-zi ni tûit-atte kamáwanài yo 'It makes no difference, whatever time you arrive.'
> Anó suutukèesu d-atte, tiísasuḡìru desyoo? 'Even if it's that suitcase, it will be too small, won't it?'

---

4. In some contexts, 'also' may be a more appropriate English equivalent than 'even.'

2. /-(a)nai uti ni/

The nominal **uti** 'interval' or 'among' has already appeared in such patterns as **tikâi uti ni** 'in the near future' and **sonó mit-tù no uti de** '(being) among those three things.'

Uti also occurs with a preceding modifier that ends with or consists of the negative of a verbal. In such cases it refers to an interval during which the action of the verbal does not occur. The implication is that it is expected to occur, and there is concern for accomplishing something (the predicate that follows) before it happens. Thus:

Mîzuno-sañ ğa kônai uti ni, dôko ni atúmàru ka kimémasyòo. 'Before Mr/s. Mi-zuno comes (*lit.* in the interval during which s/he hasn't come), let's decide where we will meet.'

Môtto tâkâku narânai uti ni, atárasìi kuruma o kaítài to omôtte (i)masu kedo, dekímàsu ka nêe. 'Before they become more expensive, I've been thinking I'd like to buy a new car, but I wonder if it will be possible.'

Kâre ğa 'yamenai uti ni, kono siğoto o zêñbu yaráseru tumori dèsu. 'I plan to make him do all this work before he quits.'

Wasurenai uti ni, soré o kakimasyòo. 'Let's write that down before we forget.'

Âme ğa 'yamanai uti ni, kaérimàsita. 'S/he went home before it stopped raining.'

The question that immediately comes to mind concerns the difference between **sinai uti ni** and **surú màe ni**. The pattern with **mâe** simply describes a time before—not after—the occurrence of its modifier. The pattern with **uti**, however, describes an interval during which something has not happened but is expected to happen, with a second activity taking place within that interval.

3. SENTENCE-PARTICLE sa

The sentence-particle **sa** occurs following direct-style final predicates. Before **sa**, the **dà** form of the copula is dropped, and **sa** never follows imperative forms. Like **nê(e)**, it may also mark the end of minor sentences. A major or minor sentence can be divided into shorter sequences to which **sa** is added, creating multiple minor sentences. **Sa** is an assertive particle—an attention-getter—that often marks obvious, accepted information. It is less strong than **yo** 'I inform you (of something new).' **Sa** may end in /!/ or /./ intonation.

Once described as typical of—or even restricted to—men's speech, **sa** is now frequently used by women as well, but it occurs only in casual speech. Examples:

Turâkut-atte sa! Sinâkyaa ikénài yo. 'Even if it's tough—you know—you've got to do it!'

Eeğo? Wakânnai sa. 'English? I don't understand it!!'

Deñwatyoo sirâbeta kedo sa! Sono namae wa dête (i)nâkatta. 'Say, I checked the phone book, but that name wasn't there.'

4. ûmì to ka mizúùmi

In lesson 27B, the utterance **Nâñ to ka narímasèñ ka** 'Won't it work out somehow?' occurred. We now meet the **to ka** sequence between nominals. **To** here is the quotative, and **ka** indicates indefiniteness (as in **nâni ka, dôo ni ka,** etc.). A series of two nominals, X and Y, with the first followed by **to ka**, is a vague kind of listing similar in meaning to **X ya Y,** with perhaps even more emphasis on imprecision: 'something like X and Y (and so on).'

In some contexts, the vagueness of the pattern resembles English 'something like X and/or Y.' An **X to ka Y** may appear in the same contexts as a nominal alone. Following an unaccented nominal, **to** is accented, as in **eńpitu tò ka pêñ** 'pencil and/or pen.' Examples:

Soó iu monò wa, hôñya to ka buñbooğuya de utte (i)rù to omoimasu. 'Things like that they sell in places like bookstores and stationery stores, I think.'

Kabúki dakè zya nâkute, nôo to ka bûñraku mo zêhi mitâi to omôtte (i)ru ñ desu. 'I've been thinking I'd like to see not just kabuki but also things like noh and the puppet theater.'

Soó iu teğami o kàku no ni wa, taípuràitaa to ka końpyùutaa ğa irû zya nai ka. 'Surely you need a typewriter or computer or something to write a letter like that?'

Konó yòo na mâñsyoñ ni sûñde (i)ru hitô wa, daitai beñgòsi to ka isyá dèsu ne! 'The people living in this kind of apartment are, for the most part, [people] like lawyers and/or medical doctors, aren't they.'

Drills

A 1. **Matá tukue uğokàsu no?**
'You mean you're going to move the desk again?'

D-âtte, uğókàse uğókàse tte, butyóo ğa iù ñ da. Iyá n(i) nâru yo.
'But (it's that) the division chief keeps telling me to move it. It gets tiresome.'

2. **Anâta ğa matíğàeta wake zya nâi no ni, ayámàri ni ikû no?**
'(You mean) you are going to go to apologize when it's not the case that *you* made the mistake?'

D-âtte, ike ikê tte, butyóo ğa iù ñ da. Iyâ n(i) nâru yo.
'But (it's that) the division chief keeps telling me to go. It gets tiresome.'

3. **seḱkaku karite kità no ni, koñpyùutaa môo modôsu;** 4. **kyaku ni ańna kotò iwáretè mo, gâmañ-suru;** 5. **ańna ni mazime de otonasìi hito, yamesaseru;** 6. **ináka no goryòosiñ ni końna monò 'okuru;** 7. **mâda ni-sáñ-do sika àtte (i)nâi no ni, kekkoñ-site simau;** 8. **sońna kotò sitâra sizéñ o kowàsu koto ni nâru no ni, mâda tuzukeru**

B 1. **Kono eeğo, hêñ desyoo?**
'This English is awkward, isn't it?'

Hêñ d-atte, syóó ğa nài sa.
'Even if it is (awkward), nothing can be done, you know.'

2. **Mâiniti ni-zîkañ mo deñsya de tuukiñ-surù no wa, turâi desyoo?**
'To commute for as long as two hours by train every day is tough, isn't it?'

Turâkut-atte, syoó ğa nài sa.
'Even if it is (tough), nothing can be done, you know.'

3. **anô ko ni ayámaseru;** 4. **eékàiwa, niğátè (da);** 5. **sońna kotò sitâra, mêewaku da to omówarèru;** 6. **Suzuki-sañ wa, señpai (da);** 7. **kono daidokoro, tyôtto kurásu-ğìru;** 8. **môtto kûuki no îi ináka ni sumitài;** 9. **kâre, sonó nyùusu kiítàra gaḱkàri-suru;** 10. **sońna kotò iḿtàra, keńka ni nàru;** 11. **môtto kańğaèru zikañ ğa hosîi**

C 1. **Moó sùg̊u syotyóo g̊a kawarù to omôu kedo . .**
'I think the head of the institute is going to change soon, but . . .' (what are we to do?)

Zyâa, kawaranai uti ni 'kono sig̊oto gańbàtte yaŕte simawanàkutya . .
'Then we must stick with this task and finish doing it before there's a change.'

2. **Raisyuu kâre g̊a 'syuttyoo kara kâette kuru to omôu kedo . .**
'I think he is going to come back from his business trip next week, but . . .' (what are we to do?)

Zyâa, kâette kônai uti ni 'kono sig̊oto gańbàtte yátte simawanàkutya . .
'Then we must stick with this task and finish doing it before he comes back.'

3. **isóg̊ànai to tyûui-sareru**; 4. **moó sùg̊u kyakú g̊a hùete, isóg̊àsìku naru**; 5. **râig̊etu 'Kimura-sañ g̊a 'yameru**; 6. **asâtte Kyôoto ni 'ikas(er)areru**; 7. **kyôo no gôg̊o aítè kara deńwa g̊a hàiru**; 8. **moó sùg̊u kâig̊i g̊a 'owaru**

D 1. **Asítà mo koŕtì ni 'oide.**
'Come here tomorrow, too.'

Asita? Hâi, kimaasu.
'Tomorrow? O.K., I will (come).'

2. **Konó keesàñki 'tukatte gorañ.**
'Try using this calculator.'

Konó keesàñki? Hâi, tukatte mimaasu.
'This calculator? O.K., I will (try using).'

3. **kono kusuri 'onomi**; 4. **obeñtoo 'motte oiki**; 5. **kono botañ 'osite gorañ**; 6. **oree 'itte oide**

E 1. **Kore, omósiròi kîzi desu yo⁀**
'This is an interesting article.'

Nâñ no kîzi desu ka⁀ Tyôtto 'haikeñ.
'An article about what? Let me see it, please.'

2. **Kore, natúkasìi syasíñ dèsu yo⁀**
'This is a photograph that brings back fond memories.'

Nâñ no syasíñ dèsu ka⁀ Tyôtto 'haikeñ.
'A photograph of what? Let me see it, please.'

3. **muzukasii syukudai**; 4. **hukúzatu na koñpyuutaa-purogùramu**; 5. **mezúrasìi doóg̊ù**; 6. **bêñri na kikâi**

F 1. **Konó kìzi, yomítàku nâi?**
'Wouldn't you like to read this article?'

Yomítài wa⁀⁵ Tyoodai.
'I would (like to read). Would you let me have it?'

2. **Kôñdo no ońg̊àkkai no kippu, hôsîku nài?**
'Wouldn't you like to have a ticket for this next concert?'

Hosîi wa⁀ Tyoodai.
'I do want one. Would you let me have it?'

3. **konáida itta hudoosañya no deńwabàñg̊oo/iranai**; 4. **Huráñsu kara moratte kìta omíyag̊e no wàiñ/nomânai**; 5. **watási g̊a señg̊àkki tukatta eékàiwa no têepu/tuka-wanai**; 6. **konó omòtya/sukî zya nâi**

G 1. **Taípuràitaa de mo waápuro dè mo îi kara . .**

Zyâa, waapuro haisyaku.
'Then let me borrow a word processor.'

---

5. The responses are feminine.

'Whether it's a typewriter or a word processor, it doesn't matter, so . . .' (you decide).

2. **Tetûğaku no nôoto de mo geñğòğaku no nôoto de mo îi kara . .**
'Whether it's philosophy notes or linguistics notes, it doesn't matter, so . . .' (you decide).

Zyâa, geñğòğaku no nôoto haisyaku.
'Then let me borrow the linguistics notes.'

3. **ané no òobaa/otóoto no zyàñpaa;** 4. **ima no deñwa/syosái nò;** 5. **tyawañ/koppu**

H 1. **Môo anó kìzi kakíhazimemàsita ka⌐**
'Have you started writing that article yet?'

E? Môo kakíowattà ñ desu yo⌐
'What? (It's that) I've already finished writing it.'

2. **Môo raíğàkki no 'yoteehyoo tukúrihazimemàsita ka⌐**
'Have you started making the schedule for next term?'

E? Môo tukúriowattà ñ desu yo⌐
'What? (It's that) I've already finished making it.'

3. **tûaa no okane atúmehazimemàsita;** 4. **raíneñ no tañtòosya erábihazimemàsita;** 5. **señsyuu syookai-sareta kyookàsyo yomíhazimemàsita;** 6. **kôñdo hiḱkòsu apâato katázukehazimemàsita;** 7. **konaida katta eékàiwa no têepu tukáihazimemàsita;** 8. **bañgòhañ tabéhazimemàsita**

I 1. **Kyoósitu to sitè wa, kurai nêe.**
'It's dark for a classroom, isn't it!'

Ñ. Kurái mamà zyaa mazûi wa yo.[6]
'Yeah. For it to be dark the way it is won't work for our purposes.'

2. **Kodómo no tamè no hôñ to sitê wa, muzukasii nêe.**
'It's difficult for a children's book, isn't it?'

Ñ. Muzúkasii mamà zyaa mazûi wa yo.
'Yeah. For it to be difficult the way it is won't work for our purposes.'

3. **owabi no teğami/mizíkài;** 4. **anó zassi no kìzi/katai;** 5. **anó zyùğyoo no sikêñ/ya-sasii;** 6. **teeburu/yowâi**

J 1. **Matíğàeta no wa, motîroñ kimí zya nài kedo . .**
'The one who made the mistake, of course, isn't you, but . . .' (you know how these things are).

Dâ no ni, dôo site watási ğa matiğàeta to ayámarànakya narânai no?
'When that's so, why is it that I have to apologize saying that _I_ made the mistake!'

2. **Kaó o tubusità no wa, motîroñ kimí zya nài kedo . .**
'The one who made [her/him] lose face, of course, isn't you, but . . .' (you know how these things are).

Dâ no ni, dôo site watási ğa tubusità to ayámarànakya narânai no?
'When that's so, why is it that I have to apologize saying that _I_ made him/her lose [face]?'

6. The responses are feminine.

3. kânozyo o 'nakaseta; 4. keésàñki o kowâsita; 5. daízi na teğami o otòsita; 6. saki ni keñka o hazimeta; 7. uéki o taòsita; 8. anô ko ni hurûi kudâmono o tabésàseta

K 1. **Kâre, waráttà ñ da tte?**
'You say (it's that) he laughed?'

Ñ, îtu mo añna hùu ni nâru to waráidàsu ñ da kara . .
'Yeah, (it's that) whenever it gets to be that way, he always bursts out laughing, so . . .' (that's how it was this time, too).

2. **Anô ko, naítà ñ da tte?**
'You say (it's that) that child cried?'

Ñ, îtu mo añna hùu ni nâru to nakídàsu ñ da kara . .
'Yeah, (it's that) whenever it gets to be that way, s/he always bursts into tears, so . . .' (that's how it was this time, too).

3. anó hutarì/keñka-sita; 4. gakúsèetati/sawâida; 5. sonó ryuuğàkusee/syabêtta; 6. otôosañ/utatta; 7. kânozyo/ki ni sita; 8. otomodati/siñpai-sita; 9. ano hurûi kuruma/uğôita

L 1. **Kawâ ni sakána ğa modòtte (i)ru soo desu kedo, ûmi ya mizúùmi wa dôo na ñ desyoo.**
'They say the fish have returned to the rivers, but how do you suppose it is for the ocean and the lakes and such?'

Âa, motîroñ ûmi to ka mizúùmi ni mo modôtte (i)ru tte iímàsu yo⌒
'Oh, they say that, of course, they have returned to places like the ocean and the lakes, too.'

2. **Sihâinin ğa naʈtoku-sita sòo desu kedo, butyóo ya katyoo wa dòo na ñ desyoo.**
'They say the managers have been persuaded, but how do you suppose it is for the division heads and section heads and such?'

Âa, motîroñ butyóo tò ka 'katyoo mo naʈtoku-sità tte iímàsu yo⌒
'Oh, they say that of course people like the division heads and section heads have also been persuaded.'

3. kodomo ğa heeki da/oyâ ya kyôodai; 4. hiráğàna o narâu/katákàna ya kañzi; 5. sîñsetu ğa taísetu na kañgaekàta da/ôñ ya girî; 6. isú o uğokasitài/tukue ya hôñdana; 7. kabúki ğa subarasìi/nôo ya bûñraku

Application Exercises

A1. Using the new **-àtte** forms, take turns getting confirmation from members of your class that it's all right (i.e., if it doesn't matter) even if (a) you read this letter; (b) you listen to this tape; (c) you use this calculator; (d) you begin the conference before the manager comes; (e) you have the secretary type this; (f) you move these chairs; (g) you don't finish this work today; (h) you don't apologize to the teacher; (i) you want more time to think; (j) your English conversation is your weak point; (k) the classroom is dark; (l) your partner isn't Japanese; (m) you don't write a letter of apology; (n) you write your thesis on a word processor. Use these questions as the basis for short conversations.

2. In response to statements about something that is going to happen, make a suggestion about what should be done before that, using the **-(a)nai uti ni** pattern. Examples: (a) Mr. Nakamura is going to come here. Suggest changing clothes. (b) The manager is going to come back. Suggest cleaning the office. (c) The conference is going to end. Suggest discussing this problem. (d) It's going to get dark. Suggest taking a walk. (e) The **siñkañseñ** is going to go up in price. Suggest going to Kyoto to see the temples.

3. Following the general pattern of CC1, practice handling situations in which one member of the class has a complaint and receives advice on how to handle it from a colleague or friend who is not personally involved. Examples of situations: (a) a foreign professional woman is being asked to make tea at the office; (b) a foreign employee is being asked to go to the airport to meet all the company's foreign visitors; (c) a foreign teacher is being asked to clean the classrooms along with the pupils; (d) a foreign employee is being asked to translate all the English letters that come to the company; (e) a foreigner is living in an apartment where the neighbors are constantly arguing and making a racket.

B. Core Conversations: Substitution

For this last set of Core Conversations, check and see to what extent you are able to substitute other patterns or forms of similar meaning that might come up in these same conversations. Follow this practice with questions and answers about content.

SECTION C

Eavesdropping

(Answer the following on the basis of the accompanying tape. A = the first speaker; B = the second speaker; C = the third speaker.)

1a. What does A want B to do?
 b. What is B's complaint?
2a. What is A's complaint?
 b. What is B's reaction to the complaint? Why?
3a. What must be done?
 b. What is B's reaction?
 c. In what connection is the **señsèe** mentioned?
4a. How is the **señsèe** described?
 b. What evidence for that description does B provide?
5a. What is about to begin?
 b. What is B's concern?
 c. According to A, how widespread is this concern?
6a. What is said to be **oisii**?
 b. According to A, when does one become aware of this?
 c. What does B suggest would be nice? What supporting evidence is mentioned?
 d. What two types of residents live in this area? Which are more numerous?
7a. Why is A angry at B?
 b. What is B's excuse?
 c. What does A want B to do? Why?
8a. Where is the company president?

   b. When is the company president due here?

   c. What is B told to do before the company president arrives?

   d. What room is B to use? Give the number, location, and size.

 9a. Where is this conversation taking place?

   b. Why are A and B upset?

   c. What does B mention to relieve the general concern?

   d. What specific concern does A mention?

   e. What would A like to find?

   f. What information does B have on this subject?

   g. What course of action does B suggest?

10a. Describe the situation. Who is indebted to whom?

   b. What does B tell A to do?

   c. In what connection is a wife mentioned?

11a. What was B made to do? When? Give details.

   b. How long did it take?

   c. How many people participated?

   d. How did B feel about the task?

12a. Who is B? What is the probable relationship between A and B?

   b. What happened to B?

   c. In what connection is Michiko mentioned?

   d. What must B do?

13a. Who is the topic of discussion?

   b. What kind of work does that person do?

   c. What is that person's weak point?

   d. What is being done to correct it? Why? Since when?

14a. What upcoming event is under discussion?

   b. What will B be made to do?

   c. Why can't B refuse?

15a. What decision is A trying to make?

   b. What suggestion does B make?

   c. What is A's concern?

   d. Why does B believe there will be no problem?

16a. What is A checking on?

   b. What information does B provide? How does B account for this answer?

   c. What is A's more specific question?

   d. What is B's problem?

   e. What does A receive permission to do?

17a. What took place last night?

   b. Who was present—both A and B, only A, or only B?

   c. What was B made to do?

   d. How does B describe what happened? Give details.

   e. In what connection does A mention B's speaking voice?

18a. What is the topic of discussion?

   b. What has B just done?

   c. What does A tell B to do?

   d. Why will B not do this?

   e. Accordingly, what is A's request?

   f. What does B plan to do?

   g. What is the language style of the conversation?

19a. What is A's question about Noguchi?

   b. What information does B provide? Give details.

   c. In what connection is Hokkaido mentioned?

   d. What is A's comment about the item under discussion?

20a. What does B want to know as A leaves the house?

   b. Why is it possible that today may be different from usual?

   c. In what connection is the telephone mentioned?

21a. What kind of part-time work is B doing?

   b. On the average, how many items does B do in one day?

   c. What is A's reaction?

   d. How does B feel at the end of a day?

   e. How does B feel about the job in general?

   f. What is B thinking about for the future?

22a. Generally speaking, how did B's interview go?

   b. What problem arose? Give details.

   c. What is A's first reaction?

   d. According to B, even assuming the problem, the situation was better than what possible alternative?

   e. What interpretation of the situation does A offer?

   f. What is B's counterinterpretation?

   g. What ritual remark by A does this lead to?

23a. Who is A?

   b. What does B feel was thoughtlessly neglected?

   c. What is A's reaction?

   d. What does B feel should have been done? What was the result of the lapse?

   e. What does A request?

   f. What does B continue to do, up to the bitter end?

24a. Describe the setting.

   b. Describe B's residence in detail.

   c. Describe the area in which it is located.

   d. What is B's complaint?

   e. How does A react to this complaint?

   f. What does B realize?

25a. What has arrived?

   b. What is B's reaction upon seeing it? Why?

   c. Why is A surprised?

   d. How does A try to reassure B?

   e. Why doesn't B find A's comment relevant?

   f. What is B's hope?

   g. What is A's reaction?

26a. Who is it that A is going to see? For what purpose?

   b. With what department is the professor under discussion connected, and what is that professor's specialization?

   c. What is A's connection with that professor?

   d. Why is A going on the errand described?

   e. In what connection does B ask about A's father?

   f. What does B learn from A in answer to that question?

27a. Where did the cake come from?

   b. How is the donor described?

   c. Why did the donor present it to B?

   d. What did B do in response?

   e. Why is A surprised?

   f. What explanation does B offer?

g. What do A and B decide to do?

28a. Where does this conversation take place?

  b. Identify A, B, and C.

  c. What does A order?

  d. What else does A ask for?

  e. What comment does A make about the item ordered?

  f. What explanation does C offer?

  g. What comment makes C happy?

  h. How does B emphasize the truth of the comment?

29a. Why didn't B take the bus?

  b. In what connection is 12 o'clock mentioned?

  c. How often do the buses run? Why so infrequently?

  d. What suggestion does A make?

  e. What is B's objection?

  f. How does A answer the objection?

  g. What is B's reaction?

  h. What is A's next suggestion?

  i. Why does B apologize?

  j. What is the relationship between A and B?

30a. What does A suggest? Why?

  b. What are B's two concerns?

  c. What three requests does A make?

Utilization

In this final exercise that will give you an opportunity to demonstrate what you have learned, make a serious attempt to create short conversations that truly reflect Japanese spoken style. Utilize the patterns you have learned to the height of your ability. Don't translate literally. Above all, indicate through your timing, gestures, facial expressions, and intonations that you are consciously thinking about the content of what you are saying. **Gańbàtte kudasai!**

1a. Check with a colleague as to whether *he* was the one who was made to do yesterday's interpreting.

  b. Your colleague replies that he was, explaining that even though his French is poor, since there was no one else who knew even a little French, there was no way out.

2a. Check with a colleague whether it was because he wanted to that he attended last week's conference.

  b. Your colleague says no, explaining that he was made to attend by the division chief.

3a. Explain to a friend, as you eat lunch together, that when you were a child, you used to be made to drink milk every day, but now you hardly drink it [at all].

  b. Your friend suggests that you should drink it every day even now, since it's good for your health.

4a. Complain to a friend that you had a sore throat and went to the hospital to have a doctor look at it; even though you went early in the morning, you were made to wait all of two hours.

  b. Your friend comments that it's always that way these days. The Japanese seem to endure this kind of thing patiently, but the foreigners do nothing but complain.

5a. Your colleague asks if you're going to introduce Mr. Nakamura to the president of Oriental Trade.

  b. You say that you are, adding that you owe Mr. Nakamura a favor, so you can't really refuse.

6a. Tell your friend that you've heard she's quitting her company and returning to her home (i.e., where she came from originally). Ask if it's true.

  b. Your friend says that it is, explaining that her father is ill and she has a duty [to return].

7a. Your friend asks if you've ever heard of a thing called "flex-time."

b. You reply that you have heard of it, but you don't understand clearly what it means.

8a. You complain to a friend that there's going to be a speech contest next month and you've been urged to participate by your teacher, but you don't want to.

b. Your friend replies that as long as your teacher is saying that, you can't really refuse. He tells you to knuckle under and participate.

9a. Your colleague confesses that she is upset because she's being made to translate a very complicated speech into English for the company president; she's worried that she will use strange English and make him lose face.

b. You suggest that since translation is her strong point, she should give it her all and try doing it.

10a. Your friend informs you that everyone will probably sing songs at the student party tonight.

b. You express concern, explaining that being made to sing in front of lots of people is something you are not good at.

11a. Ask a colleague if *he* is going to be the interpreter tomorrow.

b. Your colleague says that he is, adding that when someone like him becomes the interpreter, it ends up with the company president's losing face, so he's concerned. He points out that he isn't suited to that kind of work.

12a. You are asking directions of a policeman. Find out if the American Embassy is near the Okura Hotel.

b. The policeman replies that it is to the right of the Okura as you face it.

13a. Ask a friend how his new work is.

b. Your friend replies enthusiastically that there's no comparison with his former work; only it's a bit hard on him because he has to travel on business almost every month.

14a. A colleague asks you about the new part-time worker's English.

b. You reply that compared to the earlier part-timer, he's rather good; only his English conversation is rather stiff.

15a. A fellow student asks you how many hours a day your homework takes, on the average.

b. You reply that it differs, depending on the day; but on the average, it takes about ten hours per week—listening to tapes, memorizing the conversation portions, reading the textbook . . .

16a. A student considering taking a seminar that you have already taken asks if there is much outside preparation.

b. You reply that on the average you are made to read four or five English-language books a week, so unless you can read English quickly, it is very tough.

17a. Ask a colleague who seems to be getting ready to leave if he is going home already.

b. Your colleague says no, explaining that he is just going to see Nakamura for a moment. They had an argument yesterday, and he is going to apologize.

18a. You are complaining to a friend about a mutual acquaintance, saying that whenever you have a conversation with him, before you finish speaking, he starts to talk.

b. Your friend replies that there is nothing to be upset about. He is your superior, so you must grin and bear it.

19a. Your colleague asks if you finished reading that thesis about the natural environment.

b. You reply that—Heavens no!—you just started reading it last night.

20a. You are planning a trip with a friend. Point out that since you want to arrive before it gets dark, you'd better leave by 2 o'clock.

b. Your friend claims (assuming that you really must agree) that even if you leave at 1, you will probably arrive after dark.

21a. You are discussing an argument you had with a friend. Tell your colleague that the one at fault is your friend, so you are not going to apologize.

b. Your colleague urges you to apologize nonetheless, saying that [the situation] is no good as it is.

22a. You've just been advised by a colleague to apologize in a situation where you feel you were not at fault. Ask why you should be the one to apologize.

   b. Your colleague replies that that's the way things must be. Even if you think you can't go along with it, since your opponent is your senior, you must apologize.

23a. Complain to a colleague that your work is really hard on you these days.

   b. Your colleague advises you to give it your all even if it's tough. He encourages you by pointing out that you are often being praised by the **butyoo**.

24a. A friend tells you that there is a frightening editorial in today's paper about the air in the big cities. She asks if you saw it.

   b. You reply that there was no editorial like that in the paper you read. Ask her to let you borrow her paper.

25a. You are reading a magazine article. Your friend asks what the article is about.

   b. You tell your friend it says that Japanese colleges where (people) like Americans and/or British are teaching have gradually started to increase.

26a. An acquaintance comments that he would like to travel to Europe before he gets old.

   b. You agree, adding that you, too, want to travel while you are young.

27a. Comment to a classmate on how nice and light the classrooms in this school are.

   b. Your classmate agrees, pointing out that it's because they all face south.

28a. Your classmate tells you he's heard the professor is hoping that the students in this class will be(come) able to read things like ordinary newspaper articles and editorials by the end of this semester.

   b. You reply that if that's the case, it will be necessary to give it one's all from now on!

29a. Complain to a friend that no matter how hard you work, the manager never praises you.

   b. Your friend comments that that is how things are. If there is a problem, you're bawled out immediately, but . . .

30a. Complain to a friend that you're angry because the manager hasn't apologized in spite of having done something awful.

   b. Your friend claims that there's nothing to get angry about. Since it's the manager, there's no reason to expect him to apologize.

31a. Tell your colleague that Ms. Sugiura said she understood what you had said in English, but actually, you think she didn't.

   b. Your colleague agrees that since her English is very poor, even if she said she understood she probably didn't. He adds that she is always saying she understands even though she doesn't.

32a. Tell your friend that you tried to move this desk from here to over there, but it won't budge.

   b. Your friend offers to help, adding that (being) one person can't move it because it's too heavy.

33a. Tell your friend that no matter how tough it is, he must quit smoking for the sake of his health.

   b. Your friend agrees and says that he plans to quit starting next week.

34a. Ask a friend if she saw the 8 to 9 o'clock TV soap opera last night.

   b. Your friend did, and she assumes you agree that it was sad. She says that it made her cry.

35a. Your colleague comments that it's raining again today, adding that it's nothing but rain these days.

   b. You tell your colleague to look at the sky, pointing out that it looks as if the rain is going to stop. Add that according to today's paper, it will clear starting this afternoon.

36a. Your friend asks if you ever read anything like Japanese novels and/or poetry.

   b. You reply that you would like to, by all means, but you can't read well yet. You hope to be better at it by next year.

37a. Ask a friend for advice on how to look for a new apartment.

   b. Your friend suggests things like looking at the advertisements in the newspapers and consulting with brokers.

38a. You and a friend are on a train that has stopped between stations. Your friend wonders what has happened.

   b. You suggest that there may have been an accident up ahead. Then exclaim that you have started to move.

Check-up

1. Describe the formation and meaning of passive causative derivative verbals. How many root-extenders are involved? Which verbals have an abbreviated alternate, and what is that alternate form? What is the passive causative derivative of **kâeru** 'return'; **kaeru** 'change'; **kariru**; **kîru** 'cut'; **kiru** 'put on'; **kûru; kau; mâtu; naôsu; suru?**   (A-SP1)

2. In the sequence /**X ğa Y ni Z o** + passive causative/, describe the relationship between X, Y, and Z and the passive causative.   (A-SP1)

3. What is the difference in meaning between the passive causative and the corresponding **-(a)nakereba narânai** or **-(a)nakute wa 'ikenai** pattern?   (A-SP1)

4. What are four patterns in which quotative **(t)te** occurs?   (A-SP2)

5. Describe how, in a sequence like **Wakárànai koto ğa arímàsu ka⤴**, the breadth of meaning of **kotô** can result in there being two very different English equivalents, depending on context.   (A-SP3)

6. What is a more casual equivalent of /gerund + **mo**/? Give the corresponding equivalent for: **suru; uğôku; iku; iu; iru** 'need'; **iru** 'be located'; **turai; mazûi; îi; hirôi; yôku nâi; kawanai; sôo zya nâi; keńka dà**. How are these forms used?   (B-SP1)

7. What two patterns might occur as equivalents of 'before the professor arrives'? How do these patterns differ?   (B-SP2)

8. What is the meaning of sentence-particle **sa**? Of what speech style is it a regular feature? Describe its occurrence at the end of major and minor sentences.   (B-SP3)

9. Describe the use of **to ka** between nominals. How does **X to ka Y** differ from **X ya Y**?   (B-SP4)

Suggested review practice, before moving on: Using the accompanying video (or the textbook, if the video is unavailable), return to lesson 1 and proceed through all the CCs, *describing* what is occurring and what is being discussed in each scene. Include as much detail as possible.

OWARI

Appendix A

Summary of Verbals

Every Japanese verbal is assigned to one of four subclasses: **-ru**, **-u**, special polite, or irregular. The first two classes contain almost all verbals, since there are only five special polite verbals (**gozâru** +, **irássyàru** ↑, **kudásàru** ↑, **nasâru** ↑, and **ośsyàru** ↑) and two irregular verbals (**kûru** and **suru**). Verbals belonging to the **-u** class are further divided according to the sound that precedes final **-u**: *k, ḡ, b, m, n, s, r, t,* or a vowel other than *e.*

The table on pp. 220–21 is a summary of direct-style forms introduced in this text, with examples of each subclass. Where possible, an accented and unaccented example is given for each. In every row across, forms 2–9 are derived forms of the verbal whose citation form (the direct-style imperfective) is form 1; form 10 is a verbal derivative, but it is itself an adjectival. Its inflection is summarized below under adjectivals. Forms 11–14 are verbal derivatives that are the citation forms of new verbals belonging to the **-ru** group. These have their own inflected forms 2–9. When a particular form of a sample verbal occurs only rarely or never (for example, **yorókòbu** 'take pleasure in' does not occur in the imperative), the rare or hypothetical form is given in parentheses. Remarks about the forms follow immediately.

REMARKS ON ACCENT

FORM 1 (imperfective). Before particles **ḡa**, **ka**, **kara**, **kedo**, **si**, and **yori**,[1] sentence-particles **ka**, **yo**, and **wa**, nominal **no**, and various forms of the copula,[2] an unaccented imperfective acquires a final-mora accent. Examples: **norû kara**, **aráù kedo**, **surû no**.

FORM 3 (gerund). Before particles **kara**, **mo**, and **wa**, and sentence-particle **yo**, an unaccented gerund acquires a final-mora accent. Examples: **noťtè mo**, **aráttè wa**, **kiítè yo**.

FORM 4 (perfective). See remarks under form 1. Examples: **noťtà kara**, **aráttà kedo**, **kiítà ka**, **sitâ no**.

FORM 8 (consultative). The direct-style consultative of an unaccented verbal has an alternate accented on the next-to-last mora. Thus **nóròo**, **aráòo**, etc.

1. Alternate accent: unaccented verbal + accented **yòri**.
2. Alternate accent: unaccented verbal + accented copula. Example: **ikû desyoo** *or* **ikú desyòo**.

FORM 9 (imperative). Before sentence-particle **yo**, an unaccented imperative acquires an accent on its final mora. Thus **norê yo**, **aráè yo**, etc.

GENERAL. When, according to the regular pattern, an accent would occur on the voiceless mora of a verbal, it may shift to a neighboring voiced mora. Examples:

kûru 'come':	gerund **kitê** (*or* **kîte**)
hûru 'fall, rain':	gerund **huĺtè** (*or* **hûtte**)
kîru 'cut':	gerund **kiĺtè** (*or* **kîtte**)

Distal-style verbals are made by combining the stem (form 2 above) with **-màsu**. The inflection of **-màsu** is:

1	2	3	4	5	6	7	8	9	10
-màsu	——	-màsite	-màsita	-màsitara	-màsitari	(-masùreba)[3]	-masyòo	-màse	-masèñ

Summary of Adjectivals

An adjectival is an inflected word that ends in **-ai**, **-ii**, **-ui**, or **-oi** in its citation form (direct-style imperfective) and has a derivative perfective form ending in **-katta**.

Negative adjectivals end in **-(a)nai** and are derived from verbals; they have, in addition to a **-ku** stem, an alternate stem ending in **-(a)zu**, but they have no special polite form. Their accentuation differs from that of affirmative adjectivals.

-Tai 'want to' adjectivals are also derived from verbals; except for differences in accentuation, they are identical with **-ai** adjectivals.

A summary of adjectival forms introduced in this text appears in the table on pp. 222–23, with samples of each type. Note that form 11, the negative form of non-negative adjectivals, is the stem + **nâi**; **nâi** is itself inflected like any negative adjectival except that it has no **-(a)zu** stem. Remarks follow immediately.

REMARKS ON ACCENT

FORM 1 (imperfective). Before particles **g̃a**, **ka**, **kara**, **kedo**, **si**, and **yori**,[4] sentence-particles **ka**, **yo**, and **wa**, nominal **no**, and forms of the copula, an unaccented imperfective acquires an accent on its next-to-last mora.[5] Examples: **tumétài kara**, **ikítài kedo**, **ikánài no**.

In sentence-final position, a normally unaccented imperfective adjectival can be either accented or unaccented. Example: **Abunai.** *or* **Abúnài.**

GENERAL. Accented adjectival forms (not **-tai** adjectivals or negative adjectivals) have alternate accents in current use in the Tokyo area. These have been noted in the text. Examples:

tâkakatta	*or*	**takâkatta**
hîrokute	*or*	**hirôkute**
mizîkaku	*or*	**mizíkàku**
urêsyuu	*or*	**urésyùu**

In each case, the second form is newer.

---

3. This is an older form, rarely heard today.
4. Alternate accent: unaccented adjectival + accented **yòri**.
5. But **tooi** acquires an accent on its final mora.

Summary of the Copula **dà**

The following forms of the copula have been introduced:

	1 Imperfective	2 Pre-nominal	3 Gerund	4 Perfective	5 Conditional	6 Representative	7 Provisional	8 Tentative
Direct	**dà**	**na ~ no**	**dè**	**dàtta**	**dàttara**	**dàttari**	**nara(ba)**	**daròo**
Distal	**dèsu**	——	**dèsite**	**dèsita**	**dèsitara**	**dèsitari**	**dèsitaraba**	**desyòo**

REMARKS ON ACCENT

An accented form of the copula regularly loses its accent following an accented word or phrase.

FORM 2 (pre-nominal). This form is regularly unaccented, except that **na** following an unaccented word or phrase and preceding nominal **no** acquires an accent. Example: **byoóki nà no**.

FORM 8 (tentative). Following an unaccented verbal, the tentative has alternate accents: either the verbal remains unaccented (with **daròo/desyòo** accented) or the verbal acquires a final-mora accent (with **daròo/desyòo** unaccented). An unaccented adjectival is accented before **daròo**, and **daròo** loses its accent. Examples:

ikú daròo	*or*	**ikû daroo**
ikú desyòo	*or*	**ikû desyoo**
itta daròo	*or*	**ittà daroo**
itta desyòo	*or*	**ittà desyoo**
oisii	*but*	**oísìi daroo**
akai	*but*	**akâi desyoo**

Sample Verbals

Subclass	1 Imperfective	2 Stem	3 Gerund	4 Perfective	5 Conditional	6 Representative	7 Provisional
-ru							
(accented)	tabêru 'eat'	tâbe	tâbete	tâbeta	tâbetara	tâbetari	tabêreba
(unaccented)	ireru 'insert'	ire	irete	ireta	irétàra	irétàri	irérèba
-u							
-ku							
(accented)	arûku 'walk'	arûki	arûite	arûita	arûitara	arûitari	arûkeba
(unaccented)	kiku 'ask'	kiki	kiite	kiita	kiítàra	kiítàri	kikêba
-g̃u							
(accented)	oyôg̃u 'swim'	oyôg̃i	oyôide	oyôida	oyôidara	oyôidari	oyôg̃eba
-bu							
(accented)	yorókòbu 'take pleasure in'	yorókòbi	yorókòñde	yorókòñda	yorókòñdara	yorókòñdari	yorókòbeba
(unaccented)	yobu 'call'	yobi	yoñde	yoñda	yoñdàra	yoñdàri	yobêba
-mu							
(accented)	nômu 'drink'	nômi	nôñde	nôñda	nôñdara	nôñdari	nômeba
(unaccented)	yamu 'cease'	yami	yañde	yañda	yañdàra	yañdàri	yamêba
-nu							
(unaccented)	sinu 'die'	sini	siñde	siñda	siñdàra	siñdàri	sinêba
-su							
(accented)	hanâsu 'talk'	hanâsi	hanâsite	hanâsita	hanâsitara	hanâsitari	hanâseba
(unaccented)	kasu 'lend'	kasi	kasite	kasita	kasítàra	kasítàri	kasêba
-ru							
(accented)	tukûru 'make'	tukûri	tukûtte	tukûtta	tukûttara	tukûttari	tukûreba
(unaccented)	noru 'ride'	nori	notte	notta	nóttàra	nóttàri	norêba
-tu							
(accented)	mâtu 'wait'	mâti	mâtte	mâtta	mâttara	mâttari	mâteba
Vowel + u[a]							
(accented)	harâu 'pay'	harâi	harâtte	harâtta	harâttara	harâttari	harâeba
(unaccented)	arau 'wash'	arai	aratte	aratta	aráttàra	aráttàri	aráèba
Special Polite[b]							
(accented)	ośsyàru ↑ 'say'	ośsyài	ośsyàtte	ośsyàtta	ośsyàttara	ośsyàttari	ośsyàreba
Irregular							
(accented)	kûru 'come'	kî	kîtê	kîtâ	kîtâra	kîtâri	kûreba
(unaccented)	suru 'do'	si	site	sita	sitâra	sitâri	surêba

[a]Verbals of this class are based on a root ending in *w*. The *w* is lost everywhere in modern Japanese except before *a*.

[b]**Gozâru** belongs to this subclass but occurs only in distal-style—i.e., the stem **gozâi** always compounds with **-màsu**.

8 Consultative	9 Imperative	10 Negative Imperfective	11 Potential Imperfective	12 Causative Imperfective	13 Passive Imperfective	14 Passive Causative Imperfective
tabéyòo	tabêro	tabênai	tabé(ra)rèru	tabésasèru	tabérarèru	tabésaserarèru
ireyoo	irero	irenai	ire(ra)reru	iresaseru	irerareru	iresaserareru
arúkòo	arúke	arúkànai	arúkèru	arúkasèru	arúkarèru	arúkas(er)arèru
kikoo	kike	kikanai	kikeru	kikaseru	kikareru	kikas(er)areru
oyóğòo	oyôğe	oyóğànai	oyóğèru	oyóğasèru	oyóğarèru	oyóğas(er)arèru
yorókobòo	(yorókòbe)	yorókobànai	(yorókobèru)	(yorókobasèru)	(yorókobarèru)	(yorókobas[er]arèru)
yoboo	yobe	yobanai	yoberu	yobaseru	yobareru	yobas(er)areru
nomôo	nôme	nomânai	nomêru	nomásèru	nomárèru	nomás(er)arèru
(yamoo)	(yame)	yamanai	(yameru)	(yamaseru)	yamareru	(yamas[er]areru)
(sinoo)	(sine)	sinanai	(sineru)	sinaseru	sinareru	(sinas[er]areru)
hanásòo	hanâse	hanásànai	hanásèru	hanásasèru	hanásarèru	hanásas(er)arèru
kasoo	kase	kasanai	kaseru	kasaseru	kasareru	kasas(er)areru
tukúròo	tukûre	tukúrànai	tukúrèru	tukúrasèru	tukúrarèru	tukúras(er)arèru
noroo	nore	noranai	noreru	noraseru	norareru	noras(er)areru
matôo	mâte	matânai	matêru	matásèru	matárèru	matás(er)arèru
haráòo	harâe	haráwànai	haráèru	haráwasèru	haráwarèru	haráwas(er)arèru
araoo	arae	arawanai	araeru	arawaseru	arawareru	arawas(er)areru
(ośśyaròo)	ośśyài	ośśyarànai	ośśyarèru	(ośśyarasèru)	(ośśyararèru)	(ośśyaraserarèru)
koyôo	kôi	kônai	ko(rá)rêru	kosásèru	korárèru	kosás(er)arèru
siyoo	siro	sinai	dekîru	saseru	sareru	saserareru

Irássyàru has alternate gerunds irássyàtte and irâsite; nasâru has alternate gerunds nasâtte and nasûtte; and kudásàru has alternate gerunds kudásàtte and kudásùtte. Parallel alternation appears in forms 4–6 of these three verbals.

Sample Adjectivals

	1 Imperfective	2 Stem	3 Alternate Negative Stem	4 Special Polite (+ **gozáimàsu**)	5 Gerund
-ai					
(accented)	**takâi** 'is high'	**tâkâku**	——	**tâkôo**	**tâkâkute**
(unaccented)	**tumetai** 'is cold'	**tumetaku**	——	**tumetoo**	**tumétàkute**
-ii					
(accented)	**suzúsìi** 'is cool'	**suzûsìku**	——	**suzusyuu**	**suzûsìkute**
(unaccented)	**oisii** 'is delicious'	**oisiku**	——	**oisyuu**	**oísìkute**
-ui					
(accented)	**atûi** 'is hot'	**âtûku**	——	**âtûu**	**âtûkute**
(unaccented)	**atui** 'is thick'	**atuku**	——	**atuu**	**atûkute**
-oi					
(accented)	**hirôi** 'is wide'	**hîrôku**	——	**hîrôo**	**hîrôkute**
(unaccented)	**tooi** 'is far'	**tooku**	——	**tooo**	**toôkute**
-tai					
(accented)	**tabétài** 'wants to eat'	**tabétàku**	——	**tabétòo**	**tabétàkute**
(unaccented)	**ikitai** 'wants to go'	**ikitaku**	——	**ikitoo**	**ikítàkute**
-(a)nai					
(accented)	**tabênai** 'doesn't eat'	**tabênaku**	**tabêzu**	——	**tabênakute**
(unaccented)	**ikanai** 'doesn't go'	**ikanaku**	**ikazu**	——	**ikánàkute**

6	7	8	9	10
Perfective	Conditional	Representative	Provisional	Negative
tâkâkatta	tâkâkattara	tâkâkattari	tâkâkereba	tâkâku nâi
tumétàkatta	tumétàkattara	tumétàkattari	tumétàkereba	tumétaku nài
suzûsìkatta	suzûsìkattara	suzûsìkattari	suzûsìkereba	suzûsìku nâi
oísìkatta	oísìkattara	oísìkattari	oísìkereba	oísiku nài
âtúkatta	âtúkattara	âtúkattari	âtúkereba	âtúku nâi
atúkatta	atúkattara	atúkattari	atúkereba	atúku nài
hîrôkatta	hîrôkattara	hîrôkattari	hîrôkereba	hîrôku nâi
toôkatta	toôkattara	toôkattari	toôkereba	toóku nài
tabétàkatta	tabétàkattara	tabétàkattari	tabétàkereba	tabétàku nâi
ikítàkatta	ikítàkattara	ikítàkattari	ikítàkereba	ikítaku nài
tabênakatta	tabênakattara	tabênakattari	tabênakereba	——
ikánàkatta	ikánàkattara	ikánàkattari	ikánàkereba	——

Appendix B

na-Nominals[1]

bêñri   convenient

betu[2]   separate

daízì   valuable, important

daízyòobu   all right; safe

damê   no good

gêñki   pep, vim, high spirits; peppy, vigorous

heeki   calm, cool; indifferent; unconcerned

hêñ   strange

hetâ   unskillful; poor at

hima   free time

hityuoo   necessity; necessary

hizyoo   emergency; extraordinary, extreme

hûbeñ   inconvenient

hukuzatu   complicated

h(u)ôomaru   formal

hûu   manner style

iroiro[2] (∼ **iroñ**)   various

iyâ   unpleasant, disagreeable

kañtañ   simple

kêkko   health; healthy

kirai   displeasing; dislike

kîree   pretty, clean

kyuu   sudden, without warning; urgent

mêewaku   a nuisance; troublesome

meńdòo   bothersome, troublesome, annoying

-mìtai   as if ——

mûri   unreasonable, excessive, forced, impossible

1. The list below includes all **na**-nominals introduced in this text.
2. As the modifier of a following nominal, occurs followed by **na** or **no**.

niĝîyaka   lively, bustling; prosperous

okâsi[3]   funny; strange

ôoki[3]   big, large; loud (of voice)

rakû   relaxed; comfortable; easy

rippa   splendid, magnificent, great, eminent

sîñsetu   kind, considerate

sitûree   rudeness; rude

sîzuka   quiet; peaceful; silent

-soo[4]   looking as if ——

sukî   pleasing; like

sumûuzu   smooth

taiheñ   awful, terrible; a problem

taisetu   important

tâsika   certain, positive, reliable

têenee   polite; careful; conscientious; thorough

-teki   pertaining to

tekitoo   suitable

tîisa[3]   small, little; low, soft (of voice)

yokee   excessive, unnecessary, uncalled for

yôo   manner; resemblance; seeming

yuumee   famous; notorious

zańnèñ   regrettable; too bad; a pity

ziyûu   free, unrestricted

zyoobu   strong, rugged, sturdy

zyoózù   skillful, skilled

Examples of typical usage:

Kîree desu.   '[It]'s pretty.'

Kîree zya arímasèñ/nâi desu.   '[It] isn't pretty.'

Kîree na ozyôosañ desu.   '[She]'s a pretty girl.'

Kîree ni narímàsita.   '[She]'s become pretty.'

Kîree ni kakímàsita.   '[S/he] wrote beautifully.'

---

3. With following **na**, alternates with the **-i** form of the related adjectival as the modifier of a following nominal. Example: **ôoki na kôe** *or* **oókìi kôe** 'loud voice.'

4. For example, **hurísòo** 'looking as if it would rain,' **oisisoo** 'delicious-looking,' **geńkisòo** 'peppy-looking.'

Appendix C

Classifiers[1]

	Occurs with			Usage[c]		
	Numerals of Chinese Series[a]	Numerals of Japanese Series[b]	Irregular	Counts	Names	Counts and Names
-bañ nights		X		X		
-bañ serial numbers	X				X	
-dai vehicles and machines	X			X		
-d(e)iikee apartments (= number of rooms + dining room/kitchen)	X				X	
-do occurrences	X			X		
-doru dollars	X			X		
-eñ yen	X			X		
-ḡakki school terms	X			X		
-ḡatu months	X				X	
-ḡoositu room numbers	X				X	
-hai glassfuls and cupfuls	X			X		
-haku nights of a stay	X			X		
-heya rooms		X		X		
-hoñ long, cylindrical objects	X			X		
-huñ minutes	X					X
-huñkañ minutes	X			X		
-ka/-niti days			X			X
-kaḡetu months	X			X		
-kai floors	X					X
-kai occurrences	X			X		
-kakañ/-kaniti days			X	X		
-ken buildings and shops	X			X		
-kaneñ(kañ) years	X			X		
-ko pieces	X			X		
-mai thin, flat objects	X			X		
-mee(sama) people	X			X		
-neñ years	X					X
-neñkañ years	X			X		

1. The list below includes all the classifiers introduced in this text.

Classifiers, *cont.*

	Occurs with			Usage[c]		
	Numerals of Chinese Series[a]	Numerals of Japanese Series[b]	Irregular	Counts	Names	Counts and Names
-niñ/-ri people			X	X		
-niñmae portions	X			X		
-niti/-ka days			X			X
-ri/-niñ people			X	X		
-sai years of human age	X			X		
-satu books, magazines, etc.	X			X		
-see generations	X				X	
-señto cents	X			X		
-soku pairs of footwear	X			X		
-syoku meals	X			X		
-syuukañ weeks	X			X		
-tu units; years of human age		X		X		
-tubo[d] tsubo (two-mat area)		X		X		
-tyaku suits	X			X		
-tyoome chome	X				X	
-zi o'clocks	X				X	
-zikañ hours	X			X		
-zyoo[e] jo (one-mat area)	X			X		

[a]**Itî**, **nî**, **sañ**, etc.

[b]**Hitô**, **huta**, **mî**, etc.

[c]A number that counts tells *how many*; a number that names tells *which one*. Thus **ni-kâgetu** 'two months' counts; **ni-gâtù** 'February' names; and **nî-neñ** 'two years' or 'the year two' counts and names.

[d]Also occurs with some numerals of the Chinese series.

[e]Also occurs as a name for a room having the given number of mats.

Japanese–English Glossary

The following list contains the vocabulary introduced in Parts 1, 2, and 3 of this text—words occurring in the Miscellaneous Notes and Structural Patterns as well as those appearing in the Core Conversations. Only personal names are omitted. Numbers plus A or B following the entries refer to lesson and section; a number plus A or B alone means that the entry first occurs in the Core Conversations of that lesson and section; with a following plus sign it refers to a later part of that lesson. GUP refers to Greetings and Useful Phrases.

Except in special cases, verbals and adjectivals are listed in their citation form only. Every verbal is assigned to the appropriate subclass;[1] its perfective form is also given. For example, **tabêru /-ru; tâbeta/** identifies **tabêru** as a verbal belonging to the **-ru** subclass (i.e., the vowel-verbal subclass), with perfective **tâbeta.**

Every adjectival is identified by **/-katta/**, the perfective ending, after the citation form. Thus, the adjectival meaning 'is big' appears as: **oókìi /-katta/.**

All forms of the copula which occur in the text are listed and identified.

Nominals occur with no special designation, except that the members of the subclass of **na**-nominals[2] are identified by a following /**na**/.

Particles and the quotative are identified as /ptc/ and /quotative/, respectively.

Pre-nominals are identified by the designation /+ nom/.

Classifiers are so identified and are listed with a preceding hyphen.

Except in a few special cases, words having a polite alternate that differs from the plain alternate only in the addition of the polite prefix **o-** or **go-** are listed only in the plain form.

For purposes of alphabetizing, hyphens and the macron of **ḡ** and **ñ** are ignored.

In most cases, combinations occurring as indented sublistings match the first occurrence of the pattern in the lessons; but a simpler, more generally occurring example of the pattern is cited in cases where the combination which occurs first seems less desirable as the model for a pattern of wide general use.

For explanation of special symbols, see Introduction, Part 1.

â(a) oh! 2A

abunai /-katta/ is dangerous 7B

aḡaru /-u; aḡatta/ go/come up; rise 18A

aḡeru /-ru; aḡeta/ give (to you/him/her/them) 17A

---

1. For a description of verbal subclasses, see Lesson 9A, Structural Pattern 1, in Part 1.
2. See Lesson 5B, Structural Pattern 1, in Part 1.

kasite aḡeru lend (to you/him/her/them) 17A

nihóñḡo de hanasàsete aḡémàsita [I] let someone speak in Japanese *or* [I] had or made someone speak in Japanese, for the benefit of someone else 28A +

aḡeru /-ru; aḡeta/ raise 18A +

tê o aḡeru raise one's hand 18A +

atámà o aḡeru lift up one's head 18A +

aida interval; between-space 6A

baiteñ to dêḡuti no aida between the stand and the exit 6A

aída ni hàiru become a go-between 26B

aida ni hitó ni hàitte morau have someone become a go-between 26B

osêwa ni nâtte (i)ru aida while being under obligation; while being dependent 29B

tomodati ḡa nete (i)ru aida ni, teḡámi o yomimàsita while my friend was sleeping, I read the letter 29B +

Nihôñ ni ita aida, zutto tomódati no utì ni tomárasete moratte (i)màsita all the while I was in Japan, I stayed (was being permitted to stay) at a friend's house 29B +

kodomo no nete (i)ru aida mo, dekákerarenàkatta also/even while the children were sleeping, I couldn't go out 29B +

âidea idea 11A

ainiku unfortunate; unfortunately 12A

âisatu greeting, salutation 29A

âisatu (o) suru greet 29A

têenee na âisatu (o) sareru be greeted politely 29A

aísukurìimu ice cream 3A +

aítaḡàru /-u; aítaḡàtta/ want to meet/see; be eager *or* anxious to meet/see 28B

aítè partner; the other party 30B

akai /-katta/ is red 4A +

akarui /-katta/ is light (not dark); is cheerful (of people) 30B +

âkatyañ baby 10A +

akeru /-ru; aketa/ open [something] 16A

âki fall, autumn 19A +

akíramèru /-ru; akíràmeta/ give up, forego; resign oneself to 23A

aku /-u; aita/ become open; [something] opens 16A

aite (i)ru be vacant, available 24B

amâdo storm door 16A +

amaeru /-ru; amaeta/ presume upon; take advantage of (someone's kindness or affection); behave like a spoiled child 28A

okotoba ni amaeru take advantage of your kind words 28A

amáḡàsa (rain) umbrella 23B +

amai /-katta/ is sweet; is bland 15B +

âme rain 4A

âme ni nâru get to be rain, start to rain 22A

Amerika America 5B +

Amérika-gìñkoo Bank of America 16A

amérikàziñ an American 10B +

amî net 16A +

amîdo screen door 16A +

anâta you 2B +

ane older sister; my older sister 11A +

âni older brother; my older brother 11A +

a(ñ)mari /+ negative/ not much; not very 1B

añna that kind (of) 4B +

añna ni to that extent; like that 9B +

añnàiniñ guide 28B +

añnài-suru guide; show the way 28B

mití o añnài-suru guide along the road 28B +

Toókyoo o añnài-suru show around Tokyo 28B +

okyáku o añnài-suru show a guest around 28B +

añnaizyò information desk 28B +

ano /+ nom/ that —— over there; that —— (known to both of us) 3A

anô hitò he; she 10A +

anó kàta he; she /polite/ 10A +

|anoo| uh 4B

aôi /-katta/ is blue; is green 4A

apâato apartment; apartment house 14B

Itóo-apàato the Ito Apartments 14B

arau /-u; aratta/ wash 17B +

are that thing over there; that thing (known to both of us) 2B

aríḡatài /-katta/ is grateful; is obliged 18A

aríḡàtàku tyoodai-suru ↓ accept gratefully /humble-polite/ 18A

Arîḡatoo (gozaimasu). + Thank you. GUP

Arîḡatoo (gozaimasita). + Thank you (for what you did). GUP

âru /-u; âtta/ be located (of inanimate existence); have 4A

kesíte àru [it] has been turned off 16A

kodómo ḡa àru [I] have children 27B +

arúbàito   part-time work, usually performed by students   10A

arûku /-u; arûita/   walk   7B

  arûite iku   go on foot   7B

âsa   morning   8B+

aságòhañ   breakfast   14A+

asâtte   day after tomorrow   3B

asî   leg, foot   17A+

asítà   tomorrow   1A

asobu /-u; asoñda/   play; play around; amuse oneself; be off from work   26B

  asóñde bàkari da   it's nothing but playing   26B

asoko   that place over there; that place (known to both of us)   6B+

asû   tomorrow   1A+

asuko   /casual alternate of **asoko**/   9A

atámà   head   17A+

  atámà no hataraku hito   a bright, clever person   25A+

atárasìi /-katta/   is new; is fresh   1B+

at(á)takài /-katta/   is warm   11A

atira   that side; that way; thereabouts; there; that alternative (of two)   6A+

âto   later; remaining   8A

  dête simatta âto de   (being) after having left   19B

  âto de   (being) later on   11A

  âto ití-zìkañ   one hour left   8A

  âto gô-huñ mâtte   having waited the next five minutes   26A

-àtte   even   30B

  d-âtte   but, however, even so   30B

  itt-àtte   even if [someone] says   30B

  wârûkut-atte   even if it's bad   30B

  kîree d-atte   even if it's pretty   30B+

  dôno daiğaku ni kimét-àtte   whichever college you decide on   30B+

attì   /casual alternate of **atira**/   7B+

atui /-katta/   is thick   23B+

atûi /-katta/   is hot   11A+

atúmàrì   a meeting, a gathering   27B

atúmàru /-u; atúmàtta/   come together   19B

atúmèru /-ru; atûmeta/   bring together   19B+

àtusa   heat   24B+

âu /-u; âtta/   meet; see (a person)   11A

  X ni âu   meet person X; see person X   11A

  X to âu   meet (with) person X; see person X   11A+

âu /-u; âtta/   match up with   18A

  kutí ni àu   suit one's taste   18A

ma ní àu   be on time   20B

awateru /-ru; awateta/   become confused, disconcerted, disorganized   19B

ayámàru /-u; ayamatta/   apologize   30B

azi   taste   22B

  azi ğa suru   have a taste   22B+

azúkàru /-u; azúkàtta/   accept for temporary keeping   19A+

azúkèru /-ru; azûketa/   hand over for temporary keeping; check   19A

baai   case, circumstance   23B

  koo iu baai   cases like this   23B

  baai ni yotte   depending on circumstances   23B+

baiteñ   stand; concession; kiosk   6A

bâk(k)ari   only; only just; little else but   26B+

  asóñde bàkari da   it's nothing but playing   26B

  hikkosi-sita bàkari da   [I] just moved   26B

  hîdôku naru bâkari da   it just gets worse (*lit.* severe)   26B

  beñkyoo bàkari suru   do nothing but study   26B+

  utí no nàka ni bâkari iru   stay only inside the home   26B+

  natú bàkari ğa isóğasìi   only summers are busy   26B+

  sonó kyookàsyo bâkari o yôñde (i)ru   reads little else but that textbook   26B+

  kîree na bâkari de, yakû ni tatânai   it is only pretty; it serves no purpose   26B+

bañ   night   8B+

-bañ   /classifier for counting nights/   21A+

-bañ   /classifier for serial numbers/   3A

bañgòhañ   dinner   14A+

bañğòo   (assigned) number   12A

bañğumi   program   18B

bâsu   bus   7B+

basu-tuki   with bath   21A+

basyo   place, spot, location, site   27B

  basyó o tòtte oku   hold *or* reserve a place   27B+

  basyo o akeru   open up a place   27B+

  basyó o eràbu   choose a site   27B+

  basyó o tòru   take up space   27B+

bâta   butter   14A+

Beekoku   U.S.A.   5B+

bêekoñ   bacon   14A+

bèki: iú bèki da   [one] ought to/must/should say   26B

bêñ facilities; convenience 24B
 bêñ ǧa îi is convenient 24B
beñǧòsi lawyer 16B+
beñkyoo study 9B+
beñkyoo-suru study 9B
bêñri /na/ convenient 4A
beñtòo box lunch 14A+
Bêruriñ Berlin 12B+
bêtto/bêddo bed 17B+
betu separate; different 25B
 betú no yoozi dè because of a different/separate matter 25B+
betubetu separate 21A+
betu ni /+ negative/ not especially 9A
bîiru beer 5B+
bií-sètto the "B" meal 15B+
bikkùri-suru become surprised 11A
biñseñ stationery 4B+
bîru office building 6A
 Paáku-bìru the Park building 6A
bôku/boku I; me /M/ 2B+
 konó bòku this me right here 28B
booeki foreign trade 10A
 Oríeñtaru-bòoeki the Oriental Trading (Company) 10A
booeki-suru conduct foreign trade 10A+
boóekìsyoo foreign trader, importer-exporter 16B+
boorupeñ ballpoint pen 4B
boosi hat 23A
botañ button 26A
bôttyañ son; your son; young man /polite/ 10A+
bu division within a company 13B+
buatui /-katta/ is thick 23B
bukka (commodity) prices 24B
buñbòoǧu stationery; office supplies 7A+
buñbooǧuya stationery store; stationery dealer 7A+
bûñǧaku literature 18B+
buñǧàkùbu literature department 25B
bûñraku traditional Japanese puppet theater 28B+
burâusu blouse 23A+
butúrìǧaku physics (as an academic subject) 25B
butyoo division manager 13B+
byooiñ hospital 6B+
byooki sick; sickness 9B

dà /copula: direct imperfective/ 9A

odekake da ↑ [someone] is going out /honorific-polite/ 23A
dâ kedo however 25B
dâ kara therefore 25B+
dâ no ni in spite of that; nevertheless 30B
dâbúru(-rùumu) double room 21A+
-dai /classifier for counting vehicles and machines/ 7B+
daidokoro kitchen 17B
daídokoro-dòoǧu kitchen utensils 17B
daiǧaku university; college 7A+
daiǧakuiñ graduate school 7A+
dâiku carpenter 16B+
daitai for the most part 15B
daítòkai large city, metropolis 30B
daízì /na/ valuable, important 16A
daízyòobu /na/ all right; safe 2A
dakê just; only 5A
 soré dakè just that 5A
 kañǧàeta dakê de just having thought about it 23B
 oókìi dakê da it's just big 23B+
 dekiru dake as much as possible 23B+
damê /na/ no good 2A
dañsee man; male 19B+
dañseeǧo men's language 19B+
dañti apartment complex; housing development 24A+
dâre who? 2B
 dâre ka someone, somebody 24A
 dâre ka wakâi hito some young person 24A
 dâre mo /+ negative/ nobody 13A
daròo /copula: direct tentative/ 11A
dâsu /-u; dâsita/ put out; take out 17B+; serve 21A
 okáne o dàsu pay, put up the money 28A
 hôñ o dâsu publish a book 17B+
 teǧámi o dàsu mail a letter 17B+
 sotó ni/e dàsu put [something] outside 17B+
-dasu /-u; -dasita/ start to 30B
 narídàsu ~ naridasu start to become 30B
 uǧókidàsu ~ uǧokidasu start to move 30B
dàtta /copula: direct perfective/ 9B
dè /copula: gerund/ 8A
 de gozaimàsu + /neutral-polite equivalent of **dèsu**/ 10A
 de (i)rassyàru ↑ /honorific-polite equivalent of **dà**/ 10A
 dê mo even so, however 8B, 25B+

dotíra dè mo whichever (of two) it is; wherever it is 21B

pâat(e)ii de mo a party or something 23A

matânai de without waiting; instead of waiting 23B

matânai de kudasai please don't wait 23B

dê wa in that case, then 25B+

de /ptc/ in; at 7A; by means of 7B; because of 9B

kiśsateñ de tabèru eat at a coffee shop 7A

tâkusii de iku go by cab 7B

zîko de okureru become late because of an accident 9B

dêğuti exit 6A

-d(e)iikee /classifier for identifying apartments in terms of number of rooms + dining room and kitchen/ 24B

dekakeru /-ru; dekaketa/ go out; set out 23A

dekîru /-ru; dêkita/ become completed; can do; be possible 1A

demae home delivery of prepared food 14B

demúkaèru /-ru; demúkàeta/ meet; greet 19A

de nài: bôku de nâi it's not me 22B

dêñki electricity; electric lights 16A+

deñsya/dêñsya electric train 7B+

deñwa telephone (call) 2A

deñwa ğa tooi sound far away (on the telephone) 13A

deñwa ni dèru answer the telephone 13A

deñwa o ireru put in a call 18B

deñwa o kakèru make a telephone call 9B

deñwa ğa kakàru be called on the telephone

deñwa ğa hàiru telephone calls come in 25B

deñwabàñğoo telephone number 12A

deñwa-suru telephone 11A

deñwatyoo telephone book 19A

depâato department store 7A+

dêru /-ru; dêta/ go out; come out; leave; attend 9B

deñwa ni dèru answer the telephone 13A

têrebi ni dêru appear on television 18B

namáe ğa dète (i)ru names are carried, published, printed, etc. 20B

syokúzi ğa dèru meals are served 21A

dèsita /copula: distal perfective/ 2A

dèsu /copula: distal imperfective/ 1B, 2A

desu nê(e)| /filler/ 13B

desyòo /copula: distal tentative/ 6B

dê wa well then 13B+

-do /classifier for counting occurrences/ GUP; 12A

dôa door 16A

Dôitu Germany 5B+

doituğo German language 2A+

doítùziñ a German 10A+

dôko what place? where? 6B

dôko ka someplace, somewhere 24A

Toránomoñ no dòko where in Toranomon? what part of Toranomon? 6B

dôko no Toranomoñ the Toranomon which is where? 6B

dônata who? /polite/ 2B+

dôñdoñ in rapid succession 24A

dôñna what kind (of)? 4B

dôñna ni to what extent? in what manner? 9B+

dôno /+ nom/ which ——? 3A

dono-ğurai about how much? 8A

dô(o) /abbreviation for **doyôo(bi)**/ 8A

dô(o)·nîti Sat–Sun 8A

dôo what way? how? 2A

Dôo itasimasite. Don't mention it. GUP

dôo mo in every way; in many ways; somehow or other GUP, 13A

dôo de mo however it is 24B

dôo iu hito a person described how? what kind of person? 18B

dôo suru how will [you] act? what will [you] do? 11A

dôo site how come? how? why? 11A

âu ka dôo ka wakárànai can't tell whether it matches or not 18A

Waápuro tukattàra dôo? How about using a word processor? 26A+

Dôo sitara îi? What should I do? 26A+

doóğù tools, implements 17B

doohai colleague of equal status 26A+

dôoka /alternate of **dôozo**/ 24A

-doori: zikáñ-dòori on time 26B+

dooryoo colleague of equal status 26A+

Dôozo. Please (speaker offering something). GUP

Dôozo goyúkkùri. Take it easy! 12A+

Dôozo yorosiku. Please [treat me] favorably. 11B

dôre which thing (usually of three or more)? 2B

dôresu dress 23A+

-doru /classifier for counting dollars/ 3A+

dôtira which side? which way? whereabouts? where? which alternative (of two)? 6A
　dôtira mo both 12A
　dotíra dè mo whichever (of two) it is; wherever it is 21B
　dôtira no hoo which alternative? which direction? 6A
dôtira-sama who? /polite/ 12B
dôtti /casual equivalent of **dôtira**/ 7B +
doyôo(bi) Saturday 8A

e /ptc/ to; into; onto 7A
　hôñya e to the bookstore 7A
êe /affirmation/ GUP, 1A
êeḡa/eeḡa movie 18B +
eéḡàkañ movie theater 6B +
eeḡo English language 2A +
Eehuku-tyoo Eifuku-cho (section of Tokyo) 16B
eékàiwa English conversation 30A
Eekoku England 5B +
Eékokùziñ English person 10B +
eé-kòosu the "A" meal 14A
eé-sètto the "A" meal 15B
|**eeto**| uh 7B
eewa English–Japanese 2B
eéwa-zìteñ English–Japanese dictionary 2B
êggu egg 14A +
êki station 6A
-eñ /classifier for counting yen/ 2B
eñkai dinner party (Japanese-style) 21B
eñpitu pencil 4B +
eñryo reserve; holding back 18A
　Goéñryo nàku. Don't hold back. 18A
eñryo-suru hold back; stand on ceremony 18A +
　eñryo-site oku hold back for now; take a rain check 18A +
erâbu /-u; erâñda/ choose, select; elect 27A
erâi /-katta/ is great, eminent, superior 29A

ḡa /ptc/ 4A, 4B, 5A
gaikoku foreign country 11B +
gaikokuḡo foreign language 11B
gaíkokùziñ foreigner 10A +
gaikoo diplomacy 16B +
gaíkòokañ diplomat 16B +
gaímùsyoo Foreign Ministry 11B +
gaisyutu-suru go out 13B +
gaisyutu-tyuu da be out 13B
gaiziñ foreigner (particularly Westerner) 10A

-ḡàkari in charge of 29B +
　añnai-ḡàkari tour guide 29B +
　reñraku-ḡàkari person in charge of liaison 29B +
gakkai learned society, academic organization 20B
gaќ̀kàri-suru become discouraged; become disappointed 20B
-ḡakki /classifier for naming and counting school terms/ 28B +
gakkoo school 7A +
gakubu academic department; college (within a university) 25B +
gakusee student 2B +
gakutyoo academic president 13B +
gâmañ-suru bear, endure, put up with, suffer in silence; grin and bear it; knuckle under 30B
gañbàru /-u; gañbàtta/ exert special effort, give it one's all 30A
　gañbàtte 'yaru give it one's all and do it 30A
gâñ-neñ initial year of an era 8B +
-ḡaru /affective suffix/ 28B +
　zisíñ o kowaḡàru show fear of earthquakes 28B +
　huyû o samúḡàru find the winter cold (and show that reaction) 28B +
　syoókai o meewakuḡàru (show that) [one] finds introductions a nuisance 28B +
-ḡata /polite pluralizing suffix/ 29A
　anáta-ḡàta~anata - ḡata you (plural) 29A +
　katâ-ḡata persons /polite/ 29A +
-ḡatu /classifier for naming months/ 8B
gekizyoo theater 6B +
geñḡo language 18B +
geñḡòḡaku linguistics 25B +
gêñkañ entry hall 17B +
gêñki /na/ pep, vim, high spirits; peppy, vigorous 14B
　gêñki ḡa dêru perk up, become energetic 14B
　gêñki ḡa îi is in good spirits 14B +
　Ogêñki desu ka ✔ Are you well? 14B +
gês·sûi·kîñ Mon–Wed–Fri 8A
geta wooden clogs (for outdoors) 23A +
gêtu/gêk-/gês- /abbreviation for **getúyòo(bi)**/ 8A
getúyòo(bi) Monday 8A
giñkoo bank 7A

giṅkòoiñ banker 16B +

girî obligation, duty 30A

  seńsèe ni girî ḡa âru have an obligation to a teacher 30A

  girî o 'siranai ignore one's **girî** 30A +

  girî o tatêru recognize an obligation 30A +

  girî ni 'sibarareru be bound in obligation 30A +

gîsi engineer 16B +

gô five 2B

Gobúsata-simàsita. I've neglected to be in touch. 11B +

goeñdama ¥5 coin 19A +

Goéñryo nàku. Don't hold back. 18A

gôḡo afternoon; P.M. 8B

gôhañ cooked rice; food 14A +

  Gôhañ ḡa dekímàsita. Dinner is ready. 14A +

gohyakueñdama ¥500 coin 19A +

gohyakueñsatu ¥500 bill 19A +

gokai-suru misunderstand 29A

  îmi o 'gokai-sareru have the meaning misunderstood 29A

Gokûroosama. It's been trouble for you; Thanks for your trouble. 17B

Gomén-kudasài. Excuse me; Pardon me. 12B

Gomén-nasài Excuse me; Pardon me 29B

gomî trash; dust 17A

goórudeñ-uìiku Golden Week (April 29–May 5) 20A

-ḡoositu /classifier for naming room numbers/ 14B

gorañ↑: Kore gorañ.↑ Look at this! 28B +

goráñ ni nàru↑ look at; see /honorific-polite/ 28B

goráñ-kudasài please look at [it] 28B +

-ḡòro about (approximate point in time) 8A

  kono-ḡoro these days, nowadays 8A +

gôruhu golf 4A

goseñeñsatu ¥5000 bill 19A +

gotisoo: gotísoo ni nàru receive hospitality; be treated to food or drink 28A

gotisoo-suru entertain, treat [a person to food or drink] 28A +

Gotísoosama (dèsita). It was delicious. 5B

gozáimàsu + /neutral-polite equivalent of **âru**/ 5A

  de gozaimàsu + /neutral-polite equivalent of **dà**/ 10A

gôzeñ A.M. 8B +

gozôñzi↑ da /honorific-polite/ know 10B +

gozyuueñdama ¥50 coin 19A +

guai condition 14B

Gûamu Guam 26B

-ḡùrai about, approximately 8A

  dono-ḡurai about how much? 8A

gurêe gray 5B

gurîiñ green 5B +

gurîiñsya "green car" 19A +

gûuguu /onomatopoeia/

  gûuguu netyau fall sound asleep 19B

hâ tooth 16B +

hâa /polite affirmation/ GUP, 13B

hâai ye-es! 18A

hâha mother; my mother 11B +

hahaoya mother 11B +

-hai /classifier for counting glassfuls and cupfuls/ 14B

hâi /affirmation/; here you are GUP, 1A

haiiro gray 5B +

haikeñ↓: Kore haikeñ.↓ Let me look at this! 28B +

haikeñ-suru↓ look at; see /humble-polite/ 28B

hâikiñḡu hiking 26B +

hâiru /-u; hâitta/ go in, enter 16A

  deñwa ḡa hàiru telephone calls come in 25B

  hurô ni hâiru take a bath 21B

hâisya dentist 16B +

haisyaku↓: Eñpitu haisyaku.↓ Let me borrow a pencil! 28B +

haisyaku-suru↓ borrow /humble-polite/ 28B

hâiyaa limousine available for hire 20A +

haḱkìri clear(ly), precise(ly), exact(ly) 19A

haḱkiri-suru become exact 19A

  haḱkìri-sita zikañ exact time 19A

hako box 20A

hakobu /-u; hakoñda/ transport, carry 20A

-haku /classifier for counting nights of a stay/ 21A

  ippaku-suru stay one night 21A +

haku /-u; haita/ put (or wear) on the feet or legs 23A

  haite (i)ru be wearing (on the feet or legs) 23A

  haite iku wear (on the feet or legs) to a place 23A +

hâmu ham 14A +

hamú-sàndo ham sandwich 14A +

-hàñ- one-half 8B
  yo-zí-hàñ 4:30 8B
  yo-zíkañ-hàñ four hours and a half 8B+
  hañ-nitì half a day 27B
  hañ-tosì half a year 27B+
  hañ-tukì half a month 27B+
  hañ-zìkañ a half-hour 8B+
hana nose 17A+
hanâ flower 7A+
hanárèru /-ru; hanâreta/ become detached,
  separated 26A+
  êki o hanárèru get clear of the station
  26A+
  tê o hanárèru get to be out of one's hands
  26A+
  hanâreta matî an isolated town 26A+
  **Tookyoo kara ′deñsya de ití-zikañ-ĝùrai ha-
  nârete (i)ru** be about one hour from Tokyo
  by train 26A+
hanásì talk 13A
  X no hanásì de wa according to what X
  says 24B
  hanasi-tyuu [in] the midst of talk; 'the line is
  busy' 13A
hanásihazimèru /-ru; hanásihazìmeta/ begin
  talking 30B
hanâsu /-u; hanâsita/ talk; speak 10B
  hanásihazimèru begin talking 30B
hanâsu /-u; hanâsita/ let go, release, detach,
  separate 26A+
  mê/tê o hanâsu take one's eyes/hands off
  26A+
hanâya flower shop; florist 7A+
hañbùñ half portion; half part 14B
hañdobàggu handbag 5A+
Haneda (name of airport) 20A+
hañtai opposite 20B
  hañtai ni conversely 20B+
hañtai-suru oppose 20B+
  X ni hañtai-suru oppose X 20B+
harâ belly, abdomen 22B
  harâ ĝa tâtu become angry 22B
  harâ ĝa oókìi be big-hearted 22B+
  harâ o kimeru make up one's mind 22B+
  hitó no harà o yômu read a person's
  mind 22B+
haraĝee the art of reading the thoughts of
  others without resorting to language 22B+
harákìri ritual suicide 22B+
harâu /-u; harâtta/ pay 22B

harêru /-ru; hâreta/ become clear (of
  weather) 22A
  hârete (i)ru be clear 22A
hâru spring (season) 19A+
hâsi chopsticks 15A
hataraku /-u; hataraita/ work 25A+
  yôku hataraku work hard 25A+
  X de hataraku work at X (place) 25A+
  atámà no hataraku hito a bright, clever
  person 25A+
hâtati twenty years of age 10A+
hatî eight 2B
hatto with a start; in surprise /onomatopoeia/
  19B
  hatto ki ĝá tùku become aware with a
  start 19B
-hatu departure 19B
  Tookyoo-hatu departing Tokyo 19B+
  ití-zi hatu departing at one o'clock 19B
hatu-ka twenty days; twentieth of the
  month 8A
hayâi /-katta/ is early; is fast 9A+
hayámè ni early; in good time 10A
hâyasa speed 24B+
hazimaru /-u; hazimatta/ [something] begins
  25A+
hazime the beginning 25A+
Hazímemàsite. How do you do? 11B
hazimeru /-ru; hazimeta/ begin [some-
  thing] 11B+
-hazimeru begin —— 30B
  hanásihazimèru begin talking 30B
hazîmete the first time 11B
hazu general expectation 20B
  sitte (i)ru hazu dà it is expected that [s/he]
  knows; [s/he] should know 20B
  âtta hazu da it is expected that there was;
  there should have been 20B
hazúkasìi /-katta/ is shy; is embarrassed 19B
hazusu /-u; hazusita/ take off; let go;
  unfasten 12B
  sêki o hazusu leave one's seat 12B
hêe /exclamation of surprise/ 3B
heeki /na/ calm, cool, indifferent, unconcerned
  29A
heekiñ average, the mean 30A
Heesee the Heisei era (1989–)
heñ area; vicinity 6A
hêñ /na/ strange 13A
hetâ /na/ unskillful; poor at 9B+
heyâ room 17B

-heya /classifier for counting rooms/ 21A

hî/hi day; sun 10A+, 22A

hiatari exposure to the sun 24B

hidari left 6B

  hidári no hòo the left side; the left direction 6B

hidáridònari next door on the left 6B

hidôi /-katta/ is severe 22A

  hîdôku hûru rain (or snow) hard 22A

higásì east 19B

higasiĝuti east entrance 19B

hikidasi drawer 17B+

hikkosi-suru move (to a new residence) 26B

hikkòsu /-u; hikkòsita/ move (to a new residence) 26B

hikôoki airplane 7B+

hiku /-u; hiita/ pull 16B

  kaze o hiku catch a cold 16B

  hûne o hiku tow a boat 26A+

  kodomo o tê de hiku lead a child by the hand 26A+

  deñwa o hiku install a telephone 26A+

  kawa no mizu o hiku draw off river water 26A+

  piano o hiku play the piano 26A+

  kyaku o hiku attract customers 26A+

  zîsyo o hiku look up in a dictionary 26A+

  sâñzyuu kara zyûugo o hiku subtract fifteen from thirty 26A+

  gohyákù-eñ hiku take off five hundred yen 26A+

hima /na/ free time 13A

hiràĝànà the hiragana syllabary 28A+

hirôi /-katta/ is spacious, wide, big (of area) 24B+

hirôoeñ (wedding) reception (Japanese-style) 21B+

hîrosa area, size (of an area) 24B

hirou /-u; hirotta/ pick up 26A+

  miti de 'okane o hirou find money on the street 26A+

  hirótta monò wa, zibúñ no monò "finders, keepers" 26A+

hirû noon; daytime 14A+

hirúgòhañ lunch 14A

hisasiburi after a long interval 11B

hisyô/hîsyo secretary 13B

hitô/hito person 10A

  oñna no hitò woman 10A

  otóko no hitò man 10A

hitô-ri one person; alone; single (person) 11A

hitô-ri de iku go alone (*lit.* being one person) 11A

hitô-tu one unit 5A+

hituyoo /na/ necessary; necessity 22A

  hitúyoo ĝa nài there's no necessity 22A

hizyoo /na/ emergency; extraordinary, extreme 17B

  hizyoo ni extremely 17B

hizyóoburèeki emergency brake 17B+

hizyooĝuti emergency exit 17B+

-hodo about as much as 5B

  itû-tu-hodo about five (units) 5B

hodo extent 15A

  sore hodo to that extent 15A

  sore hodo yôku nâi isn't that good 15A

  koré o yòmu hodo omósìròku nâi isn't as interesting as reading this 20A+

  sûmeba sûmu hodo the more [I] reside 27B

  ôókìkereba oókìi hodo îi the bigger, the better 27B+

  sîzuka nara sîzuka na hodo îi the quieter, the better 27B+

hoka other, another, other than 5A, 15B

  Hoká ni nàni ka? Anything else? 5A

Hokkàidoo Hokkaido (northernmost main island of Japan) 11A

Hokudai Hokkaido University 11B+

homêru /-ru; hômeta/ praise 29B+

hôñ book 2B+

-hoñ /classifier for counting long, cylindrical objects/ 4B

hoñ: hoñ no kimoti only feeling; no more than feeling 18A

hôñdana bookshelf 16A

Hôñsyuu Honshu (a main island of Japan) 11A+

hoñtoo true; truth 2B

hôñya bookstore; book dealer 7A

hoñyaku translation 25A

  hoñyaku-suru translate 25A+

  eeĝo kara 'nihoñĝo ni hoñyaku-suru translate from English into Japanese 25A+

hôo direction; way; side; alternative 6A

  hidári no hòo left side; toward the left 6A

  miĝí no hòo right side; toward the right 6A

  hâsi no hoo the alternative of chopsticks 15A

  hâsi no hoo ĝa tabéyasùi chopsticks are easier to eat with 15A

  sonó hòo ĝa îi that alternative is better 15A

itta hòo ḡa îi [you]'d better go 20A
kurúma de iku hòo ḡa hayâi going by car is faster 20A+
hooḡaku law, jurisprudence 25B+
hoómudòrama soap opera 18B+
hôra look! hey! 22A
hooritu a law, the law 25B+
hosíḡaru (show that one) wants 28B+
hosîi /-katta/ want; is wanted 25A
  sité hosìi want to have it done 25A
  sinâi de hosîi want not to have it done 25A+
  Dâre ḡa hosîi? Who wants it? 25A+
  Nâni ḡa hosîi? What do you want? 25A+
hôteru hotel 6B
  Oókura-hòteru Hotel Okura 6B
hotôñdo almost; nearly; all but 3B
hudoosañya real estate broker 24B
huêru /-ru; hûeta/ [something] increases 27B
huku /-u; huita/ wipe 17B+
hûku /-u; hûita/ blow 22A
hukû clothing 23A
Hukûoka Fukuoka 8A+
hukuzatu /na/ complicated 29A
-huñ /classifier for counting and naming minutes/ 8A
hûne boat, ship 8B+
-huñkañ /classifier for counting minutes/ 8A+
h(u)ôoku fork 15A
h(u)ôomaru /na/ formal 23B
Hurañsu France 5B+
hurañsuḡo French language 2A+
huráñsùziñ French person 10B+
hurô bath 21B
  hurô ni hâiru take a bath 21B
huróbà bathroom 17B+
hurosiki square wrapping cloth 4A
hûru /-u; hûtta/ fall (of rain, snow, etc.) 22A
hurûi /-katta/ is old (i.e., not new) 1B+
husúmà sliding door (opaque) 16A+
hutá-tù two units 5A
hutoñ futon (Japanese-style quilt for sleeping) 21B
  sikíbùtoñ bottom quilt 21B+
  kakébùtoñ top quilt 21B+
hutuu ordinary, regular, usual 19A
  /+ predicate/ ordinarily, regularly, usually 24A
  hutuu ni suru do in the usual way 19A+
  hutuu wa suru usually (at least) do [it] 19A

hutúu(rèssya) regular train (a local) 19A+
hùu /na ~ no/ manner, way, style 29A
  koó iu hùu ni wa 'iwanai does not say in thi[s] way, at least 29A
huyâsu /-u; huyâsita/ increase [something] 27B+
huyû winter 19A+
hyakû one hundred 2B
-hyaku /counter for hundreds/ 2B
hyakueñdama ¥100 coin 19A+

i stomach 17A+
iê house, home; household 7B+
iêie /negation/ 1B
îḡaku medicine (as a subject) 25B
Iḡirisu England 5B+
iḡírisùziñ English person 10B+
îi /yôkatta/ is good, fine, all right; neve[r] mind 1B
  yôku dekîru can do well 1B
  yôku suru do often 1B
  Dôo sitara îi? What should I do? 26A+
  Hâyâku owaru to/owárèba îi desu ḡa nêe. [I] hope it ends early. 26A+
  Hâyâku owáttàra yôkatta no ni .. I wish [i]t had ended early. 26A+
i(i)e /negation/ GUP, 1A
iíkaèru /-ru; iíkàeta/ rephrase, say again in [a] different way 20B+
iikata: kimatta iikata a set way of saying 29A
iíowàru /-u; iíowàtta/ finish saying 30B
iiwake excuse, explanation 26B+
  iiwake o iu provide an excuse 26B+
  umâi/mazûi iiwake a good/poor excuse 26B+
  iíwake ḡa zyoozù/hetà da is good/poor a[t] making excuses 26B+
  Hoóritu o siranai kotò wa, iíwake nì wa na[ra]rânai. Ignorance of the law is no ex[cuse.] cuse. 26B+
ikâḡa how? /polite/ 4A
ikâsu /-u; ikâsita/ bring to life; make the mos[t] of; bring into use 25A
  eeḡo to nihoñḡo o ikâsita siḡoto work tha[t] has brought English and Japanese into use 25A
  hima o ikâsite tukau use leisure wisely 25A+
ikê pond 18A+
ikenai /-katta/ it won't do; it's too bad 14B
  sitê wa 'ikenai [one] must not do 22B
ikîru /-ru; îkita/ live, be alive 27B+

iku /-u; itta/ go 1A
  kikâete iku go having changed; change and go; change before going 23B
îkura how much? 2B
îku-tu how many units? 5B; how old (of people)? 10A
îma now 7A
imâ (Western-style) living room 17B+
îmi meaning 18B
imôoto younger sister 11A
inaka the country 30B+
Îndo India 5B+
iñdòziñ an Indian (from India) 10B+
iñtabyuu-bàñgumi interview program, talk show 18B
iñtyoo hospital director 13B+
inû dog 17B+
ippai full 15A
ippaku-suru stay one night 21A+
irássyàru ↑ /-aru; irássyàtta ~ irâsita/ be located (of animate existence) 7A; come 4B; go 8B /honorific-polite/
  de (i)rassyàru ↑ /honorific-polite equivalent of dà/ 10A
  Irássyài(màse). ↑ Welcome! 4B
ireru /-ru; ireta/ put into; insert 16A
  otya o ireru make tea 17B
  deñwa o ireru put in a call 18B
iriĝuti entrance 6A+
irô color 5B
iroiro /no ~ na/ various 20B
  iroiro beñkyoo-suru study about all kinds of things 20B
iroñ /na/ various 20B+
iru /-ru; ita/ be located (of animate existence) 7A
  Tookyoo ni iru be in Tokyo 7A
  kekkoñ-site (i)ru be married 10B
  hanâsite (i)ru be talking 10B
iru /-u; itta/ need; be required 5A
iru /-u; itta/ enter 23A
  ki ni iru appeal 23B
isóĝasìi /-katta/ is busy 9A
  Oísoĝasii tokorò (o) arîĝatoo gozaimasita. Thank you for giving me your time when you are busy. 25B+
isóĝu /-u; isôida/ be in a hurry, make haste 20B
  isôide iku go hurriedly 20B
ìs-see first generation (used in reference to Japanese who have moved abroad) 10B+

issyo togetherness 11A
  issyo ni suru do together 11A
  tomodati to issyo together with a friend 11A
iśsyookèñmee with all one's might; whole-heartedly 30B
isu chair 17B+
isya medical doctor 16B
  isyá no tokorò the doctor's (place) 16B
itadaku /-u; itadaita/ ↓ drink; eat; accept; receive /humble-polite/ 1A, 17B
  tetúdàtte itadaku ↓ receive help, be helped 17B
  Ozîkañ o itádakemasèñ ↓ ka◞ Can('t) I have [some of] your time? /polite/ 25B
  Kitê itádakemàsu ↓ ka◞ Will I be able to have you come? /polite/ 25B
  Yomâsete itádakemasèñ ka◞ Can('t) I please have [you] let me read this? /polite/ 28A+
  Osáki ni kaeràsete itadakimasu. I'm going to take the liberty of going home before you. /polite/ 28A+
itâi /-katta/ is painful; hurts 17A
  itâkute 'naku cry in pain 29B+
Itaria Italy 5B+
itariaĝo Italian language 2A+
itáriàziñ an Italian 10B+
itasu /-u; itasita/ ↓ do /humble-polite/ 12B
itî one 2B
itibañ most, to the greatest degree 15B
  itíbañ sukì da is most pleasing; likes best 15B
iti-d(e)iikee 1-DK (i.e., one room + dining area/kitchen) 24B
itieñdama ¥1 coin 19A+
itímañèñsatu ¥10,000 bill 19A+
iti-niti-zyuu all day long 24B
itôko cousin 11B+
Ítte (i)rassyài(màse). ↑ Goodbye (said to person leaving home). /honorific-polite/ 7A
Ítte kimàsu. Goodbye (said by person leaving home). 7A
Ítte mairimàsu. ↓ Goodbye (said by person leaving home). /humble-polite/ 7A+
îtu when? 3B
  îtu mo always 11A
itû-tu five units 5A
iu /-u; itta/ be called, be named 12A; say 18B
  X to iu be called or named X 12A

X to//(t)te iu   be named X   12A; say, "X"
18B
X to//(t)te iu Y   a Y named or called X   18B
Soó itte kudasài.   Please say that.   12A
surú yòo ni iu   tell [someone] to do   24A
—— **to iû no**   the thing described as ——
25A
iya   /negation/   1A
iyâ /na/   unpleasant, disagreeable   11A
izure   someday, sometime   12A

ka   /question particle/   1A
dôko ka   someplace, somewhere   24A
dôko ka îi tokoro   some good place   24A
kosyoo kâ mo sirenai   maybe it's out of
order   13A
âu ka dôo ka wakárànai   can't tell whether it
matches or not   18A
dâre ga dêru ka 'kiku   ask (or hear) who will
attend   18B
—— **ka sira**   I wonder if —— /gentle/   25B
—— **ka nâa**   I wonder if —— /blunt/   25B+
ka /ptc/   or   27A
sigoto ka 'katee   work or the home   27A
kâ   section within a company   13B+
-ka/-niti   /classifier for naming and counting
days/   8A
kâ(a)   /abbreviation for **kayôo(bi)**   8A
kâa·môku   Tues–Thurs   8A
kabañ   bag, suitcase   5A
kabuki   kabuki (traditional Japanese theater)
28B
kabûru /-u; kabûtta/   put (or wear) on the
head   23A
kâdo   street corner   7B
kaérì   a return   8A
kaeru /-ru; kaeta/   change [something]   20B+
noríkaèru   transfer to another vehicle
20B+
atárasìi no ni kaeru   change to new
ones   23B
kâeru /-u; kâetta/   return (home)   7A
kâette kuru   come back; come home   23A
Okáeri-nasài(màse).   Welcome back!   7A
kâesu /-u; kâesita/   give back, return [some-
thing]   28A
X o Y ni kâesu   return X to Y   28A+
kâette   on the contrary; instead   26B
kâgaku   science   25B+
kâgaku   chemistry   25B+
-kagetu   /classifier for counting months/   8B

kagî   key   16A
kagî o kakêru   lock [something]   16A
kagî ga kakâru   be(come) locked   16A
kâgu   furniture   17B+
kagûya   furniture store   17B+
kâi   floor   26B
-kai   /classifier for naming and counting floors/
7A
-kai   /classifier for counting number of times/
19A
kâigi   conference, meeting   3B
kaígìsitu   conference room   10B
kaimono   shopping   14A+
kaisatu   ticket checking   19B+
kaísatùguti   ticket-checking gate, wicket   19B
kaisya   a company, a firm   11A
kaísyàiñ   company employee   16B+
kaiwa   conversation   30A
eékàiwa   English conversation   30A
kaíwàbuñ   conversation text *or* portion   30A
-kakañ/-kaniti   /classifier for counting days/
8A+
kâkari (no hito)   person in charge   21A
kakâru /-u; kakâtta/   be required   8B
zikáñ ga kakâru   it takes time   8B+
kakâru /-u; kakâtta/   become suspended   16A
kagî ga kakâru   be(come) locked   16A
omé ni kakâru ↓   meet, see [a person] /hum-
ble-polite/   13B+
kakébùtoñ   top quilt   21B+
kakénaòsu /-u; kakénaòsita/   suspend
again   13A
deñwa o kakenaòsu   telephone again   13A
-kakeru /-ru; -kaketa/   set about ——ing   23A
dekakeru   go out; set out   23A
ikikakeru   be about to go   23A+
kakêru /-ru; kâketa/   suspend (something)   9B;
sit down   19B+
deñwa o kakèru   make a telephone call   9B
kagî o kakèru   lock [something]   16A
kakíkaèru /-ru; kakíkàeta/   rewrite   20B+
kâku /-u; kâita/   write; draw   7A
kamâu /-u; kamâtta/   mind; care; concern oneself about   10A
Okámai nàku.   Don't bother; Don't go to any
trouble.   18A
kamáwànai /-katta/   it doesn't matter   10A
kâmera   camera   16A
kamî   paper   4B
kamínarì   thunder   22A+
kana   Japanese written syllabary   28A+

Kânada Canada 5B+

kânai my wife 10B+

kanarazu surely, positively, without fail 28A

kânari fairly, rather, quite 19B

kañgaèru /-ru; kañgàeta/ think over, consider, ponder 23B

   kañgàete simau think twice about a matter 23B+

kañgòhu nurse 16B+

kâñgo-suru nurse, care for 16B+

kañkee connection 18B

   keézai-kàñkee a connection with economics 18B

Kâñkoku South Korea 5B+

kañkokùziñ a South Korean 10B+

kañkyoo environment 30B

   sizeñ no kañkyoo natural environment 30B

kanoosee possibility 29A

kânozyo she 10A

kañriniñ apartment manager, superintendent 26B

kañtañ /na/ simple 29A

kañzi Chinese character 28A+

kañzyoo the check 15A+

kao face 14B+; expression 24B

   kao o suru assume an expression 24B

   iyâ na kao o site (i)ru have a disagreeable expression 24B+

kaoiro (facial) color 14B

kâppu (coffee) cup 15B+

kara /ptc/ from 8B; because 11A; after 16B

   gôgo kara from the afternoon 8B

   koko kara from here 8B

   iyâ da kara because it's displeasing 11A

   tûite kara after arriving 16B

karada body 17A+

karâi /-katta/ is spicy; is salty 15B+

karaoke orchestration without singers 29B+

kâre he 10A+

kariru /-ru; karita/ borrow; rent (from someone) 10B

   tomodati ni (or kara) kariru borrow or rent from a friend 10B

karui /-katta/ is light (of weight) 20A+

kâsa umbrella 4A

Kasíkomarimàsita. Certainly. I'll do as you asked. 4B

kasu /-u; kasita/ lend; rent (to someone) 10B+

-kata way of ——ing 22B+

   sikata way of doing 22B+

   hanasikata way of talking 22B+

kâta shoulder 17A+

katâ person /polite/ 10A+

katai /-katta/ is hard; is stiff; is tough 15B+

katâkàna the katakana syllabary 28A+

katázukèru /-ru; katázùketa/ make tidy; put in order 17A+

katázùku /-u; katázùita/ become tidy; be(come) put in order 17A

katee household, the home 27A

katyoo section manager 13B+

kau /-u; katta/ buy 1B

kawâ river 18A+

kawáìi /-katta/ is cute 10A

kawâku /-u; kawâita/ become dry 14A+

   nôdo ğa kawâku become thirsty 14A+

kawari a change 11B; substitute, replacement 24A

   kawari ni as a substitute, instead 24A

   kawári ni sùmu reside as a substitute, house-sit 24A

kawaru /-u; kawatta/ undergo change 11B+; change places 13B

   X ni kawaru change into X 13B+

   X to kawaru (ex)change with X 13B+

   deñwa o kawaru make a replacement on the telephone 13B+

kayôo(bi) Tuesday 8A

kayou /-u; kayotta/ commute 20A+

kaze a cold 16B

   kaze o hiku catch a cold 16B

kaze wind 22A

kâzi a fire 9B+

kâzoku family; my family 11A

kedo /ptc/ 4B

keekeñ experience 21A

   bôku no keékeñ dè wa in my experience (at least) 21A

keekeñ-suru experience, go through 21A+

kêeki cake 3A

Keeoo Keio University 12B+

keésàñki calculator 17B

keesañ-suru calculate 17B+

kêezai economics; economy 18B+

   keezai-teki /na/ economic 25A+

kekka result 22B

keḱkòñsiki wedding ceremony 23A

keḱkoñ-sèekatu married life 27B+

kekkoñ-suru get married 10B

kekkon-site (i)ru be married 10B
kêkkoo /na/ fine, great 13B
-keñ /classifier for counting buildings and shops/ 7B
keñka-suru argue, have a quarrel; fight 30B
keñkoo /na/ health; healthy 14B
  keñkoo ni ìi is good for one's health 14B
keñkyuu research 13B+
keñkyùusitu laboratory 13B+
keñkyuu-suru do research 13B+
keñkyuuzyo research institute 13B
keñtiku architecture 16B+
keñtikuka architect 16B+
kêsa this morning 9A+
kêsiki scenery 18A+
kesu /-u; kesita/ turn off; extinguish; erase 16A
ki mind, spirit; feelings; attention 19B+
  ki ğá tùku notice; become aware 19B
  ki ó tukèru pay attention; be careful 19B+
  ki ni iru appeal 23A
  ki ğa suru have a feeling 26A
  ki ó wàrùku suru be(come) displeased, offended; have one's feelings hurt 28B
  ki ni suru mind; worry about, concern oneself about 24A
  ki ní nàru weigh on one's mind; become a cause for concern 24A+
kî tree 17B+
kibísìi /-katta/ is strict, stern, rigorous 29A
kiboo-suru hope 29B+
kieru /-ru; kieta/ go out; be(come) turned off; be(come) extinguished 16A
kiiroi /-katta/ is yellow 4A+
kikáèru ~ kiğáèru /-ru; kikâeta ~ kiğâeta/ change clothing (worn on the body) 23B
kikâi machine 19A
kikóenikùi /-katta/ is difficult to hear 13A
kikoeru /-ru; kikoeta/ can hear; be audible 13A
kikóeyasùi /-katta/ is easy to hear 13A+
kiku /-u; kiita/ ask 7B; hear; listen 10B
kimaru /-u; kimatta/ become decided 17B+
  kimatta mono things that have been decided 21A
  kimatta iikata a set way of saying 29A
kimeru /-ru; kimeta/ decide [something] 17B
kimi you /familiar/ 9A+
kimono kimono 23B
kimoti feeling, mood 18A

hoñ no kimoti only feeling; no more than feeling 18A
kimóti ğa ìi is pleasant; feels well 21B
kimóti ğa warùi is unpleasant; doesn't feel well 21B+
kîñ /abbreviation for **kiñyòo(bi)**/ 8A
  gês·sûi·kîñ Mon–Wed–Fri 8A
kinódòkù pitiable; unfortunate 29B
  Okínodoku desu nêe. *or* **Okinodokusama.** That's too bad. 29B+
kinódokuğàru /-u; kinódokuğàtta/ feel sorry (for someone) 29B+
kinôo yesterday 1A
kiñyòo(bi) Friday 8A+
kîñzyo neighborhood 17A
kippu ticket 19A
kippu-ùriba ticket counter 19A+
kirai /na/ displeasing; dislike 15B
kirâsu /-u; kirâsita/ exhaust the supply 12A
  meési o kiràsite (i)ru be out of business cards 12A
kîree /na/ pretty; clean 2A
kiru /-ru; kita/ put (or wear) on the body 23A
  kite (i)ru be wearing 23A
  kite iku wear (to a place) 23A
kîru /-u; kîtta/ cut, cut off; hang up (the telephone) 13A
kisêtu season 26B
  kisêtu no mono seasonal things 26B+
kisetu-teki /na/ seasonal 26B+
kissateñ/kissàteñ coffee shop; tearoom 7A
kisyâ (steam) train 7B+
kitâ north 19B+
kitánài /-katta/ is dirty, squalid, obscene, sordid, stingy 28A
kitto surely, certainly, undoubtedly 24B
kîzi news article 30B
kizûkai concern 18A
kke /question particle of recall/ 25B
  Nâñ te (i)tta kke. What *was* his/her name (I can't recall)! 25B
-ko /classifier for counting pieces/ 20A
ko child 10A
  okosañ child /polite/ 10A+
  oñnà no ko little girl; young girl 10A+
  otókò no ko little boy; young boy 10A+
kodomo child 10A+
kôe voice 13A
  ôoki na kôe loud voice 13A
  tîisa na kôe low voice 13A+

kôi /-katta/   is thick (of liquids); is strong (of coffee, tea, etc.); is dark (of colors)   15B +

koko   this place, here   6B

kokó no tosyòkañ   the library here   6B

kokôno-tu   nine units   5A +

kokuğo   the mother-tongue of the Japanese   2A +

kokutetu   national railway (until 1987)   19A

komákài /-katta/   occurs in small units; is small, is detailed   17B

komákài âme   drizzle   17B +

komâru /-u; komâtta/   become upset; become a problem   1B

komê   uncooked rice   14A +

komêya   rice shop   14A +

kômu /-u; kôñda/   become crowded, congested, filled up   20A

konaida   the other day, recently   18A +

konáidà kara   starting recently   29B

kôñbañ   this evening, tonight   9A +

Koñbañ wa.   Good evening.   GUP

kôñdo   this time; this next time   25A

kône (konêkusyoñ)   connections   25A +

koñğakki   this (school) term   28B +

koñğetu   this month   9A +

koñna   this kind (of)   4B

koñna ni   to this extent, like this   9B +

Koñniti wa.   Good afternoon.   GUP

kono /+ nom/   this ——   3A

konó màe   (in) front of this   6A +

kono-ğoro   these days, nowadays   8A +

kôñpa   (student) party (Japanese-style)   21B +

koñpyùutaa   computer   3A

koñpyuutaa-puroguramu   computer program   29B

koñsàrutañto   consultant   16B +

koñsyuu   this week   9A +

koñtakuto(-rèñzu)   contact lens(es)   23B

koñtakuto(-rèñzu) o suru   put in contact lenses   23B

kôñya   this evening, tonight   10A +

koobañ   police box   6A +

Kôobe   Kobe   8A +

kooeñ   park   6B +

kooeñ   speech, lecture   18B +

koóèñkai   lecture meeting   28A +

koogaku   engineering   25B +

kôoği   lecture   18B +

koohai   junior colleague   26A

oóhìi   coffee   3A +

oóhiikàppu   (coffee) cup   15B +

kookoku   advertisement   30B +

kookoo   high school   7A +

koómùiñ   government employee   16B +

koori   ice   14A +

koósàteñ   intersection   7B

kôosu   meal with fixed menu   14A

kôoto   coat   30A

koósyuudèñwa   public telephone   6A

kootuu   transportation   24B

koótuu no bèñ ğa îi   transportation facilities are good   24B

kootya   black tea   5B +

koozitu   excuse, explanation, pretext   26B +

koózitu o tukùru   concoct an excuse   26B +

hoñ no koozitu   a mere pretext   26B +

kôpii-suru   copy   28A

kôppu   drinking glass   15B +

kore   this thing   2B

kore kara   from this point, after this   8A

kôro   approximate time   29A

watási ğa kodomo no kòro   around the time when I was a child   29A

kôru /-u; kôtta/   become stiff   17B

kôsa   strength (of tea, coffee, etc.); depth (of a color)   24B +

kosî   lower back   17A +

(kosí)kakèru /-ru; (kosí)kàketa/   sit down   19B +

kòso /ptc/   11B

Kotíra kòso.   I'm the one.   11B

kosyôo   pepper   14A +

kosyoo   out of order   13A

kosyoo-suru   break down   13A +

kotâe   answer   26A

kotáèru /-ru; kotâeta/   answer   26A +

teğámi ni kotáèru   answer a letter   26A +

hitô ni kotáèru   answer a person   26A +

iíè to kotáèru   answer "no"   26A +

kotira   this side; this way; hereabouts; here; this alternative (of two)   6A

kotíra no hòo   this direction; this alternative   6A

kotô   fact; act   21A

miñsyuku no kotò   facts concerning tourist homes   21A

nokôru koto ni suru   decide on remaining   24A

ikú kotò ni nâru   be(come) decided that [someone] will go   24A

ikú kotò ğa âru   there are occasions when [I] go   25A

ikú kotò wa nâi there are no occasions when I go 25A

ikú kotò ğa dekîru the act of going is possible; can go 25A+

ikú kotò wa 'iku . . [I] *do* go, but . . .

kotóbà (spoken) language; utterance; phrase; word 22B

kotosi this year 8B

kotówàru /-u; kotówàtta/ refuse 29B

  nâñ to ka itte kotówàru refuse, saying something or other; fabricate an excuse 29B+

kotti /casual alternate of **kotira**/ 7B

kowâi /-katta/ is fearsome, frightening, terrible 26B+

kowáréru /-ru; kowâreta/ become broken, damaged, destroyed; fall apart 24B

  kowáreyasùi is breakable, fragile 24B+

  kowaremono fragile article 24B+

kowâsu /-u; kowâsita/ break [something]; demolish, destroy 24B+

  karada o kowasu ruin one's health 24B+

  onaka o kowasu develop stomach trouble 24B+

kû nine 2B

kubi neck 17A+

kudâmono fruit 15A+

kudásài /imperative of **kudásàru**/ give me 4A

  Koré o kudasài. Please give me this one. 4A

  Kitê kudasai. Please come. 4A

  oáğari-kudasài please go/come up 18A

kudásàru↑ /-aru; kudásàtta ~ kudásùtta/ give me /honorific-polite/ 4A

  tetúdàtte kudasaru give help (to me/us/you) 17A

  Kâite kudásaimasèñ ka⌐ Would (*lit.* won't) you be kind enough to write for me? 7A

  (watasi ni) haráwàsete kudasai please let me pay 28A

kumôru /-u; kumôtta/ become cloudy 22A

  kumôtte (i)ru be cloudy 22A

-kuñ /suffix attached to male names; familiar/ 9A

kuni a country, nation; one's native land or area 15A+

kurabemono a comparable thing; a match 30A

  kurábemono ni narànai is no match 30A

kuraberu /-ru; kurabeta/ compare 30A+

kurai /-katta/ is dark; is gloomy (of people) 30B

kûrasu class 30A

kureru /-ru; kureta/ give (to me/us/you) 17A

  kure give (to me/us)! /command/ 29B

  tetúdàtte kureru give help (to me/us/you) 17A

  mîte kureru? will you look at (for me/us/you)? will he/she/they look at (for me/us/you)? 17A

kurôi /-katta/ is black 4A

kûroo toil, hardship 17B+

kûru /irreg; kîtâ/ come 1A

  hârete kuru come to be clear; begin to clear 22A

  itte kùru come, having gone (i.e., go and then come) 7A

  Itte kimàsu. 'So long!' (said leaving one's own quarters) 7A

  kâette kuru come back; come home 23A

kuruma car 5B

kusuri medicine 14B

  kusúri o nòmu take medicine 14B+

kusuriya drugstore 14B+

kutábirèru /-ru; kutábìreta/ become fatigued 24B

kuti mouth 17A+

  kutí ni àu suit one's tasate 18A

kut(t)akuta worn out, exhausted, dog-tired 24B

kutû shoes 23A

kutûsita socks; stockings 23B

kûuki air 30B

kuukoo airport 7B

kuwásìi /-katta/ is detailed 24A

  kuwásìi koto details, particulars 24A

  X ni kuwásìi is well versed in X; has detaile knowledge of X 24A+

kyaku guest; visitor; customer 10B

kyôneñ last year 10A+

kyôo today 1A

Kyoodai Kyoto University 11B+

kyôodai brothers and sisters, siblings 11A+

kyooiku education 27A+

  kyoóikùğaku education (as a subject) 27A+

  kyoóiku no àru/nài hito an educated/uned ucated person 27A+

  kyoóiku-màma "education mother" 27A +

kyookai church 6B+

kyoókàsyo textbook 10B

kyôosi instructor 13B+

kyoositu classroom 10B

kyoósyuku dà   is grateful, appreciative; is obliged; is apologetic   25B

Kyôoto   Kyoto   2A+

kyoóyooğàkùbu   liberal arts department or college   25B+

kyoozyu   professor   13B+

kyôri   distance   26A

kyôri ğa dekîru   distance develops   26A

kyûu   nine   3A

kyuu /na/   sudden, without warning; urgent   26A

Kyuudai   Kyushu University   11B+

kyuukoo   express   19A+

kyuúkòokeñ   express ticket   19A+

Kyûusyuu   Kyushu (a main island of Japan)   11A+

ma ní àu   be on time   20B

mâa   /expression of qualified agreement/   1B

mâa   /expression of persuasion/   15B+

mâa   oh, my! /exclamation of surprise; F/   18A

mâa·mâa   so-so   1A

mâda /+ negative predicate/ not yet   14A /+ affirmative predicate/   still   14B

mâda da   not yet (lit. it is yet [to happen])   14A

màde   /ptc/ as far as; up to and including   7A; until   8B

giñkoo màde   as far as the bank   7A

nâñ-zi made   until what time?   8B

sâñ-zi made ni   by 3 o'clock   9A

koko made ûmâku syabêru   speak well as far as this level   24A

kâeru made   until [someone] returns   28A

kâeru made ni   by the time [someone] returns   28A

mâdo   window   16A

madôğuti   ticket window   20B

mîdori no madôğuti   ticket window for green-car tickets   20B

mâe   front   6A; time before; past time   8A+

toó-ka màe   ten days ago   10B

go-hûñ-mae   five minutes before the hour   8A

dêru mâe   before going out   19A

mağaru /-u; mağatta/   make a turn   7B; [something] bends   26A+

miti ğa mağatte (i)ru   the road is curved   26A+

nêkutai ğa mağatte (i)ru   [his] necktie is twisted   26A+

kosí no mağatta tosiyòrì   an old person with a bent back   26A+

mağátta kotò o suru   do something not aboveboard   26A+

mağeru /-ru; mağeta/   bend [something]   26A+

kotóbà no îmi o mağeru   twist the meaning of words   26A+

-mai   /classifier for thin, flat units/   4B

mâiasa   every morning   8B+

mâibañ   every evening; every night   8B+

maido   every time   4B

Maido arîgatoo gozaimasu.   Thank you again and again.   4B

maiğetu   every month   8B+

maineñ   every year   8B+

mâiniti   every day   8B

mâiru ↓ **/-u; mâitta/**   come   7A; go   8B /humble-polite/

maisyuu   every week   8B+

maitosi   every year   8B+

maituki   every month   8B+

maiyo   every evening; every night   10A+

makáseru /-ru; makâseta/   trust [someone] with [a matter]; leave [a matter] to [someone]   28B

mamà   condition just as it is   29A

konó mamà da to   when it is like this, without being changed   29A

sonó mamà de kêkkoo da   is fine as it is, like that   29A+

tumétai mamà de îi   is fine as it is, cold   29A+

-mañ   /counter for ten thousands/   3B

mâñsyoñ   apartment; apartment house   24A

mañzài   cross-talk comedy   28B+

maru   circle; zero   12A

maśsùğu   straight   7B

mata   again   4B

matâ wa   or on the other hand   12A

matî   town, small city   20A+

matíğaèru /-ru; matíğaeta/   make a mistake   20B

mití o matíğaèru   mistake the road   20B+

X o Y ni/to matíğaèru   mistake X for Y   20B+

matíğàu /-u; matíğàtta/   be(come) wrong, get to be in error   20B+

mattaku   precisely, totally, entirely   22B

mâtu /-u; mâtta/   wait   8A

mâtu   pine   14B+

Matuzusi /name of sushi shop/ 14B+

mawaru /-u; **mawatta**/ go around; be(come) passed around; be(come) transferred 21A+

  Nihôñ omawaru go around Japan 21A+

mawasu /-u; **mawasita**/ send around; pass around; transfer 21A

mazêru /-ru; **mâzeta**/ mix [something] 26A+

  mizú o mazêru dilute 26A+

  gurêe ni gurîiñ o mazêru blend green into the gray 26A+

  nihôñgo o màzeta eeğo English that has mixed in Japanese 26A+

mazime /**na**/ serious; steady; conscientious 29B

mazírì mixture; impurity; adulteration 26A+

mazîru /-u; **mazîtta**/ [something] gets mixed; [something] mixes 26A+

  ûmâku mazîru irô colors that blend well 26A+

  yukî no mazîtta âme rain mixed with snow 26A+

  eéğo to nihôñgo ğa mazìtte (i)ru hanásì talk in which English and Japanese are mixed 26A+

mazûi /-katta/ tastes bad 7A+; is inadvisable; is poor at 30B

mê eye 16B+

medétài /-katta/ is auspicious 27A

  omédetoo gozaimàsu+ congratulations /neutral-polite/ 27A

-mee(sama) /classifier for counting people/ 15A

meesi calling card; business card 12A

  meesi no motiawase cards on hand 12A

(go)mêewaku nuisance, annoyance 28B

  mêewaku ni nâru become a nuisance 28B+

  mêewaku o kakêru cause inconvenience, annoy [someone] 28B+

mêewaku-suru be(come) troubled, annoyed 28B+

Mêezi the Meiji era (1868–1912) 8B+

mêğane eyeglasses 23B

  mêğane o kakêru put on eyeglasses 23B

mêisya eye doctor 16B+

meńdòo /**na**/ bothersome, troublesome, tiresome 29B

  meńdòo ni nâru become a bother 29B+

meńdòo o kakêru cause trouble (for someone) 29B+

meńdòo o mîru care (for someone) 29B+

goméñdoo-nàğara while it's a bother for you 29B+

meñsetu job interview 28A+

  meñsetu o ukêru have an interview; be interviewed 28A+

mesiağaru ↑ /-u; **mesiağatta**/ eat; drink; smoke /honorific-polite/ 15B

mêsseezi message 12B

Mêziro (section of Tokyo) 7B

mezúrasìi /-katta/ is amazing, surprising, unexpected 19B

mîdori green 5B+

  mîdori no madôğuti ticket window for green-car tickets 20B

miêru /-ru; **mîeta**/ be visible; can see 18A; appear, seem 23A

  tiğáu hitò ni miêru appear as if a different person 23A

miğî right 6B

  miğí no hòo right side, right direction 6B

miğídònari next door on the right 6B

mimî ear 17A+

minami south 19B+

minâsañ everyone /polite/ 5B+, 11B

minato harbor 18A+

miníkùi /-katta/ is hard to see with or look at 23B

mi(ń)nà all; everyone; everything 5B

miñsyuku tourist home 21A

miokuru /-u; **miokutta**/ see off 19A

mîru /-ru; **mîta**/ look at; see 5B

  kiíte mìru try asking, ask and see 19A

mîruku milk 5B+

misê store, shop 6A+

misêru /-ru; **mîseta**/ show 4A

-mìtai /**na**/ as if ——; ——like 24A

  kimátta-mìtai da it seems as if it was decided 24A

  anâta-mitai ni nihôñgo ğa zyoozù da is good in Japanese the way you are 24A

miti street; road 6A+

mit́-tù three units 5A

mitukaru /-u; **mitukatta**/ be(come) found; be(come) discovered 23A

mitukeru /-ru; **mituketa**/ find, locate, turn u [something] 23A+

miyağe souvenir 15A

miyağeya souvenir shop 15A+

izíkài /-katta/ is short 9B+

izu cold water 14A+

izúùmi lake 18A+

o /ptc/ also, too 4B

dôo mo in every way; in many ways GUP; somehow or other 13A

dôtira mo both 12A

îtu mo always 11A

kore mo this one too 4B

kore mo sore mo both this one and that one 5B

mâe ni mo in the front too 6A

sitê mo also (or even) having done 21B

sinâkute mo also (or even) not having done 22A

Sitê mo îi? May [I] do [it]? Will it be all right even/also if [I] do [it]? 21B

Sinâkute mo îi? Will it be all right even/also if [I] don't do it? 22A

dotíra dè mo whichever it is 21B

nâni o sitê mo whatever [someone] has done 21B

dôko e ittè mo wherever [someone] has gone 21B

pâat(e)ii de mo a party or something 23A

rokû-neñ mo even six years; as much as six years 27B

hañ-nitì mo even half a day; as much as half a day 27B

nâñ-neñ mo mâe ni any number of years ago 27B

hito-ri mo /+ negative/ not even one person 27B

ano kooeñ wa sukôsi mo wakárànakatta I didn't understand that lecture at all (even a little) 27B+

huta-ri to mo both people 27B

odôru /-u; modôtta/ return; go/come back; back up 13B

odôsu /-u; modôsita/ put back, send back; throw up 30B+

ku/môk- /abbreviation for **mokúyòo(bi)**/ 8A+

ku·dôo Thurs–Sat 8A+

kuteki purpose 22B

kúyòo(bi) Thursday 8A+

ñbùsyoo Ministry of Education 11B

ñdai problem 24B

ñku complaint 26B

môñku o iu complain 26B

nô thing 14A+

surú monò da [one] is to do; the regular procedure is to do 29A

kibîsìku sitúkeràreta mono da used to be brought up strictly 29A

monô person(s) (in my in-group) 28A

utí no monò person(s) in my home or in-group 28A

Watasi Oríeñtaru-bòoeki no monô de gozaimasu. I'm an employee (person) of Oriental Trade. 28A+

monórèeru monorail 20A+

monósuğòi /-katta/ is dreadful, awful 20A

monósùğòku omoi is awfully heavy 20A

moo /+ quantity expression/ more; additional 5A

moó mit-tù three more units 5A

moó sukòsi a little more; a few more 5A+

môo /+ affirmative predicate/ already, yet 14A

/+ negative predicate/ no more 14B

moosiwake excuse, explanation 12A

Moósiwake arimasèñ. I'm very sorry. (*lit.* There is no excuse.) GUP

môosu ↓ /-u; môosita/ say; be called, be named 12A; say 18B /humble-polite/

X to moósimàsu ↓ my name is X 12A

X to/(t)te môosu ↓ be called, be named X 12A; say, "X" 18B

morau /-u; moratta/ receive 17B

naôsite morau have something fixed 17B

kâite moraeru can have it written 25B

Kâite moraenai? Can('t) I have it written? 25B

môsi supposing 26A

môsi ka suru to perhaps; it may be the case that 26A

môsimosi hello (on the telephone); say there! 12A

Mosukuwa Moscow 8A

motiawase things on hand 12A

meési no motiawase ğa nài have no business cards on hand 12A

motiawaseru /-ru; motiawaseta/ have on hand 12A+

motîroñ of course, certainly 15A

motte iku take (to a place) (said of things) 15A+

motte kùru bring (said of things) 15A+

môtto more; a larger amount 5A

môtto yasûi no one that is cheaper 5A

mukae a meeting; a greeting; a welcoming 16B

mukaeru /-ru; mukaeta/ meet; greet; welcome 16B

mukau /-u; mukatta/ face; confront; proceed to 30A +

  mukatte miǧí no hòo da it's on the right as [you] face it 30A +

mukeru /-ru; muketa/ point [something] toward 30A +

-muki facing toward; aimed at; suitable for 24B

  nisi-muki facing west 24B

  gaiziñ-muki aimed at foreigners 24B +

  huyu-muki suitable for winter 24B +

mukôo/mukoo over there 6A; abroad 9B

mukooǧawa opposite side, the other side 6B +

muku /-u; muita/ be(come) turned toward; face 24B +; look out on; suit; be inclined 30A

  aá iù no ni 'muku be inclined toward that sort of thing 30A

munê chest 17A +

murâ village 20A +

mûri /na/ unreasonable, excessive, forced, impossible 21B

  mûri o suru strain; lean over backward 21B +

mûsiro rather; more than that 20B

  mûsiro X no hôo ǧa hayâi rather, X is faster 20B

musuko son 10A +

musúmè daughter 10A +

muí-tù six units 5A

muzukasii /-katta/ is difficult 3B

  muzúkasii hitò a person hard to get on with 11A +

muzukasisa difficulty 24B +

myôobañ tomorrow night 12B +

myoóǧòniti day after tomorrow 12B +

myôoniti tomorrow 12B

myootyoo tomorrow morning 12B +

ñ /casual-style affirmation/ 8A

ñ /contraction of nominal **no**/ 7B

  abúnài ñ da it's that it's dangerous 7B

ñ? yeah? 27A

na /pre-nominal alternate of **dà**/ 5B

-na /negative command/ 29B

  mûri surû-na don't strain! 29B

nâa /sentence-particle of confirmation, agreement, or deliberation/ 13A

nâdo: X nâdo X, etc.; X, and so forth; X, for example 26A +

naǧâi /-katta/ is long 9B

-nàǧara while 27A

  otyá o nominàǧara soodañ-suru consult at the same time, drink tea 27A

  wakâru to iínàǧara, hoñtoo wa wakárànai while saying she understands, actually she doesn't understand 27A +

Nâǧoya Nagoya 8A

nâihu knife 15A +

naiseñ extension 12A

naiyoo contents; subject matter, substance 22B

nâka inside, within 15B

  A to B to C no nâka de (being) among A and B and C 15B

  konó mit-tù no nâka de (being) among the three things 15B

nakanaka quite; rather; more than one might expect 4A

naku /-u; naita/ cry 29B +

  itâkute 'naku cry in pain 29B +

  mîruku ǧa hôsîkute 'naku cry for milk 29B +

nakunaru /-u; nakunatta/ die; disappear (inanimates) 27B

  ryôosiñ ǧa nakúnàtta my parents died 27B +

  tokée ǧa nakunàtta my watch disappeared 27B +

namae name 7A

nami regular 14B +

nâñ what? 2A

  nâñ to ka somehow 25A

  nâñ to ka nâru become something; things will work out somehow 27B

  nañ to nàku somehow, in some (vague) way 26A

  Nâñ to iítàra îi? What should I say? 26A

  nâñ da ka something or other 29B

nâna seven 3A

nanâ-tu seven units 5A

nâni what? 4A

  nâni ka something 5A

  nani mo /+ negative/ nothing 13A +

  nâni o sitê mo whatever [someone] does, be done 21B

naniǧo what language? 2A +

naniiro   what color?   5B

naniziñ   what nationality?   10B+

nâñka: X nâñka   X, etc.; X, and so forth; X, for example   26A

nañni mo   /emphatic equivalent of **nani mo**/ 24B

naôru /-u; naôtta/   become repaired; recover   17B

naôsu /-u; naôsita/   fix, repair; correct   13A

nàra   /provisional form of **dà**/   27A

naraberu /-ru; narabeta/   place in line   19A+

narabu /-u; narañda/   form a line; get in line   19A

narânai   [it] won't come to anything   22B+

  sitê wa narânai   [one] mustn't do   22B+

narâu /-u; narâtta/   learn; study; take lessons   25A

narêru /-ru; nâreta/   become accustomed, become used to   23A

  zîipañ ni narêru   become accustomed to blue jeans   23A

narídàsu ~ naridasu /-u; narídàsita ~ naridasita/   start to become   30B

Nârita   (name of airport)   20A

naru /-u; natta/   sound   22A+

  kamínarì ğa naru   it thunders   22A+

nâru /-u; nâtta/   become; get to be   9A

  onári ni nàru ↑   /honorific-polite equivalent of **nâru**/   10A

  osóku nàru   become late   9A

  rokú-syùukañ ni nâru   get to be six weeks 9B

  ki ní nàru   weigh on one's mind; become a cause for concern   24A+

  ikú kotò ni nâru   be(come) decided that [someone] will go   24A

  syabêru yoo ni nâru   reach the point of speaking   24A

  inaku naru   disappear (of animates)   no.?

narubeku   as much as possible   15B

  narúbeku hàyàku   as fast as possible   15B

naruhodo   to be sure! of course! indeed!   9A

nasâru ↑ /-aru; nasâtta/   /honorific-polite equivalent of **suru**/   do   12B

nattoku-suru   become persuaded or convinced; consent to   27A

nattoku-site kureru   become persuaded (for the benefit of the in-group)   27A

  kono yoteehyoo ni nattoku-suru   consent to this schedule   27A+

yotéehyoo o tukau kotò o nattoku-suru   be persuaded to use a schedule   27A+

  konó yoteehyoo o tukattà to wa naítoku-dekìnai   [I] can't be persuaded that [s/he] used this schedule   27A+

natû   summer   19A+

natúkasìi /-katta/   is nostalgic   26B+

  Toókyoo ğa natukasìi   [I] miss Tokyo 26B+

nâze   why?   11A+

nedañ   price   21A

nê(e)   /sentence-particle of confirmation, agreement, or deliberation/   1A, 1B, 2A

nekasu /-u; nekasita/   put to sleep; put to bed; lay [something] on its side   19B+

nêko   cat   17B+

nêkutai   necktie   23A+

  nêkutai o simêru/suru   put on a necktie 23A+

nemui /-katta/   is sleepy   19B+

-neñ   /classifier for naming and counting years/ 8B

nêñ   care, caution   23B

  nêñ no tame   for the sake of caution; to be on the safe side   23B

  nêñ o ireru   use care; use caution   23B+

-neñkañ   /classifier for counting years/   8B+

neru /-ru; neta/   go to sleep; go to bed   19B

nî   two   2B

ni   /ptc/ in; on; at   6A; into; onto; to   7A; from   10B

  usíro ni àru   be located in back   6A

  zyûu-zi ni kûru   come at ten o'clock   8B

  hôñya ni iku   go to the bookstore   7A

  Kimura-sañ ni deñwa o kakèru   telephone Mr/s. Kimura   9B

  rokú-syùukañ ni nâru   get to be six weeks 9B

  tomodati ni kariru   borrow from a friend   10B

  soñna ni   to that extent; like that   9B

  hayámè ni kûru   come early   10A

  keñkoo ni ìi   is good for the health   14B

  miyağe ni kau   buy as a souvenir   15A

  mukae ni iku   go to meet   16B

  tanósimì ni suru   consider to be a pleasure   16B

  ikû no ni wa   for the purpose of going   20A

  matâzu ni   without waiting; instead of waiting   23B

  kêezai ni tuite   concerning economics   25A

tuyú ni tùite no hôn   a book about the rainy season   25A+

soré ni sitè mo   even so, nevertheless   26A

niâu   suit, become [someone]   23B

   X ni niâu   suit X, be becoming to X   23B+

niĝátè ~ niĝate   weak point; one's downfall   30A

niĝiyaka /na/   lively; bustling; prosperous   21B

nihaku-suru   stay two nights   21A+

Nihôñ/Níppòñ   Japan   5B+

nihoñgo/nippoñgo   Japanese language   2A

nihoñma   Japanese-style room   21A+

nihoñsyoku   Japanese-style food   15A+

nihóñzìñ/níppoñzìñ   Japanese person   10B+

nikkèeziñ   person of Japanese ancestry   10B

nikû   meat   15A+

-nikui /-katta/   is marked by difficulty   13A

   siníkùi   is hard to do   13A

nîmotu   luggage; things to be carried   19A

-niñ/-ri   /classifier for counting people/   11A

niñĝyoo   doll   29A+

-niñmae   /classifier for counting portions/   14B

niôi   smell   22B+

   niôi ĝa suru   have a smell   22B+

nî-see   second generation (used in reference to offspring of native Japanese who have moved abroad)   10B+

nisi   west   19B+

-niti/-ka   /classifier for counting days and naming dates/   8A

nitíyòo(bi)   Sunday   8A

niwa   garden   17B

n̂n̂   /casual-style negation/   9A

no   /nom/   3B

   oókìi no   a big one   3B

   kawárù no de   being the case that [I]'ll change; [I]'ll change so . . .   13B

   ikû no ni wa   in the process of going   20A

   atúmàru no   the gathering   19B

no   /ptc/   5B

   tomodati no kuruma   a friend's car   5B

   kinoo no siñbuñ   yesterday's newspaper   5B

   kokó no tosyòkañ   the library here   6B

nò   /ptc **no** + nominal **no**/   5B

   kyôo no da   it's today's (one)   5B

no ~ ĝa   /ptc/

   Tanáka-sañ no mottè kita nîmotu   luggage that Mr/s. Tanaka brought   19A

   ít̀(e) òita no ni   in spite of having said in advance   26A

nihóñzìñ na no ni   even though s/he i̇ Japanese   26A+

aá iu hitò to tukíàetara yôkatta no ni   i̇ would have been great if you could have as̆ sociated with that kind of person   26A+

Môtto suzûsìkattara îi no ni.   I wish (it woulḏ be good if) it were cooler.   26A+

dâ no ni   in spite of that; nevertheless   30B

no   /pre-nominal form of **dà**/

   uńtèñsyu ĝa zyosée no tàkusii   a taxi whosȇ driver is a woman   19B

nobâsu /-u; nobâsita/   lengthen, extend, stretcḫ [something]; postpone; prolong   27B

nobîru /-ru; nòbita/   [something] extends, stretches; is postponed, is prolonged   27B

nôdo   throat   14A+

   nôdo ĝa kawâku   become thirsty   14A+

nokorimono   leftovers   24A+

nokôru /-u; nokôtta/   be(come) left behind; rȇ main, stay on   24A

nokôsu /-u; nokôsita/   leave behind; hold in rȇ serve; save   24A+

nomîmono   drink, beverage   14A

nômu /-u; nôñda/   drink   1A; take (of medi̇ cine)   14B

noo   no(h) (traditional Japanese theater)   28B

nôoka   farmer   16B+

Noósuèsuto   Northwest (airline)   19A

nôoto   notebook   4B; notes   28A

noótobùkku   notebook   4B+

norikae   a transfer to another vehicle   20B

noríkaèru /-ru; noríkàeta/   transfer to anothȇ vehicle   20B+

noru /-u; notta/   get on; board a vehiclȇ ride   19B

   tâkusii ni noru   take a taxi   19B

noseru /-ru; noseta/   place on [something]; takȇ on board; give a ride   19B+

notihodo   later   12B

nûĝu /-u; nûida/   take off (of clothing)   23A+

nyûusu   news   16A

Nyuúyòoku   New York   8A

o   /ptc/   4A

   kore o iku   go along this one (e.g., street)   7̇

   kore o kau   buy this one   4A

oba   aunt; my aunt   11B+

obâasañ   grandmother; your grandmother; olḏ woman /polite/   11B

obasañ   aunt; your aunt; woman /polite/   11B

ôbi   kimono sash   14A+

ôbi o simêru/suru   put on an obi   23B+

obóeru /-ru; obôeta/   commit to memory; learn by heart   12B+

Odaizi ni.   Take care of yourself.   16B

Oháyoo (gozaimàsu). +   Good morning.   GUP

ohîru   noon; noon meal   14A; daytime   18B

oíde ni nàru ↑   go; come; be located (animate) /honorific-polite/   10A+

oisii /-katta/   is delicious   5B

oitokosañ   cousin /polite/   11B+

oka   hill   18A+

okâasañ   mother; your mother /polite/   11B+

Okáeri-nasài(màse).   Welcome back!   7A

okaḡesama de   thanks to you; thanks for asking   11B

Okámai nàku.   Don't bother; Don't go to any trouble.   18A

okane   money   19A+

okâsi   cake; candy; sweets   15A+

okásìi /-katta/   is funny; is strange   13A

okâsi na /+ nom/   funny; strange   13A+

okîru /-ru; ôkita/   wake up; get up   21B+

okôru /-u; okôtta/   become angry   22B+

okosañ   child /polite/   10A+

   okósañḡata   children /polite/   29A

okôsu /-u; okôsita/   wake [someone] up   21B

oku /-u; oita/   put, place   16A

   iret(e) oku   put in for future use, put in and leave   16A

   tôtt(e) oku   put aside, set aside   21A

   oite (i)ku   leave behind   16A

okureru /-ru; okureta/   become late or delayed   9B

   okúrete kùru   come late   9B

okuru /-u; okutta/   send; send off, see off   16B

ôkusañ   wife; your wife /polite/   10B

Omátase-itasimàsita. ↓   I've caused you to wait /humble-polite/   12B

omáti-kudasài   please wait   4B

omâwarisañ   policeman   7B+

omé ni kakàru ↓ **/-u; kakâtta/**   meet, see (a person) /humble-polite/   13B

   Hazîmete omé ni kakarimàsu.   How do you do.   13B+

omédetoo gozaimàsu   congratulations   27A

omoi /-katta/   is heavy   20A

omóidàsu /-u; omóidàsita/   recall   25B

omósiròi /-katta/   is interesting; is amusing; is fun   1B

omósìrosa   interest, enjoyment   24B+

omótè   front side   7B+

omôtya   toy   29A+

omôu /-u; omôtta/   think   11A

   kâette (i)ru to omôu   think [someone] is or will be back   11A

   deyôo to omôu   [I] think [I]'ll leave   20A

ôñ   obligation, debt of gratitude   30A+

   ôñ o 'siranai   ignore one's ôñ   30A+

   ôñ ni nâru   become indebted   30A+

   ôñ o 'wasureru   forget a favor   30A+

   ôñ o kâesu   return a favor   30A+

onaka   stomach   14A

   onaka ḡa suku   become hungry   14A

onazi   same   5B

   onazi zassi   same magazine   5B

   koré to onazi tàipu   a type the same as this   17B

(o)nêesañ   older sister; your older sister /polite/   11A+

Onéḡai-simàsu. ↓   I make a request of you. /humble-polite/   GUP

ôñḡaku   music   28B+

oñḡàkùkai   concert   28B+

(o)nîisañ   older brother; your older brother /polite/   11A

oñnà   female   10A

   oñna no hitò   woman   10A

   oñna no katà   woman /polite/   10A+

   oñnà no ko   little girl; young girl   10A+

ôobaa   (over)coat, topcoat   23B

oôi /-katta/   are many; are frequent   20A

   nîmotu ḡa oôi   there is lots of luggage   20A

oókìi /-katta/   is big   1B+

ôoki na /+ nom/   big, large; loud (of voice)   13A

ôokisa   size (bulk)   24B+

Oókura-hòteru   Hotel Okura   6B

oókuràsyoo   Finance Ministry   11B+

oómìzu   flood   22A+

Oosaka   Osaka   8A+

Oósutorària   Australia   5B+

oósutorariàziñ   an Australian   10B+

oózèe   large numbers of people; crowd   19A

oree   reward; thanks, expression of appreciation   17A   See **rêe**.

orîru /-ru; ôrita/   descend; get off (a vehicle)   19B

orôsu /-u; orôsita/   lower; unload; let off (a vehicle)   19B+

ôru ↓ **/-u; ôtta/**   be located (of animate existence) /humble-polite/   7A

Toókyoo ni òru ↓   be in Tokyo (animate)
7A

keќkoñ-sit(e) òru ↓   be married   10B

hanâsit(e) oru ↓   be talking   10B

kotíra ni nàtte orimasu ⁺   [it] has come to be
here /neutral-polite/   15B

Osaki ni.   (Excuse me for going) ahead of you.
/polite/   9B

  Dôozo, osaki ni.   Please go ahead. /polite/
9B

Osewasama.   (Thank you for) your helpful assistance.   6B

osieru /-ru; osieta/   teach; give instruction or
information   7A

osiire   closet   17B +

osoi /-katta/   is late; is slow   9A

  osóku nàru   become late; become slow   9A +

  osókute mo   even/also if it's late; at the
latest   21B

osókù   late (time)   11A

  osókù made   until late   11A

Osôre-irimasu.   I'm sorry; Thank you.   12B

ośsyàru ↑ **/-aru; ośsyàtta/**   be called, be
named   12A; say   18B /honorific-polite/

  X to/(t)te ośsyàru ↑   be named X   12B;
say, "X" /honorific-polite/   18B

osu /-u; osita/   push   26A

otaku   home; household /polite/   7B

otîru /-ru; ôtita/   [something] drops, falls
26A +

  hî ğa nisí ni otìru   the sun sets in the
west   26A +

  aráttè mo otînai   it doesn't come out even if
you wash it   26A +

  sikêñ ni otîru   fail in an exam   26A +

otókò   male   10A

  otóko no hitò   man   10A

  otóko no katà   man /polite/   10A +

  otókò no ko   little boy; young boy   10A +

otona   adult   10A +

otôosañ   father; your father /polite/   11B +

otóotò   younger brother   11A +

otôsu /-u; otôsita/   drop [something]   26A +

  sará o otòsu   drop a plate   26A +

  kôe o otôsu   lower one's voice   26A +

  namáe o otòsu   drop (omit) a name   26A +

  ki ó otòsu   lose heart   26A +

otótòi   the day before yesterday   3A

otôtosi   the year before last   10A +

ôtto   husband; my husband   10B +

Otúkaresama (dèsita).   (You must be
tired!)   GUP

oturi   change (money returned)   4B

otya   tea   3A +

  otya o ireru   make tea   17B

(o)wabi   apology   30B +

  (o)wabi o iu   apologize   30B +

  (o)wabi no teğami   letter of apology   30B +

owari   the end   25B +

owaru /-u; owatta/   finish, terminate   25B

-owaru   finish ——   30B

  iíowàru   finish saying   30B

oyâ   parent   11B +

oyağosañ   parent; your parent /polite/   11B +

Oyásumi-nasài.   Goodnight.   GUP

oyóğì   swimming   26B +

oyôğu /-u; oyôida/   swim   26B +

oyu   hot water   14A +

ozi   uncle; my uncle   11B +

ozîisañ   grandfather; your grandfather; old
man /polite/   11B +

ozisañ   uncle; your uncle; man /polite/   11B +

ozyôosañ   daughter; your daughter; young
woman /polite/   10A

Paáku-bìru   the Park building   6A

pâat(e)ii   party   21B +

pâi   pie   3A +

pâñ   bread   14A

pâñtaroñ   slacks   23A +

pâñtu   slacks   23A +

Pâri   Paris   8A

Pâruko   Parco (name of department store)   7

pêñ   pen   4B +

perapera   fluent; glib, voluble   25B

  nihóñğo ğa perapera no hitò   person whos
Japanese is fluent   25B

pîkunikku   picnic   22A

pûriñ   custard pudding   3A +

purógùramu   program   20B

-ra /pluralizing suffix/   29A

  bôkura   we (masculine)   29A +

raíğakki   next (school) term   28B +

râiğetu   next month   9A +

raineñ   next year   9A +

râisu   cooked rice   14A

raisyuu   next week   9A

rakû /na/   relaxed; comfortable; easy   8A

  rakû ni suru   make comfortable   18A

rakuğo   traditional Japanese comedy monologue   28B +

rańti-sàabisu   special lunch   14A

-rasìi /-katta/   apparently is; seems to be   24B
  kitá-rasìi   apparently has come   24B
  yasúi-rasìi   is apparently cheap   24B
  kimí-rasìi   is typical of you; seems to be
    you   24B

rassyu-àwaa   rush hour   11A

râzio   radio   16A +

rêe   zero   12A
  rêe-zi   zero o'clock, midnight   19A +

rêe   reward; thanks, expression of
  appreciation   17A
  rêe o siranai   rude, ill-mannered   17A +
  oree o iu   express thanks   17A +
  oree o suru   reward   17A +
  omiyağe no oree ni   in return for a souvenir
    received   17A +

rêe no X   that very X; that X known to both of
  us   24A

rekisi   history   25B +

eńraku-suru   get in touch; make contact   12B

eńsyuu-suru   practice   22B

essya   a train   19A +

esutorań   restaurant (Western-style)   14B +

ri/-niń   /classifier for counting people/   11A

ikoń-suru   get divorced   10B +

imúziń-bàsu   limousine bus   20A

Rińkaań-dàiğaku   Lincoln University/Col-
lege   25B

ippa /na/   splendid, magnificent, great,
  eminent   20B

okû   six   2B +

ońbuń   article, essay; thesis   30B +

Rôńdoń   London   8A

oodoo-suru   labor   16B +

oódòosya   laborer   16B +

ooka   corridor, hall   17B +

oómàzi   romanization   28A +

osiağo   Russian language   2A +

osíàziń   Russian person   10A +

ûsu   absence from home   9B

usubań   a caretaker   13A
  rusubań o suru   act as a caretaker   13A +

usúbań-dèńwa   telephone answering
  machine   13A

yokań   Japanese-style inn   6B

yokoo   trip; travel   20A
  ryokóo ni dèru   leave on a trip   20A

yokoo-suru   take a trip   20A +

Amerika o ryokoo-suru   travel through
  America   20A +

ryoóğàeki   money-changing machine   19A

ryôoğae-suru   make change; exchange
  money   19A

ryôori   cooking   15B

ryôori-suru   prepare food   15B +

ryoórìya   restaurant (Japanese-style)   15B +

ryôosiń   both parents   11B +

ryôozi   consul   13B +

ryoózìkań   consulate   6B
  Amérika-ryoozìkań   American con-
    sulate   6B

ryuúğákùsee   student studying abroad   25B

sa   /sentence- particle of assertion/   30B

sâa   hmmm!   6A

sâa   here, now! come, now! /exclamation of urg-
  ing/   18A

sâabisu   service; item or service offered "on the
  house"   15A

sabísìi /-katta/   is sad, desolate, lonely, solitary   26B +
  sabísìi tokórò   a lonely place   26B +
  sabísìi kao   a cheerless face, expression
    26B +
  sabísìi kêsiki   desolate scenery   26B +
  kânozyo ğa inâkute sabísìi   it's lonely with
    her not being here   26B +

sàe   /ptc/   even   27B
  isú sàe nâi   there aren't even any chairs
    27B +
  tukî ni sae 'iku   go even to the moon   27B +
  kodómo de sàe   even being a child   27B +
  basyó sàe kimárèba   if only the place is
    decided   27B
  soré o sitte sàe irêba   if only [s/he] knows
    that   27B +
  osí sàe surêba   if only [you]'ll push it   27B +
  omósìròku sae âreba   if only it's inter-
    esting   27B +
  yasásii nihoňğo de sàe âreba   if only it's easy
    Japanese   27B +

sağasu /-u; sağasita/   look for; locate; track
  down   24A

-sai   /classifier for counting years of human age/
  10A +

saikoo   the highest, the maximum   26B

sakana   fish   13B

sakaya   liquor store   14B +

saki   ahead (of time or place)   6A, 21B

saṅ-syùukaṅ-hodo saki about three weeks ahead (from now) 25A
sakihodo a while ago /formal/ 18B
sâkki a while ago 16A
sakura cherry 18A+
-sama Mr.; Mrs.; Miss; Ms. /polite suffix/
samêru /-ru; sâmeta/ get cold 18A
samûi /-katta/ is cold (of atmosphere only) 11A+
sâmusa cold(ness) 24B+
saṅ three 2B+
-saṅ Mr.; Mrs.; Miss; Ms. /polite suffix/ 2A
saṅdo/saṅdoìtti sandwich 14A+
Saṅhurānsìsuko San Francisco 8A
sâṅkyuu thank you 17A
saṅpo a walk 26B+
saṅpo-suru take a walk 26B+
sâṅ-see third generation (used in reference to grandchildren of native Japanese who have moved abroad) 10B+
Sapporo Sapporo 8A+
sara plate 15B+
saraiḡetu month after next 10A+
saraineṅ year after next 10A+
saraisyuu week after next 10A+
sarárìimaṅ salaried employee 16B+
sasiaḡeru↓ /-ru; sasiaḡeta/ give (to you/him/her/them) /humble-polite/ 17A+
  kasite sasiaḡeru↓ lend (to you/him/her/them) 17A+
sasímì raw fish dish 14A+
sasou /-u; sasotta/ invite (to do something) 28A
satôo sugar 5B
-satu /classifier for counting books, magazines, etc./ 4B
satu a bill (currency) 19A+
sawâḡu /-u; sawâida/ make a noise; raise a racket; revel 29B+
sayoo /formal equivalent of **sôo**/ 13B
Sayo(o)nara. Goodbye. GUP
sebiro man's suit 23A
sêebutu living things 25B+
seébutùḡaku biology 25B+
seekatu daily life, living 27B
  kekkoṅ-sèekatu married life 27B+
  syakái-sèekatu social life 27B+
  seékatu no tamè ni hataraku work to make a living 27B+
seekatu-suru pursue daily life; make a living 27B+

seereki Christian era; A.D. 8B
sêetaa sweater 23B
seezi politics 16B+
seezi-teki /na/ political 25A+
  seezi-teki na moṅdai ~ seeziteki-moṅdai political problems 25A+
seezika politician 16B+
sêki seat; assigned place 12B
  sêki o hazusite (i)ru be away from one's seat 12B
sekiniṅ responsibility 27A
  oyâ to site no 'sekiniṅ responsibility as a parent 27A
  sekíniṅ ḡa àru have responsibility 27A+
  sekíniṅ o tòru/môtu take/assume responsibility 27A+
sekíniṅsya responsible person, person in charge 27A+
sekkakù with special trouble or effort 15A
  Sekkakù desu ḡa .. It's especially [kind of you] but . . . 15A+
  sekkaku no pìkkunikku a picnic involving special effort 22A
semâi /-katta/ is cramped, narrow, small (of area) 24+
sêminaa seminar 25A
sêṅ one thousand 2B
-seṅ /counter for thousands/ 2B
senaka back (part of the body) 17A+
seṅeṅsatu ¥1000 bill 19A
seṅḡàkki last (school) term 28B+
sêṅḡetu last month 10A
seṅkyòosi missionary 16B+
seṅmeṅzyo washroom 24B+
seṅmoṅ specialization 25A
  X o seṅmoṅ ni suru make X a specialty, specialize in X 25A+
seṅmoṅḡo specialized vocabulary 25A+
seṅmoṅ-teki /na/ specialized 25A
seṅpai senior colleague, superior colleague 26A
seṅsèe teacher; doctor 2B
seṅsèṅḡetu month before last 10A+
seṅsèṅsyuu week before last 10A+
seṅsyuu last week 10A
-seṅto /classifier for counting cents/ 3A+
seṅyaku previous appointment 28B
seṅzitu the other day 18A
setto-mèṅyuu set menu 15B
setumee explanation no.?
setumee-suru explain 18B+

sewâ helpful assistance 11B

sewâ ni nâru become obliged for assistance 11B

si /ptc/ and (what is more) 23A

mitúkaranài si it isn't found, and (what is more) 23A

si poem; poetry 30B+

sî four 2B+

sî city 20A+

Siâtoru Seattle 19A

sibai a show, a play 18B+

sibâraku a while (of indeterminate length) 11B+, 18A+

Sibâraku desu. It's been a while (since our last meeting). 18A+

sibâru /-u; **sibâtta**/ bind, tie up 26A+

sî-go-niti four or five days 20A

sigoto work 8B

sihâiniñ manager 29B+

sîizuñ the season 21B

sika /ptc/ except for 21A

âsa sika dasânai not serve except in the morning, serve only in the morning 21A

miñsyuku nì sika tomárànai not stay except in tourist homes, stay only in tourist homes 21A

sikaru /-u; **sikatta**/ scold 29A+

sikasi but 24B

sikata way of doing 22B+

sikáta ğa nài nothing can be done; it can't be helped 22B+

sikêñ exam, test 25B

sikéñ-mòñdai test problem, test question 25B

sikî ceremony, rite 23A+

sikíbùtoñ bottom quilt 21B+

Sikôku Shikoku (a main island of Japan) 11A+

siku /-u; **siita**/ spread out 21B

simâ island 18A+

simâru /-u; **simâtta**/ become closed; [something] closes 16A

simâtta damn! oh, dear! 21A

simau /-u; **simatta**/ put away; store 16A

wasurete simau/wasuretyau forget completely; end up forgetting 16B

simêru /-ru; **sîmeta**/ close [something] 16A

sînai within a city (a **sî**) 20A+

siñbuñ newspaper 2B+

siñbuñkìsya journalist 16B+

siñğakki new (school) term 28B+

siñğoo traffic light 7B

siñğuru(-rùumu) single room 21A

siñkàñseñ bullet train 7B+

siñpai worry, concern 20B

siñpai o kakèru cause [someone] to worry 20B+

siñpai-suru worry 20B+

siñrìğaku psychology 25B+

siñsetu /na/ kind, considerate 28B

sîñsetu ni suru act kindly 28B+

gosîñsetu ni amaete taking advantage of your kindness 28B+

siñsitu bedroom 17B+

sinu /-u; **siñda**/ die (of humans and animals) 27B+

siñzoo heart 17A+

Siñzyuku Shinjuku (section of Tokyo) 8B

siô salt 14A+

sirábèru /-ru; **sirâbeta**/ look into, investigate, check 14B

sirôi /-katta/ is white 4A+

siru /-u; **sitta**/ get to know 10B; give heed to, be concerned with 28A

sitte (i)ru know 10B

wakárànakute mo 'siranai [I]'ll pay no attention even if [you] don't understand 28A

sita bottom; down; below, under 17B+

sitaği underwear 23A+

sitásìi /-katta/ is familiar, intimate, close 26A

sitásisuğìru be too familiar 26A

sitêeseki reserved seat 19A+

sitî seven 2B+

situke training; discipline; upbringing 29A+

sitúkèru /-ru; **sitûketa**/ train; discipline; teach manners 29A

situmoñ question 29A+

situmoñ-suru ask a question 29A

sitûree /na/ rude; rudeness 12B

Sitûree-simasita. Excuse me (for what I have done). GUP

Sitûree-simasu. Excuse me (for what I am about to do). GUP

siyoo way of doing 22B+

siyóo ğa nài nothing can be done; it can't be helped 22B+

sizeñ nature; natural 30B

sizeñ no kañkyoo natural environment 30B

sîzuka /na/ quiet, calm, placid 26B+

sôba nearby 6B

êki no sôba near the station 6B

sôba buckwheat noodles 14A+

sobâya noodle shop 14B+
Sobíeto /see **Sôreñ**/ 5B+
sôbo (my) grandmother 11B+
sodáteru /-ru; sodâteta/ bring up, raise 27A+
sodâtu /-u; sodâtta/ grow up, be raised 27A
sôhu (my) grandfather 11B+
soko that place (near you or just mentioned) 6B+
-soku /classifier for counting pairs of footwear/ 23A+
soñna that kind (of) 4B+
  soñna ni to that extent; like that 9B
sono /+ nom/ that —— near you; that —— just mentioned 3A
-soo /na/ looking as if 24B
  kowáresòo /na/ looking as if it would break 24B
  hirósòo ni mieru appear spacious-looking 24B
sôo that way; like that 2A
  âru soo da I hear that there are, it is said that there are 21A
soodañ-suru consult; talk over 11A
Sôoru Seoul 8A+
soozi-suru clean 17A+
sôra sky 30B+
sore that thing (near you or just mentioned) 2B
  sore kara after that; and then 4B
  sore ni onto that; on top of that; in addition 11A
  soré dè (wa) that being the case 13B
  soré ni sitè mo even so, nevertheless 26A
Sôreñ Soviet Union 5B+
soréñzìñ Soviet citizen 10B+
sôrosoro slowly; gradually 18A
sorya /contraction of **sore wa**/ 14B
sotira that side; that way; thereabouts; there; that alternative (of two) 6A+
sôto outside 17B
sot́tì /casual equivalent of **sotira**/ 7B+
sotuğyoo graduation 27A+
sotúğyòosee a graduate 27A+
sotuğyoo-suru graduate 27A+
  daiğaku o sotuğyoo-suru graduate from college 27A+
subárasìi /-katta/ is splendid, wonderful, magnificent 26B+
-suği past; after 8A
  go-hûñ-suği five minutes after the hour 8A

suğîru /-ru; sûğita/ go past, go beyond 15A+
-suğiru /-ru; -sûğita/ go to excess 15A
  tabesuğiru overeat 15A
suğôi /-katta/ is awful, wonderful, weird, terrific 11A
  suğôku zyoózù da is awfully skilled/skillful 11A
sûğu soon; immediate 5B
  sûğu kûru will come soon 5B
  sûğu sôba immediate vicinity 6B
sûi /abbreviation for **suíyòo(bi)**/ 8A
  gês·sûi·kîñ Mon–Wed–Fri 8A
suíyòo(bi) Wednesday 8A
sukâato skirt 23A+
sukî /na/ pleasing; like 15B
sukiyaki sukiyaki (description in 14A) 14A+
suḱkàri completely, utterly 17A
sukôsi a little; a few 5A
suku /-u; suita/ become empty 14A
  onaka ğa suku become hungry 14A
sukúnài /-katta/ are few; is rare; is infrequent 20A+
  kâzi ğa sukúnài there are few fires 20A+
sumásèru /-ru; sumâseta/ bring to an end, finish 21B
Su(m)ímasèñ. I'm sorry; Thank you. GUP
Su(m)ímasèñ desita. I'm sorry (for what I did); Thank you (for the trouble you took). GUP
sûmu /-u; sûñda/ come to an end 21B+
sûmu /-u; sûñda/ take up residence, reside 24A
sumûuzu /na/ smooth 26B
  sumûuzu ni iku go smoothly 26B
Supêiñ Spain 5B+
supeiñğo Spanish language 2A+
supéiñzìñ Spaniard 10B+
supíiti-kòñtesuto speech contest 30A
supóotu-bàñğumi sports program 18B+
supóotùkàa sportscar 5B
suṕpài /-katta/ is sour 15+
supûuñ spoon 15A+
surâkkusu slacks 23A+
surîppa slippers 23A+
suru /irreg; **sita**/ do; play (of games) 1A
  âtûku nattari sâmûku nattari suru alternate between getting hot and getting cold 26B
  eé-kòosu ni suru make [it] (to be) the "A" meal; decide on the "A" meal 14A
  ki ni suru mind; worry about; concern oneself about 24A

tukau yoo ni suru act so as to use 24A

nokôru koto ni suru decide on remaining 24A

deyôo to suru be about to leave; try to leave 25B

deyôo to sita tokórò ni at the very moment when I had been about to leave 25B

konó heñ no utì to sitê wa yasûi for a house in this area, it's cheap 26A+

soré ni sitè mo even so 26A+

arûite kuru ni sitê mo, osôi even granted that s/he's walking here, s/he's late 26A

usî sushi (description in 14A) 14A+

usîya sushi shop 14B+

usumeru /-ru; susumeta/ recommend; encourage; urge 29B+

utañdo lamp 17B+

uteru /-ru; suteta/ throw away 17A

uu /-u; sutta/ smoke (cigarettes, cigars, etc.) 14B

uuğaku mathematics 25B+

ûúpaa(màaketto) supermarket 7B+

ûutu man's or woman's suit 23A

uútukèesu suitcase 5A+

uuzi number(s) 12A

uwaru /-u; suwatta/ sit down 19B+

uzúsìi /-katta/ is cool 11A+

yabêru /-u; syabêtta/ speak, talk, chat 24A

yâiñ staff member 16B+

yakâiğaku sociology 18B+

yakái-sèekatu social life 27B+

yasetu editorial 30B+

yasiñ photograph 16A

  syasíñ o tòru take a picture 16A

yâtu shirt 23A+

yatyoo company president 13B

syoku /classifier for counting meals/ 21A

  ni-syoku-tuki with two meals, two meals included 21A

yokudoo dining room; restaurant 14A+

yokuzi dining; meal 16B

  syokúzi ğa dèru meals are served 21A

  syokuzi ni suru make it dinner; have dinner 21B

yokuzi-suru dine, have a meal 16B+

yoo way of doing 22B

  syoó ğa nài nothing can be done; it can't be helped 22B+

yooğo noon 18B

  syoóğo-suğì after noon 18B

yookai-suru introduce 11B

syoosetu a novel 30B+

syôosyoo a little 4B

syôotai-suru invite (to an event) 28A+

syooti-suru agree to; consent to 21B

Syoowa the Showa Era (1926–89) 8B+

syooyu soy sauce 14A+

syoozi sliding door (translucent) 16A+

syoṕpiñğubàggu shopping bag 5A+

syosai study (room) 17B+

syotyoo institute director 12B

syukkiñ attendance at the office 22A+

  zisá-syùkkiñ staggered work hours; flextime 22A

syukudai homework; outside assignment 30A

  syukúdai ğa dèru homework is assigned 30A

syuttyoo business trip 9B

syuttyoo-suru go away on a business trip 9B+

syuu week 10A+

-syuukañ /classifier for counting weeks/ 8B+

syûukyoo religion 25B+

syuúkyòoğaku religion (as a subject) 25B+

syuumatu weekend 21A+

syuusyoku-suru find or seek employment 25A

syûziñ husband; my husband 10B+

tabako cigarette 14B

tabakoya cigarette shop, tobacconist 14B+

tabémòno food 14A+

tabêru /-ru; tâbeta/ eat 1A

tabésuğìru /-ru; tabésùğita/ overeat 15A

tâbi bifurcated socks (Japanese-style) 23B+

tâbuñ probably 21A

tâda only, merely; free (of charge), gratis 30A

  tâda tetúdàu tamê ni sita I did it only to help 30A+

  tâda da it's free 30A+

  tâda de morau get [it] free 30A+

Tadaima. Hello, I'm back. 7A

taiheñ /na/ awful; terrible; a problem 9B

taíhùu typhoon 22A

tâipu type, style, variety; typing 17B

taípuràitaa typewriter 3A

taisetu /na/ important 13A

tâisi ambassador 13B+

taísìkañ embassy 6B

  Amérika-taisìkañ American embassy 6B

Taisyoo the Taisho Era (1912–26) 8B

taitee usually 8B+

Taíwàñ Taiwan 5B+

takâi /-katta/ is expensive; is high 1B

take bamboo 18A+

takkyuubiñ (special baggage service) 20A

takúsàñ much; many 5A

tâkusii taxi 7B

tamâḡo egg 14A+

tamê reason, sake; benefit 23A

  tamê ni nâru mono a thing which is beneficial 23A+

  kyôosi ni nâru tamê (ni) in order to become a teacher 23A

  byóóki ni nàtta tamê (ni) because of having become sick 23A+

  nêñ no tame for the sake of caution; to be on the safe side 23B

tana shelf 16A+

tanî valley 18A+

tanômu /-u; tanôñda/ request, ask for 14A+

tanósìi /-katta/ is enjoyable, pleasant; is joyous 26B

  Tanôsìkatta. It was fun! 26B+

tanósìmì a joy; a pleasure 8B

tanósìmu /-u; tanósìñda/ take pleasure in 8B+

tañsu chest (furniture) 17B+

tañtoo-suru take charge of 27A+

tañtòosya person in charge 27A

  tañtòosya no Mîraa-sañ Mr/s. Miller who is the person in charge 27A

taórèru /-ru; taôreta/ fall down, collapse 26A+

  zisiñ de iê ḡa taórèru houses collapse in earthquakes 26A+

  kazé de taòreta kî a tree that toppled over in the wind 26A+

  taóresòo na kaisya a company that looks as if it will fail 26A+

taôsu /-u; taôsita/ fell, knock down 26A+

  kî o taôsu fell a tree 26A+

  iê o taôsu raze a house 26A+

  hitô o taôsu throw a person down 26A+

  kaísya no syatyoo o taòsu unseat the president of a company 26A+

tâsika /na/ certain, positive, reliable 20A

  tâsika ni /+ predicate/ certainly, positively, surely 20A+

  tâsika /+ predicate/ if I'm correct, if I remember correctly, most likely 20A+

tasúkàru /-u; tasúkàtta/ be(come) rescued, saved 17B

tasúkèru /-ru; tasûketa/ rescue, save 17B+

  Tasuketeeee. Help!!! 17B+

tasyoo more or less; somewhat 25A

tatâku /-u; tatâita/ beat, knock, tap 26A+

  dôa o tatâku knock on a door 26A+

  kâta o tatâku pound [someone's] shoulder (to promote relaxation) 26A+

  tê o tatâku clap hands 26A+

  teéburu o tatâku drum on a table 26A+

  taípuràitaa o tatâku peck away at a typewriter 26A+

  hitó no kao o tatàku slap [someone's] face 26A+

  gakútyoo o tatàku (verbally) attack the university president 26A+

tatami (Japanese-style floor mat) 17B

  tatámi no heyà room with mats 17B

tatêmòno building 6B

tatêru /-ru; tâteta/ stand [something] up; erect [something] 19B+

  yakû ni tatêru put to use 20B+

  X o yakû ni tatêru put X to use 20B+

-tati /pluralizing suffix/ 29A

  watá(ku)sìtati we 29A+

  bôkútàti we (masculine) 29A+

  anâtatàti you (plural) 29A+

  Nakámura-sañ-tati Mr/s. Nakamura and his/her group 29A+

  hitôtati persons 29A+

tatôeba for example 26B

tâtu /-u; tâtta/ stand up; get built 19B

  yakû ni tâtu be of use 20B

  hará ḡa tàtu become angry 22B

tâtu /-u; tâtta/ depart 19B+

tê hand 17A+

teârai toilet 6A

teeburu table 17B

têenee /na/ polite; careful, conscientious, thorough 28A+

têepu tape 3A

teesyoku meal with a fixed menu 14A

teḡami letter 2A

Tekísasu-òiru Texas Oil 15A

-teki /na/ pertaining to, derived from, related to 25A+

tekitoo /na/ suitable 24B

temae this side (of) 7B

Teñhana (name of tempura restaurant) 15A

teñiñ salesperson 16B+

tênisu tennis 4A

têñki weather; good weather 22A

(îi) têñki ni nâru get to be good weather 22A

eñki-yòhoo weather forecast 18B+

eñpura batter-fried fish and vegetables 14A+

eñpuraya tempura shop 14B+

erâ Buddhist temple 6B+

êrebi television 16A

têrebi ni dêru appear on television 18B

etúdài help, assistance 27B

otêtudai ni iku go to help [you]; give [you] a hand 27B

etúdàu /-u; tetúdàtta/ help, lend a hand 17A

etûğaku philosophy 25B+

iğau /-u; tiğatta/ be different; be wrong 1A

îtu mo to tiğau be different from [what is] always [normal] 23A

iísài /-katta/ is small 1B+

îisa na /+ nom/ small, little; low, soft (of voice) 13A+

ikâ underground 7A

ikâi /-katta/ is near 13B

tikâi uti ni in the near future 30B+

ikâku vicinity 13B+

ikatetu subway 7B+

ikázukèru /-ru; tikázùketa/ bring close; associate with 22A+

ikázùku /-u; tikázùita/ approach, draw near; become acquainted 22A

îri geography 25B+

itî father; my father 11B+

itioya father 11B+

íttò mo even a little 28B

îzu map 7B

ô the city of Tokyo 20A+

o /ptc/ and; with 3B; as if /manner/ 25B

kore to sore this and that 3B

tomódati to hanàsu talk with a friend 10B

tomodati to issyo together with a friend 11A+

A to B to, dôtira ğa îi? Which is better, A or B? 15A

îtu mo to tiğau be different from [what is] always [normal] 23A

—— **ni yoru to** according to —— 22A

soo suru to (with) that being the case 26A+

—— **to iu to?** What do you mean by ——? 26A

himá dà to whenever s/he's free 26A+

deyôo to suru be about to leave; try to leave 25B

deyôo to sita tokórò ni at the very moment when I had been about to leave 25B

tomodati to site in the capacity of a friend, as a friend 26A

konó heñ no utì to sitê wa yasûi for a house in this area, it's cheap 26A+

to /quotative/ 11A

îi to omôu think that it's good 11A

deyôo to omôu [I] think [I] will leave 20A

Tanaka to iu be named Tanaka 12A

X to iu ~ ośsyàru ↑ ~ môosu ↓ be named X 12A; say, "X" 18B

to iu kotò wa that is to say 21B

to iù yori more than saying what was just said; that is to say, rather 22B

—— **to iû no** the thing described as —— 25A

nañ to nàku somehow, in some (vague) way 26A

to door 16A+

todana cupboard 17B

todókèru /-ru; todôketa/ deliver; report, notify 20A+

todôku /-u; todôita/ be delivered; reach; extend 20A+

tôire toilet 6A+

to ka and/or 30B

ûmi to ka mizúùmi the oceans and/or the lakes and the like 30B

tokai city 30B

tokee clock; watch 8A

tokî occasion, time 13A

himá na tokì ni at a time when [someone] is free 13A

kodómo no tokì the time when [I] was a child 13A+

tokídokì sometimes 19A

Tokíwa-hòteru Tokiwa Hotel 21A

tokkyuu special express 19A+

tokkyùukeñ special express ticket 19A+

tokonoma alcove 21B

tokórò place; location 10B; stage in a sequence; the very moment (of an activity) 25B

tukûtte (i)ru tokórò da is just now making 25B

omôtte (i)ta tokórò da is the very moment when I was just thinking 25B

deyôo to sita tokórò ni at the very moment when I had been about to leave 25B+

nôñde (i)ru tokórò o mîru see [him/her] at the moment when s/he is drinking 25B+

Oísoğasii tokorò (o) arîğatoo gozaimasita. Thank you for giving me your time when you are busy. 25B+

tokubetu special 19A+

tokúbetu-kyùukoo/tokkyuu special express 19A+

tokûi/tokui one's specialty, one's forte 30A+

tokuzyoo super-deluxe 14B+

tomaru /-u; tomatta/ come to a halt; stop over 8A

miñsyuku ni tomaru stay in a tourist home 21A

tomeru /-ru; tometa/ stop (something); bring to a halt 7B

to mo 27B

huta-ri to mo both people 27B

Îi to mo. Of course [it's] good! 28B

tomodati friend 2B+

tônai within the city of Tokyo 20A

tonari next door; adjoining place 6B

Toñde mo nài. Heavens, no! 8B

tônikaku at any rate, in any case 27B

tôo ten units 5A+

Toodai Tokyo University 11B

tooi /-katta/ is far 13A

deñwa ğa tooi sound far away (on the telephone) 13A

toókù the faraway 13A+

Tookyoo Tokyo 2A

toórì road, thoroughfare, avenue 26B+

tôori way; in accordance with 26B+

sonó tòori that way; [just] like that 26B

yakúsoku no tòori accordance with a promise made 26B+

ossyàtta↑ tôori da it's just as you said /polite/ 26B+

kâre no iú tòori ni suru do in accordance with what he says 26B+

tôoru /-u; tôotta/ go through; pass through [something] 26A+

koóeñ o tòoru go through the park 26A+

mití o tòoru pass through a street 26A+

gakkoo no usiro o tòoru pass in back of the school 26A+

Mêziro o tôotte iku go by way of Mejiro 26A+

sikêñ o tôoru pass an exam 26A+

îmi ğa tôoru the meaning is understood 26A+

Suzúki to iu namae de tòoru pass as (go by the name of) Suzuki 26A+

tôosu /-u; tôosita/ pass [something] through 26A+

âme o tôosu let in the rain 26A+

mizú o toosànai be waterproof 26A+

kaíğìsitu ni okyákusàma o tôosu show guest to the conference room 26A+

mê o tôosu glance at 26A+

tûuyaku o tôosite hanâsu speak through an interpreter 26A+

rokú-syùukañ tôosite 'asoko de hataraita worked there for an uninterrupted period of six weeks 26A+

toozitu the very day, the day in question 19B

torâñku trunk 16A

Toranomoñ (section of Tokyo) 6B

tori chicken 15A+

torikaeru /-ru; torikaeta/ exchange 20B+

tôru /-u; tôtta/ take up; take away 16A

syasíñ o tòru take a picture 16A

huráñsuğo o tòru take French 16A+

satôo o tôru pass the sugar 16A+

tôtt(e) oku put aside, set aside 21A

tosî year 8B+

tosíyòrì old person 10A+

tosyôkañ library (a building) 6B

tosyôsitu library (a room) 8B

tot(t)emo very, extremely 1B

(t)te /quotative/ 18B

X (t)te iu ~ ossyàru ~ môosu be named X say, "X" 18B

X (t)te. Someone says, "X." 18B

-tu /classifier for counting units and years of human age/ 5A, 10A

tûaa tour 19B

-tubo /classifier for counting tsubo (= the area covered by two tatami mats)/ 24B+

tubureru /-ru; tubureta/ become crushed; collapse 30A+

kao ğa tubureru lose face; become disgraced 30A+

tubusu /-u; tubusita/ crush, smash, mash 30A

kao o tubusu destroy face; disgrace 30A

tuğî next 7B

tuğoo convenience 13B

tuğóo ğa ìi is convenient 13B+

tuğóo ğa warùi is inconvenient 13B+

tûi unintentionally, carelessly, by accident, involuntarily 27A

tuíñ(-rùumu) twin room 21A+

tuítatì first day of the month 8A

tûite: X ni tuite concerning X 25A

tukárèru /-ru; tukâreta/ become tired 17B

tukau /-u; tukatta/ use 3A

tukêru /-ru; tukêta/ attach [something]; turn on 16A

　ki ó tukèru pay attention; be careful 19B+

　-tuki attached 21A

　　ni-syoku-tuki with two meals, two meals included 21A

tukî month; moon 8B+

-tuki /classifier for counting months/ 27B+

　hitô-tuki one month 27B+

tukiatari end of the street, corridor, etc. 7B+

tukíàu /-u; tukíàtta/ associate, interact, socialize 26A

　tomódati to site tukiaèru be able to associate as a friend 26A

tûku /-u; tûita/ arrive 16B

tûku /-u; tûita/ become attached; become turned on 16A

　kêezai ni tuite concerning the economy 25A

　tuyú ni tùite no hôn a book about the rainy season 25A+

ki ğá tùku notice; become aware 19B

Tukuba Tsukuba University 12B+

tukue desk 17B+

tukûru /-u; tukûtta/ make, construct 1A

　komê o tukûru grow rice 14A+

tûma wife; my wife 10B+

tumárànai /-katta/ is boring; is trifling 1B

tumetai /-katta/ is cold 14A

tumori plan, intention 20A

　ikú tumori dà I plan to go 20A

　minámiğuti no tumori dàtta I expected it to be the south entrance 20B

　kâre ğa mâtte kureru tumori de ita I was of the expectation that he would wait for me 20B+

　sonó tumori de kùru come with that intention 28A

tuná-sàñdo tuna fish sandwich 14A+

turai /-katta/ is hard; is a strain; is **tureru /-ru; tureta/** take along (of people) 15A

　turete iku take (a person to a place) 15A+

tutómèru /-ru; tutômeta/ become employed 25A+

　depâato ni tutômete (i)ru be employed in behalf of a department store; work for a department store 25A

tuuğaku-suru commute to school 25A+

tuukiñ commuting to work 19B

tuukiñ-suru commute to work 19B+

tuúkiñ-zìkañ commuting time 19B

tûuyaku interpreter; interpretation 25A

　tûuyaku no hito interpreter 25A+

　X no tûuyaku de Y to hanâsu speak with Y, with X interpreting 25A+

tûuyaku-suru interpret; serve as an interpreter 25A+

tuuziru /-ru; tuuzita/ make oneself understood, get through 13A

tuyôi /-katta/ is strong 12A+

tûyosa strength 24B+

tuyu rainy season 22A

tuzukeru /-ru; tuzuketa/ continue [something] 26B

　hanásì o tuzukeru continue a talk 26B+

tuzuku /-u; tuzuita/ [something] continues 26B

　tuzúita sèki adjoining (continuous) seats 26B+

tya tea 5B+

tyairo brown 5B+

-tyaku arriving 19A

　Tookyoo-tyaku arriving in Tokyo 19A+

　itî-zi-tyaku arriving at one o'clock 19A

-tyaku /classifier for counting suits/ 23A+

-tyañ /polite suffix added to children's and young people's names/ 10A

tyanoma (Japanese-style) living room, sitting room 17B+

tyañto properly; exactly; neatly 17A

tyawañ bowl (for rice) 15B+

tyokusetu direct 26B

　tyokusetu iu say directly 26B

tyoodai↓: Mizu tyoodai.↓ Let me have some water! 28B+

tyoodai-suru↓ accept /humble-polite/ 18A

　aríğátàku tyoodai-suru↓ accept gratefully 18A

tyoodo exactly 4B

-tyoome /classifier for naming chome/ 14B

tyôtto a bit; a little 1A

　Tyotto.. I'm afraid not . . . /polite refusal/ 1A

-tyuu [in] the middle of 13A; throughout 24B

hanasi-tyuu [in] the middle of talk; 'the line is busy' 13A

gozeñ-tyuu all morning long 24B

gozeñ-tyuu ni within the morning

Tyûuğoku China 5B+

tyuuğokuğo Chinese language 2A

tyuúğokùziñ a Chinese 10B+

tyûui caution; advice; warning 29A+

tyûui o harâu pay attention 29A+

tyûui o hiku attract [someone's] attention 29A+

komákài tyûui meticulous attention 29A+

tyûui-suru pay attention, be careful of; advise, warn 29A

keñkoo ni tyûui-suru pay attention to one's health 29A+

kuruma ni tyûui-suru be careful of the cars 29A+

soó sinai yòo ni tyûui-suru warn not to do that 29A+

tyuúka-ryòori Chinese cooking 15B

tyuumoñ an order (for something) 14A+

tyuumoñ-suru place an order 14A

udê arm 17A+

uê/ue top; up; over 17B

ueki plant 17B+

uekiya gardener 17B+

ueru /-ru; ueta/ plant 17B+

uğókàsu /-u; uğókàsita/ move [something] 30B+

uğôku /-u; uğôita/ [something] moves 30B

ukağau /-u; ukağatta/↓ inquire, ask 6A; visit 13B /humble-polite/

ukêru /-ru; ûketa/ undergo; take (of courses, exams, etc.) 27A+

uketuke receptionist 10B

umâi /-katta/ is skilled; is delicious 24A

ûmâku mazîru irô colors that blend well 26A+

umareru /-ru; umareta/ be born 27B+

ume plum 15A+

Umeteñ (name of tempura restaurant) 15A

ûmi ocean, sea 15A

umu /-u; uñda/ lay (eggs); give birth 29A+

kodomo o umu give birth to a child 29A+

uñteñ-suru drive a vehicle 16B+

uñtèñsyu driver, chauffeur 16B+

urâ reverse side; rear 7B

urésìi /-katta/ is happy, glad 26B+

urésisòo na kao happy-looking face/ expression 26B+

uru /-u; utta/ sell 19A

urúsài /-katta/ is noisy, harassing, a nuisance 26B

urúsài señsèe a teacher who is a nuisance 26B+

urúsài moñdai a bothersome problem 26B+

usiro back; rear 6A

usui /-katta/ is thin (of liquids); is weak (of coffee, tea, etc.); is pale (of colors) 15B+; is thin (of flat objects) 23B+

utâ song 29B+

utau /-u; utatta/ sing 29B+

utâ o utau sing songs 29B+

uti interval 13B; among 15B

tikâi uti ni in the near future 13B

A to B to C no uti de (being) among A and B and C 15B

konó mit-tù no uti de (being) among these three things 15B

osóku narànai uti ni while it hasn't become late; before it gets late 30B

utî house, home; household; in-group 7B

uti no /+ nominal/ our household's, our 7B

ûtu /-u; ûtta/ hit, strike; impress 26A+

taípuràitaa o ûtu use a typewriter 26A+

pisútoru o ùtu shoot a pistol 26A+

tokee ğa kû-zi o ûtta the clock struck nine 26A+

uwaği jacket 23B

wa /assertive sentence-particle/ 9A

wa /ptc/ in regard to; at least; comparatively speaking 4A

Tanáka-sañ wa wakarimàsu. Mr/s. Tanaka (at least) understands. 4A

Siñbuñ wa kaimasèñ desita. A paper (in contrast) I didn't buy. 4A

Konó heñ nì wa arímasèñ. It's not around here (at least). 6A

sitê wa having done 22B

sitê wa 'ikenai/narânai [one] must not do 22B

sinâkute wa 'ikenai/narânai [one] must do 22B

hoká no hitò de wa dekînai being (i.e., if it is) another person, it can't be done 22B

waapuro word processor 3A+

wabi apology 30B+ *See* **(o)wabi**

waee Japanese–English 2B

waée-zìteñ Japanese–English dictionary 2B

wahuku Japanese-style clothing 23A+

wâiñ wine 5B+

waisyatu man's dress shirt 23A+

wakâi /-katta/ is young 10A+

wakâru /-u; wakàtta/ be(come) comprehensible; understand 1A

wâke reason, cause, grounds 27B

  wâke no wakàrànai koto things that are meaningless 27B+

  môñku o iú wàke ğa âru there is cause for complaint 27B+

  Dôo iu wâke de okôtta? For what reason did you get angry? 27B+

  nobâsu wake ni wa 'ikanai can't really postpone 27B

  ikú wàke ni mo 'ikanai can't really even/also go 27B

wañrùumu one-room unit; studio apartment 24B

warau /-u; waratta/ laugh 29B+

wareware we 29B

  waréware nihoñzìñ we Japanese 29B+

warûi /-katta/ is bad; is wrong 7A

Wâseda Waseda University 12B+

Wasîñtoñ Washington 8A

wasitu Japanese-style room 21A+

wasuremono thing forgotten and left behind 14A+

wasureru /-ru; wasureta/ forget 12B

wasyoku Japanese-style food 15A

wata(ku)si I; me 2B

wataru /-u; watatta/ go over, go across 19B+

watasu /-u; watasita/ hand over 19B

wâzawaza purposely, specially 18A

ya /particle/

  susî ya sasímì things like sushi and sashimi 15A

yahâri /see **yappàri**/

yakámasìi /-katta/ is noisy, loud; is fault-finding, strict 26B+

  yakámasìi moñdai a much-discussed problem 26B+

  yakámasìi titioya a strict father 26B+

yakeru /-ru; yaketa/ get burned, baked, roasted 23A

  hi ni yakeru get sunburned 23A+

yakû duty, role, office 20B+

yakû ni tâtu be of use 20B

yakû ni tatêru put to use 20B+

  watákusi de oyaku ni tàtu koto things that will be of use to you because of me; something for which I'll be of use 28A

X o yakû ni tatêru put X to use 20B+

yaku /-u; yaita/ burn [something]; bake; roast 23A+

  tê o yaku burn one's fingers 23A+

yakusoku appointment; promise 10A

yakusoku-suru make an appointment; promise 10A+

yamâ mountain 15A

yameru /-ru; yameta/ quit; give up 8B

yamu /-u; yañda/ stop (of rain, snow, etc.) 22A+

yânusi landlord 24B

yaoya vegetable store 7B+

yappàri after all 3B

yarínaòsu /-u; yarínaòsita/ redo 16B+

yaru /-u; yatta/ do 16B

yaru /-u; yatta/ give (to you/him/her/them) 17A+

  kasite yaru lend (to you/him/her/them) 17A+

yasai vegetable 15A+

yasasii /-katta/ is easy 3B+

  yasásii hitò a person who is gentle, kind, nice 11A

yasûi /-katta/ is cheap 1A

-yasui /-katta/ is marked by ease 13A+

  siyásùi is easy to do 13A+

yasúmì vacation; holiday; time off 8A

yasûmu /-u; yasûñde/ rest; take time off 8A+

yâsusa cheapness 24B

yâtiñ rent 24B

yatto finally, with difficulty; barely, only, just 25A

yaí-tù eight units 5A+

yawárakài /-katta/ is soft; is tender 15B+

yo /informative sentence particle/ 1A

yobu /-u; yoñda/ summon, call 9A

yôi /-katta/ is good 1B+

yokee /na/ excessive, unnecessary, uncalled for 29A

yoko side 17B+

  yoko ni oku place on its side or at the side of 17B+

Yokohama Yokohama 8A+

yôku /see **ii**/

Yôku irássyaimàsita. Welcome! 18A

yômîkaki reading and writing 25A

yômu /-u; yôñda/ read 12A+

yôñ four 2B

yoo way of ——ing 22B

    siyoo/syoo way of doing 22B+

yôo /na/ manner; resemblance; seeming 24A

    aíte (i)ru yòo seeming to be open or available 24A+

    anâta no yoo na hito a person like you 24A+

    anâta no yoo ni nihóñgo ga zyoozù da is good in Japanese the way you are 24A+

    surú yòo ni iu tell [someone] to do 24A

    tukáu yòo ni suru try to use; act so as to use 24A

    syabêru yoo ni nâru reach the point of speaking 24A

yoohuku Western-style clothing 23A+

yooma Western-style room 21A+

Yoóròppa Europe 8B

yoosu the state of things; manner; appearance 26A

yoosyoku Western-style food 15A+

yoozi matters to attend to 9B

    yoozi de iku go on business 12B

yori /ptc/ more than 15A

    sasímì yori more than sashimi; compared to sashimi 15A

    sasímì yori îi is better than sashimi 15A

    koré o yòmu yori omósiròi is more interesting than reading this 20A+

yorókòbu /-u; yorókòñda/ take pleasure in 16B

    yorókòñde ukagau ↓ visit with pleasure 16B

yorosii /-katta/ is good, fine, all right; never mind 5B

    Yorosiku. (May things go well.) 11B+

    Ôkusañ ni yorosiku. Regards to your wife. 11B+

yoru /-u; yotta/ stop in 16B

yoru /-u; yotta/ rely, depend; lean 22A

    X ni yoru to according to X 22A

    X ni yotte depending on X 22A

yôru evening; night 8B+

yotee plan, program, schedule 27A

    yotée o tatèru set up a plan 27A+

    yotée yòri hâyâku/osoku ahead of/behind schedule 27A+

yoteehyoo (written) schedule 27A

yoꞋ-tù four units 5A+

yowâi /-katta/ is weak 12A

    suúzi ni yowài is poor at numbers 12A

yoyaku reservation 21A

yoyaku-suru make a reservation 21A+

yu hot water 14A+

yubî finger 17A+

yukata light cotton kimono 23B+

yukî snow 4A+

yukꞋkùri slowly; leisurely 12A

    Dôozo, goyúkkùri. Take it easy! 12A+

yuúbè last night 10A+

yuúbìñkyoku post office 6B

yuugata evening 25B

yuumee /na/ famous; notorious 20B

yuútàañ U-turn 7B

yuútàañ-suru make a U-turn 7B

zadâñkai round-table discussion; symposium 18B+

zañꞋnèñ /na/ regrettable; too bad; a pity 2A

zassi magazine 2B+

zêhi by all means 24A

zêmi seminar 10A

zêñbu all; the whole thing 3B

zeñzeñ /+ negative/ not at all 3B

zêro zero 12A+

zettai ni absolutely 22B

zi written symbol; letter; character 28A

-zi /classifier for naming the o'clocks/ 8A

zibuñ oneself 17A+

    zibuñ de yaru do by oneself 17A+

    zibuñ no kuruma one's own car 17A+

z(i)eé-àaru Japan Railway 19A+

ziipañ blue jeans 23A

zikañ time 8A+

    zikáñ ga àru have time 8A+

    zikáñ ga kakàru take time 15B

    zikáñ-dòori on time 26B+

-zikañ /classifier for counting hours/ 8A+

zîko accident 9B

zikokuhyoo timetable 19A

zimûsyo office 11A+

ziñrùigaku anthropology 25B+

zîñzya Shinto shrine 6B+

zîsa time difference 22A+

zisá-syùkkiñ staggered work hours; flextime 22A

zisiñ earthquake 9B+

zîsyo dictionary 2B

zitêñsya bicycle 7B+

zitû truth, reality 13B

  zitû o iu speak the truth 13B+

  zitû wa in reality, the fact is 13B

zyûu /na/ free, unrestricted 16B+

zyûugyoo freelance worker 16B+

zyûuseki free (unreserved) seat 19A+

zizyoo circumstances, conditions; the situation 27A

  zizyoo ga tigau circumstances are different 27A+

  zizyóo ni yòtte depending on circumstances 27A+

  katee no zizyoo household situation 27A+

zoñzìru ↓ **/-ru; zôñzita/** get to know /humble-polite/ 10B+

  zôñzite (i)ru ↓ [I] know /humble-polite/ 10B+

  gozôñzi da ↑ [you] know /honorific-polite/ 10B+

zoori sandals (for outdoors) 23A+

zuibuñ awfully; very 8B

zutto by far 10B; without interruption 26B

  zutto màe way before; long ago 10B

  konó hòo ga zutto ìi this one is much better 15A

  zutto beñkyoo-sitè (i)ta [I] was studying the whole time, without interruption 26B+

zutu of each; for each; at a time 5B

zyâ(a)/contraction of **dê wa**/ that being the case, in that case, then 2B

  sôo zya nâi it's not so 2A

Kîree ni kâite âru zya nai ka. Isn't it written neatly? Surely you agree that it's written neatly! 28A

Dekîru zya nai ka. Surely you can do it! 28A+

Yasásìi zya nai ka. Don't you agree it's easy? 28A+

zyama nuisance, bother; interruption 17B

  Ozyáma desyòo ga.. Excuse me for interrupting you. 17B+

  Ozyáma-(ita)simàsita. Excuse me for having interrupted you. 17B+

zyâñ·kêñ·pôñ "rock, paper, scissors" (game) 29A+

zyâñpaa windbreaker; jacket 23A

zyogiñgu jogging 26B+

-zyoo /classifier for counting jo (= the area covered by one tatami mat) 24B+

zyôo deluxe 14B

zyoobu /na/ strong; rugged; sturdy 12A+

zyoósyàkeñ passenger ticket 19A+

zyoózù /na/ skillful; skilled 9B

  zyoózù ni nâru become skillful; become skilled 9B

zyosee woman, female 19B

zyoseego women's language 19B+

zyûgyoo schooltime; classtime 8A

zyugyoo-suru teach classes; give lessons 9B+

-zyuu throughout 13A+

  iti-neñ-zyuu all year long 13A+

  kotosi-zyuu ni within this year 13A+

zyûu ten 2B

zyuueñdama ¥10 coin 19A+

zyûusyo address 25B

English–Japanese Glossary

This glossary, which includes vocabulary introduced in Part 1, Part 2, and Part 3 of this text, is intended as a reminder list for use when vocabulary items have been temporarily forgotten. It is not intended as a means of acquiring new vocabulary. On those occasions when both an item and the patterns in which it occurs have been forgotten, the Japanese equivalent should be located in this glossary and then further checked by using the Japanese–English glossary and the index.

Verbals are identified by a hyphen, the location of which identifies the verbal class: **X-u** = consonant verbal; **X-ru** = vowel verbal; **X-aru** = special polite verbal (cf. Lesson 9A-SP1 in Part 1).

Adjectivals are identified by a hyphen separating the root from **-i**, the imperfective ending: **X-i**.

Na-nominals are identified by /**na**/ immediately following the item: **X** /**na**/.

Polite alternates are included in cases where their use is particularly common and/or is in some way unusual or unpredictable in form.

A.M. **gôzeñ**
abdomen **harâ**
about (approximate amount) **-ĝùrai**
about (approximate point in time) **-ĝòro**
about as much as **-hodo**
about how much? **dono-ĝurai**
absence from home **rûsu**
absolutely **zettai ni**
academic department **gakubu**
academic organization **gakkai**
accept **mora-u; itadak-u ↓; tyoodai-suru ↓**
accept for temporary keeping **azúkàr-u**
accident **zîko**
accidentally **tûi**
according to X **X ni yoru to**
accustomed: become ~ **narê-ru**
acquainted: become ~ **tikázùk-u**
act **kotô**
address **zyûusyo**
adjoining place **tonari**
adjoining seats **tuzúita sèki**
adulteration **mazírì**

advertisement **kookoku**
advice **tyûui**
advise **tyûui-suru**
after **kara** /ptc/
  ~ that; and then **sore kara**
after (past) **-suĝi**
  ten ~ one **itî-zi zíppùñ-suĝi**
after all **yahâri/yappàri**
after a long interval **hisasiburi**
afternoon **gôĝo**
again **matâ**
ago **mâe**
  a while ~ **sakihodo; sâkki**
agree to **syooti-suru**
ahead **saki**
  (Excuse me for going) ahead of you. **Osaki ni.**
aimed at **-muki**
air **kûuki**
airplane **hikôoki**
airport **kuukoo**
alcove **tokonoma**

266

ll   mińnà; zeñbu

ll day long   iti-niti-zyuu

ll right   daízyòobu /na/

  is ~   îi/yô-i; yorosi-i

lmost   hotôñdo

lone   hitô-ri (de)

lready   môo

lso   mo /particle/

lternative   hôo

lways   îtu mo

mazing: is ~   mezúrasì-i

mbassador   tâisi

merica   Amerika

merican (person)   amérikàziñ

merican Consulate   Amérika-ryoozìkañ

merican Embassy   Amérika-taisìkañ

mong ——   —— no nâka/uti

muse oneself   asob-u

nd/or   to ka

ngry: become ~   okôr-u; harâ ğa tât-u

nnoy [someone]   mêewaku o kakê-ru

nnoyance   mêewaku

  become an ~   mêewaku ni nâr-u

nother   hoka

nswer (verb)   kotáè-ru

nswer   kotâe

nswer the telephone   deńwa ni dè-ru

nthropology   zińrùiğaku

ny time   itú dè mo

partment (house)   apâato; mâñsyoñ

partment manager, superintendent   kañriniñ

pologetic: is ~   kyoósyuku dà

pologize   ayámàr-u; (o)wabi o i-u

pology   (o)wabi

pparently is X   X-rasì-i

ppeal   ki ni ir-u

ppear   miê-ru

ppearance   yoosu

ppear on television   têrebi ni dê-ru

ppointment   yakusoku

  make an ~   yakusoku-suru

  previous ~   señyaku

ppreciation: expression of ~   (o)ree

ppreciative: is ~   kyoósyuku dà

pproach   tikázùk-u

rchitect   keñtikuka

rchitecture   keñtiku

rea (vicinity)   heñ; (size) hîrosa

rgue   keñka-suru

rm   ude

round: go ~, be passed ~   mawar-u

send ~, pass ~   mawas-u

arrive   tuk-u

arriving (at a time or place)   -tyaku

article, thesis   roñbuñ

as: ~ a friend   tomodati to site

as if X   X-mìtai /na/

as much as possible   narubeku; dekiru dake

ask   kik-u; ukağa-u ↓

ask for   tanôm-u

assistance   tetúdài

associate   tukíà-u

associate with   tikázukè-ru

at any rate   tônikaku

attach   tukê-ru; be(come) attached   tûk-u

attached   -tuki

attend   dê-ru

attendance at the office   syukkiñ

attention   ki

  pay ~   ki ó tukè-ru; tyûui-suru

aunt   oba; obasañ /polite/

auspicious: is ~   medétà-i

Australia   Oósutorària

Australian (person)   oósutorariàziñ

autumn   âki

available: be ~   aite (i)-ru

avenue   toórì

average, the mean   heekiñ

aware: become ~   ki ğá tùk-u

awful: is ~   taíhèñ /na/; monósuğò-i; suğô-i

awfully   zûibuñ; taiheñ

baby   âkatyañ

back   usiro; urâ

back (body part)   senaka

  lower ~   kosî

back up   modôr-u

bacon   bêekoñ

bad: is ~   damê /na/; warû-i

bag   kabañ

baggage service   takkyuubiñ

bake [something]   yak-u; get baked   yake-ru

ballpoint pen   boorupeñ

bamboo   take

bank   giñkoo

Bank of America   Amérika-gìñkoo

banker   gińkòoiñ

barely   yatto

bath   hurô

  with ~   basu-tuki

bathroom   huróbà

bear   gâmañ-suru

beat **tatâk-u**
be called **i-u; ośsy-àru** ↑ **; môos-u** ↓
be in a hurry **isôĝ-u**
be located (of animate existence) **i-ru; irássy-àru** ↑ **; ôr-u** ↓ **~ +**
be located (of inanimate existence) **âr-u; goz-âru +**
be named **i-u; ośsy-àru** ↑ **; môos-u** ↓
be on time **ma ní à-u**
be possible **dekî-ru**
because **kara** /ptc/
become **nâr-u**
bed **bêtto/bêddo**
  put to ~ **nekas-u**
  go to ~ **ne-ru**
bedroom **siñsitu**
beer **bîiru**
before **mâe**
begin [something] **hazime-ru;** [something] begins **hazimar-u**
  begin —— **-hazime-ru**
begin (gradually) to —— **-te kuru**
beginning **hazime**
behave like a spoiled child **amae-ru**
belly **harâ**
below **sita**
bend [something] **maĝe-ru;** [something] bends **maĝar-u**
benefit **tamê**
between **aida**
beverage **nomîmono**
beyond **mukôo/mukoo**
  go ~ **suĝî-ru**
bicycle **zitêñsya**
big: is ~ **oókì-i; ôoki na** /+ nom/; (of area) **hirô-i**
bill (currency) **satu**
  ¥500 ~ **gohyákuèñsatu**
  ¥10,000 ~ **itímañèñsatu**
bind **sibâr-u**
biology **seébutùĝaku**
birth: give ~ **um-u**
  give ~ to a child **kodomo o um-u**
black: is ~ **kurô-i**
bland: is ~ **ama-i**
blouse **burâusu**
blow **hûk-u**
blue: is ~ **aô-i**
blue jeans **ziipañ**
board (a vehicle) **nor-u**
boat **hûne**

body **karada**
book **hôñ**
bookshelf **hôñdana**
bookstore; book dealer **hôñya**
boring: is ~ **tumáràna-i**
born: be ~ **umare-ru**
borrow **kari-ru; haisyaku-suru** ↓
both **dôtira mo**
  ~ parents **ryôosiñ; goryôosiñ** /polite/
  ~ people **huta-ri to mo**
  ~ this one and that one **kore mo sore mo**
bother **zyama**
  while it's a ~ for you **goméñdoo-nàgara**
  become a ~ **méñdòo ni nâr-u**
bothersome **méñdòo** /na/
bottom **sita**
bowl (for rice) **tyawañ;** (for soup) **(o)wañ**
box **hako**
box lunch **beñtòo**
boy **otókò no ko**
bread **pâñ**
break [something] **kowâs-u;** [something] breaks **kowárè-ru**
break down **kosyoo-suru**
breakable: is ~ **kowáre-yasù-i**
breakfast **aságòhañ**
bright person **atámà no hatarak-u hito**
bring together **atúmè-ru**
bring to life, bring into use **ikâs-u**
bring up **sodátè-ru**
broken: become ~ **kowárè-ru**
brother: older ~ **âni; (o)nîisañ** /polite/
  younger ~ **otóotò; otootosañ** /polite/
brown **tyairo**
Buddhist temple **terâ**
build **tatê-ru;** get built **tât-u**
building **tatêmòno; bîru**
bullet train **siñkàñseñ**
burn [something] **yak-u;** get burned **yake-r**
bus **bâsu**
business card **meesi**
  cards on hand **meesi no motiawase**
business trip **syuttyoo**
bustling **niĝiyaka** /na/
busy: is ~ **isóĝasì-i**
  Thank you for giving me your time when y(are ~. **Oísoĝasii tokorò (o) arîĝatoo g zaimasu. +**
but **sikasi; d-âtte**
butter **bâta**
button **botañ**

buy **ka-u**
by all means **zêhi**
by far **zutto**

cake **kêeki; okâsi**
calculate **keesañ-suru**
calculator **keésàñki**
call (summon) **yob-u**
call on the telephone **deñwa o kakè-ru; deñwa-suru**; be called on the telephone **deñwa ğa kakàr-u**
be called, be named **i-u; ossy-àru ↑**; **môos-u ↓**
calm **heeki /na/; sîzuka /na/**
camera **kâmera**
candy **okâsi**
car **kuruma**
care **nêñ**
use ~ **nêñ o ire-ru**
Take ~ of yourself. **Odaizi ni.**
careful **têenee /na/**
be ~ **ki ó tukè-ru; tyûui-suru**
carelessly **tûi**
caretaker **rusubañ**
act as a ~ **rusubañ o suru**
carpenter **dâiku**
carry **hakob-u**
case, circumstance **baai**
cat **nêko**
catch a cold **kaze o hik-u**
cause **wâke**
caution **tyûui**
certain, positive **tâsika /na/**
certainly **kitto; tâsika ni**
Certainly. I'll do as you asked. **Kasí-komarimàsita.**
chair **isu**
change **kawari**
change: make ~ **ryôoğae-suru**
change (= money) **oturi**
change [something] **kae-ru;** [something] changes **kawar-u**
change clothing **kikáè-ru/kiğáè-ru**
change places **kawar-u**
character: written ~ **zi**
chat **syabêr-u**
chauffeur **uñtèñsyu**
cheap: is ~ **yasû-i**
cheapness **yâsusa**
check, look into **sirábè-ru**
check, the bill **kañzyoo**

cheerful: is ~ (of people) **akaru-i**
chemistry **kâğaku**
cherry **sakura**
chest (body part) **munê**
chest (furniture) **tañsu**
chicken **tori**
child **kodomo; ko; okosañ** /polite/
China **Tyuuğoku**
Chinese (person) **tyuúğokùziñ**
Chinese character **kañzi**
Chinese language **tyuuğokuğo**
choose **erâb-u**
chopsticks **hâsi**
Christian era, A.D. **seereki**
church **kyookai**
cigarette **tabako**
cigarette shop **tabakoya**
circle **maru**
circumstance **baai**
circumstances **zizyoo**
city **tokai**
small ~ **matî**
large ~ **sî; daítòkai**
class **kûrasu**
classifiers *See* Appendix B
classroom **kyoositu**
classtime **zyûğyoo**
clean (verb) **soozi-suru**
clean **kîree /na/**
clear: become ~ (of weather) **harê-ru**
clear(ly) **hakkìri**
clever person **atámà no hatarak-u hito**
clock **tokee**
clogs **geta**
close: bring ~ **tikázukè-ru**
close [something] **simê-ru;** become closed **simâr-u**
closet **osiire**
clothing **hukû**
Western-style ~ **yoohuku**
cloudy: become ~ **kumôr-u**
coat **ôobaa; kôoto**
coffee **koóhìi**
coffee shop **kissàteñ/kissateñ**
coin: ¥5 ~ **goeñdama**
¥100 ~ **hyakueñdama**
cold: get ~ **samê-ru**
cold: is ~ **tumeta-i;** (of atmosphere only) **samû-i**
cold: a ~ **kaze**
cold(ness) **sâmusa**

collapse **taórè-ru; tubure-ru**
colleague: ~ of equal status **doohai; dooryoo**
  junior ~ **koohai**
  senior ~ **seṅpai**
collect (bring together) **atúmè-ru**; (come together) **atúmàr-u**
college **daiǧaku;** (within a university) **gakubu**
color **irô**
  facial ~ **kaoiro**
  what ~? **naniiro; dôṅna irô**
come **kú-ru** /irreg/; **irássy-àru** ↑ ; **mâir-u** ↓
come back; come home **kâette ku-ru**
comedy monologue (traditional Japanese) **rakuǧo**
come out **dê-ru**
come together **atúmàr-u**
come up **aǧar-u**
comfortable **rakû /na/**
communicate **tuuzi-ru**
commute **kayo-u**
  ~ to school **tuuǧaku-suru**
  ~ to work **tuukiṅ-suru**
commuting time **tuúkiṅ-zìkaṅ**
commuting to work **tuukiṅ**
company **kaisya**
company employee **kaísyàiṅ**
company president **syatyoo**
comparable: a ~ thing **kurabemono**
compare **kurabe-ru**
complain **môṅku o i-u**
complaint **môṅku**
completed: become ~ **dekî-ru**
completely **suḱkàri**
complicated **hukuzatu /na/**
comprehensible: become ~ **wakâr-u**
computer **koṅpyùutaa**
computer program **koṅpyuutaa-purogùramu**
concern **kizûkai**
  become a cause for ~ **ki ní nàr-u**
  ~ oneself about **ki ni suru**
concerning —— —— **ni tûite**
concert **oṅǧàkùkai**
condition **guai**
condition just as it is **mamà**
conditions **zizyoo**
conference **kâiǧi**
conference room **kaíǧìsitu**
confront **muka-u**
confused: become ~ **awate-ru**
Congratulations. **Omédetoo gozaimàsu. +**
connection **kaṅkee**

connections **kône**
conscientious **mazime /na/; têenee /na/**
consent to **syooti-suru; nattoku-suru**
consider **kaṅgaè-ru**
considerate **sîṅsetu /na/**
consul **ryôozi**
consulate **ryoózìkaṅ**
consult **soodaṅ-suru**
consultant **koṅsàrutaṅto**
contact **reṅraku-suru**
contact lens(es) **kôṅtakuto(-rèṅzu)**
contents **naiyoo**
continue [something] **tuzuke-ru**; [somethin】 continues **tuzuk-u**
convenience **tuǧoo; bêṅ**
convenient **bêṅri /na/**
  is ~ **tuǧóo ǧa ìi; bêṅ ǧa îi**
conversation **kaiwa**
conversely **haṅtai ni**
convinced: be(come) convinced **nattoku-suru**
cook, prepare food **ryôori-suru**
cooking **ryôori**
cool: is ~ **suzúsì-i**
copy **kôpii-suru**
corner: street ~ **kâdo**
correct **naôs-u**
corridor **rooka**
country, nation **kuni**
  the ~ **inaka**
cousin **itôko; oitokosaṅ** /polite/
cramped: is ~ **semâ-i**
cross-talk comedy **maṅzài**
crowd: a ~ **oózèe**
crowded: be(come) ~ **kôm-u**
crush **tubus-u**; become crushed **tubure-ru**
cry **nak-u**
cup: coffee ~ **kâppu;** tea ~ **yunómì**
cupboard **todana**
custard pudding **pûriṅ**
cut, cut off **kîr-u**
cute: is ~ **kawâi-i**

damaged: become ~ **kowárè-ru**
damn! **simâtta**
dangerous: is ~ **abuna-i**
dark: is ~ (of colors) **kô-i;** (gloomy) **kura-i**

daughter **musúmè; musumesaṅ, ozyôosaṅ** /polite/
day **hî/hi**
  ~ after tomorrow **asâtte; myoóǧòniti**

~ before yesterday **otótòi**
the other ~ **konaida; señzitu**
the very ~, the ~ in question **toozitu**
daytime **hirû**
decide **kime-ru;** be(come) decided **kimar-u**
~ on X **X ni suru/kime-ru**
~ to X **X kotô ni suru/kime-ru**
be(come) decided that [someone] will X **X
kotô ni nâr-u/kimar-u**
delicious: is ~ **oisi-i; umâ-i**
It was ~. **Gotísoosama (dèsita).**
deliver **todókè-ru;** be delivered **todôk-u**
delivery (of prepared food) **demae**
deluxe (of food orders) **zyôo**
dentist **hâisya**
depart **tât-u; dê-ru**
departing **-hatu**
department store **depâato**
depend **yor-u**
depending on X **X ni yotte**
depth (of color) **kôsa**
derived from **-teki /na/**
descend **orî-ru**
describe: the thing described as —— —— to
i-û no
desk **tukue**
desolate: is ~ **sabísì-i**
destroy face **kao o tubus-u**
detach **hanâs-u;** become detached **hanárè-ru**
detailed: is ~ **kuwásì-i; komákà-i**
details **kuwásìi koto**
dictionary **zîsyo**
English–Japanese ~ **eéwa-zìteñ**
die (of humans and animals) **sin-u; nakunar-u**
different: be ~ **tiğa-u**
difficult: is ~ **muzukasi-i**
difficulty **muzúkasìsa**
with ~ **yatto**
is marked by ~ **-nikù-i**
dilute **mizú o mazè-ru**
dine **syokuzi-suru**
dining **syokuzi**
dining room **syokudoo**
dinner **bañgòhañ**
dinner party (Japanese-style) **eñkai**
diplomacy **gaikoo**
diplomat **gaíkòokañ**
direct **tyokusetu**
direction **hôo**
dirty **kitánà-i**
disagreeable **iyâ /na/**

disappear (of inanimates) **nakunar-u;** (of animates) **ináku nàr-u**
disappointed: become ~ **gaḱkàri-suru**
discipline (verb) **sitúkè-ru**
discipline **situke**
disconcerted: become ~ **awate-ru**
discouraged: become ~ **gaḱkàri-suru**
disgrace **kao o tubus-u;** become disgraced
kao ğa tubure-ru
dislike **kirai /na/**
disorganized: become ~ **awate-ru**
displeased: be(come) ~ **ki ó wàrùku suru**
displeasing **kirai /na/**
distance **kyôri**
division (of a company) **bû/bu**
division manager **bûtyoo/butyoo**
divorced: get ~ **rikoñ-suru**
do **suru** /irreg/; **nas-âru** ↑; **itas-u** ↓; **yar-u**
can ~ **dekî-ru**
doctor **señsèe**
doctor (medical) **isya; señsèe**
dog **inû**
doll **niñğyoo**
Don't bother. **Okámai nàku.**
Don't mention it. **Dôo itasimasite.**
door **dôa; to**
sliding, opaque ~ **husúmà**
sliding, translucent ~ **syoozi**
screen ~ **amîdo**
storm ~ **amâdo**
double room **dâbúru(-rùumu)**
down **sita**
draw **kâk-u**
drawer **hikidasi**
dreadful: is ~ **suğô-i; monósuğò-i**
dress **dôresu**
drink **nôm-u; mesiağar-u** ↑; **itadak-u** ↓
drink, beverage **nomîmono**
drive (a vehicle) **uñteñ-suru**
driver **úñtèñsyu**
drop [something] **otôs-u;** [something] drops
otî-ru
drugstore **kusuriya**
dry: become ~ **kawâk-u**
dust **gomî**
duty **girî**

each: of ~, for ~ **-zutu**
ear **mimî**
early, in good time **hayámè ni**
early: is ~ **hayâ-i**

earthquake **zisiñ**
ease: is marked by ~ **-yasù-i**
east **hiǧásì**
east entrance **hiǧasiǧuti**
easy: is ~ **yasasi-i**
eat **tabê-ru; mesiaǧar-u** ↑ ; **itadak-u** ↓
economic **keezai-teki /na/**
economics, economy **kêezai**
editorial **syasetu**
education **kyooiku;** (as a subject)
　kyoóikùǧaku
　~ mother **kyoóiku-màma**
　an educated/uneducated person **kyoóiku no
　àru/nài hito**
effort: with special ~ **seḱkakù**
egg **tamâǧo; êggu**
eight **hatî**
　~ days; eighth of the month **yoo-ka**
　~ units **yaṫ-tù**
either one **dotíra dè mo**
elect **erâb-u**
electric train **deñsya/dêñsya**
electricity; electric lights **dêñki**
embarrassed: is ~ **hazúkasì-i**
embassy **taísìkañ**
emergency **hizyoo /na/**
eminent **rippa /na/;** is ~ **erâ-i**
employed: become ~ **tutómè-ru**
　work for a department store **depâato ni tu-
　tômete (i)-ru**
empty: become ~ **suk-u**
end (verb) **owar-u**
end: bring to an ~ **sumásè-ru;** come to an
　~ **sûm-u**
end: the ~ **owari**
end of the street, corridor, etc. **tukiatari**
endure **gâmañ-suru**
energetic **gêñki /na/**
engineer **gîsi**
engineering **kooǧaku**
England **Eekoku; Iǧirisu**
English conversation **eékàiwa**
English–Japanese **eewa**
　~ dictionary **eéwa-zìteñ**
English (person) **iǧírisùziñ; eékokùziñ**
English language **eeǧo**
enjoyable: is ~ **tanósì-i**
enjoyment **omósìrosa**
enter **hâir-u**
entertain **gotisoo-suru**
entirely **mattaku**

entrance **iriǧuti**
entry hall **gêñkañ**
environment **kañkyoo**
erase **kes-u;** be(come) erased **kie-ru**
erect [something] **tatê-ru**
essay **roñbuñ**
etc. **nâdo; nâñka**
Europe **Yoóròppa**
even **mo /ptc/; -àtte; sàe /ptc/**
even so **dê mo; d-âtte; soré ni sitè mo**
evening **bañ; yôru; yuuǧata**
every day **mâiniti**
every month **maituki; maiǧetu**
every morning **mâiasa**
every night **mâibañ; maiyo**
every time **maido**
every week **maisyuu**
every year **maitosi; maineñ**
everyone **mińnà; minâsañ /polite/**
everything **mińnà; zêñbu**
exactly **tyoodo; haḱkìri; tyañto**
　exact time **haḱkìri-sita zikañ**
exam **sikêñ**
example: for ~ **tatôeba**
excess: go to ~ **suǧî-ru**
excessive **yokee /na/**
exchange **torikae-ru**
exchange money **ryôoǧae-suru**
excuse **moosiwake; iiwake; koozitu**
　a good/poor ~ **umâi/mazûi iiwake**
Excuse me. **Goméñ-nasài.**
exert special effort **gańbàr-u**
exhaust a supply **kirâs-u**
exhausted, tired out **kut(t)akuta**
exit **dêǧuti**
expectation: general ~ **hazu**
expensive: is ~ **takâ-i**
experience (verb) **keekeñ-suru**
experience **keekeñ**
explain **setumee-suru**
explanation **setumee**
explanation, excuse **moosiwake; iiwake; kooz
　itu**
exposure to the sun **hiatari**
express **kyuukoo**
　special ~ **tokúbetu-kyùukoo; tokkyuu**
　~ ticket **kyuúkòokeñ**
expression **kao**
extend [something] **nobâs-u;** [something] ex
　tends **nobî-ru; todôk-u**
extension **naiseñ**

extent **hodo**
  to that ~, that much **sore hodo; soñna ni**
extinguish **kes-u;** be(come) extinguished
  kie-ru
extraordinary **hizyoo /na/**
extreme **hizyoo /na/**
extremely **hizyoo ni**
eye **mê**
eye doctor **mêisya**
eyeglasses **mêğane**
  put on ~ **mêğane o kakê-ru**

face (verb) **muk-u; muka-u**
face **kao**
facilities; convenience **bêñ**
facing toward **-muki**
fact **kotô**
fairly **kânari**
fall: [something] falls **otî-ru**
fall (of rain, snow, etc.) **hûr-u**
fall (season) **âki**
fall apart **kowárè-ru**
fall down **taórè-ru**
fall sound asleep **gûuguu netya-u**
familiar: is ~ **sitásì-i**
  be too ~ **sitásisuğì-ru**
family **kâzoku; gokâzoku** /polite/
famous **yuumee /na/**
far: as ~ as **made** /ptc/
  is ~ **too-i**
  the ~ away **toókù**
  sound ~ away on the telephone **deñwa ğa
    too-i**
farmer **nôoka**
father **titî; titioya; otôosañ** /polite/
fatigued: become ~ **kutábirè-ru**
fault-finding: is ~ **yakámasì-i**
fearsome: is ~ **kowâ-i**
feel unwell **kimóti ğa warù-i**
feel well **kimóti ğa ìi**
feeling **kimoti**
  have a ~ **ki ğa suru**
fell **taôs-u**
female **oñnà**
few: are ~ **sukúnà-i**
fight **keñka-suru**
finally **yatto**
Finance Ministry **oókuràsyoo**
find **mituke-ru;** be(come) found **mitukar-u**
find employment **syuusyoku-suru**
find out **sir-u; gozôñzi da** ↑ **; zoñzì-ru** ↓

fine **kêkkoo /na/**
  is ~ **îi/yô-i; yorosi-i**
finger **yubî**
finish [something] **sumásè-ru;** [something]
  finishes **sûm-u**
finish ——: ~ saying **iíowàr-u**
fire (conflagration) **kâzi**
first day of the month **tuítatì**
first generation **îs-see**
first time **hazîmete**
fish **sakana**
five **gô**
  ~ units **itû-tu**
  ~ days; fifth of the month **itu-ka**
fix **naôs-u;** be(come) fixed **naôr-u**
flex-time **zisá-syùkkiñ**
flood **oómìzu**
floor **kâi**
floor mat (Japanese-style) **tatami**
flower **hanâ**
flower shop; florist **hanâya**
fluent **perapera**
food **tabémòno; gôhañ**
  Japanese-style ~ **nihoñsyoku; wasyoku**
foot **asî**
for the most part **daitai**
foreign country **gaikoku**
foreign language **gaikokuğo**
Foreign Ministry **gaímùsyoo**
foreign trade **booeki**
foreign trader **boóekìsyoo**
foreigner **gaiziñ, gaíkokùziñ**
forget **wasure-ru**
fork **h(u)ôoku**
formal **h(u)ôomaru /na/**
forte: one's ~ **tokûi/tokui**
four **sî; yôñ**
  ~ units **yoť-tù**
  ~ days; fourth of the month **yok-ka**
fragile: is ~ **kowáre-yasù-i**
fragile article **kowaremono**
France **Hurañsu**
free (of charge) **tâda**
free (unrestricted) **ziyûu /na/**
free time **hima /na/**
freelance work(er) **ziyûuğyoo**
French (person) **huráñsùziñ**
French language **hurañsuğo**
frequent: are ~ **oô-i**
fresh: is ~ **atárasì-i**
Friday **kiñyòo(bi)**

friend **tomodati**
frightening: is ~ **kowâ-i**
from **kara** /ptc/
front **mâe; omótè**
fruit **kudâmono**
full **ippai**
funny: is ~ **okásì-i; okâsi na** /+ nom/; **omó-sirò-i;** (= strange) **okásì-i; okâsi /na/; hêñ /na/**
furniture **kâg̃u**
furniture store **kag̃ûya**

garden **niwa**
gardener **uekiya**
gathering: a ~ **atúmàrì**
geography **tîri**
German (person) **doítùziñ**
German language **doitug̃o**
Germany **Dôitu**
get **mora-u; itadak-u** ↓
get off (a vehicle) **orî-ru**
get on **nor-u**
get through, make oneself understood **tuuzi-ru**
get up **okî-ru;** get [someone] up **okôs-u**
girl **oñnà no ko**
give: ~ (to the in-group) **kure-ru, kudás-àru** ↑
~ (to the out-group) **ag̃e-ru; sasiag̃e-ru** ↓ ;
yar-u
give a ride **nose-ru**
give back, return **kâes-u**
give up, forgo; resign oneself to **akíramè-ru**
give up, quit **yame-ru**
glad: is ~ **urésì-i**
glass (for drinking) **kôppu**
glib **perapera**
gloomy: is ~ (of people) **kura-i**
go **ik-u; irássy-àru** ↑ ; **mâir-u** ↓
~ on foot **arûite iku**
go across **watar-u**
go-between: become a ~ **aída ni hàir-u**
go in **hâir-u**
go out; leave **dê-ru**
go out (of the office or home) **gaisyutu-suru**
be out **gaisyutu-tyuu da**
go out; set out **dekake-ru**
go over **watar-u**
go through **tôor-u**
go up **ag̃ar-u**
Golden Week **goórudeñ-uìiku**
golf **gôruhu**
good **kêkkoo /na/**

is ~ **îi/yô-i; yorosi-i**
Good afternoon. **Koñniti wa.**
Good evening. **Koñbañ wa.**
Good morning. **Oháyoo (gozaimàsu).**
Goodnight. **Oyasumi-nasai.**
Goodbye. **Sayo(o)nara.**
Goodbye. (said by person leaving home) **Ítte ki-màsu; Ítte mairimàsu.** ↓
Goodbye. (said to person leaving home) **Ítte (i)rassyài(màse).** ↑
government employee **koómùiñ**
gradually **sôrosoro**
graduate (from school) **sotug̃yoo-suru**
graduate: a ~ **sotúg̃yòosee**
graduation **sotug̃yoo**
grandfather **sôhu; ozîisañ** /polite/
grandmother **sôbo; obâasañ** /polite/
grateful: is ~ **aríg̃atà-i; kyoósyuku dà**
gratitude: debt of ~ **ôñ**
gray **gurêe; haiiro**
great **kêkkoo /na/; rippa /na/;** is ~ **erâ-i**
green **guríiñ; mídori**
green car **guríiñsya**
greet **mukae-ru; demukae-ru; âisatu (o) suru**
greeting **âisatu**
grow [something] **tukûr-u**
grow up **sodât-u**
guest **kyaku; okyakusañ** /polite/
Guam **Gûamu**
guide **añnàiniñ**
guide, show the way **añnài-suru**

half **-hañ**
~ day **hañ-nitì**
~ month **hañ-tukì**
~ year **hañ-tosì**
half part, half portion **hañbùñ**
hall **rooka**
ham **hâmu**
ham sandwich **hamú-sàndo**
hand **tê**
lend a ~ **tetúdà-u**
hand over **watas-u**
~ for temporary keeping **azúkè-ru**
handbag **hañdobàggu**
Haneda (airport) **Haneda**
hang (something) **kakê-ru**
hang up (on the telephone) **kîr-u**
happy: is ~ **urésì-i**
harassing: is ~ **urúsà-i**
harbor **minato**

hard: is ~ (= difficult) **muzukasi-i; tura-i;**
 (=stiff) **katâ-i**
hardship **kûroo**
hat **boosi**
have **âr-u; môtte (i)-ru**
he **kâre; anô hitò; anó kàtà** /polite/
head **atámà**
health(y) **keñkoo** /na/
hear **kik-u**
heart **siñzoo**
heat **âtusa**
Heavens, no! **Toñde mo nài.**
heavy: is ~ **omo-i**
Heisei Era (1989–) **Heesee**
hello (on the telephone) **môsimosi**
 Hello, I'm back. **Tadaima.**
help (verb) **tetúdà-u**
help **tetúdài**
Help!!! **Tasuketeeee.**
helpful assistance **sewâ**
 Thank you for your ~. **Oséwasama (dèsita).**
here **koko; kotira; kottì**
hereabouts **kotira; kottì**
hey! **hôra**
high school **kookoo**
hiking **hâikiñgu**
hill **oka**
hiragana syllabary **hirâgànà**
history **rekisi**
hit **ût-u**
hmmm! **sâa**
hold back, stand on ceremony **eñryo-suru**
hold in reserve **nokôs-u**
holiday **yasúmì**
home **utî; iê; otaku** /polite/
home delivery (of prepared food) **demae**
homework **syukudai**
hope **kiboo-suru**
 I ~ it ends early. **Hâyâku owaru to/owárèba
 îi desu ğa nêe.**
hospital **byooiñ**
hospital director **îñtyoo**
hospitality: receive ~ **gotísoo ni nàr-u**
hot: is ~ **atû-i;** (= spicy) **karâ-i**
hotel **hôteru**
house; household **utî; iê; otaku** /polite/
house-sit **kawári ni sùm-u**
housing development **dañti**
how? **dôo; ikâğa** /polite/
 How do you do? **Hazímemàsite.**
however **d-âtte; dâ kedo; dê mo**

how many ——? **nañ-/iku-** + classifier
how many units? **îku-tu**
how much? **îkura**
how old? (of people) **îku-tu; nâñ-sai**
hundred **hyakû**
hungry: become ~ **onaka ğa suk-u**
hurts; is painful **itâ-i**
 cry in pain **itâkute 'nak-u**
husband **syûziñ, otto; gosyûziñ** /polite/

I; me **wata(ku)si; bôku**
ice **koori**
ice cream **aísukurìimu**
idea **âidea**
immediately **sûğu**
implements **doóğù**
important **taisetu** /na/; **daízì** /na/
importer-exporter **boóekìsyoo**
impurity **mazírì**
inadvisable: is ~ **mazû-i**
in any case **tônikaku**
in charge of **-ğàkari**
 person in charge of liaison **reñraku-ğàkari**
inclined: be ~ **muk-u**
included: X ~ **X-tuki**
inconvenience: cause ~ **mêewaku o kakê-ru**
inconvenient: is ~ **hûbeñ** /na/; **tuğóo ğa
 warù-i**
increase [something] **huyâs-u;** [something] increases **huê-ru**

India **Îñdo**
Indian (person from India) **iñdòziñ**
indifferent **heeki** /na/
information desk **añnaizyò**
infrequent: is ~ **sukúnà-i**
inn (Japanese-style) **ryokañ**
inquire **kik-u; ukağa-u** ↓
insert **ire-ru**
inside **nâka**
in spite of that **dâ no ni**
instead, on the contrary **kâette**
institute director **syotyoo**
instructor **kyôosi**
intention **tumori**
interact **tukíà-u**
interest **omósìrosa**
interesting: is ~ **omósirò-i**
interpret **tûuyaku-suru**
interpretation **tûuyaku**
interpreter **tûuyaku; tûuyaku no hito**

interruption **zyama**
intersection **koósàteñ**
interval **aida**
interview: job ~ **meñsetu**
  have a job ~ **meñsetu o ukè-ru**
in that case, then **dê wa; zyâ(a)**
intimate: is ~ **sitásì-i**
introduce **syookai-suru**
investigate **sirábè-ru**
invite (to an event) **syôotai-suru**
invite (to do something) **saso-u**
involuntarily **tûi**
island **simâ**
it won't do; it's too bad **ikena-i**
Italian (person) **itáriàziñ**
Italian language **itariağo**
Italy **Itaria**

jacket **uwaği**; (windbreaker) **zyâñpaa**
Japan **Nihôñ/Níppòñ**
Japan Railway **z(i)eé-àaru**
Japanese–English **waee**
Japanese (person) **nihôñzìñ/níppoñzìñ**
Japanese language **nihoñğo/nippoñğo**
jeans **ziipañ**
jogging **zyogiñğu**
journalist **siñbuñkìsya**
joy: a ~ **tanósìmì**
joyous: is ~ **tanósì-i**
junior colleague **koohai**
just; exactly **tyoodo**
just (no more than) **dakê**
  ~ having thought about it **kañğàeta dakê de**
  it's ~ big **oókìi dakê da**
  That's all (= It's ~ that.) **Soré dakè desu.**
just now **tadâima**

kabuki (traditional Japanese theater) **kabuki**
Keio [University] **Keeoo**
key **kağî**
kimono **kimono**
  cotton ~ **yukata**
kimono sash **ôbi**
  put on a ~ **ôbi o simê-ru/suru**
kind, gentle **sîñsetu /na/**
kindly: act ~ **sîñsetu ni suru**
kiosk **baiteñ**
kitchen **daidokoro**
kitchen utensils **daídokoro-dòoğu**
knife **nâihu**
knock **tatâk-u**

knock down **taôs-u**
know **sitte (i)-ru; gozôñzi da** ↑ **; zôñzite (i)**
  ru ↓
  come to ~ **sir-u**
Kyoto **Kyôoto**
Kyoto University **Kyoodai**

labor **roodoo-suru**
laboratory **keñkyùusitu**
laborer **roódòosya**
lake **mizúùmi**
lamp **sutañdo**
landlord **yânusi**
language **geñğo**
  spoken ~ **kotóbà**
large: is ~ **oókì-i; ôoki na** /+ nom/; (of area)
  hirô-i
last month **sêñğetu**
last night **yuúbè**
last week **señsyuu**
last year **kyôneñ**
late: is ~ **oso-i**
  ~ (= behind) **okure-ru**
  get to be ~ **osóku nàr-u**
  until ~ **osókù made**
later **âto de; notihodo** /formal/
latest: at the ~ **osôkute mo**
laugh **wara-u**
lawyer **beñğòsi**
lay (eggs) **um-u**
lay [something] on its side **nekas-u**
lean **yor-u**
learn **narâ-u**
learned society **gakkai**
leave **dê-ru; tât-u**
leave behind **oite ik-u; nokôs-u**; be(come) left
  behind **nokôr-u**
leave one's seat **sêki o hazus-u**
lecture **kôoği; kooeñ**
lecture meeting **koóèñkai**
left (direction) **hidari**
  ~ side **hidári no hòo**
left (remaining) **âto**
  one hour ~ **âto ití-zìkañ**
leg **asî**
leisurely **yukkùri**
lend **kas-u**
lengthen **nobâs-u**
let [someone] off (a vehicle) **orôs-u**
letter **teğami**

liberal arts department *or* college **kyoóyooğak-ùbu**

library (a building) **tosyôkañ**

library (a room) **tosyôsitu**

life **seekatu**

  social ~ **syakái-sèekatu**

light: is ~ (of weight) **karu-i**

  is ~ (not dark) **akaru-i**

like, love **sukî /na/**

like X, X-like **X-mìtai /na/**

limousine available for hire **hâiyaa**

limousine bus **rimúziñ-bàsu**

Lincoln University **Riñkaañ-dàiğaku**

line is busy **hanasi-tyuu da**

line up, form a line **narab-u;** place in line **narabe-ru**

linguistics **geñğòğaku**

liquor store **sakaya**

listen **kik-u**

literature **bûñğaku**

  ~ department **buñğàkùbu**

little: is ~ **tiísà-i; tîisa na /+ nom/**

  a ~ **sukôsi; tyôtto**

live (be alive) **ikî-ru**

live (reside) **sûm-u**

lively **niğiyaka /na/**

living: make a ~ **seekatu-suru**

living room (Japanese-style) **tyanoma;** (Western-style) **imâ**

living things **sêebutu**

locate [something] **mituke-ru; sağas-u**

located: be ~ (of inanimate existence) **âr-u; goz-âru +**

  (of animate existence) **i-ru; irássy-àru↑; ôr-u↓**

location **basyo**

lock [something] **kağî o kakê-ru;** [something] locks **kağî ğa kakâr-u**

lonely: is ~ **sabísì-i**

long: is ~ **nağâ-i**

look! **hôra**

look, seem **miê-ru; yôo /na/; -mitài /na/**

look at **mî-ru; goráñ ni nàr-u↑; haikeñ-suru↓**

look for **sağas-u**

look into **sirábè-ru**

looking as if **-soo /na/**

look out on **muk-u**

lose face **kao ğa tubure-ru**

loud voice **ôoki na kôe**

loud: is ~ **yakámasì-i**

low voice **tîisa na kôe**

lower (verb) **orôs-u**

lower back **kosî**

luggage **nîmotu**

lunch **hirúgòhañ; ohîru**

  box ~ **beñtòo**

machine **kikâi**

magazine **zassi**

magnificent **rippa /na/;** is ~ **subárasì-i**

mail a letter **teğámi o dàs-u**

make **tukûr-u**

make a turn **mağar-u**

make an appointment **yakusoku-suru**

make haste **isôğ-u**

make tea **otya o ire-ru**

make the most of, bring into use **ikâs-u**

male **dañsee; otókò**

male language **dañseeğo**

man **otóko no hitò; otóko no katà /polite/; ozisañ; dañsee**

manager **sihâiniñ**

manner **hûu /na ~ no/; yoosu**

many **takúsàñ**

  are ~ **oô-i**

  ~ people **oózèe**

map **tîzu**

marry **kekkoñ-suru**

  married life **kekkoñ-sèekatu**

mash **tubus-u**

match up with **â-u**

mathematics **suuğaku**

matter (verb) **kamâ-u**

  it doesn't ~ **kamáwàna-i**

matters to attend to **yoozi**

maximum **saikoo**

maybe X **X ka mo sirenai**

may do (= permission) **sitê mo îi**

meal **syokuzi**

  fixed ~ **teesyoku; kôosu; sètto-mèñyuu**

  the "A" ~ **eé-kòosu; eé-sètto**

  meals are served **syokúzi ğa dè-ru**

meaning **îmi**

meat **nikû**

medicine **kusuri**

medicine (as a subject) **îğaku**

meet **â-u; omé ni kakàr-u↓**

meet; greet **mukae-ru; demukae-ru**

meeting: a ~ **atúmàrì; kâiği**

Meiji Era (1868–1912) **Mêezi**

merely **tâda**

message **mêsseezi**
metropolis **daítòkai**
midnight **rêe-zi**
midst of talk **hanasi-tyuu**
milk **mîruku**
mind **ki**
Ministry of Education **moñbùsyoo**
missionary **señkyòosi**
mistake: make a ~ **matígaè-ru**
misundertand **gokai-suru**
mix [something] **mazê-ru;** [something] mixes-
    mazîr-u
mixture **mazírì**
Monday **getúyòo(bi)**
money **okane**
money-changing machine **ryoóğàeki**
monorail **monórèeru**
month **tukî**
    last ~ **sêñğetu**
    ~ before last **señsèñğetu**
    this ~ **koñğetu**
    next ~ **râiğetu**
    ~ after next **saraiğetu**
    one ~ **iḱ-kàğetu; hitô-tuki**
mood **kimoti**
moon **tukî**
more **môtto**
    /+ quantity expression/ **moo**
    a little ~ **moó sukòsi**
    ~ than that **mûsiro**
    the bigger, the better **ôókìkereba oókìi hodo**
    îi
more or less **tasyoo**
morning **âsa**
    this ~ **kêsa**
    tomorrow ~ **asíta no àsa; myootyoo**
most **itibañ**
mother **hâha, hahaoya; okâasañ** /polite/
mountain **yamâ**
mouth **kuti**
move [something] **uğókàs-u;** [something] mov-
    es **uğôk-u**
move (to a new residence) **hikkosi-suru;**
    hiḱkòs-u
movie **eeğa**
movie theater **eéğàkañ**
Mr.; Mrs.; Miss; Ms. **-sañ** /polite suffix/
much **takúsàñ**
music **ôñğaku**

Nagoya **Nâğoya**

name **namae**
    be named **i-u; ośsy-àru** ↑ **; môos-u** ↓
narrow: is ~ **semâ-i**
national railway (until 1987) **kokutetu**
native land **kuni**
natural **sizeñ**
nature **sizeñ**
near: is ~ **tikâ-i**
    in the ~ future **tikâi uti ni**
nearby **sôba**
neatly **tyañto**
necessary **hituyoo /na/**
necessity **hituyoo /na/**
neck **kubi**
necktie **nêkutai**
    put on a ~ **nêkutai o simê-ru/suru**
need **ir-u**
neighborhood **kîñzyo**
net **amî**
never mind **îi/yô-i; yorosi-i; kêkkoo da**
nevertheless **dâ no ni; soré ni sitè mo**
new: is ~ **atárasì-i**
news **nyûusu**
news article **kîzi**
newspaper **siñbuñ**
next **tuğî**
next door **tonari**
    ~ on the left **hidáridònari**
    ~ on the right **miğídònari**
next month **râiğetu**
next week **raisyuu**
next year **raineñ**
night **bañ; yôru**
    last ~ **yuúbè**
    tonight **kôñbañ**
    tomorrow ~ **asita no bañ; myoobañ**
nine **kû; kyûu**
    ~ units **kokôno-tu**
    ~ days; ninth of the month **kokóno-kà**
no **i(i)e; iya; iêie; ñ̂ñ**
no good **damê /na/**
no(h) (traditional Japanese theater) **noo**
no more **môo** /+ negative/
nobody **dâre mo** /+ negative/
noise: make a ~ **sawâğ-u**
noisy: is ~ **urúsà-i; yakámasì-i**
noodles: buckwheat ~ **sôba**
noodle shop **sobâya**
noon **hirû/ohîru; syooğo**
north **kitâ**
Northwest (airline) **noósuèsuto**

nose **hana**
nostalgic: is ~ **natúkasì-i**
  [I] miss Tokyo **Toókyoo ğa natukasì-i**
not at all **zeñzeñ** /+ negative/
not especially **betu ni** /+ negative/
not much; not very **a(ñ)mari** /+ negative/
not yet **mâda** /+ negative/
notebook **nôoto**
notes **nôoto**
notice **ki ğá tùk-u**
notify **todókè-ru**
novel (book) **syoosetu**
now **îma**
nowadays **kono-ğoro**
nuisance **zyama; mêewaku**
  become a ~ **mêewaku ni nâr-u**
number(s) **suuzi**
  assigned ~ **bañğòo**
nurse **kañğòhu**
nurse, care for **kâñğo-suru**

obligation **girî; ôñ**
obliged: be(come) ~ for assistance **sewâ ni nâr-u**
obscene, dirty: is ~ **kitánà-i**
occasion **tokî**
ocean **ûmi**
of course; to be sure **naruhodo; motîroñ**
  ~ [it's] good. **Îi to mo.**
offended: be(come) offended **ki ó wàrùku suru**
office **zimûsyo**
office building **bîru**
oh! **â(a)**
old: is ~ (not new) **hurû-i**
old man **ozîisañ** /polite/
old person **tosíyòri**
old woman **obâasañ** /polite/
older brother **âni; (o)nîisañ** /polite/
older sister **ane; (o)nêesañ** /polite/
one **itî**
  ~ unit **hitô-tu**
  ~ day **ití-nitì**
  ~ person **hitô-ri**
one hundred **hyakû**
oneself **zibuñ**
  do by ~ **zibuñ de suru**
only **tâda**
only, only just **bâ(k)kari**
only: nothing except X **X sika** (+ negative)
only X; no more than X **hoñ no X**
on time: be ~ **ma ní à-u**

open [something] **ake-ru;** [something] opens **ak-u**
oppose **hañtai-suru**
opposite **hañtai**
opposite side **mukooğawa**
or **ka** /ptc/
or on the other hand **matâ wa**
orchestration without singers **karaoke**
order: an ~ for something **tyuumoñ**
  place an ~ **tyuumoñ-suru**
ordinary **hutuu**
other **hoka**
  Anything else? **Hoka ni nâni ka?**
  ~ than X **X no hoka**
  ~ X **hoka no X**
  the ~ party **aítè**
ought to/must/should **bèki**
  [one] ought to/must/should say **iú bèki da**
our household's; our **uti no** /+ nom/
out: be(come) ~ of **kirâs-u**
out of order **kosyoo**
over **uê**
over there **asoko; atira; aʼtì; mukoo**
overcoat **ôobaa; kôoto**
overeat **tabésuğì-ru**
own: one's ~ X **zibuñ no X**

P.M. **gôğo**
painful: is ~ **itâ-i**
pale: is ~ **aô-i;** (of colors) **usu-i**
paper **kamî**
Pardon me. **Goméñ-nasài.**
parent **oya; oyağosañ** /polite/
  both parents **ryôosiñ; goryôosiñ** /polite/
park **kooeñ**
partner **aítè**
part-time work(er) **arúbàito**
party **pâat(e)ii**
  student ~ **kôñpa**
pass [something to someone] **tôr-u**
pass [something] through **tôos-u**
pass through **tôor-u**
past **-suği**
  ten (minutes) ~ **zíp-pùñ-suği**
pay **harâ-u**
pay attention **ki ó tukè-ru; tyúui-suru**
pedagogy **kyoóikùğaku**
pen **pêñ**
pencil **eñpitu**
pep; peppy **gêñki** /na/
pepper **kosyôo**

perhaps   **môsi ka suru to**
perk up   **gêñki ğa dê-ru**
person   **hitô; katâ** /polite/
person (in my in-group)   **monô**
person in charge   **kâkari (no hito); tañtòosya**
person of Japanese ancestry   **niḱkèeziñ**
persuaded: be(come) ~   **nattoku-suru**
pertaining to   **-teki** /na/
philosophy   **tetûğaku**
photograph   **syasiñ**
phrase   **kotóbà**
physics (as a subject)   **butúrìğaku**
pick up   **hiro-u**
picnic   **pîkkunikku**
picture (photograph)   **syasiñ**
   take a ~   **syasíñ o tòr-u**
pie   **pâi**
pine   **mâtu**
pitiable   **kinódòkù**
pity: a ~   **zańnèñ** /na/
place (verb)   **ok-u**
place   **tokórò; basyo**
place on [something]   **nose-ru**
placid   **sîzuka** /na/
plan   **tumori; yotee**
plant (verb)   **ue-ru**
plant   **ueki**
plate   **sara**
play (= a show)   **sibai**
play, play around   **asob-u**
pleasant: is ~   **kimóti ğa ìi; tanósì-i**
Please (speaker offering something)   **Dôozo.**
   (speaker requesting something)   **Onéğai-simàsu.**
pleasing   **sukî** /na/
pleasure: a ~   **tanósìmì**
   take ~ in   **yorókòb-u**
   do with ~   **yorókòñde suru**
plum   **ume**
poem   **si**
poetry   **si**
point [something] toward   **muke-ru**
police box   **koobañ**
policeman   **omâwarisañ** /polite/
polite   **têenee** /na/
political   **seezi-teki** /na/
politician   **seezika**
politics   **seezi**
pond   **ikê**
ponder   **kañğaè-ru**
positive   **tâsika** /na/

positively   **tasika ni; kanarazu**
possibility   **kanoosee**
possible: the act of X is possible   **X kotô ğa dekî-ru**
post office   **yuúbìñkyoku**
postpone   **nobâs-u;** [something] is postponed   **nobî-ru**
practice   **reñsyuu-suru**
praise   **homê-r̩u**
precise(ly)   **hakkìri; tyañto; mattaku**
president of a company   **syatyoo**
presume upon   **amae-ru**
pretext, excuse   **koozitu**
   a mere ~   **hoñ no koozitu**
pretty   **kîree** /na/
price   **nedañ**
   commodity prices   **bukka**
probably   **tâbuñ**
problem   **moñdai**
professor   **kyoozyu**
program   **bañğumi; puróğùramu**
prolong   **nobâs-u;** [something] is prolonged   **nobî-ru**
promise   **yakusoku**
   make a ~   **yakusoku-suru**
properly   **tyañto**
psychology   **sińrìğaku**
public telephone   **koósyuudèñwa**
publish books   **hôñ o dâs-u;** books are published   **hôñ ğa dê-ru**
pull   **hik-u**
punctual   **zikáñ-dòori**
puppet theater (traditional Japanese)   **bûñraku**
purpose   **mokuteki**
purposely   **wâzawaza**
push   **os-u**
put   **ok-u**
put aside   **oite ok-u**
put away   **sima-u**
put back   **modôs-u**
put in order   **katázukè-ru;** be(come) put in order   **katázùk-u**
put into   **ire-ru**
put on: ~ the body   **ki-ru**
   ~ the head   **kabûr-u**
   ~ the feet or legs   **hak-u**
put out   **dâs-u**
put up the money   **okáne o dàs-u**
put up with   **gâmañ-suru**

quarrel   **keñka-suru**

question **situmoñ**
  ask a ~ **situmoñ-suru**
quiet **sîzuka /na/**
quilt (for sleeping) **hutôñ**
  bottom ~ **sikíbùtoñ**
  top ~ **kakébùtoñ**
quit **yame-ru**
quite **nakanaka; kânari**

radio **râzio**
rain **âme**
rain check: take a ~, hold back for now **eñryo-site ok-u**
rainy season **tuyu**
raise **aǧe-ru**
raise (bring up) **sodátè-ru;** be raised **sodât-u**
rapid: in ~ succession **dôñdoñ**
rare: is ~ **sukúnà-i**
rather **nakanaka; kânari; mûsiro**
reach **todôk-u**
reading and writing **yômîkaki**
real estate broker **hudoosañya**
reality: in ~ **zitû wa**
rear **usiro; urâ**
reason **tamê; wâke**
recall **omóidàs-u**
receive **mora-u; itadak-u ↓; tyoodai-suru ↓**
recently **kon(o)aida**
  starting ~ **konáidà kara**
reception **hirôoeñ**
receptionist **uketuke**
recommend **susume-ru**
recover **naôr-u**
red: is ~ **aka-i**
redo **yarínaòs-u**
refuse **kotówàr-u**
  refuse, saying something or other; fabricate an excuse **nâñ to ka itte kotówàr-u**
regrettable **zaññèñ /na/**
regular **hutuu**
  ~ train **hutuu(ressya)**
  ~ (order of food) **nami**
related to **-teki /na/**
release **hanâs-u**
reliable **tâsika /na/**
religion **syûukyoo;** (as a subject) **syuúkyòoǧaku**
rely **yor-u**
remain behind **nokôr-u**
rent **yâtiñ**

rent (from someone) **kari-ru;** (to someone) **kas-u**
repair **naôs-u;** be(come) repaired **naôr-u**
rephrase **iíkaè-ru**
replacement **kawari**
report **todókè-ru**
request **tanôm-u**
required: be ~ (of time and money) **kakâr-u**
rescue **tasúkè-ru;** be(come) rescued **tasúkàr-u**
research **keñkyuu**
  do ~ **keñkyuu-suru**
  ~ institute **keñkyuuzyo**
reservation **yoyaku**
reserve, holding back **eñryo**
reside **sûm-u**
resign oneself to **akíramè-ru**
responsibility **sekiniñ**
  responsible person **sekíniñsya**
restaurant (Western-style) **rêsutorañ;** (Japanese-style) **ryoóriya**
result **kekka**
return: a ~ **kaérì**
return, give back **kâes-u**
return, go back **modôr-u**
  ~ (home) **kâer-u**
revel **sawâǧ-u**
reverse side **urâ**
reward **rêe/oree**
rewrite **kakíkaè-ru**
rice: cooked ~ **gôhañ**
  uncooked ~ **komê**
rice shop **komêya**
ride **nor-u**
right **miǧi**
  ~ side **miǧí no hòo**
rigorous: is ~ **kibísì-i**
rise **aǧar-u**
river **kawâ**
road **miti; toórì**
roast [something] **yak-u;** get roasted **yake-ru**
"rock, paper, scissors" **zyâñ·kêñ·pôñ**
romanization **roómàzi**
room **heyâ**
  Japanese-style ~ **nihoñma, wasitu**
  Western-style ~ **yooma**
round-table discussion **zadâñkai**
rude **sitûree /na/; rêe o 'sirana-i**
rush hour **raśsyu-àwaa**
Russian (person) **rośiàziñ; soréñziñ**
Russian language **rosiaǧo**

sad: is ~ **sabísì-i**

safe **daízyòobu /na/**

safe side: to be on the ~ **nêñ no tame**

sake **tamê**

saké (rice wine) **sake**

salaried employee **sarárìimañ**

salesperson **teñiñ**

salt **siô**

salty: is ~ **karâ-i**

salutation **âisatu**

same **onazi**

sandals (for outdoors) **zoori; geta**

sandwich **sâñdo(ìtti)**

Saturday **doyôo(bi)**

save, hold back **nokôs-u**

save, rescue **tasúkè-ru;** be(come) saved, rescued **tasúkàr-u**

say **i-u; ośsy-àru ↑; môos-u ↓**

a set way of saying **kimatta iikata**

finish saying **iíowàr-u**

schedule **yotee**

written ~ **yoteehyoo**

scenery **kêsiki**

school **gakkoo**

school term: this ~ **koñgàkki**

last ~ **señgàkki**

new ~ **siñgàkki**

next ~ **raígàkki**

schooltime, classtime **zyûgyoo**

science **kâgaku**

scold **sikar-u**

sea **ûmi**

season **kisêtu**

the ~ (for something) **sîizuñ**

seasonal **kisetu-teki /na/**

seat (assigned place) **sêki**

reserved ~ **sitêeseki**

leave one's ~ **sêki o hazus-u**

Seattle **Siâtoru**

second generation **nî-see**

secretary **hîsyô**

section (within a company) **kâ**

section manager **katyoo**

see (a person); meet (with a person) **â-u; omé ni kakàr-u ↓**

see: can ~ **miê-ru**

see (look at) **mî-ru; goráñ ni nàr-u ↑; haikeñ-suru ↓**

see off **okur-u; miokur-u**

seek employment **syuusyoku-suru**

seem **miê-ru**

seems to be X **X-rasì-i**

select **erâb-u**

sell **ur-u**

seminar **zêmi; sêminaa**

send, send off **okur-u**

send back **modôs-u**

separate (verb) **hanâs-u;** become separated **hanárè-ru**

separate **betubetu; betu**

serious **mazime /na/**

serve (a meal) **dâs-u**

meals are served **syokúzi ğa dè-ru**

service **sâabisu**

set aside **tôtt(e) ok-u**

set out **dekake-ru**

seven **nâna; sitî**

~ units **nanâ-tu**

~ days; seventh of the month **nano-ka**

severe: is ~ **hidô-i**

she **kânozyo; anô hitò; anó kàtà /polite/**

shelf **tana**

ship **hûne**

shirt **syâtu**

dress ~ **waisyatu**

shoes **kutû**

shop **misê**

shopping **kaimono**

shopping bag **syoppíñğubàggu**

short: is ~ **mizíkà-i**

shoulder **kâta**

show **misê-ru**

show (= a play) **sibai**

Showa Era (1926–89) **Syoowa**

shy: is ~ **hazúkasì-i**

sick; sickness **byooki; gobyooki /polite/**

side **hôo; yoko**

simple **kañtañ /na/**

sing **uta-u**

single (unmarried) **hitô-ri**

single room **sîñguru(-rùumu)**

sister: older ~ **ane; (o)nêesañ /polite/**

younger ~ **imôoto; imootosañ /polite/**

sit down **suwar-u; (kosí)kakè-ru**

site **basyo**

sitting room **tyanoma**

situation **zizyoo**

six **rokû**

~ units **muí-tù**

~ days; sixth of the month **mui-ka**

size (bulk) **ookisa;** (of an area) **hîrosa**

skillful; skilled **zyoózù /na/; ozyoozu /polite/**

is ~ **umâ-i**

kirt **sukâato**

ky **sôra**

lacks **surâkkusu; pâñtu; pâñtaroñ**

leep: put to ~ **nekas-u;** go to ~ **ne-ru**

leepy: is ~ **nemu-i**

lippers **surîppa**

lowly **yuḱkùri; sôrosoro**

mall: is ~ **tiísà-i; tîisa na** /+ nom/

is ~ (occurs in small units) **komákà-i**

is ~ (of area) **semâ-i**

mash **tubus-u**

mell, odor **niôi**

have a ~ **niôi ḡa suru**

moke (verb) **su-u; (tabáko o) nòm-u/**
mesiaḡar-u ↑

nooth **sumûuzu /na/**

ɔap opera **hoómudòrama**

ɔcial life **syakái-sèekatu**

ɔcialize **tukíà-u**

ɔciology **syakâiḡaku**

ɔcks **kutûsita**

bifurcated ~ **tâbi**

ɔft: is ~ **yawárakà-i**

ɔlitary: is ~ **sabísì-i**

ɔmebody **dâre ka**

ɔmeday **îtu ka; izure** /formal/

ɔmehow or other **nâñ to ka; nań to nàku; dôo**
ni ka

ɔmeplace **dôko ka**

ɔmething **nâni ka**

ɔmething or other **nâñ da ka**

ɔmetime **îtu ka; izure** /formal/

ɔmetimes **tokídokì**

ɔmewhat **tasyoo**

ɔmewhere **dôko ka**

ɔn **musuko; musukosañ, bôttyañ** /polite/

ɔng **utâ**

ɔon **sûḡu**

ɔrdid, dirty: is ~ **kitánà-i**

ɔrry: I'm ~ **su(m)ímasèñ; moósiwake ari-**
masèñ

feel ~ (for someone) **kinódokuḡàr-u**

ɔ-so **mâa·mâa**

ɔund, make a noise **nar-u**

ɔund far away (on the telephone) **deñwa ḡa**
too-i

ɔur: is ~ **suppà-i**

ɔuth **minami**

ɔuth Korea **Kâñkoku**

ɔuth Korean (person) **kañkokùziñ**

souvenir **miyaḡe**

souvenir shop **miyaḡeya**

Soviet Union **Sôreñ; Sobíèto**

soy sauce **syooyu**

space: take up ~ **basyó o tòr-u**

spacious: is ~ **hirô-i**

Spain **Supêiñ**

speak **hanâs-u; syabêr-u**

special **tokubetu**

specialization **señmoñ**

specialized **señmoñ-teki /na/**

specialized vocabulary **señmoñḡo**

special lunch **rañti-sàabisu**

specially, purposely **wâzawaza**

specialty: one's ~ **tokûi/tokui**

speech **kooeñ**

speech contest **supíiti-kòñtesuto**

speed **hâyasa**

spicy: is ~ **karâ-i**

spirit **ki**

splendid **rippa /na/**

is ~ **subárasì-i**

spoon **supûuñ**

sports program **supóotu-bàñgumi**

sportscar **supóotùkàa**

spread out **sik-u**

spring (season) **hâru**

squalid, dirty: is ~ **kitánà-i**

staff member **syâiñ**

staggered work hours **zisá-syùkkiñ**

stand (= concession) **baiteñ**

stand up **tât-u;** stand [something] up **tatê-ru**

start: with a ~ **hatto**

start to: **-das-u; -hazime-ru**

state of things **yoosu**

station **êki**

stationery **biñseñ**

writing supplies **buñbòoḡu**

stationery store; stationery dealer **buñbooḡuya**

stay on **nokôr-u**

stay one night **ippaku-suru**

stern: is ~ **kibísì-i**

stiff: become ~ **kôr-u**

is ~ **katâ-i**

still **mâda**

stingy: is ~ **kitánà-i**

stockings **kutûsita**

stomach **onaka; i**

stop; bring to a halt **tome-ru;** come to a halt;
stop over **tomar-u**

stop (of rain, snow, etc.) **yam-u**

stop in **yor-u**
store (verb) **simâ-u**
store **misê**
storm door **amâdo**
straight **maśsùg̣u**
strain **mûri o suru**
  is a ~ **tura-i**
strange: is ~ **okásì-i; okâsi na /+ nom/; hêñ**
  /na/
street **miti**
street corner **kâdo**
strength **tûyosa**; (of coffee, tea, etc.) **kôsa**
stretch [something] **nobâs-u**; [something] stretches **nobî-ru**
strict: is ~ **kibísì-i; yakámasì-i**
strike **ût-u**
strong: is ~ **tuyô-i**; (of coffee, tea, etc.) **kô-i**;
  (sturdy) **zyoobu /na/**
student **gakusee**
  ~ studying abroad **ryuúg̣akùsee**
studio apartment **wańrùumu**
study (verb) **beñkyoo-suru; narâ-u**
study (a room) **syosai**
sturdy **zyoobu /na/**
style **hûu /na ~ no/**
substitute **kawari**
subway **tikatetu**
sudden **kyuu /na/**
sugar **satôo**
suit **sûutu**
  (man's) ~ **sebiro**
suit, become [someone] **niâ-u**
suit, match up with **â-u; muk-u**
  ~ one's taste **kutí ni à-u**
suitable **tekitoo /na/**
  ~ for **-muki**
suitcase **suútukèesu**
summer **natû**
summon **yob-u**
sun **hì/hi**
sunburned: get ~ **hi ni yake-ru**
Sunday **nitíyòo(bi)**
super-deluxe (order of food) **tokuzyoo**
superintendent, apartment manager **kañriniñ**
superior: is ~ **erâ-i**
superior colleague **señpai**
supermarket **sûupaa**
supposing **môsi**
surely **kitto; kanarazu; tasika ni**
surprise: become surprised **biḱkùri-suru**
surprising: is ~ **mezúrasì-i**

sushi **susî**
sushi shop **susîya**
suspend (something) **kakê-ru**
sweater **sêetaa**
sweet: is ~ **ama-i**
sweets **okâsi**
swim **oyôg̣-u**
swimming **oyóg̣ì**
syllabary, Japanese written **kana**
symbol: written ~ **zi**
symposium **zadâñkai**

table **teeburu**
Taisho Era (1912–26) **Taisyoo**
take (a train, taxi, etc.) **nor-u**
take (of medicine) **nôm-u**
take (require) **kakâr-u**
take, take up, take away **tôr-u**
take a bath **hurô ni hâir-u**
take advantage of (someone's kindness or affection) **amae-ru**
take charge of **tañtoo-suru**
take lessons **narâ-u**
take off (of clothing) **nûg̣-u**
take on board **nose-ru**
take out **dâs-u**
take to a place (of things) **motte ik-u**; (of people) **turete ik-u**
talk (verb) **hanâs-u; syabêr-u**
talk **hanásì**
talk show **ińtabyuu-bàñgumi**
tap **tatâk-u**
tape **têepu**
taste **azi**
  have a ~ **azi g̣a suru**
taxi **tâkusii**
tea **otya**
  black ~ **kootya**
teach **osie-ru**
teach manners **sitúkè-ru**
teacher **señsèe**
teacup (Japanese-style) **yunómì**
telephone (verb) **deñwa-suru; deńwa o kakèru**
telephone: ~ call **deñwa**
  ~ answering machine **rusúbañ-dèñwa**
  ~ book **deñwatyoo**
  ~ number **deńwabàñgoo**
television **têrebi**
  appear on ~ **têrebi ni dê-ru**
tempura **teñpura**

mpura shop **teñpuraya**

n **zyûu**

~ units **tôo**

~ days; tenth of the month **too-ka**

nder: is ~ **yawárakà-i**

nnis **tênisu**

rminate **owar-u**

rrible: is ~ **suǧô-i; kowâ-i; taíhèñ /na/**

rrific: is ~ **suǧô-i**

st **sikêñ**

~ problem **sikéñ-mòñdai**

xtbook **kyoókàsyo**

hank you. **Ariǧatoo (gozaimasu).** + ;
Su(m)ímasèñ.

Thanks for your trouble. **Gokûroosama de-sita.**

thanks to you; thanks for asking **okaǧesama de**

at —— near you; that —— just mentioned
sono / + nom/

at —— over there; that —— (known to both of us) **ano** / + nom/

at being the case **(soré) dè wa; (soré) zyà(a)**

at is to say **to iu kotò wa**

at kind of —— **soñna, añna** / + nom/

at place **soko; asoko, asuko**

at side **sotira, sottì; atira, attì**

at thing (near you or just mentioned) **sore**

at thing over there (or known to both of us) **are**

at way; like that **sôo, âa**

eater **gekizyoo**

movie ~ **eéǧàkañ**

ere **soko; asoko, asuko; sotira, sottì; atira, attì**

ereabouts **sotira, sottì; atira, attì**

erefore **dâ kara**

esis **roñbuñ**

ick: is ~ **atu-i, buatu-i;** (of liquids) **kô-i**

in: is ~ (of liquids) **usu-i**

ing **monô; kotô**

ings on hand **motiawase**

have no business cards on hand **meési no motiawase ǧa nài**

ink **omô-u**

ink over **kañǧaè-ru**

ird generation **sâñ-see**

irsty: become ~ **nôdo ǧa kawâk-u**

is —— **kono** / + nom/

is kind of —— **koñna** / + nom/

is place **koko**

this side **kotira, kottì**

this side of **temae**

this thing **kore**

this way **kôo**

thorough **têenee /na/**

thoroughfare **toórì**

thousand **sêñ**

three **sañ**

~ units **mit-tù**

~ days; third of the month **mik-ka**

throat **nôdo**

throughout **-tyuu, -zyuu**

~ the morning **gozeñ-tyuu**

~ Japan **Nihoñ-zyuu**

all day long **iti-niti-zyuu**

throw away **sute-ru**

throw up **modôs-u**

thunder **kamínarì**

it thunders **kamínarì ǧa nar-u**

Thursday **mokúyòo(bi)**

ticket **kippu**

express ~ **kyuúkòokeñ**

special express ~ **tokkyùukeñ**

passenger ~ **zyoósyàkeñ**

ticket checking **kaisatu**

~ gate **kaísatùǧuti**

ticket counter **kippu-ùriba**

tidy: make ~ **katázukè-ru;** be(come) ~ **katázùk-u**

tie up **sibâr-u**

time **zikañ**

have ~ **zikáñ ǧa àr-u**

take ~ **zikáñ ǧa kakàr-u**

—— at a ~ **-zutu**

time: approximate ~ **kôro**

time: be on ~ **ma ní à-u**

time: free ~ **hima /na/**

time, occasion **tokî**

this ~; this next ~ **kôñdo**

time difference **zîsa**

timetable **zikokuhyoo**

tired: become tired **tukárè-ru**

tiresome **meñdòo /na/**

to be sure! **naruhodo**

today **kyôo**

together **issyo**

~ with a friend **tomodati to issyo**

do ~ **issyo ni suru**

toil **kurôo**

toilet **tôire; teârai**

tomorrow **asítà, asû; myôoniti**

tools **doógù**
tooth **hâ**
top **uê**
totally **mattaku**
touch: get in ~ **reñraku-suru**
tough: is ~ **katâ-i**
tour **tûaa**
tourist home **miñsyuku**
town **matî**
toy **omôtya**
trader: foreign ~ **boóekìsyoo**
traffic light **siñǧoo**
train (verb) **sitúkè-ru**
train: (electric) ~ **deñsya/dêñsya**
    (steam) ~ **kisyâ**
    a ~ **rêssya/ressya**
training **situke**
transfer (to another vehicle) **noríkaè-ru**
translate **hoñyaku-suru**
    ~ from English into Japanese **eeǧo kara 'ni-**
    hoñǧo ni hoñyaku-suru
translation **hoñyaku**
transport **hakob-u**
transportation **kootuu**
trash **gomî**
travel **ryokoo-suru**
treat [a person to food or drink] **gotisoo-suru**
tree **kî**
trip **ryokoo**
troublesome **meñdòo** /na/
true; truth **hoñtoo**
trunk **toráñku**
trust [someone] with [a matter] **makásè-ru**
truth, reality **zitû**
try: ~ going **ítte mì-ru**
    ~ to go **ikú yòo ni suru**
    ~ (unsuccessfully) **-(y)oo to suru**
Tuesday **kayôo(bi)**
tuna fish sandwich **tuná-sàñdo**
turn: make a ~ **maǧar-u**
turn off **kes-u;** be(come) turned off **kie-ru**
turn on **tukê-ru;** be(come) turned on **tûk-u**
twenty days; twentieth of the month **hatu-ka**
twenty years of age **hâtati**
twin room **tuíñ(-rùumu)**
two **nî**
    ~ units **hutá-tù**
    ~ days; second of the month **hutu-ka**
type **tâipu**
typewriter **taípuràitaa**
typhoon **taíhùu**

typing **tâipu**

U-turn **yuútàañ**
    make a ~ **yuútàañ-suru**
uh |anoo|; |eeto|
umbrella **kâsa; amáǧàsa**
uncle **ozi; ozisañ** /polite/
unconcerned **heeki** /na/
under **sita**
underground **tikâ**
underwear **sitaǧi**
undoubtedly **kitto**
unexpected: is ~ **mezúrasì-i**
unfasten **hazus-u**
unfortunate **kinódòkù**
    That's ~. **Okínodòku desu; Okinodok**
    sama.
unfortunately **ainiku**
unintentionally **tûi**
uninterruptedly **zutto**
university **daiǧaku**
unload **orôs-u**
unnecessary **yokee** /na/
unpleasant **iyâ** /na/
    is ~ **kimóti ǧa warù-i**
unreasonable **mûri** /na/
unreserved seat **ziyûuseki**
unrestricted **ziyûu** /na/
unskillful, poor at **hetâ** /na/
    is ~ **mazû-i**
until **màde** /ptc/
up **uê**
upbringing **situke**
upset: become ~ **komâr-u**
urge **susume-ru**
urgent **kyuu** /na/
use (verb) **tuka-u**
use: be of ~ **yakû ni tât-u;** put to ~ **yakû**
    tatê-ru
used to: become ~ **narê-ru;** ~ do **sitá mon**
    da
usual **hutuu**
usually **taitee**
utterance **kotóbà**
utterly **sukkàri**

vacant: be ~ **aite (i)-ru**
vacation **yasúmì**
valley **tanî**
valuable **daízì** /na/
variety **tâipu**

various   **iroiro** /no ~ na/; **iroñ** /na/

vegetable   **yasai**

vegetable store   **yaoya**

very   **tot(t)emo; taiheñ; zûibuñ**

  that ~ X   **rêe no X**

vicinity   **heñ; sôba; tikâku**

village   **murâ**

visible: be ~   **miê-ru**

visit   **ukaḡa-u** ↓

visitor   **kyaku; okyakusañ** /polite/

voice   **kôe**

voluble   **perapera**

wait   **mât-u**

wake up   **okî-ru**; wake [someone] up   **okôs-u**

walk (verb)   **arûk-u**

walk: a ~   **sañpo**

  take a ~   **sañpo-suru**

want, is wanted   **hosî-i**

want to ——   **-tai**

  ~ do   **sita-i**

warm: is ~   **at(á)takà-i**

warn   **tyûui-suru**

warning   **tyûui**

wash   **ara-u**

washroom   **señmeñzyo**

watch; clock   **tokee**

water: cold ~   **mizu**; hot ~   **(o)yu**

way (manner)   **hûu** /na ~ no/; **tôori**

way (direction)   **hôo**

way before; long ago   **zútto mày**

way of ——ing   ——**kata**

  way of doing   **sikata**

we: **watá(ku)sì-tati; bôkú-tàti, bôku-ra** /masculine/

we Japanese   **waréware nihoñzìñ**

weak: is ~   **yowâ-i**; (of coffee, tea, etc.)   **usu-i**

weak point   **niḡátè/niḡate**

wear: on the body   **ki-ru**

  ~ on the head   **kabûr-u**

  ~ on the feet or legs   **hak-u**

weather: good ~   **têñki**

weather forecast   **teñki-yòhoo**

wedding ceremony   **kekkòñsiki**

wedding reception   **hirôoeñ**

Wednesday   **suíyòo(bi)**

week   **syuu**

  this ~   **koñsyuu**

  last ~   **señsyuu**

  ~ before last   **señsèñsyuu**

  next ~   **raisyuu**

~ after next   **saraisyuu**

welcome (verb)   **mukae-ru; demukae-ru**

Welcome!   **Irássyài(màse); Yôku irássyaimàsita.**

Welcome back!   **Okáeri-nasài.**

welcoming: a ~   **mukae**

well, healthy   **gêñki** /na/

well then   **dê wa; zyâ(a)**

west   **nisi**

what?   **nâñ/nâni**

  What do you mean by ——?   —— **to iu to?**

what ——?   **dôno** /+ nom/

what color?   **naniiro; dôñna irô**

whatever [you] do   **nâni o sitê mo**

what kind of ——?   **dôñna** /+ nom/

what language?   **naniḡo**

what nationality?   **naniziñ**

What should I do?   **Dôo sitara îi?**

when?   **îtu**

where?   **dôko; dôtira, dôtti**

whether:

  can't tell ~ there is any or not   **âru ka dôo ka wakárànai**

  doesn't matter ~ there is any or not   **âtte mo nâkute mo kamáwànai**

which ——?   **dôno** /+ nom/

which side?   **dôtira (no hoo); dôtti (no hoo)**

which thing? (usually of three or more)   **dôre**

  (of two alternatives)   **dôtira (no hoo), dôtti (no hoo)**

while: a ~ (of indeterminate length)   **sibâraku**

white: is ~   **sirô-i**

who?   **dâre; dônata, dôtira-sama** /polite/

whoever it is   **daré dè mo**

whole: the ~ thing   **zêñbu**

wholeheartedly, with all one's might   **issyookèñmee**

why?   **dôo site; nâze**

wicket   **kaísatùḡuti**

wide: is ~   **hirô-i**

wife   **kânai, tûma; ôkusañ** /polite/

windbreaker   **zyâñpaa**

window   **mâdo**

  ticket ~   **madôḡuti**

wine   **wâiñ**

  rice ~   **sake**

winter   **huyû**

wipe   **huk-u**

wish: I ~ it had ended early   **hâyâku owáttàra yôkatta no ni**

within: ~ a city   **sînai**

~ Tokyo **tônai**
~ this year **kotosi-zyuu ni**
woman **oǹna no hitò; oǹna no katà, obasañ**
    /polite/
women's language **zyoseeḡo**
wonderful: is ~ **suḡô-i; subárasì-i**
work (verb) **hatarak-u**
    ~ hard **yôku hatarak-u**
work **siḡoto**
worry **siñpai**
    cause worry **siǹpai o kakè-ru**
worry about **siñpai-suru; ki ni suru**
wrapping cloth **hurosiki**
write **kâk-u**
wrong: be ~ **tiḡa-u; matiḡa-u**

yeah **ñ**
year **tosi**
    this ~ **kotosi**

next ~ **raineñ**
~ after next **saraineñ**
last ~ **kyôneñ**
~ before last **otôtosi**
initial ~ of an era **gâñ-neñ**
yellow: is ~ **kiiro-i**
yes **hâi, êe; hâa** /polite/
yesterday **kinôo**
yet **môo** /+ affirmative/
    not ~ **mâda** /+ negative/
you **anâta; kimi** /familiar/
you (plural) **anâta-tàti; kimî-tati** /familiar/;
    anáta-ḡàta ~ anata-ḡata /polite/
young: is ~ **wakâ-i**
younger brother **otóotò; otootosañ** /polite/
younger sister **imôoto; imootosañ** /polite/

zero **rêe, zêro, maru**
zero o'clock (midnight) **rêe-zi**

ndex

References are to Lesson, Section, and Structural Pattern: for example, 11B-3 refers to Lesson 11, Section B, Structural Pattern 3. MN refers to Miscellaneous Notes; GUP refers to Greetings and Useful Phrases in the Introduction.

Items designated simply as particles (ptc) are phrase-particles. /Ḡ/ and /n̄/ are alphabetized as /g/ and /n/.

adjectivals, 1B-1,2; special polite forms, 17B-3, 18A-2; /+ nominal/, 3B-1; sentence modifiers ending in, 19A-1; ending in **-tai** 'want to ——,' 7B-4; /+ **nâru**/, 9A-5. *See also under individual forms*

adjectival stem + **wa**, 29A-4

adversative passive, 29A-1

affective predicates, 5A-1, 15A-2, 16A-1, 19B-2, 24A-4

affects: primary and secondary, 5A-1

affirmative: distal-style: verbal, 1A-1; adjectival, 1B-1; /nominal + copula/, 2A-1; direct-style: verbal, 9A-1, 9B-1; adjectival, 1B-1; /nominal + copula/, 9A-2, 9B-2

affirming, 1A-4

age, counting, 10A-1

g̃eru 'give (to out-group),' 17A-1; /gerund +/, 17A-2

ida: /predicate +/, 29B-2

alternate negative stem in **-(a)zu**, 23B-1; use of, 23B-2

alternate questions, 12A-4; embedded, 18A-3

(a)nài de, 23B-2

(a)nakereba narânai ~ ikenai, 27A-3

nâta 'you,' 2B-2

n̄na 'that kind of ——,' 4B-3; /+ **ni**/, 9B-5

no 'that ——,' 3A-2

noo| 'uh,' 4B-5

anticipatory **no**, 19A-2

approximate numbers, 20A-5

approximation: **-hodo**, 5B-3; **-g̃òro** and **-g̃ùrai**, 8A-3

re 'that thing,' 2B-1

ru 'be located (inanimate),' 'have,' 4A-5, 5A-1, 27B-MN; /transitive gerund +/, 16A-2; **kotô g̃a ~**, 25A-3

soko 'that place,' 6B-1

tira 'that direction,' 'that alternative,' 6A-2

to: /sentence-modifier +/, 19B-4

tte, 30B-1

bâkari, 26B-1

bèki, 26B-3

Blunt-style, 9A-3

bôku 'I,' 'me,' 3B-2

Careful-style, 8A-4, 9A-3

Casual-style, 8A-4, 9A-3

Causative, 28A-1,2

Chinese series of numerals, 2B-3

Classifiers, 2B-3; time, 8A-1, 8B-4. *See also Appendix B and individual listings in Japanese–English glossary*

Clause-particles, 4B-4

Comparison: of two items, 15A-1; of three or more items, 15B-2; of activities, 20A-2

Compounds, 6A-1, 13A-4; verbal compounds in **-suru**, 9B-6; in **-sug̃iru**, 15A-3; nominal compounds in **-kata** and **-yoo**, 22B-3; in **-sa**, 24B-1; in **-soo**, 24B-2

Conditional, 26A-2

Connectors: sentence ~, 25B-3

Consonant verbals, 9A-1

Consultative: distal-style, 7B-1; direct-style, 20A-6; /+ **to suru**/, 25B-4

Copula, 2A-1; following a particle, 8B-2, 11A-2; polite equivalents, 10A-2. *See also under individual forms*

Counting: digits, 2B-3; hundreds, 2B-3; thousands, 2B-3; ten thousands, 3B-2

dà /copula/, 9A-2

dakê 'just,' 5A-2, 23B-3

daròo /copula/, 11A-5

Dates, 8B-4

dàtta /copula/, 9B-2

dè /copula/, 8A-5

de /ptc/ 'by means of,' 7B-2

de /ptc/ 'at,' 7A-1

de gozaimàsu⁺, 10A-2

289